Finance Capitalism and Germany's Rise to Industrial Power

Based on a wide array of new data collected by the author, the book uses clear, theoretically motivated economic analysis to explain the structure, performance, and influence of universal banks and securities markets on firms during industrialization. The German universal banks played a significant but not overwhelming role in the ownership and control of corporate firms. Banks gained access to boards via a confluence of their underwriting and brokerage activities, the legal phenomena of bearer shares and deposited voting rights, and the flourishing securities markets of the turn of the twentieth century. In general, bank relationships had little impact on firm performance; stock market listings or ownership structure was more important. The findings show that securities markets can thrive within a civil-law universal-bank system and suggest that financial system complexity can favor rapid industrial expansion.

Caroline Fohlin is a research professor of economics at Johns Hopkins University. She previously taught at the California Institute of Technology. Professor Fohlin is the author of the forthcoming book *Financial System Design and Industrial Development: International Patterns in Historical Perspective*, which was awarded the 1999 Japan–U.S. Center UFJ Bank Monographs in International Financial Research prize and which will be published by Cambridge University Press. Professor Fohlin's research has appeared in publications such as the *Journal of Finance, European Review of Economic History, Business History, Economic History Review, Explorations in Economic History*, and *Business and Economic History*.

Studies in Macroeconomic History

SERIES EDITOR: Michael D. Bordo, *Rutgers University*

EDITORS: Forrest Capie, *City University Business School, U.K.*
Nick Crafts, *London School of Economics*
Barry Eichengreen, *University of California, Berkeley*
Angela Redish, *University of British Columbia*

The titles in this series investigate themes of interest to economists and economic historians in the rapidly developing field of macroeconomic history. The four areas covered include the application of monetary and finance theory, international economics, and quantitative methods to historical problems; the historical application of growth and development theory and theories of business fluctuations; the history of domestic and international monetary, financial, and other macroeconomic institutions; and the history of international monetary and financial systems. The series amalgamates the former Cambridge University Press series *Studies in Monetary and Financial History* and *Studies in Quantitative Economic History*.

Other books in the series:

Howard Bodenhorn, *A History of Banking in Antebellum America*
[0-521-66285-0; 0-521-66999-5]
Michael D. Bordo, *The Gold Standard and Related Regimes* [0-521-55006-8]
Michael D. Bordo and Forrest Capie (eds.), *Monetary Regimes in Transition*
[0-521-41906-9]
Michael D. Bordo and Roberto Cortés-Conde (eds.), *Transferring Wealth and
Power from the Old to the New World* [0-521-77305-9]
Trevor J. O. Dick and John E. Floyd, *Canada and the Gold Standard*
[0-521-40408-8]
Barry Eichengreen, *Elusive Stability* [0-521-44847-6]
Barry Eichengreen (ed.), *Europe's Postwar Recovery* [0-521-48279-8]
Michele Fratianni and Franco Spinelli, *A Monetary History of Italy*
[0-521-44315-6]
Mark Harrison (ed.), *The Economics of World War II* [0-521-62046-5]
Kenneth Mouré, *Managing the Franc Poincaré* [0-521-39458-9]

Continued after the Index

Finance Capitalism and Germany's Rise to Industrial Power

CAROLINE FOHLIN
Johns Hopkins University

CAMBRIDGE
UNIVERSITY PRESS

CAMBRIDGE UNIVERSITY PRESS
Cambridge, New York, Melbourne, Madrid, Cape Town,
Singapore, São Paulo, Delhi, Tokyo, Mexico City

Cambridge University Press
32 Avenue of the Americas, New York, NY 10013-2473, USA

www.cambridge.org
Information on this title: www.cambridge.org/9780521396608

First published 2007
First paperback edition 2011

A catalog record for this publication is available from the British Library

Library of Congress Cataloging in Publication data
Fohlin, Caroline, 1966–
Finance capitalism and Germany's rise to industrial power / Caroline Fohlin.
p.   cm. (Studies in macroeconomic history)
ISBN 0-521-81020-5 (hardcover)
1. Banks and banking – Germany.   2. Universal banks – Germany.   3. Industrialization –
Germany.   1. Fohlin, Caroline.   11. Series
HG3048.F655   2006
322.10943 22–pcc   2005032691

ISBN 978-0-521-81020-3 Hardback
ISBN 978-0-521-39660-8 Paperback

For John

Contents

Acknowledgments

This book has evolved over many years, and I have therefore accumulated a list of intellectual debts too long to enumerate here. There are a few people who stand out, particularly for their input during the formative stages of this project. First among these is Barry Eichengreen, who steered me toward the topic of universal banking and industrialization and who has been an adviser, mentor, and friend ever since. Richard Tilly, who provided several months of hospitality at his institute at the University of Münster, offered much-needed guidance and assistance in my early forays into German libraries and archives. Gianni Toniolo, who first got me thinking about the writings of Alexander Gerschenkron when I served as teaching assistant in his undergraduate course in European economic history at Berkeley, provided enthusiastic help in carrying out my research in Italy. I thank them heartily but in no way implicate them for any errors or shortcomings.

For their advice and assistance, comments and criticisms, cajoling and encouragement, I thank variously Michael Bordo, Lance Davis, Gerald Feldman, Lou Galambos (whose input vastly improved the book's conclusion), Thomas Gehrig, Martin Hellwig, Harold James, Geoffrey Jones, Morgan Kousser, David Romer, and Richard Sylla (who rightly suggested that I add the chapter on stock markets). I am also grateful to Peter Bossaerts for graciously allowing me to include in Chapter 7 some previously unpublished results of our joint research. Cumulatively, I have spent several of the past fifteen years in Germany undertaking the research for this book, and I am thankful for the warm hospitality with which I have been received by my hosts and the staff at numerous libraries, archives, museums, universities, and other institutions, including most especially the Wissenschaftszentrum Berlin (David Soskice), the Free University of Berlin (Carl-Ludwig Holtfrerich), the University of Mannheim (Martin Hellwig), and the American Academy in Berlin (Gary Smith).

Many research assistants have contributed to this project, and I thank in particular Gerald Böke and Hendry Susanto Ng for coding hundreds of thousands of balance sheet items and names of bank board members; several California Institute of Technology undergraduates, including Jean Kim, Ernest Yeung, and especially Sueanne Lee for much additional data entry, database organization, and help in matching bank and company board members; Juan Contreras and Mircea Trandafir for assistance with statistical analysis; Thies Clausen, Julia Förster, Anne Jacobs, Henrike Lichtenberg, Annette Lohmann, Steffen Reinhold, and Julia Schneider for help in gathering sources in Germany; and Damien Kempf for help with literature review and editing. Most of this assistance has been made possible by funding from the National Science Foundation (NSF), and I thank Dan Newlon for his guidance and the many NSF grant reviewers for their constructive comments and critiques. I acknowledge with many thanks fellowship and grant funding from the Social Science Research Council, the Center for German and European Studies (the University of California, Berkeley), the Economic History Association, the American Academy in Berlin (Berlin Prize Fellowship), the Fulbright Foundation, the German Marshall Fund of the United States, the Alexander von Humboldt Stiftung (TransCoop Fellowship), and the California Institute of Technology.

For their patience and expertise in seeing this book through, I am grateful to Michael Bordo and Scott Parris as well as to Brianne Millett and Andy Saff at Cambridge University Press and to the anonymous reviewers who offered helpful comments.

Finally, and above all, I owe abundant thanks to my children – Benjamin and Helen – and to my husband – John – for making life better in so many ways.

1

Introduction

The activity of the banks in the economic life of society has often been likened to that of the heart in the human body.... For just as it is the function of the heart to regulate by means of certain organs the circulation of the blood, which through countless arteries and veins flows through the human body and returns to the heart, so ... it is the function of the banks to regulate by certain economic measures the circulation of capital, which flows from them and returns to them, and which may properly be regarded as the life blood of the modern economic organism.[1]

Nearly a century ago, this declaration appeared, in defense of the German universal banks, in the well-known treatise of Jakob Riesser – himself a director of a Berlin great bank. By the last quarter of the nineteenth century, after industrialization had progressed through textiles, steam power, and railroads, populist voices – stemming mostly from agrarian or socialist quarters – criticized the banks for wielding excessive power over industry. Riesser argued, on the contrary, that the banks played a facilitating or sustaining role in the economy. In constructing his argument, he laid out the details of the German universal banking system, as he saw them and as he garnered from the writers and scholars of the time.[2] The U.S. Monetary Commission, having translated Riesser's book into English during its campaign to understand the major financial systems of the world following the 1907 financial crisis, then propelled this work into the mainstream of American thinking on the German financial system.

---

[1] Riesser (1910 [1911]), p. 186. An earlier, if more reserved, circulatory system reference can be found in *Der Deutsche Ökonomist* of June 23, 1883.

[2] For much of his exposition on the role of banks in corporate governance of industrial firms, Riesser (1910 [1911]) relied heavily on the dissertation of Otto Jeidels (1905). The latter also worked in a large universal bank in the first part of the twentieth century.

After World War II, when economists turned their attention to "backward" or "underdeveloped" economies, Alexander Gerschenkron began to formulate his ideas on the patterns of development and industrialization in continental Europe. Having temporarily shed the mantle of the bank-power critique, the predominant view now built up the universal banks as the great engine of industrialization. Amid the economic boom of West Germany in the decades following the war, the German universal banking system appeared to many to possess beneficial characteristics that allowed it to perform efficiently, provide relatively inexpensive capital to industry, and promote overall economic growth – in both the post-war reconstruction and in the pre–World War I industrialization. In the 1980s, many felt that the United States was falling behind Germany and Japan; the search for explanations turned up the structure of national financial systems as a key point of divergence. True, Germany's financial markets, especially stock exchanges, barely existed; and industry, furthermore, coordinated activities to a high and probably anticompetitive degree. Yet these features appeared to be benefits, since they seemingly promoted the sort of long-term investment perspective that rampant market-orientation lacked.

While the historical and contemporary economics strands of literature interact hardly at all, the underlying tenor of the research stems largely from the same source: the general success of the German economy during industrialization and during the first four post–World War II decades. Only in the last decade, since the post-reunification recession set in and a number of scandals involving customers of universal banks came to light, has the sentiment about the current German financial system shifted considerably. The now orthodox view of the pre–World War I era, however, has changed more slowly.

Banks are seen as part and parcel of the German industrialization; the great bankers are commonly held up as the master promoters of technology and enterprise. This book tells a more nuanced story. To be sure, the universal banks played a major role in the German industrial economy during the forty years leading up to World War I. But they constituted one part of a rapidly developing financial system – one that included a variety of financial institutions and, surprisingly to some, active and well-functioning stock markets. By delving deeper into this particular case, this book contributes to a number of debates: some large, some small; some in economics, some in history, yet others at the boundaries of various other disciplines. A few big questions motivate the research and help structure the investigation.

WHAT IS THE ROLE OF THE FINANCIAL SYSTEM IN ECONOMIC GROWTH?

At the heart of this research is the desire to understand the nature of the relationship between financial systems and economic growth. While most economists recognize that the financial system is a crucial component of any economy, there is much disagreement over the manner in which financial and real variables interact. Even the early writers on the financial system took as a given both the asymmetry of information between investors and entrepreneurs and the role of the financial system in ameliorating such information problems. Joseph Schumpeter (1912), for example, stressed the role of bankers in screening and then funding entrepreneurs, as well as the stimulus that these activities provided to innovative activity and economic growth. Modern growth theory highlights the acquisition of human capital and the productivity of economic units (firms and entrepreneurs) as well as the traditionally emphasized expansion of the physical capital stock. This literature has also made strides in incorporating the financial system into models of endogenous growth.

Expansion of the financial sector has proven to go hand in hand with economic growth, but the direction of causality is still uncertain.[3] Joan Robinson (1952) suggested that financial systems develop in response to prospects in the real sector, yet the literature over the last decade has tended to argue that the real sector responds to financial development. The evidence seems to support the view that the extent and depth of the financial system positively correlates with future economic growth, but problems of omitted variables and robustness undermine such findings.[4] Jeremy Greenwood and Bruce Smith (1997) offer what may be the most reasonable compromise: a model in which financial markets arise after some period of real development, and the expansion of those markets fuels further real growth.[5]

These sorts of questions suggest the need for a finer-grained understanding of how financial systems evolve and how this institutional growth

---

[3] Early studies include Goldsmith (1969), McKinnon (1973), and Shaw (1973).

[4] The more recent literature considering the causal relationship between finance and growth includes King and Levine (1993), Jappelli and Pagano (1994), Jayaratne and Strahan (1996), and Rajan and Zingales (1998). Robert Lucas (1988), perhaps not surprisingly, expresses doubt about the importance of financial factors and excludes these considerations in his model of development.

[5] A logical implication of this model is that exogenous creation of a financial system with advanced features may not spur real growth. The problem then for implementing development policy is determining how to get poor countries to the point at which financial systems will arise endogenously.

influences the real economy at the firm level. In other words, even more useful than knowing *if* financial development pushes real economic growth is understanding the mechanisms by which that process unfolds.

DOES THE STRUCTURE OF FINANCIAL SYSTEMS MATTER?

The first overarching question leads directly to the second: Does the structure of financial systems matter? Determining how the development of financial systems yields real growth effects hinges on knowing why financial systems develop the characteristics and practices that they do, whether certain financial systems perform more efficiently or generate and mobilize higher quantities of capital than others. As the primary example of Gerschenkron's paradigm on the importance of institutional organization, Germany is of central significance. There is also a widespread sense in the United States and the United Kingdom that banking systems of the sort found in Germany offer advantages for industrial development and economic growth. These views persist in some circles despite the poor showing of the German economy in the 1990s. Thus, one fundamental goal of this book is to explore the development of specific features of German banking and their impact on individual firms and on the German economy at large.

Universal versus Specialized Banking

Much of the discussion in this book centers around the structure of certain classes of financial institutions and the organization of the financial system more generally. The book focuses on the parts of the system that serve industry and commercial enterprises, particularly those of the corporate form. In the German system, the universal banks as well as certain private banks have filled this role since their inception. Universal banking is often discussed as if it were a well-defined and static principle. In reality, the concept of universal banking has evolved gradually over time and the practices associated with this style of banking have also changed. Benston (1994, p. 121) articulated the common notion that "Germany today and before the second World War offers the best example of universal banking." Similar financial institutions certainly existed—and possibly even slightly earlier—in other continental European countries, but German banks took a leading role and have become synonymous with universal banks as we know them today.

The forerunners of German universal banking arose mostly in the 1830s and 1840s.[6] The universal banks of this era, however, were private banks

---

[6] See Tilly (1995) and the discussion in Chapter 2.

that bore little resemblance to the twentieth-century universal bank. Even ignoring the question of demand for industrial finance at the time, strict regulations on incorporation and limited liability proscribed both the possibility of externally financed banks and the potential coporate clientele for universal banking services. By the time that the German Empire was formed in 1871, after much relaxation of corporate regulations and a strong wave of industrialization, the universal banks began to organize under the joint-stock form and were unregulated except by the general laws applying to German share companies (*Aktiengesellschaften* or *Kommanditgesellschaften auf Aktien*). It is really from this point that the German universal banks began to take on their modern form.

The fundamental characteristic of universal banking is the joint provision of a range of financial services by the same institution. Universal banks have thereby earned the appellation of "supermarkets of corporate finance." True universal banks are allowed to provide virtually any product, but most typically combine traditional commercial banking functions (short-term credit, deposit taking, payments clearing, bill discounting) with underwriting and trading of securities. Modern universal banks also sell insurance, mortgages, and investment funds, though they usually do so through affiliates. Additional practices have become identified with universal banking, mainly because they have often appeared in tandem with universality of services. Examples include branching over extensive geographic areas, holding securities – particularly equity stakes – of nonfinancial firms, voting shares in proxy for their customers, and sitting on the boards of directors of client firms.

Thus, it is useful to delineate two sets of bank characteristics, universal banking and relationship banking, whose coexistence may offer synergies, but which may in practice exist independently of one another. Universal banking can be defined as the joint production of multiple financial services (investment banking, commercial banking, retail securities business, mortgage, and insurance). The provision of many services over several phases of firms' development may tend to lead to long-term relationships between firms and financial institutions, but formalized relationships depend on a further set of activities. Relationship banking can be viewed as a separate category involving practices related to the ownership and control of firms (long-term debt and equity stakes, proxy voting of shares, and interlocking directorates between banks and firms). Not all universal banks perform the complete range of allowable functions, and not all financial institutions that provide some of these functions are universal banks.

History offers a number of examples. Japanese banks have at times operated as universal banks while being prohibited from holding equity stakes and board positions in underwritten firms; they have also been permitted to engage in interlocking directorates with industry while being restricted in the scope of their financing services. Likewise, banks in the United States were permitted to combine investment and commercial banking until the passage of the Glass-Steagall Act in 1933; however, interlocking directorates had been progressively restrained at the turn of the twentieth century and then essentially prohibited by the Clayton Act in 1914. Furthermore, not all specialized or arm's-length systems result from prohibitions on universal or relationship banking: British commercial banks, for example, have always been permitted to engage in universal and relationship banking, but for the most part have remained specialized and at arm's length until recently.

The question of branching, though sometimes seen as connected to universal banking, is really a separate issue. While the practicality of universal banking may hinge on size, it is not clear that branching is a necessary condition. Indeed, the first universal banks were unit banks, and those in Germany operated as such for several decades before beginning to branch. Moreover, since the principal benefit of geographic dispersion is diversification potential, branching may be equally beneficial to specialized banks.

Banking structure is also commonly seen as going hand in hand with the structure of the overall financial system. Universal banking is typically associated with bank-dominated systems (those with weak securities markets) and are normally contrasted with market-based systems in which specialized institutions have largely provided investment and commercial banking services. The United States and Great Britain provide the foremost examples of market-based systems, given the predominance of secondary securities markets in these two countries. The banking systems of the two countries differ in many ways, though the practice of separating the provision of commercial and investment banking services into distinct financial institutions, particularly until recently, constitutes an important similarity.

Financial systems vary, however, in their degrees of banking specialization and in their use of securities markets relative to banking institutions. Thus, it proves difficult to classify all systems in one of two categories.[7] The diversity of experiences further hints at the multiplicity of influences on system design and on the possible absence of a clearly optimal system.

Motivation for the Study

Albeit with varying intensity over the past century, the German universal banking system has become well-trod research ground. Perhaps most

---

[7] See Fohlin (forthcoming).

prominently, Gerschenkron heartily advanced the notion that the universal banking system played a crucial role in the German industrialization, but a number of other scholars have delved more deeply into narrower areas of the field. Gerschenkron's ideas have held sway over many, particularly in the United States, but numerous scholars have made significant corrections and reevaluations over the years. Gerschenkron himself recognized that he could not answer the broader question, whether financial institutions are generally able to promote the kind of mobilization and efficient utilization of capital that is thought of as a prerequisite for industrial development, and this is the kind of question that economists find the most compelling. Motivating this book, therefore, is the sense that there is still much to learn both about the history and from the history.

Economics research on modern universal banking understandably reflects current themes in regulatory debates in the United States, negotiations over European unification, and efforts toward industrial development in many regions of the world. Just as naturally, but also in contrast, the historical literature tends to focus on the power and importance of specific individuals and institutions. Rarely do the modern and historical strands meet. Thus, in attempting to answer questions about financial structure and industrial development, economists, historians, and economic historians all stand to gain from more extensive linking between recent theoretical and empirical work on financial institutions and historical research on the German experience.

CLEARER UNDERSTANDING OF THE GERMAN EXPERIENCE

The purpose of this book, at its core, is to shed a brighter light on the past. By scrutinizing the German corporate finance and governance system of the late industrialization period, the investigation provides a clearer understanding of the German experience at that time. By uncovering new evidence and reevaluating already available sources, the following chapters set out to paint the most accurate and balanced portrait of the system and in so doing take on a range of debates that have persisted for several generations of scholarship. The findings often support a number of plausible interpretations of the history and, in those cases, call a draw to the debate. The book may not answer every open question, but it at least elucidates many previously unlit corners of the literature. The upshot of the book is that interactions among the various actors and institutions are complex and sometime contradictory. Thus, clarifying often means making the story a bit messier – identifying multiple paths of causation, rejecting some prevailing beliefs, and opening up new interpretations of the history.

LESSONS FOR TODAY

Historical debates on their own provide substantial motivation for the current study, but history may have lessons for today as well – for newly industrializing or transitional economies as well as for highly advanced western economies. Much of the current structure of financial institutions originates in the institutions and systems of the nineteenth century. Understanding the past may therefore enrich our understanding of the present. Clearly, much has changed over the past century, and the experiences of Germany before World War I may not be directly applicable to modern-day developers. But the basic problems of creating effective means of mobilizing capital and ensuring relatively efficient utilization of that capital translate quite clearly into modern-day economies with nascent banking systems and a dire need for investment. Having a clear picture of past development experiences and understanding the actual role of particular institutions within those contexts can warn of possible pitfalls and illustrate the complexity of the issues at hand. The results of this study in particular may help determine whether creating banks that establish formalized governance relationships with industry will encourage investment and growth in these countries.

The analysis may also improve our understanding of the role of financial institutions in contemporary western economies. Despite its recent trials, many still believe that Germany's banking system is effective in promoting economic growth, particularly in certain sectors of the economy. Such apparent success has often led to debates over regulatory policy and system design in the United States and Great Britain. Much of the discourse over banking reform, both past and present, hinges on the assumption that certain types of financial systems allocate an economy's resources more efficiently than others. Although the United States has liberalized banking law significantly over the past decade, economists and policy makers continue to consider more dramatic reductions in regulation. The question remains whether such loosening would encourage universal, relationship-oriented banking in the United States, and whether this development would stimulate productive investment and higher growth. At the same time, ongoing banking crises in Japan and bank-related scandals in Germany have raised doubts about and tempered enthusiasm for relationship-oriented systems.

Whether or not historical cases teach specific lessons for today, the additional knowledge gained can only help in seeing the bigger picture. Since each economic epoch presents different challenges for financial systems and economies, adding new periods of observation increases the number of data points available for analysis. This broader range of cases demonstrates the

variety of paths that past development has taken, permits greater general-
ization when common patterns appear, and might also dampen cycles or
fads in thinking about financial system design.

REFINING THEORIES

Because historical investigation offers a long-term view of the evolution of
systems, it provides an expansive testing ground for financial theories. The
German case in particular, because of the significant systemic changes and
repeated shocks that its financial system has suffered over the past 150 years,
offers a potential wealth of experience to inform and help refine theories of
financial system structure and firm decision making. As this book reveals,
empirical research often fails to support current theoretical thinking. If theories explain the present but not the past, then we are left to wonder about the
future. Theoretical work can benefit from historical research, particularly if
we understand the importance of underlying assumptions – how they affect
the theories and how well they apply in different situations. The historical
research may recommend some adjustment to existing theoretical models
of financial system design and its connections to the real economy, if those
models are to prove useful for producing forecasts or policy prescriptions.

The Plan of the Book

The first part of the book – Chapters 2 and 3 – explores both historical
studies and modern theories and, in the process, ties together a wide range
of research on universal banking. Combining the models and methods of
economics and history raises new questions and helps restructure unresolved
debates about financial systems and their possible role in economic growth.
Driven by these motivations, the second part of the book – Chapters 4
through 7 – turns to the reassessment of the German corporate finance and
governance system within a modernized conceptual framework.

Chapter 2 begins with a brief review of the development of German industry and corporate finance over the second half of the nineteenth century
and the beginning of the twentieth. The chapter then sets out the traditional
conception of German universal banking during industrialization. Much of
the current understanding of the German system during industrialization
comes from Gerschenkron's work, which in turn derives largely from early-
twentieth-century writers such as Jakob Riesser, Otto Jeidels, and Werner
Sombart. As this chapter points out, despite heavily entrenched views on
the role of universal banking in Germany, certain areas have often been

debated. Chapter 2 evaluates these debates and closes with a discussion of logical and empirical inconsistencies in the orthodox, Gerschenkron-inspired paradigm. The chapter concludes that stronger theoretical under-pinnings can move the historical debates forward in fruitful new directions.

Building on the historical survey, Chapter 3 then lays the theoretical groundwork for an evaluation of financial intermediation and corporate finance. This chapter shows that despite copious research on the subject, the theoretical literature has as yet arrived at no consensus on the relative costs and benefits of universal or relationship banking, nor on a theoretical basis for the commonly perceived dichotomy of bank-based versus market-based financial systems. Theoretical research on financial systems and economic growth is no more conclusive, though the existence of a financial system is seen as spurring growth by raising the quantity, quality, and efficiency of capital provision. Still, available theories are unable to define an optimal design of financial systems – even a conditional one. Thus, the theoretical literature leaves much to be explored empirically.

At the microeconomic level, the recent theoretical literature emphasizes the role of financial institutions in resolving uncertainty through the revela-tion and intermediation of information about individual firms as well as in balancing and diversifying risks that remain even when firms and potential investors are symmetrically informed. These fundamental tenets of finan-cial theory provide a framework for new lines of inquiry – for example, whether certain types of financial institutions gather and disseminate infor-mation more effectively than others, whether close ties between firms and banks resolve information asymmetries and alter firms' decision making, or whether universal banking systems encourage superior risk management compared to specialized banking systems.

Bringing together the theory and history, the second part of the book poses new lines of research based both on restructuring traditional debates around modern banking and finance theory and raising new questions not often addressed in the previous literature. The first phase of the empirical analysis (Chapter 4) involves quantifying and detailing the overall growth of the financial system, and of the joint-stock universal banks in particular. The findings suggest that many of the practices considered integral to the German banks – such as widespread deposit taking and branching, positions on company boards, and equity stakes in industrial companies – took place only to a limited extent during industrialization; and those that did may have had little to do with the banks' universal structure. At the aggregate level, the chapter shows that the universal banking sector developed late in the development process, expanding most rapidly in concert with the final push of industrialization in the 1890s and the early-twentieth century.

The results tend to undermine the traditional emphasis on institutional peculiarities and motivate further detailed analysis of the role of universal and relationship banking institutions once the system developed more fully.

Chapters 5 and 6 turn to a microlevel analysis of firm behavior and outcomes based on a large dataset of company financial data. The first of these two chapters investigates possible motivations for different types of formal associations between banks and firms – not simply bank representation on firm supervisory boards, but also indirect links via common representatives on bank and company boards. In doing so, the chapter reveals both differences and similarities between bank affiliated and independent firms. Of particular interest are comparisons of industrial investment, rates and volatility of return, listings on stock exchanges, and firm survival rates. Chapter 6 focuses more heavily on the financing patterns of industrial firms, examining the capital structure, liquidity sensitivity, and debt maturity of industrial firms, and then inquiring into the role of universal bank relationships in such decisions and experiences. The results indicate that firms' financial choices vary systematically with certain characteristics, usually in line with theoretical predictions. Despite theoretical arguments in favor of significant effects of bank relationships, however, the findings of both chapters generally suggest little alteration of these patterns due to formal bank oversight. Together, the analysis in the first three chapters of the second part yields little support for the common perception that the German universal banks offered marked advantages over other forms of banking, especially through close, formal relationships with industrial firms.

The findings therefore argue for a closer examination of the potential costs of such a financial system, especially the idea that universal banking, and the German banks in particular, undermined the development of active securities markets. The final chapter of this section, Chapter 7, investigates precisely this question. The chapter starts with an overview of stock market development, its regulation and taxation by governing bodies, and its relationship to the universal banking industry. The second part of the chapter investigates the role of stock market listings in firm finance and governance, the costs of issuing shares in the markets, the determinants of stock returns, and the efficiency of price discovery in the Berlin market in particular. The findings indicate the presence of a surprisingly large, active, and efficient stock market in the later industrialization period, suggesting quite convincingly that Germany supported lively markets *because of*– rather than *despite*– the participation of the universal banks in the corporate finance system.

The final part of the book comprises two concluding chapters. Chapter 8 brings the story of German financial and economic development up to the present, recounting the changing fortunes of the German financial system from its propitious start in the industrialization period to the upheaval of the First World War, the Weimar Republic, and the Nazi years. The chapter then follows the developments through reconstruction to reunification to recession. The final chapter draws together the finely detailed portrait of the second part of the book with Chapter 8's broad survey of the past ninety years and offers some general conclusions on the importance of history in shaping financial systems and on the role of financial systems in the real economy.

Limitations of the Analysis

The topic of this book is one on which most economic historians and many economists have, if not detailed knowledge, then at least some notion of the received wisdom. It is a subject, however, that has received little systematic, comprehensive, economics-based analysis. As a result, there exists a wide variety of divergent views on the fundamental questions to ask and on the appropriate means and method of analysis. Thus, while this book covers significant ground, it cannot address every potentially important issue in detail. Some exclusions result from a desire to keep the book within certain thematic and space limits; others stem purely from a lack of relevant data sources.

On the latter point, a number of limitations appear immediately. First, statistical analysis of corporate finance patterns must use joint-stock firms, because private firms reported results sporadically, if at all. Confining the analysis to joint-stock companies may bias the results, if such firms behave significantly differently from private firms. In 1905, however, there existed approximately 5,500 German share companies, and many of these firms were very small. Thus, while public firms are likely larger on average than private firms, the coverage of the joint-stock population is greater than one might imagine. The sampling population also imposes hardly any constraint on the analysis, since universal banks served corporate firms most of all. Since only joint-stock companies were required to convene a supervisory board, such companies comprise the principal targets of formalized bank–firm relationships. By the standard of most modern studies, this book actually considers an unusually broad population, since it includes unlisted companies, not solely those with stocks traded on an exchange.

Still, there are data that would be useful to have but that are generally unavailable. For example, despite the general availability of financial and governance data for corporations, German law required no ownership reporting at the time. Hence, we can determine ownership structure only in cases where historians have happened upon the data, and the number of such cases is exceedingly small – too small to be useful in statistical analysis.

And even for readily available data on share companies, the data, of course, are not perfect or complete. Financial data arise from company reports and therefore may contain errors and omissions that are difficult to identify. In addition, in the prewar period, accounting standards were laxer, and firms were not required to report highly detailed information. The scarcity of archival material for many firms and banks compounds the difficulty of compiling more comprehensive qualitative information. Despite these constraints, the book provides a wealth of new data and fresh analysis of previously available data and offers important insights into many questions of interest to economists, historians, and economic historians.

The Primary Conclusions in Brief

The empirical analysis in this book reveals a number of specific findings about the development of universal banking and securities markets in Germany and the financing of industry during the later stages of industrialization. Together, the results generate new ideas about the institutional features we observe in the German financial system; the coexistence of markets and powerful, universal banks; and the role of financial systems in economic growth more broadly. In particular, the results here suggest that key characteristics of universal and relationship banking emerged late in the industrialization process and yielded little discernable influence on industrial firms as a group. The impact of increasingly available financing, both through the mobilization of capital in the universal banking system and via expanding secondary markets for securities, seems to overshadow the impact of specific institutional features of the German system. To be sure, the German universal banks made a palpable impact on the German economy; but the findings here indicate that this influence came from something other than the formalized relationships they maintained with firms. Moreover, the importance of universality – the combination of investment and commercial banking – appears mostly in the active use of securities markets, not in the domination of industry nor in the dramatic alteration of firm behavior or performance.

At the more general level, the book also argues that social, political, and regulatory environments play key roles in shaping financial systems. If rational, economic considerations do not drive financial institution structure, or if some institutional arrangements are infeasible under certain conditions, then it will be difficult to dictate an optimal system design. For similar reasons, it is difficult to determine the effects of importing a structure from one context to another, even if that system has proven to offer significant advantages in the home country. In addition, it seems that even institutional designs that were once beneficial may become entrenched and outlive their usefulness to the economy, complicating evaluation of the long-term efficiency and desirability of given financial systems.

One primary conclusion of this book, therefore, is that in focusing on international differences among financial systems, widely held beliefs about the relative benefits of German-style universal banking may underestimate both the impact of political, social, and cultural factors on development experiences and the similarities in the ultimate economic effects of disparate systems. In this light, it appears that traditional views of the importance of financial structure, and of the benefits of the universal, relationship system of banking in particular, require rethinking. If the specific institutions that comprise universal and relationship banking did not result in more rapid technological change, greater productivity, or more efficient investment at the firm or economywide level, then we are left to determine what other factors played a part in transforming Germany into a modern, industrial nation. As usual, there is much left to learn about and from history.

The Development of the German Corporate Finance System until 1913

Germany began the nineteenth century as a collection of thirty-eight sovereign states with a predominantly agrarian economy.[1] In Prussia, the largest of the German states, the agricultural sector comprised approximately two-thirds of the population, while those in industry and commerce made up less than 25 percent.[2] In Württemberg, also an overwhelmingly agrarian state in 1840, over 80 percent of the state's wealth found its origin in agrarian pursuits, while only 8 percent of assets were based in handwork and a scant 0.6 percent made its way to factories.[3] These numbers suggest a dearth of modern industrial activity before the middle of the nineteenth century; yet the decades prior to 1870 were characterized by a marked move out of agrarian and into industrial sectors – a process brought about by several distinct factors.

THE EARLY INDUSTRIAL PERIOD (1848–1870)

Laying the foundation for the transition to industry was the relatively strong capital accumulation that took place between 1815 and 1848 – the first extended period of calm since the start of the Thirty Years' War (1618–48).

---

[1] Much of the first section of this chapter originates from Fohlin (1994).

[2] Computed from *Preussische Statistik* (1865). Similar numbers can be found in Hoffman (1965), p. 204. See also von Reden (1848), p. 995, and *Vergleichende Kulturstatistik*, by the same author in the same year, as reported in Riesser (1911), p. 33. The difficulty with computing the proportions of the population engaged in industry and agriculture in the mid-nineteenth century is that the early census numbers do not differentiate various types of handwork, and all handworkers are counted under the industrial sector. It is probably safe to say that the numbers for industry are thus overstated and for agriculture are understated, but it is not possible to say to what extent this is true. For a discussion of other obstacles to accurate population accounting, see Hoffman (1965), pp. 180–8.

[3] Computed from Loewenstein (1912), p. 5 and included sources. These sources do not discuss the composition of the agrarian sector. Though handwork is categorized separately,

Productivity advances in agriculture between the 1820s and 1870s, particularly after the publication of Liebig's manual on the uses of chemistry in agriculture in 1840, allowed the release of labor from agrarian pursuits. The 1834 creation of a customs union among the German states (the *Zollverein*) increased the extent of the market for all producers and "dealt the death blow to the medieval economic system in Germany."[4] Expanding markets, together with the efficiency enhancements of the new steam energy, began to spur industrial growth – particularly in textiles.

Railroads began to spread across Germany in the 1840s, marking what many have termed a new era in the German economy. The London exhibition of 1851, showcasing the latest advances in technology, spurred on Germany's emerging entrepreneurs. Within five years, one of these new technologies, the Bessemer process, revolutionized the German iron and steel industry and provided a further stimulus to railroad construction. This new process for manufacturing steel from molten pig iron produced less brittle steel, and also greatly improved the efficiency of production, thus increasing the quantity and quality of steel available for heavy industry and railroads. Of the 25,664 kilometers of track laid between 1845 and 1875, 20,000 kilometers were built after 1855.[5]

Railroads directly affected the economy through their requirement of capital for constructing rails and cars as well as for supporting industries. Equally important, however, railroads encouraged investment in other industries, because they signaled increased profitability due to cheaper, more reliable transport. In this manner, railroads arguably prompted the founding of many new companies in the 1850s.[6] The newly formed firms were concentrated in mining, insurance, and banking, as well as in the railroads themselves, together absorbing about 92.7 percent of all capital invested in Prussian joint-stock companies during these twenty years.[7] Through their demand for large outlays of capital over extended periods of time,

---

some cottage industry may nonetheless be disguised as agriculture. Thus, the breakdown between agriculture and industry may be slightly distorted.

[4] Riesser (1911), p. 29. On the Zollverein, see Dumke (1976, 1981, and 1991, and references cited therein); see also the survey by Henderson (1984). Ziegler (2000a) argues that the interpretation of the Zollverein as a conscious step toward unity is a myth. On the contrary, the fear of losing their sovereignty caused especially small and medium-sized states to join the union.

[5] Sombart (1909), p. 541.

[6] See Krengel (1980), Riesser (1911), Tilly (1967), and Wagenblass (1973).

[7] Riesser (1911), p. 48. Riesser's numbers imply the following breakdown of capital investment: railroads, 71.6 percent; mines, foundries, and salt works, 11.5 percent; insurance companies, 6.6 percent; and banks, 3.9 percent.

the railroads are also thought to have been the catalyst for the development of large-scale, mixed banking techniques – the combination of short- and long-term finance that would ultimately become the hallmark of the German universal banking system.[8]

The financial institutions of the early industrial period reflected the agrarian nature of the economy as well as the dispersion of political power. The traditional elements of the financial system included agricultural credit institutions (*Landschaften*), government securities, and short-term trading capital for international and interregional trade.[9] Agricultural credit institutions began in the eighteenth century and issued interest-bearing mortgage bonds (*Pfandbriefe*). The conservative, agrarian-influenced political majority shunned industrialization and exercised strict control over money and joint-stock corporate charters. Through their rigid regulation, the governments of Prussia and Saxony, in particular, minimized outside competition for their note-issuing banks. Because of tight government control over banks of issue, the majority of financial intermediaries were private banks. These institutions executed a substantial share of the economy's payments, linked savers with investment opportunities, and helped found new businesses. As such, the private banks constituted perhaps the most important class of financial intermediaries in the half-century before the formation of the German Empire. Although they could not issue notes, private bankers granted acceptance credits (like IOUs), which increased economywide liquidity and weakened government control over the money supply.

Interregional and international trade aided the accumulation of capital and provided a substantial stimulus to German economic development. The important private banks, nearly all based in merchant families, set up shop in older commercial and political centers. This combination of merchant activities and banking business renders it nearly impossible to distinguish between trade and industrial capital or the flow from trade to industry.[10] The private banks of the early- to mid-nineteenth century developed new banking techniques, such as conversion of short-term loans into long-term securities. This form of maturity transformation and securitization represented precursors to both modern industrial credit and government finance.

While increasing needs for government finance first propelled the transition from merchant to banker, it likely also crowded out some industrial

---

[8] See Fremdling (1975, 1983) on the contribution of the railroads to financial and economic development in Germany.

[9] Tilly (1967), pp. 154–5.

[10] See, for example, Heyn (1981 [1969]), pp. 120 ff, on the transition from merchant to banker.

finance in the short term. The availability of relatively secure government business made the conservative banking elite reluctant to finance riskier new business; and among investors generally, government securities attracted substantial capital because of their low risk relative to investment in industrial enterprise (in particular, in joint-stock companies). Private bankers played an essentially passive role in industrial undertakings – the exception being those in the Rhineland, who did not have an active business with government and were far less timid about financing industry. Thus, most private financing of industry before the 1840s flowed through local banks.[11]

Joint-stock credit banks began to emerge at midcentury. These institutions formed under corporate charters primarily as a means of increasing their capital base. The first of these banks, A. Schaaffhausen'schen Bankverein (ASB) of Cologne, established in 1848, resulted from the reorganization of the old private-banking firm of Abraham Schaaffhausen during the economic upheaval of the 1848 revolution. Within a few years, several other German credit banks took shape; the largest of which were the Disconto-Gesellschaft of Berlin (1851); the Bank für Handel und Industrie of Darmstadt (1853), also known as the Darmstädter Bank; the Mitteldeutsche Creditbank of Meiningen (1856); and the Berliner Handelsgesellschaft of Berlin (1856).[12]

Whether these banks constitute a unique innovation remains something of a question, as the German bankers seem to have based some of their organizing principles on the French Crédit Mobilier of 1852. Indeed, one of the French institution's founders, Abraham Oppenheim, also helped found the Darmstädter Bank. Furthermore, one of the high officials in the Crédit Mobilier was an early director of its German counterpart. Rondo Cameron asserts that "Although the initiative for the bank came from Germany, the inspiration, the idea, most of the capital and a large part of the practical experience both in promoting it and in organizing its operations came from the

---

[11] See Heyn (1981 [1969]) on private banking and industrialization in Frankfurt am Main. See also Tilly (1965, 1966) as well as Neuberger (1977 [1974]), pp. 57–61, giving the example of the private-banking firm Gebrüder Bethmann. Loewenstein (1912) provides some details on the private bankers in Württemberg.

[12] See von Poschinger (1971 [1879]), p.122 et. seq., on the formation – and attempted formation – of what he refers to as Crédit Mobilier–type banks prior to 1870. See also Hübner (1968 [1853], II) on the founding of the earliest credit banks. See also Henderson (1975), pp. 123–9. The latter notes that, "Most of the credit banks established in the 1850s were located in northern and central Germany and served the main industrial and commercial regions of the country" (p. 129). According to Riesser (1910), p. 892, fourteen credit banks, with capital ranging from 600,000 to 42,936,000 marks, were founded between 1848 and 1856.

Crédit Mobilier."[13] Perhaps lacking in impartiality, Jakob Riesser emphasizes the essentially German nature of the new credit banks, though he does acknowledge the many operational similarities between them and the Crédit Mobilier. The bylaws of the Darmstädter Bank, he contends, were copied "not from those of the Crédit Mobilier, but consciously, and in some cases literally, from the statutes of the A. Schaaffhausen'schen Bankverein. Consequently, they rest essentially on a German, and not a French foundation, and were the product of German business customs and views."[14] Whatever Riesser's potential biases, even the eminently reasonable P. B. Whale concurs:

> It is known that the Pereires, founders of the Crédit Mobilier, took a part in promoting the Darmstädter Bank, and that the "statutes" of the latter follow closely those of the French institution. But the Schaaffhausen'scher Bankverein, earlier than either of these, had much the same programme; and in any case the practice of the German banks diverged very early from that of the Crédit Mobilier.[15]

Beyond historical curiosity, however, the placing of credit for the invention of this style of banking is of questionable importance, as Whale (1930, p. 10), also notes: ". . . the question of how far the Kreditbanken were copies of the Crédit Mobilier has been the subject of much sterile dispute."

More important for the issues addressed in this book is the level and pace of institutional development over time within Germany. In that regard, the emergence of this new class of institutions is crucial, as it marks one of the most significant steps in the formation of Germany's modern commercial banking industry. True, not all of the new credit banks met with the same fortune as the A. Schaaffhausen'schen Bankverein or the Darmstädter Bank, but the credit banks as a class of institutions were firmly established by the mid-1860s.

Low levels of capital accumulation, along with erratic or cyclical profits, meant that producers frequently needed to borrow even for very short-term needs. Such credit often came in the form of bills of exchange (IOUs with government securities as collateral) or real estate mortgages. The need for the joint-stock banks increased, as joint-stock companies began to form after 1840. Kurt Bösselmann (1939, pp. 199–200) counts 118 joint-stock companies founded in Prussia between 1800 and 1850, 90 of which were formed after 1835. W. O. Henderson (1975, p. 131) reports that "over 270 joint-stock companies were set up in the 1850s." Corporate firms used the universal banks (both private and joint-stock) for most of their financial

---

[13] See Cameron (1961), pp. 150–1, and Henderson (1975).
[14] See Riesser (1911), pp. 48–56, on the Crédit Mobilier and its connections to German banking.
[15] Whale (1930), p. 10, note 1.

intermediation needs. The practice of offering short-term credit was carried over from government finance, but it is thought that finance was flexible and often ended up financing the accumulation of fixed capital. Their use of share capital, instead of short-term deposits, enabled the credit banks to provide these rolled-over credits to industrial enterprises with less fear of illiquidity.

The joint-stock banks, of course, operated within the broader financial system and contributed to and depended upon its continued development. Those changes came, but progress remained slow over the first half of the century. The German capital market of the 1820s and 1830s was a loose network of local markets, heavily based on personal contacts and family connections. As capital markets developed and as incorporation spread, credit banks played an active role in the promotion and placement of corporate securities – alongside their government business. Richard H. Tilly (1966) finds that private placement by the credit banks was important for all joint-stock firms, but was particularly so in the mining and metallurgical sectors. Metallurgy, he argues, was a "relatively untried branch of activity before 1870, and 'blind capital' could not be found for them as easily as it could for railroad companies or governments."[16]

At least in the case of the Rhineland, universal bankers filled what seems to have been a wide information gap between the investing public and entrepreneurs. It may therefore be more apt to describe the placement functions of these banks as a solution for market failures than as a circumvention of a highly functioning market.[17] Given the newness of some of the technology that the banks financed at this time, these early joint-stock banks took on a role not unlike that of modern venture capitalists. The apparent prevalence of direct placements and trading within banks has often led to the characterization of the German stock exchanges as relatively unimportant for channeling capital into industry. The markets did remain extremely small and thin until the last quarter of the nineteenth century, but they did not substantially lag those of other countries at similar levels of industrial and economic development at that time. The question of securities placements points to the connections between stock market functioning and the operations of the universal banks as well as to the potential influence of regulation on the functioning of securities markets – topics

---

[16] Tilly (1966), p. 119.

[17] Since the credit banks were both underwriters and brokers, however, this interpretation implies that the credit banks were ineffective quality signalers. That is, if the advice of the banks was generally dependable, investors should have simply purchased the market shares that were issued by a trustworthy bank. Personal placement would have been unnecessary.

that receive extensive further attention in subsequent chapters of this book.

THE KAISERREICH (1871–1914)

The events around 1870, particularly the formation of the Empire in 1871, are thought by some to have marked the beginning of a new era in the economic development of Germany. For the first time, the country was unified under one government. Within five years, it both consolidated its more than seven independent coinage systems into one currency (1873) and formed a single central note bank, the Reichsbank (beginning on January 1, 1876). The loosening of restrictions on the founding of joint-stock companies throughout the 1860s and 1870s abolished important barriers to business formation.[18] Meanwhile, the Prussian victory over France had brought in 5 billion francs in war indemnity – the largest such transfer in history, amounting to about one-quarter of the German gross domestic product (GDP).[19] Political and institutional conditions seemed favorable for industrialization.

The liberalization of incorporation law, compounded by the burst of industrial activity, led to a rapid increase in joint-stock foundings after 1871.[20] In the thirty-eight years between 1871 and 1908, fifteen times more joint-stock firms, with about three times the capital, were founded than in the previous forty-five years. The ranks of *Aktiengesellschaften* swelled from a total of approximately two hundred before 1870 to over one thousand shortly thereafter. The numbers exceeded three thousand by 1890 and stayed well over five thousand from the late 1890s until at least World War I. To be sure, many of these new joint-stock companies resulted from the transformation of existing private firms, but the creation of new businesses also played a major role. The use of the joint-stock form allowed firm founders to disperse ownership, diversify their financial assets, and tap financial markets for external finance – all of which lent the potential for further growth. Thus, evolution toward the modern industrial enterprise moved rapidly forward.[21]

---

[18] See Loewenstein (1912), pp. 60 et seq., on the battle over the founding of joint-stock companies, particularly in Württemberg.

[19] See the recent dynamic macroeconomic analysis of the indemnity transfer in Devereux and Smith (2004) and sources cited there. There remains some uncertainty over what role the indemnity payment played, if any, in Germany's boom-and-bust cycle of the early 1870s.

[20] A table of yearly foundings with average capital stocks appears in Riesser (1911), p. 119. See also *Handbuch der deutschen Aktiengesellschaften*, annually from 1895, and the longer-run picture of corporate formation and ownership in Fohlin (2005).

[21] According to Whale (1930), at the end of the nineteenth century, the proportion of joint-stock foundings resulting from new undertakings was approximately equal to that which

As industry expanded, the Prussian agricultural workforce naturally declined – from about 66 percent of the population in 1861 to 40 percent by 1882. In the same years, the industrial labor force increased from 26 percent to 36 percent.[22] The changes in the distribution of labor in the Reich as a whole followed a similar path: The agricultural workforce decreased from 43.4 percent in 1882 to 37.5 percent in 1895 and to 35.2 percent in 1907. Over the same period, the proportion of workers in industry, trade, and transport grew from 42 percent to 48.1 percent and then to 52.5 percent.[23] The mining sector maintained its preeminence in the post-1870 period: Metals assumed the largest share of German manufacturing in the first decade of the new century, growing from 19.8 percent in 1895 to 25.1 percent in 1907.[24]

New industries began to emerge as well, and among these, two attained particular prominence. The first, the electrotechnical industry, came into being in 1883, when Emil Rathenau formed the Deutsche Edisongesellschaft für angewandte Elektrizität with Siemens & Halske. In 1884, the firm became independent of Siemens & Halske, and in 1887 it became Allgemeine Elektrizitäts-Gesellschaft (better known as A.E.G.). By the turn of the century, well over thirty joint-stock electric companies were operating with a capital of 436 million marks. The second new industry, chemicals, experienced a less dramatic beginning. A few chemical companies appeared in the 1850s, but they had all but vanished by the 1870s. The start of the modern German chemical industry, and its prominence in world markets, came between 1870 and 1874, when at least forty-two new firms were created. By 1896 there were over a hundred joint-stock chemical companies, as well as thousands of small (one to five employees) and medium-sized (six to fifty employees) private companies.[25]

Progress toward the modern enterprise became the most pronounced after the turn of the twentieth century: Scale, product diversification, and functional integration all increased. Of the largest one hundred German firms in 1887, only thirty-six were engaged in five or more product groups,

---

was based on conversions of existing firms. By 1907, the share of new joint-stock firms created out of preexisting companies was 72 percent, and by 1912, that number was 91 percent (the average for the period 1907–12 was 83.5 percent). The proportion of share capital in converted firms tended to be slightly lower and averaged 82 percent for the same period. See Weber (1915), as cited in Whale (1930), p. 42 (note).

[22] *Preussische Statistik, Statistik des Deutschen Reichs,* and *Statistisches Jahrbuch für das Deutsche Reich,* various volumes.

[23] Statistisches Bundesamt (1972), p. 142.

[24] Trebilcock (1981), p. 47.

[25] See sources cited in Riesser (1911), pp. 123–8, on the electrotechnical and chemical sectors. See also Henderson (1975), pp. 186–98.

whereas in 1907, this number had risen to fifty-one. Similarly, the number of firms involved in marketing or in cartels as well as in production and or raw materials grew from thirteen to sixty-four between 1887 and 1907. Also, the share capital of the top one hundred firms ranged from 3.8 to approximately 40 million marks in 1887, but varied from 10 to 180 million marks in 1907.[26] These organizational and operational changes led to a more hierarchical corporate structure, which brought with it salaried managers and the separation of ownership and control. Increasing financial independence and organizational complexity led to changes in corporate finance practices and in the relationships between banks and non-financial firms – topics that subsequent chapters take up in detail.

Though many of the future great banks were already founded before the establishment of the Second Empire, it was during the Kaiserreich that the universal banks evolved into their full-fledged form. By maintaining its restrictive monetary policy, particularly its tight control over note issue, the government unintentionally spurred the development of the financial sector as more entrepreneurial bankers created alternatives to the note-issuing banks (*Notenbanken*).

After the introduction of the unified currency in 1873, the number of note-issuing banks declined considerably. The Bank Act of 1875 nonetheless authorized certain banks to issue currency and also regulated their activities.[27] Government-imposed liquidity requirements limited the investment opportunities of the note-issuing banks, while expansion of the Reichsbank eroded the market for their notes. Most of these banks ultimately abdicated their note-issuing privileges, and after 1905 there were only four *Notenbanken* apart from the Reichsbank.

Since banks of issue needed to remain highly liquid, the less liquid investment opportunities were left to other institutions, especially to the credit banks.[28] The credit banks (*Kreditbanken*) were both private and joint-stock firms that provided many forms of credit mainly to industry. With minor exceptions, they were unregulated except by the general laws applying to German companies (*Aktiengesellschaften* or *Kommanditgesellschaften auf*

---

[26] From Kocka and Siegrist (1979), pp. 80–1. Given the moderate inflation during the period, the real increase is still significant – over three-fold. See also Kocka (1978) on the changes in German corporate structure at the turn of the century.

[27] See Lotz (1976 [1888]) on the development of German note-issuing banks and for a critical analysis of the Bank Act of 1875 that regulated such banks.

[28] See Verdier (2002) for a more detailed argument linking liquidity and universal bank development and Fohlin (forthcoming) for an international comparison of political, economic, and legal factors in financial system development.

Aktien). The private banks were naturally exempt even from these regulations. It is into this category of financial institutions, which later became more widely known as universal banks, that the great banks fall.

Several other types of financial institutions served other segments of the imperial economy. Joint-stock mortgage banks (*Hypothekenbanken*), whose scope was regulated by the *Hypothekenbank* law of 1899, confined their business mainly to mortgages on urban real estate. To raise funds, they issued interest-bearing mortgage bonds known as *Pfandbriefe*. Agricultural credit unions (*Landschaften*), found predominantly in Prussia beginning in the eighteenth century, provided credit to agriculture through *Pfandbriefe*. Provincial government banks (*Landesbanken*), maintained by provincial governments, also offered agricultural mortgage credit and, in addition, helped finance local authorities and acted as regional central banks to the savings banks.[29]

Municipal authorities created, regulated, and guaranteed the savings banks (*Sparkassen*), whose lending was small-scale and conservative. Effectively segmented from the commercially oriented universal banks, these institutions served mainly working-class clientele, whose main purpose in using a financial institution was to earn interest on deposits.[30] Cooperative credit societies (*Creditgenossenschaften*) offered yet another distinct alternative for primarily working-class customers. Small-business owners, farmers, and laborers – who normally had difficulty proving their creditworthiness to a large bank – often pooled their resources into these cooperative credit societies in order to fund their own investment projects collectively.[31] They were required to register by the *Genossenschaft* laws of 1889 and 1896.

By 1913, the savings banks, mortgage banks, and joint-stock credit banks comprised 32.7, 19.1, and 27 percent of financial system assets, respectively, each far outweighing the cooperative societies. These figures raise the generally underemphasized point that the credit banks, while responsible for a large share of the economy's intermediation, were nonetheless just one part of a diversified financial system. Indeed, the savings banks maintained the largest share of bank-held assets throughout the period.[32] Nonetheless,

---

[29] Whale (1930), p. 3.

[30] For a picture of the clientele of savings banks, see *Statistisches Amt der Stadt Frankfurt a.M.* (1903, 1906). See Schönitz (1912) on the provision of credit by savings banks to small- and medium-scale businesses.

[31] See Schönitz (1912) for comprehensive details on the *Genossenschaften*. For a modern analysis of the functions of the credit cooperatives, see Guinnane (2001).

[32] Data comes from Deutsche Bundesbank (1976), via Fohlin (1994).

the credit banks stand out due to the size of the largest institutions in the sector, especially relative to banks of other types. While accounting for less than 1 percent of banking institutions in 1900, joint-stock universal banks held over a quarter of the country's banking assets and over 17 percent of financial institution assets more broadly.[33] The size disparity of universal banks endured, and even grew slightly, over the period. By 1913, these banks averaged over 100 million marks in assets, with the nine great banks each holding over nine times that amount on average. In contrast, the savings banks averaged just over 6 million marks of liabilities apiece.[34]

The Credit Banks

The functions performed by the credit banks extended to many realms of corporate finance. They provided current accounts, acceptances, discounting, Lombards and reports, brokerage, and promotions (that is, transformations, foundings, issuings, syndications, and securities).[35] Their combination of credit and off-balance-sheet operations distinguished the German universal banks from the other types of financial institutions, but their mix of services also evolved over time, as the discussion in Chapter 4 details at length. Small business gained limited access to the larger universal banks, but there were many small joint-stock banks and private banks that supplied credit to these small borrowers. While the majority (130) of the joint-stock universal banks held paid-in capital of 100,000 to 1 million marks as of 1908, there still remained 80 such institutions with share capital less than 100,000 marks.[36]

---

[33] The data for banking institutions come from Deutsche Bundesbank (1976), while those for total financial institutions come from Goldsmith (1969), mostly originating in Hoffmann (1960). The Bundesbank figures exclude the central bank and insurance companies. When they are included, the universal banks' share in total financial assets falls significantly for earlier years but decreasingly so up through 1913.

[34] According to Sheppard (1971), the forty-three joint-stock banks of England and Wales held approximately 420 million marks of assets on average in 1913. These banks, of course, provided primarily commercial services. Capie and Webber (1985) provide newer, more comprehensive estimates, especially for the period before 1891. Chapter 4 investigates the structure of the German banking industry, and Fohlin (2000b) provides further comparisons with the United States and the United Kingdom, along with an estimation of the degree of market power in commercial lending.

[35] There is an enormous literature describing both debit and credit operations. See, for example, Bosenick (1912), Buchwald (1909), Jeidels (1905), Motschmann (1915), Riesser (1910 [1911])), and Whale (1930). In Riesser (1911), see pp. 191–406 for an exhaustive discussion.

[36] Many of these small joint-stock banks had converted from cooperatives (*Genossenschaften*). For more on the small joint-stock banks and provision of credit to small business, see Lansburgh (1909) and Schönitz (1912).

The universal banks provided short-term credit by offering acceptances, discounting bills, and floating Lombard loans. Acceptances themselves served three purposes: offering liquidity for domestic and foreign commodities transactions, providing funds for current operating expenses (and sometimes for working capital), and supplying cash for stock exchange speculation. Banks discounted bills by taking on at a discount the obligations owed to firms, and in doing so, allowed firms to mobilize liquid resources. Lombard loans provided similar flexibility, in the form of short-term personal credit to trade, agriculture, industry, and private capital. Throughout the period, however, current account services arguably constituted the most important line of business for the credit banks. A current account with a credit bank afforded the firm many services, such as facilities for making and receiving payments, undersigning of commercial paper, bill acceptances, Giro accounts (payments made and received between customers of one bank), foreign bills of exchange, current account credits or discounting of bills and outstanding business accounts, and information on business connections (including individuals, firms, and foreign markets). The current account business not only provided the banks' primary sources of commissions, it also often led to the provision of other services – and thus more commissions – for the same firms.[37] Banks competed vigorously for their current account customers, since establishing a steady stream of business through the current account meant that "a direct road is opened to power and profit for the bank."[38] These additional commissions and "power" came typically from the banks' brokerage and investment business. Indeed, the banks earned about a quarter of their gross profits from such commissions. Much of this activity involved small purchases of merchandise and securities for third parties, so that a substantial portion of the income came from the brokerage side.[39]

Commissions (particularly for the great banks) also flowed in from investment services. The credit banks played a key role in underwriting securities of all types. From their beginnings in the early industrial period, they handled transformations and foundings of share companies and issued industrial securities of other types. Contemporary observers credited the universal

---

[37] Since most firms accumulated debits and credits to current accounts seasonally, and since seasons differed for the various industries, a large, well-diversified bank would have little need for its own capital in covering current accounts. But for poorly diversified banks, current account credits could prove risky.

[38] Riesser (1911), p. 260.

[39] *Der Deutsche Ökonomist,* covering banks with capital of at least 1 million marks, as cited in Riesser (1911). More evidence appears in Chapter 4 of this book.

banks for the post-1870 boom in joint-stock foundings, and certainly the banks organized a majority of new companies at that time.[40] The large credit banks underwrote many of the new issues of corporate securities, particularly in the mining, machinery, and electrical industries. The largest banks also took part in major underwriting projects, such as arranging the French war indemnity payment of 1871–2, nationalizing the railway companies, and financing large government loans. For underwriting large or risky projects such as these, banks often combined into syndicates, allowing them to offer substantial amounts of credit while safeguarding against illiquidity or insolvency. As a result of many of these promotional operations, the banks are thought to have held, both voluntarily and otherwise, the securities of their client firms, thereby providing further sources of liquidity.[41]

The Credit Banks and the Stock Exchanges

Because of their promotional operations, and because of the peculiar institutional organization of the German securities markets, the universal banks, particularly the largest ones, were closely tied to the exchanges. Throughout the pre–World War I period, a substantial proportion of joint-stock firms listed their shares on one or more of the several German stock exchanges. According to available estimates, virtually all of the registered *Aktiengesellschaften* had listings on the Berlin exchange in the first half of the nineteenth century. Listings grew rapidly over the century, but the ranks of new share companies expanded even faster: The Berlin exchange listed approximately half of joint-stock firms by the early 1870s, and fewer than a third for most of the 1890s and early 1900s. The increasing use of the joint-stock form, in addition to the expansion of many firms' share capital via secondary equity offerings, also altered the balance of exchange business, especially at the larger bourses. Berlin, for example, traded mainly state bonds and other government paper until 1870 but shifted toward industrial securities once they became more widely used. Smaller, provincial exchanges retained their focus on local issues, though joint-stock companies gained ground throughout Germany.

---

[40] During the ensuing depression, critics then blamed the credit banks for engaging in and fomenting stock market speculation. For a range of polemics, see Glagau (1876), Lansburgh (1909), and Sattler (1977 [1890]). Even Riesser (1911), a great-bank director, acknowledged some bank culpability.

[41] Subsequent chapters elaborate on this theme and argue that, particularly during the late industrial period (c. 1880–1913), such stock holdings were typically temporary and did not result in long-term equity stakes in industrial enterprises.

Securities and commodities exchanges emerged in all corners of the country, most serving the needs of a particular region.[42] Several dealt only in securities (Augsburg, Dresden, Frankfurt, Hanover, Munich, Stuttgart, and Zwickau), but even more traded commodities as well (Berlin, Bremen, Breslau, Cologne, Düsseldorf, Essen, Hamburg, Königsberg, Leipzig, Lübeck, Mannheim, and Stettin). At least for the first half of the nineteenth century, Frankfurt and Hamburg, the old commercial centers, remained the leading stock exchanges in Germany. The consolidation of the German Empire shifted not just political but also economic and financial power toward the new center and in the process lifted the Berlin exchange to national prominence. Before long, the latter took over as the country's premier exchange, surpassing Frankfurt and Hamburg in trading volume, tax receipts, and numbers of listings by the 1880s.

Government regulation of the German securities exchanges began in earnest in the nineteenth century. Before that, local businesspeople generally controlled the bourses through chambers of commerce (*Handelskammern*) or similar trade organizations. The excesses of the early 1870s, the so-called *Gründerjahre*, and the bust that followed brought calls for reform: greater protection for shareholders and tighter restrictions on the stock exchanges. Company law, regulating the founding and governance of joint-stock firms, also changed out of similar motivations. While the right to incorporate with limited liability became almost universal by 1870, the government retained a variety of controls over firms' organization, operation, and financing. Thus, given the natural interdependence of the stock markets and joint-stock companies, regulation of the two institutions was intimately linked. Moreover, because of the intertwining of commodities and securities trading (especially in Berlin, but elsewhere as well), agrarian interests, and their reactions to conditions in agriculture, played a major role in debates over regulatory changes.

Yet even after government intervention in the mid-nineteenth century, private business organizations maintained a firm grasp. Private bankers, because of their involvement in both government and industrial finance, became involved in the exchanges early on in their formation. Later, the universal banks, largely the progeny of private bankers, naturally also found a significant place in exchange governance. The interrelationship between the securities exchanges and these larger mixed banks intensified only after the flourishing of share companies more generally.

---

[42] See Fohlin (2002b) and Chapter 7 of this book.

TRADITIONAL VIEWS ON GERMAN UNIVERSAL BANKING
BEFORE WORLD WAR I

The Gerschenkron-Inspired Paradigm

By the end of the nineteenth century, economists and historians had begun to emphasize the role of the universal banks in Germany's industrialization, particularly during the period of heavy industrialization beginning with the railroad boom. Despite significant reevaluations of the universal banks' involvement in German industrialization, traditional views persist in recent research in the area. A number of authors have written on the subject over the past several decades; but Gerschenkron's work remains the standard statement of the orthodox paradigm – perhaps because it boils down many complex issues into a few simple points. Many economic historians speak of a "Gerschenkron hypothesis," yet it proves difficult to articulate such a hypothesis that is both nontrivial and feasible to test empirically. Indeed, as appealing as it is to have a unified, cogent statement of the role of financial systems in industrial development, the literature so far, including that of Gerschenkron, does not provide one.

Gerschenkron's work did spur later scholars to seek more detailed evidence to support or refute his claims, and many of his followers have gone on to recount and refine his stories in their own research and teaching. Between Gerschenkron's original work and the subsequent retelling and reworking of it, a certain set of ideas about financial systems and European industrialization has evolved into what I refer to as the "Gerschenkron-inspired paradigm" or the "orthodox paradigm." Gerschenkron himself held that the role of financial institutions in industrialization related to the extent of "economic backwardness" on the eve of industrial takeoff.[43] According to his schema, financial institutions played a critical role in the industrialization of "moderately backward" economies – meaning much of northwestern continental Europe. In situations of extreme underdevelopment, as in Russia, financial institutions alone could not support the transition to modernized industrial activity. Such cases demanded supplementary, centralized institutional intervention, mostly from government.

But the importance of financial institutions comprises only part of Gerschenkron's overall thesis; he saw banking as one factor in many that

---

[43] Gerschenkron (1962, 1970). Sylla (1991) gives a nice retrospective on Gerschenkron's theories and some related work. P. K. O'Brien (1986) also addresses and explains Gerschenkron's typology of European industrialization.

varied with general economic conditions. Gerschenkron (1970) summarized those conditions thus:

> ... what was found to vary in direct relation to the degree of backwardness were: 1) the speed of industrial growth; 2) the stress on bigness of plant and enterprise; 3) the composition of the nascent output, that is, the degree to which "heavy" industries were favored; 4) the reliance on technological borrowing and perhaps financial assistance from abroad; 5) the pressure on levels of consumption; 6) the passive role of agriculture; 7) the role of banks and state budgets; 8) the virulence of ideologies, under the auspices of which the industrialization proceeded.[44]

Because of its ability to adopt technologies developed in already-industrialized Britain, Germany is argued to have arrived faster at modernization than had its role model. Yet the scale of factories and firms needed to compete internationally was so large as to require investment funds from beyond the typical entrepreneur's circle of family and associates. This relative shortage of financial capital is thought to have necessitated institutions capable of mobilizing a high volume of resources from disparate sources and also able to compensate for a scarcity of human capital, specifically managerial or entrepreneurial. The universal banks are traditionally viewed as just such an institution:

> The German investment banks – a powerful invention, comparable in economic effect to that of the steam engine – were in their capital-supplying functions a substitute for the insufficiency of the previously created wealth willingly placed at the disposal of entrepreneurs. But they were also a substitute for entrepreneurial deficiencies.[45]

Though only one piece of his overall paradigm, Gerschenkron clearly depicts the universal banks as an integral part of the industrialization process – and he is not alone. Many economic historians believe that the universal banks provided the underpinnings, and were even a necessary condition, for German industrialization. Qualifications of the role of the banks have been surfacing for some time, yet the consensus – at least through the 1990s – remained on the side of the banks.[46] The orthodox view of universal banking, whether originating with Gerschenkron or not, credits these institutions with contributing in many ways to the growth of German industry. At the most fundamental level, the universal banks are thought to have

---

[44] Gerschenkron (1970), pp. 98–9.

[45] Idem (1968), p. 137.

[46] See, for example, Calomiris (1995), Chandler (1990), Da Rin and Hellmann (2002), Kennedy (1987), or Tilly (1994b). Subsequent sections discuss ongoing debates and doubts further.

mobilized the financial resources that made industrialization possible. As Alfred D. Chandler explains, "... these banks provided initial capital for new industrial ventures and helped guide them through their early years of growth.... They supplied much of what today would be called venture capital."[47]

Such views may have originally derived from a literal reading of the statutes of the new joint-stock banks themselves. The original statutes of the Bank für Handel und Industrie (Article III K), for example, empowered the bank "to bring about or participate in the promotion of new companies, the amalgamation or consolidation of different companies, and the transformation of industrial undertakings into joint stock forms."[48] But most of the orthodox paradigm, built up in the mid-twentieth century, originates in the literature of the late-nineteenth and early-twentieth centuries; for example, the well-known writings of Werner Sombart includes the following: "Doubtless, a good portion of the increase in economic life in Germany is attributable to this interest of the banks and bankers in productive, economic activities. The banks have become the direct promoters of the spirit of enterprise, the pacemakers for industry and trade."[49] The sentiment of Sombart (1909) was widely shared by his contemporaries and finds continued support among modern economists and historians – many of whom use the German case to illustrate the great benefits of universal-relationship banking.

W. P. Kennedy (1987) exemplifies such thinking:

Germany and America were compensated for their deficiencies in short-term and high-grade securities markets...by a superior ability to concentrate resources in areas strategic for rapid development at moments crucial to the evolution of new products and techniques.... The German banking system, therefore, provided much more elaborate formal facilities for concentrating financial resources than either the U.S. or British counterparts.[50]

He goes on to attribute apparently superior growth performance in Germany (and the United States) to differences in financial structure:

... capital markets in the U.S. and Germany, by making resources available to a large group of technologically progressive industries on a scale unequaled in Britain,

---

[47] Chandler (1990), pp. 417–19.
[48] Translated and quoted by Whale (1930), p. 12.
[49] Sombart (1909), p. 203, my translation. For a thorough bibliography of contemporary literature, primarily in German, see Riesser (1910 [1911]). Whale's (1930) bibliography is a useful supplement and covers later works.
[50] Kennedy (1987), p. 116. See also Chandler (1990), pp. 417–19.

account for much of the difference in the economic growth performance between those two countries and Britain in the half century after 1865.[51]

Similar views on German banking also emerged much earlier. Frederick Lavington (1921), for example, stressed screening, monitoring, risk management, venture capital activities, and economies of scale and scope:

An organization of this kind, intermediate between the sources of enterprise and the sources of capital, must evidently possess machinery for investigating business ventures, financial strength adequate to sustain the heavy risks to which it is exposed and the reputation and business connexions necessary for the efficient sale of securities to the public. An organization such as the Deutsche Bank possesses these qualities to a high degree.... It is easy to see that, with able management and machinery of this kind, the risks of industrial banking are greatly reduced; business ventures in need of capital can be thoroughly investigated and the development of the more pioneering enterprises may be promoted with a reasonable prospect of success.[52]

At the same time, these authors overlook some contrarian views, particularly that of Robert Liefmann (1921) on the early industrialization period:

It is not to be supposed that the formation of such financial companies will increase the influence of the banks on industry, but rather the contrary. In opposition to a widely held opinion, I have always disputed that one could speak of a growing influence of the banks on German industry as a general phenomenon, and anyone who has closely studied the history of the investment bank in the period from 1850– 1870, must agree with me. The development of the financial companies seems to me now to be a further circumstance which tends in the opposite direction of a greater independence of industry in relation to the banks.[53]

Liefman's commentary notwithstanding, the German universal banks are thought to have developed special institutional features, both in their organizational structure and in their policies. The orthodox paradigm, albeit not always in these terms, credits the universal banks with mobilizing capital through large networks of branches, screening potential entrepreneurs, promoting and reorganizing whole industries, deciding on investment and production strategies, monitoring the progress of clients' investments, arranging and enforcing propitious industrial combinations, and diversifying away the risk associated with such innovative activities.

[51] Kennedy (1987), p. 120.
[52] Lavington (1921), p. 210.
[53] Liefman (1921), p. 491. Quoted and translated by Whale (1930), pp. 58–9.

The universal banks' combination of the full range of financial services is thought by many to have given German bankers advantages in providing substantial and efficient finance throughout firms' lives. Such efficiency has been argued in turn to have reduced the costs of finance and thus promoted industrial investment.[54] In a related vein, the German banks have been credited with promoting efficient allocation of the economy's investment portfolio, particularly in comparison with Britain.[55]

Efficiency gains hinge not just on the reusability of information but on its quality as well. Thus, close, long-term relationships between banks and industrial firms are seen as central to the banks' acquisition and transfer of useful information – not just financial, but also strategic and entrepreneurial. Moreover, the banks are thought to have gained significant say in the use of funds and therefore the types of investments made by firms. Such involvement and oversight is argued to have reduced banks' uncertainty about borrowers, mitigated risks of moral hazard or simple bad judgment, and facilitated long-term lending. Long-term bank lending usually took the form of short-term credits on current accounts that were rolled over repeatedly. Sidney Pollard and Dieter Ziegler (1992) sum up the widely accepted view "that the rolling short-term credit, perpetually renewed, could be the equivalent of long-term capital, or could be used to free the firm's resources for long-term investments."[56]

Even more than the universality of banking functions itself, the historical literature has focused in on the formation of relationships between banks and nonfinancial firms. Gerschenkron, among others, claimed that "the German banks, and with them the Austrian and Italian banks, established the closest possible relations with industrial enterprises."[57] Formal ties between banks and firms were established and maintained through placement of bank representatives on firms' supervisory boards (*Aufsichtsrat*).[58] In fact, Otto Jeidels (1905) argued that ". . . the power of the Great Banks is exercised

---

[54] Economies of scope is a modern interpretation of the traditional accounts. Calomiris (1995), for example, advances such an argument and has argued that German companies faced lower costs of issuing new equity compared with their American counterparts. Tilly (1994b) produces similar figures for Germany.

[55] See Tilly (1986) and Kennedy and Britton (1985), discussed subsequently at greater length.

[56] Pollard and Ziegler (1992), p. 21.

[57] Gerschenkron (1962), p. 14. Chandler (1990), Jeidels (1905), Riesser (1910 [1911]), Schumpeter (1930), Wallich (1905), Whale (1930), and Tilly (1994b), and most others writing on the subject, also emphasize this point.

[58] German joint-stock firms are governed by two boards. The supervisory board is elected by and represents shareholders and also appoints the firm's executive board. The latter,

via the legal institution of the supervisory board, rather than through direct influence of financial strength."[59] Gerschenkron echoed Jeidels:

... through development of the institution of the supervisory boards to the position of most powerful organs within corporate organizations, the banks acquired a formidable degree of ascendancy over industrial enterprises, which extended far beyond the sphere of financial control into that of entrepreneurial and managerial decisions.[60]

Thus, bank seats on supervisory boards are traditionally thought to have permitted not just oversight, but also direct control over firms' operations and decisions. Chandler (1991) notes, "The representatives of the German Großbanken participated to a greater extent in the top-level decision-making of new industrial companies than did representatives of financial institutions in the United States and Britain." He goes on to report that "... the banks often had a significant say (particularly in the early years of a company's history) in investment decisions, in the selection of top and even middle managers, in establishing administrative procedures, and in reviewing the internal financial management of the enterprises that they had helped to finance."[61]

The idea persists that for individual firms and whole industries, bank intervention improves operational efficiency, managerial effectiveness, industrial organization, and, ultimately, profitability. In this connection, the universal banks are often also characterized as marriage brokers: identifying advantageous combinations, in the form of cartels or mergers. As Wilfried Feldenkirchen describes, noting the difficulty of enforcing output and pricing agreements during the 1880s, "... the banks, with the Disconto-Gesellschaft in the lead, promoted the expansion of big enterprises such as the Gelsenkirchener Bergwerks AG and the Harpener Bergbau AG, expecting to achieve their aims more easily once industrial concentration had taken place."[62] In a related vein, Norbert Reich (1979, pp. 266–7) argues, in the context of the 1884 law, that the placement of the same individual in multiple board positions – particularly directors of banks or "friendly" companies – increased the tendency for industrial concentration. Reich bases his analysis on the finding of Rudolf Wiethölter (1961, p. 287), similar to Jürgen Kocka's,

---

comprising firm managers, oversees day-to-day operations. Most other types of companies are not required to have a supervisory board.

[59] Jeidels (1905), p. 145, author's translation.

[60] Gerschenkron (1962).

[61] See the more extensive discussion in Chandler (1990), pp. 417–19.

[62] Feldenkirchen (1991), p. 127 and references cited there.

that in 1906, 70 people held a total of 1,184 supervisory board positions, for an average of 17 positions each. One banker even held 35 positions. Klaus Hopt (1996, p. 244) finds that the six great banks in Berlin were represented in other joint-stock companies 344 times by directors and 407 times by members in the supervisory board.

One further advantage often attributed to the universal banking system, and to formal bank–firm relationships in particular, is the long-term perspective of bankers in helping firms solve financial difficulties and get through more general economic downturns. Feldenkirchen (1991) gives the example of Hoerder Bergwerks- und Hüttenverein, which, because of its exclusive relationship with the Schaaffhausen'schen Bankverein (and the private banker Deichmann & Co.), received crucial restructuring help and survived a brush with bankruptcy.[63] Harkening back to the less benevolent bank-power hypotheses, however, Feldenkirchen also suggests that such help could enable bankers to extend their direct influence on company policy:

In particular the ten million thaler loan granted to Krupp in 1874, after he had financed new plant with short-term credit, which was later recalled after the downturn in the business cycle, illustrates how the banks used the dependency generated by new credit provision to extend their influence. They issued the loan with an interest rate of six per cent at a premium of 86, while Krupp had to repay it at 110 within nine years. Additionally, a representative of the banks became a member of the company's board in order to directly monitor further developments.[64]

More generally, the conventional view of German universal banking emphasizes the cradle-to-grave relationships between banks and firms and the beneficial mutual commitment that resulted. Jeidels (1905) commented, from the banks' perspective, that it was "in the interest of the security, profitability, and longevity of a credit institution to provide for all of the credit needs of a firm, from its formation to its liquidation."[65]

Taken in its entirety, the traditional paradigm of German finance and industrialization holds that universal banking activities and accompanying formalized bank–firm relationships raised the quantity, quality, and efficiency of investment in the latter half of the nineteenth century and the start of the twentieth. This view implicitly compares the German system to others, and distinguishes sharply between the early industrialization experiences of

---

[63] Ibid.

[64] Ibid., p. 126. Feldenkirchen relies here on primary sources coming from Krupp. But it is useful to note the early date of the evidence – from a decade before the 1884 company law. Moreover, the case of Krupp may not provide a good representation of broader patterns.

[65] Jeidels (1905), p. 63, author's translation. See also Gerschenkron (1962) and, for a modern restatement, Mayer (1988).

Germany and England in particular. As the first European country to indus-
trialize, England constitutes the basis to which to compare subsequent experiences. In the Gerschenkronian account, English industrial development
proceeded gradually enough, and innovations required small enough infu-
sions of capital, that entrepreneurs depended little on external financing
from banks.[66] Though such notions are currently debated, Britain is traditionally thought to have lost ground relative to its continental neighbors
at the turn of the century, and this relative slowdown is often attributed
to a failure to innovate and invest at the forefront of technology. Noting
Germany's significant advantage over Britain in world exports of chemicals, electrical equipment, and industrial machinery, Chandler concludes as
follows:

. . . these figures emphasize that although Britain was holding its own in traditional
industrial goods and materials, textiles, iron shapes, iron ships, and steam engines,
Germany had decisively outpaced Britain in producing and exporting the products
of the Second Industrial Revolution.[67]

Chandler voices a common view, in which the British financial system
bears most of the blame for what is seen as the decline of the British economy for much of the past century. Lack of capital is thought to have constrained British industry, and the banks, it is argued, held back the finance
that would have permitted innovation. Many have chastised the British
banks for avoiding engagement with domestic industry and leaving firms
to find finance from other sources. The banks' involvement in foreign and
imperial ventures is claimed to have drained away funds from domestic
industry; firms' resultant recourse to securities markets is argued to have
advanced investors' short-term profit motives at the expense of long-term
growth.[68]

Thus, the German banks are thought not only to have engaged in all
of the activities seen as central to the promotion of economic growth, but
to have executed these functions more effectively and efficiently than the
British banks. In echoing the common perception that the British banks and
securities markets heavily favored short-term and gilt-edged instruments,

---

[66] Some question the standard view. See, for example, Cameron (1967, 1972), Cottrell (1980),
and Mathias (1973, 1989).

[67] Chandler (1990), pp. 410–11. See this same work for in-depth discussion of British, American, and German forms of industrial organization. On the relative productivity of Britain
and Germany, see Broadberry (1997, 2003).

[68] For a review of the literature on British banking and industrial development, see Collins
(1991, 1998). Also see Capie and Collins (1992). For a critical appraisal of the British
banking system, see Edwards (1987).

Kennedy (1987) attributes the lack of long-term lending and venture capital to the "informational weaknesses" of the British system. Kennedy and R. Britton (1985) argued moreover that the German system's superior risk diversification placed that country closer to its efficient portfolio frontier than did the British system. Kennedy concludes that "What was unique in Britain was not the existence of imperfect sharing of risk and control among those with a stake in corporate ventures but rather the unusually slow development of recognition of the extent of the problem and of effective means to rectify it."[69]

Yet more recent research has begun to undermine the sharp distinction between the operations of the British deposit banks and the German universal banks, particularly in the realm of commercial lending. Michael Collins (1998), for example, argues convincingly that the English banks offered much more long-term finance through rolled-over credits than previously thought and suggests that the English banks discriminated less among customers compared to the lending practices of bank-industry groups (*Konzern*) in Germany. Moreover, it seems that British bankers did provide significant oversight functions and also aided distressed firms, with which the banks maintained long-term relationships.[70] Nonetheless, a significant contingent still holds that the British system promoted short-termism and less efficient distributions of risk compared to German-style banking.[71] Similarly, the American banking system has come under frequent attack for its relative inefficiency. As in the English case, the basis of comparison is usually Germany (and, up until the 1990s, Japan).

Traditional Areas of Debate in the Historical Literature

The German joint-stock universal banks, since their appearance in the middle of the nineteenth century, have engendered extensive discussion and debate among academics, practitioners, and politicians. Strong views, both positive and negative, persist. Yet the orthodox view of banking and industrial development, though predominant and enduring, has not gone unchallenged. Recent work confronts Gerschenkron's hypothesis at the broadest level. For example, it is now recognized that the orthodox view underemphasizes the role of political and legal factors in the development of financial

---

[69] Kennedy (1987), p. 127.
[70] Watson (1995) also argues, based on financing of the beer brewing and steel industries, that criticism of the British banks is exaggerated.
[71] This position is stated in Tilly (1994b), p. 4.

systems, and not just in the German case. Notably, the Bubble Act of 1720 and the monopoly of the Bank of England over limited liability banking until 1825 kept the English banks smaller and more conservative than they likely would have been based only on demands for industrial finance.[72] Moreover, the lack of a dependable lender of last resort reinforced the reluctance of English bankers to take on financial risk – particularly the risk associated with transforming short-term liabilities into potentially illiquid assets.[73] The German Reichsbank, in contrast, both squeezed other banks out of much of the short-term commercial business and facilitated those banks' provision of riskier investment services. Moreover, regulation of securities markets and of joint-stock companies possibly encouraged the dependence on and expansion of the universal banking system in Germany.[74]

Daniel Verdier (1997) generalizes such critiques and takes direct aim at Gerschenkron's hypothesis about the relationship between the extent of economic backwardness and the role of financial institutions. He argues that political structure, not relative backwardness, determines the shape of financial systems. As Verdier concedes, though, political centralization was neither solitary nor decisive in determining financial structure in most cases. Furthermore, political structure is not clearly independent of economic backwardness, and the two factors may be mutually enhancing, rather than mutually exclusive. Thus, Verdier's point, whether it correctly characterizes the relationship between political and financial development, does not clearly subvert Gerschenkron's hypothesis. Nonetheless, this line of work raises important points about the role of political and legal factors in financial and economic development.[75]

Most debates in this area focus more directly on the connection between financial institutions and industrial development. In this vein, perhaps most damaging to the orthodox view of universal banking's role in the industrialization of continental Europe is the criticism that this form of banking often developed after the first push of industrialization. This point is particularly relevant for the German case. Since German state governments tightly restricted the formation of joint-stock companies until 1870, few companies organized themselves under this form during the first wave of industrialization in the late 1830s and 1840s or even during the first big push

---

[72] Tilly (1994b) makes this point, as have others.

[73] See Kennedy (1992) and Ziegler (1993) on this point.

[74] See Chapter 7 for more on the securities markets and the impact of regulation.

[75] For more on legal issues, see the edited volume by Horn and Kocka (1979), especially those chapters by Horn, Friedrich, and Reich.

(in the 1850s) of heavy industry in the Ruhr.[76] Moreover, Germany's first joint-stock universal bank appeared in 1848, and several more formed in the 1850s, so that they could not have played any role in the significant steps toward industrialization taken in the first half of the nineteenth century.[77]

To counter the anachronism critique, researchers have pointed to Tilly's (1966, 1967, 1986) work showing that the private bankers of the Rhineland began to develop universal banking techniques as early as the 1830s. The activities and involvement of private bankers varied considerably, however, with most concentrating their resources on government finance and safer investments.[78] As Feldenkirchen notes, German financial institutions developed slowly: "Indeed in hardly any other field of the German economy in the mid-1850s was there such a general degree of backwardness as in the banking sector."[79] Thus, it appears that much of the financing of the first wave of industrialization flowed not through universal banks, but from the personal savings of entrepreneurs, their families, and friends.[80] The debate over the timing of industrialization and the development of the banking sector raises another potential problem for the Gerschenkron school: geographic and sectoral heterogeneity within Germany. The orthodox view of German industrialization derives largely from the experiences of the Rhineland and Westphalia and of heavy industry and, much later, electrotechnicals. The first wave of heavy industrialization sprang largely from the advent of railroads; and investment in this sector produced growth-enhancing spillovers in input sectors (mining and metal products) as well as in industries that could benefit from improved transport. Railroad companies themselves soaked up almost three-quarters of all capital invested in Prussian joint-stock companies prior to 1870.[81] While banks played a significant role in early railroad financing in parts of Prussia and Saxony, however, state governments financed the vast majority of such investment in other areas.[82]

Furthermore, industrial production began much earlier in Germany than the standard view supposes; and much of the industrial growth of the first

---

[76] See Böesselman (1939) and Thieme (1960) on joint-stock companies in Germany.

[77] Cameron (1972) and Edwards and Ogilvie (1996) make the more general point about the timing of industrialization and the development of joint-stock banking.

[78] See Donaubauer (1988), Kocka (1978), as well as studies cited in those works.

[79] Feldenkirchen (1991), p. 119.

[80] Kocka (1978), p. 538.

[81] Figures estimated by Fremdling (1977), p. 588. But, of course, joint stock capital grew much faster after 1870 than before.

[82] Borchardt (1968) estimates government investments at nearly three-quarters of railroad finance before 1850, and Vagts (1979), p. 614, indicates that by 1900, Prussia had 33,000 kilometers of state lines and only 2,257 kilometers of private lines.

half of the nineteenth century derived from small and medium-sized producers in metalworking, textiles, and other light industries.[83] Such industries spread throughout what became the pre–World War I German Empire, while mining naturally concentrated in a narrow swath of middle Germany – primarily the Ruhr, Saxony, and Silesia (now part of Poland). In many regions, small-scale industry was tied closely to agriculture, and factory production evolved only slowly.[84] Clearly, industrial development varied considerably among the German regions. Yet proponents of the orthodox view have insisted that, despite their small share in the economy, the universal banks and their principal clientele comprised such a crucial segment of the economy that they still provided the underpinnings of the industrial revolution; in Charles P. Kindleberger's view, "the great banks constituted less than a tenth of the total assets of financial institutions ... but were found at the critical margin affecting economic growth."[85]

The focus of the universal banks on a narrow range of industries has also prompted debate over the overall effects of the banks on economic growth and the suggestion that this effect, contrary to Kindleberger's assertion, may actually have been unfavorable. Indeed, Neuberger and Stokes (1974) found a negative relationship between the extent of aggregate bank lending via current accounts and economic growth in Germany between 1883 and 1913. The paper sparked some controversy, and debates over its methodology ended without a firm conclusion for or against the growth distortion hypothesis.[86]

Debates have spread even to the orthodox views of relations between large firms and banks in the later stages of industrialization. One part of the traditional paradigm holds that the universal banks exploited their positions of power to manipulate and control industrial firms to the banks' advantage.[87] As Tilly (1994) concludes, "the 'facts' of financial control of industry also seem clear. That investment and mixed banks of the Belgian, French or German and Austrian type consciously and actively pursued the goal of controlling the railroads and industrial enterprises they financed is documented in hundreds of individual episodes."[88]

---

[83] See Fischer (1968) and Hans Pohl (1986).

[84] On regional differences, see Herrigel (1996) and the many case studies cited there. Fremdling and Tilly (1979) and the paper by Megerle in that book are particularly informative. For a more general view of regional differences in Europe, see Pollard (1979).

[85] Kindleberger (1984a), p. 129, quoted in Edwards and Ogilvie (1996). So far, no general evidence exists to support Kindleberger's claim.

[86] See Fremdling (1977) and Komlos (1978).

[87] Hilferding (1910), a well-known socialist critic, energetically promoted such an idea.

[88] Tilly (1994b), p. 4, citing also Cameron (1961), Kocka (1978), Levy-Leboyer (1964), März (1968), Pohl (1982), and Tilly (1966).

The banks' detractors denounce the universal banks for exercising disproportionate power over industrial enterprises and using their positions to enforce unwanted takeovers and collusive agreements. Several scholars emphasize the role of the 1884 company law in the development of the supervisory board and in spurring the creation of interlocking directorates that provided banks with formal access to corporate decision making. Tilly (1999), for example, claims that "perhaps the new law's most important feature was its strengthening of suppliers of capital relative to company promoters and managers. It did this by strengthening the supervisory board (*Aufsichstrat*) at the expense of managers."[89] Similarly, Feldenkirchen (1991) explains that "[the banks'] means of control and supervision [over firms] took the form of a stronger representation on the supervisory board, especially after the Companies Act had been revised in 1884. . . . After 1884 the supervisory board hired the directors of the company and had the right to call an extraordinary general meeting."[90]

Kocka (1999, p. 167) draws somewhat different conclusions, despite striking figures on bank-held supervisory board positions:

Bank directors were the single largest group among the members of supervisory boards in German industrial joint-stock companies, and in 1913/14 they made up 20 percent. The Deustche Bank, for example, had representatives in 186 other companies. Leading bank directors individually held as many as forty-four representative board seats in 1914, and as many as one hundred in 1930.

Nevertheless, for him, "figures likes these do not indicate domination of bank finance over industrial capital, as numerous analyses have attempted to prove."[91]

Kocka is justified in such a conclusion, given that previous authors provide no clear evidence that the bank positions created the hypothesized impact. Indeed, researchers have uncovered little evidence in support of the bank-power hypothesis for the prewar period, and the consensus opinion of specialists now holds that the banks were losing their grip on industry by 1900. Bank critics refer to the mining and smelting concern Phoenix, a company thought to have been forced into cartelization and merger by bankers sitting on the company supervisory board, as a prime example

---

[89] Tilly, however, does not provide specifics to illustrate this point.

[90] Feldenkirchen (1991), p. 126, and note 74, p. 141. Here again, Feldenkirchen does not cite supporting evidence for the argument that banks were increasing their control.

[91] See also Kocka (1978), pp. 565–70, as well as Augustine (1992), p. 162, who finds that "one-sixth [of the the bankers in Wilhelmine Germany] were directors or chairmen of the board of joint-stock companies."

of bank power.[92] Volker Wellhöner's (1989) research, however, overturns the standard view on the Phoenix case and casts doubt on the bank dominance hypothesis for heavy industry more generally. Though bankers did use their votes on the Phoenix supervisory board to force the company into the Steelworks Association (*Stahlwerksverband*) against the wishes of the firms' top managers, the banks did so under pressure from other firms in the Association. The banks, one of which was a great bank, acted as a lever for the competitors of Phoenix; the powerful industrialist Fritz Thyssen, not the banks, took the lead. Similar events surrounded the fusion of Phoenix with a number of other mining and metal firms in the decade before World War I.[93]

Gerald Feldman's work also demonstrates that industrialists, notably Hugo Stinnes, played a major role in initiating mergers and acquisitions and even had to pull the bankers together at times.[94] Banks may have attempted to use their positions to extract rents from their clients, but industrialists could often fight back and exert their independence. Indeed, in many cases, it seems the banks' primary motivation lay in their competition with one another. A telling example is Hugo Stinnes' attempts to secure financing for the acquisition of Dortmunder Union by his firm, Deutsch-Luxemburg, in 1910. The chief difficulty seems to have been the banks' haggling with one another over their shares in the underwriting consortium. Feldman (1997) quotes from Stinnes' wife's diary:

Hugo tries to get the D-Banks under one roof with regard to the fusion of the Union and Deutsch-Luxemburg, so far without success, even if they are coming closer. No one is willing to allow the other a little bit more. Schoeller does not want to let himself be put into a minority by the others, while the Deutsche and Dresdner Banks believe that the Disconto is making too much on the business anyway.[95]

Broder and Wengenroth (1991) and Wessel (1990) also support the idea that bank power was waning (at least in the steel industry), and that especially large firms were mostly independent of the universal banks, well before 1900.[96] Most of the research on bank power has focused on the mining and steel sectors, and probably for good reason. If bank power was exerted

---

[92] See Feldenkirchen (1979a) and Kunze (1926). Both are cited in Wellhöner (1989).

[93] Wellhöner (1989), pp. 83–7. Also see Jeffrey Fear's (2005) recent work on Thyssen.

[94] See Feldman (1997), p. 7.

[95] Feldman (1997), pp. 7–8, quoting Stinnes' wife's diary of August 6, 1910. See also Feldman (1998). The D-banks were the four largest great banks: Disconto-Gesellschaft and the Dresdner, Deutsche, and Darmstädter banks.

[96] See also Wengenroth's (1986) comparative study of technological progress and strategy in the British and German steel industry from 1865 to 1895.

through their positions on firm supervisory boards, then it is clear that the influence of the largest banks was confined primarily to the mining, transport, and electrotechnical industries.[97]

Certainly between the largest banks and firms, power flowed in both directions. Yet this line of historical research has not yet determined how well these prominent counterexamples to claims of bank power generalize to the larger population. Thus, while the traditional views clearly over-state the imbalance between banks and firms, more research is needed to determine the extent of bank influence more broadly. If the paradigm fits poorly in the heavy industrial sectors, though, it probably fits even less well among the sectors that hardly engaged with the great banks. Provincial banks covered much of the geographical and industrial territory ignored by the big Berlin banks, however, and researchers have tended to neglect that segment of the banking sector. These gaps are filled in the next chapters of this book, in which the analysis directly considers the provincial banks and their role, along with the great banks and their clientele. Given the extant research, Kocka so far seems correct in concluding that "the banks acted like large flywheels; they did not initiate most changes, but, rather, reflected and strengthened existing trends."[98]

Based on this newer research, it now seems as though bank power had declined even before the concentration movement began gathering steam in Germany. On the other end of the timeline, the era of formal bank control must also have been shorter than the traditional account suggests. Since there were few joint-stock companies to control before 1870, and since half of the great banks were founded after 1870, the period of universal bank domination, if it ever existed, could have spanned at most two decades – the 1870s and 1880s. It is therefore difficult to reconcile the idea of bank power with the actual timing of events. Moreover, some observers accept that a tradition of bank control emerged, but argue that by rationalizing industrial structure, bank influence benefited German industry. For example, Harold James interprets Gerschenkron's claims as indicating that the banks "used their influence on supervisory boards (Aufsichtsräte) to influence firms' policies and especially to regulate competition and promote cartels and

---

[97] Chapter 5 in this book gives the sectoral breakdown of all kinds of bank board positions, and of interlocking directorates more generally, for a random sample of all joint-stock companies in Germany. Sombart (1909) reports on all seats of the great banks, and the findings are also summarized in Fohlin (1997a).

[98] Kocka (1980), p. 92, cited also in Herrigel (1996), p. 83. Such a sentiment was expressed much earlier by Whale (1930) and even to some extent – albeit with a defensive intent – by Riesser (1910 [1911]).

mergers."[99] Thus, whether or not the literature can agree on the existence of bank power and influence, debates continue on the costs and benefits of such control. Subsequent chapters, particularly Chapter 6, investigate these issues of bank influence on firm behavior and performance.

Difficulties in the Gerschenkron-Inspired Paradigm

Existing debates over universal banking, though certainly of importance, have typically been structured in a manner that makes it difficult to draw general principles or lessons from them.[100] With the goal of drawing such principles or lessons in mind, the traditional literature would benefit from greater attention to a number of areas: achieving theoretical cogency, constructing useful methodological specifications, gathering sufficient evidence, and amending persistent anachronisms. The research in the next chapters resolves many of these difficulties, though there will always exist limits to the availability of certain important data.

The most troubling difficulties of Gerschenkron's work are the specificity of his theories to a narrow range of cases and the limited scope for empirical testing. There is, in fact, no formal, falsifiable Gerschenkron theory in itself. Gerschenkron's views on the German case, in particular, come in large part from his own observations of the way in which banking seemed to operate. As Richard Sylla (1991) aptly describes, Gerschenkron's experiences growing up in interwar Vienna colored his view of banking and industrialization. For example, Gerschenkron reminded his readers that

... [he had] had a close personal opportunity of watching how, in the 1920s, the representatives of the Credit Anstalt appeared weekly at two machinery factories in a little industrial town near Vienna. They participated most intimately not just in all entrepreneurial decisions, but in many managerial decisions, and their word was received as command by the directors of the two firms.[101]

There are several obvious reasons why Gerschenkron's personal experiences may prove insufficient for understanding Austrian industrialization, much less that of Germany and the rest of continental Europe. First, the observations he made on a small number of companies may not fit more generally even in interwar Austria. Second, the Austrian experience cannot be

---

[99] James (1992), p. 263.
[100] This section is based on Fohlin (1999c).
[101] Gerschenkron (1977), p. 55. Quoted in Sylla (1991), p. 46.

generalized to Germany or the rest of Europe. Third, the 1920s provide an inaccurate portrait of the pre–World War I experiences in many cases.[102]

Clearly, Gerschenkron's views on German industrialization did not rely exclusively on his own observations in interwar Austria, but he did not avail himself of broad-based evidence for pre–World War I Germany either. Yet it would be unfair to single out Gerschenkron on this point. For details of the German case, many authors (apparently including Gerschenkron) rely on the accounts of such contemporaries of the late industrialization period as Riesser (1910 [1911]), Rudolf Hilferding (1910), and Jeidels (1905). These authors had even greater stakes in the debates over universal banking in Germany: Riesser was a director of one of the largest universal banks, Jeidels was an employee of another such bank, and Rudolf Hilferding was a well-known socialist critic of capitalism and the power of the banks. Perhaps more important than ideological biases, however, these older studies are largely based on a small, nonrepresentative set of firms over a limited period of time. Such biases become problematic when the resulting works are extrapolated to the rest of the economy or to different time periods.

As a result, Gerschenkron's hypothesis (or the orthodox paradigm of German industrialization that has developed from it) includes a number of ill-supported notions about what functions the universal banks performed, when the characteristic features of universal banking developed, how much influence the banks had over industry, and the ultimate effects of the structure of the German financial system on industrialization and economic growth. While the fact that Gerschenkron's work rests on little empirical evidence or analysis does not automatically invalidate his thesis, it does leave his hypotheses open to revision. The apparent generality and sweep of Gerschenkron's theories on financial institutions and industrialization also invite criticism and skepticism.[103]

Problems with the earlier historical literature have often resurfaced in more recent work, as many simply accepted Gerschenkron's claims and those of the earlier writers. If the structure and function of financial institutions do not fit the orthodox view, however, then the foundation of the Gerschenkron hypothesis is fundamentally unstable. In particular, marked changes in the organization and operations of the German joint-stock banks between 1850

---

[102] For more on the post–World War I period in Germany, see Chapter 8 in this book as well as Fohlin (2005).

[103] Early skepticism emerges in Cameron (1972) and Rudolph's chapter (on Austria) in the same book. Tilly's (1967) work on Germany also offers moderation, though he is generally supportive.

and 1913 mean that these institutions reached the Gerschenkronian ideal long after the main phases of industrialization, if ever. Recent studies have made use of theoretical advances in economics in an attempt to place the historical experience in a more modern framework.[104] Yet, because the theoretical analyses often rely on the sometimes anachronistic and often inaccurate accounts given in the older historical literature, the resulting models are not very informative.

The orthodox view of German universal banking stresses the size and structure of the banks, the involvement of the banks in the formal governance of industrial firms, and to some extent the efficiency of intermediation and diversification provided by the banks. Less tangible, but equally crucial to this paradigm, are the entrepreneurial spirit, informal oversight and control, and willingness to take risks that are also attributed to the directors of the German industrial banks (all of which are usually supported on the basis of a handful of prominent cases). The fundamental lesson of the historical literature is that the universal banks were powerful institutions that played an important role at least in the later stages of the German industrialization. Thus, while institutional structure is central to widely held beliefs about German banking, most views of universal banking in German economic development also hinge crucially on characteristics unrelated to financial system organization: culture, time and place, and individual personalities, for example.

The modern economics literature, however, looks to the historical record for insight into the consequences of the organization of financial systems for industrial growth and development. The existing historical literature therefore may prove insufficient for deriving such economic implications: Even if banks did play a crucial role in German industrialization, their effectiveness may not have resulted from their structure as universal banks. Likewise, perceived failures of other systems – the British, for example – may be due to idiosyncratic characteristics. Given the current state of knowledge, therefore, it may be impossible to replicate the German experience in other contexts or to determine whether such a goal would be desirable. This problem, in particular, underscores the need for economic theory in providing testable generalizations that might be used in understanding modern

---

[104] See Calomiris (1995), DaRin (1996), Fohlin (1994), and Hauswald (1995) for examples using the newer theoretical literature on information asymmetry and agency theory. The DaRin and Fohlin works essentially recast the Gerschenkronian paradigm in modern language. Kennedy and Britton (1985) and Tilly (1986, 1992, 1994) use the standard capital asset pricing model (CAPM) and portfolio theories to test the efficiency of the German system (in comparison with the British). These papers are discussed subsequently.

problems. Theoretical underpinnings can reveal potential flaws in the standard arguments and offer new ways to approach the long-standing questions and debates about the German experience with universal banking.

The bank power debate is just one example of a historical debate that might benefit from insights of modern theoretical work on banking and financial contracting as well as further empirical research. Much historical work focuses on the question of the dominance of banks over firms with limited reference to the economic effects of that power. Other work has emphasized the efficiency enhancements engendered by the banks' control with little supporting evidence and without theoretical justification of the need for formal bank relationships in the process of rationalization. To understand the economic importance of bank power, one needs to draw a connection between bank control and systematic differences in firms' behavior and outcomes.[105] Such is the goal of Chapters 5 and 6.

---

[105] Tilly (1994b), p. 104, also makes this point: "[This literature] has only rarely made use of economic theory, which thus limits the generalizations which can be made from it." Baskin and Miranti (1997) also argue for the use of theory in interpreting the evolution of financial institutions and corporate finance since medieval times.

Theoretical Perspectives on Banking and Financial System Structure

THE MODERN VIEW OF FINANCIAL INTERMEDIATION

Recent debate over the optimal structure of financial systems has produced a lively discussion over the motivation for and impact of universal banking, along with an active literature working to analyze institutional structure in the context of modern theories of corporate finance and banking. To understand the theoretical implications of universal banking, it is useful first to place these institutions in the more general context of financial intermediation.[1]

The Existence and Functions of Intermediaries

Financial institutions intermediate between the sources and uses of financial capital in the economy. Financial intermediaries arise because they can provide these services at lower cost than individual savers and borrowers can on their own.[2] In doing so, they may or may not change the fundamental characteristics of assets involved. They may, for example, simply broker transactions when the primary constraint on capital provision is the lack of information about opportunities: Those holding wealth are often unacquainted with those in need of funds. Much as a real estate agent facilitates the transfer of property, a financial intermediary can act as a broker simply by

---

[1] If you are already familiar with the theoretical debates over universal banking and financial system design, you might want to skip this chapter.

[2] This chapter is based on a section of Fohlin (1999c) but incorporates numerous updates, additions, and revisions. Bhattacharya and Thakor (1993) provide a nice review of the theoretical banking literature up to the early nineties. Allen and Santomero (1998) offer a critical assessment of traditional theories of intermediation in light of institutional changes in financial markets.

providing an easily identifiable place for buyers and sellers to transact. This service lowers transactions costs and broadens the accessibility of finance, thus raising the quantity of capital available.

The work of intermediaries also involves qualitative asset transformation (QAT), that is, changing the characteristics of financial claims. Individuals use their wealth to buy deposits at financial institutions, and those institutions invest the funds in a wide range of projects. In many cases, the maturity and liquidity of deposit contracts differ from that of loans or other assets that are created. Liquidity and maturity transformation therefore stem from the mismatch between the needs of debtors and creditors. Relative to deposits or cash, capital investment is assumed to yield higher average per-period returns, but requires more time to pay off. Assets are best invested in capital if they are not needed for a significant period of time, but should be held in more liquid form if they may be needed on short notice. The difficulty is that wealth holders rarely know the precise timing of their cash needs over their lifetimes; thus, intermediaries pool deposits and invest in an asset portfolio that reflects the expected distribution of future demands for liquidity. By mobilizing resources that would otherwise sit idle in the hands of wealth holders, financial intermediaries expand the quantity of assets available to entrepreneurs. By investing in a range of projects, financial institutions also effectively diversify depositors' portfolios.

Much of the intermediary's theoretical cost advantage over individual investors stems from problems of asymmetric information between entrepreneurs and their potential sources of finance. Incomplete or imperfect information may open the door for suboptimal use of funds or misreporting of returns that may be most efficiently diminished by a financial intermediary. Even when information problems involve no malfeasance, the process of intermediation can also help diversify depositors' portfolios. Since capital investment often requires outlays in substantial minimum increments, most individuals face limits on the number of different projects to which they can contribute. By financing a range of entrepreneurs with independent return streams, an intermediary reduces the agency costs associated with using external funding directly from less-informed outsiders.[3] Traditionally, the literature has analyzed the case in which the intermediary

---

[3] Diamond (1984) is the classic model of the existence of risk-neutral financial intermediaries based on delegated monitoring services. In this case, viability hinges on size in order to allow diversification. A useful exposition on this and related models appears in the textbook of Freixas and Rochet (1997).

is risk-neutral, but even if the intermediary is risk-averse, it may remain viable due to its ability to diversify.[4]

Intermediaries may still find it difficult to identify the best targets for investment. Poor information about entrepreneurs' quality, and thus the distribution of potential payoffs, can lead to the refusal of financing at any price. If an intermediary cannot distinguish among loan applicants, then it charges a single interest rate to all borrowers. Under certain assumptions about the distributions of project returns, the maximum acceptable interest rate increases with the riskiness of the borrower, and increases in rates cause the safest borrowers to exit first. Thus, when unobservably heterogeneous borrowers are pooled, it is impossible to find an interest rate at which all risks are priced properly, and the intermediary rations credit.[5] In a similar fashion, investors may also ration equity, not just debt. The two kinds of rationing may occur separately and simultaneously when investors (specializing in debt or equity financing) are heterogeneous and when asymmetric information affects both the expected return and the riskiness of the project. Competition between markets may drive such rationing, while the incentive for rationing diminishes as the ability to estimate returns improves.[6] Thus, if those with superior abilities to differentiate among potential borrowers – or among firms wishing to issue equity – become financial intermediaries, then such institutions may partially alleviate rationing. In that respect, information sharing among financial intermediaries (through credit bureaus) may ameliorate adverse selection problems by providing valuable information.[7]

The Pecking Order of Financial Instruments

So far, the discussion has not differentiated among the types of claims that financial intermediaries create and trade in the process of financing investment. In a tax-free world with free markets, perfect competition, and symmetric information, the choice among financial instruments has little consequence for firms. Under such conditions, Modigliani and Miller (1958) proved their now well-known proposition that firms cannot alter the total

---

[4] Hellwig (2000) shows that the main result of the literature is still valid under risk aversion in the intermediary.

[5] Stiglitz and Weiss (1981) address this problem, and much further research follows from that article.

[6] Hellman and Stiglitz (2000) provide a model of debt and equity rationing.

[7] Jappelli and Pagano (2000) analyze the case for information sharing very thoroughly by looking at its effect on default rates, informational rents, moral hazard stemming from hidden action after lending, and related issues.

value of their securities by varying the mix between debt and equity. That is, capital structure is irrelevant. The stringent Modigliani-Miller conditions, however, rarely hold; consequently, firms do differ in their choice of financing instruments.

Many theories of capital structure, most hinging on problems of asymmetric information and agency problems, have appeared in the past several years. In this literature, information and preference gaps between firms (or managers) and potential investors create differences in the desirability of various types of financing. Because such problems arise inherently from the use of any outside funds, recourse to external finance may raise financing costs. In the extreme, firms may be able to finance new investment solely from internally generated funds. External finance becomes viable only if firms find some mechanism to transmit credible information and ameliorate conflicts between managers and investors.[8]

Firms seeking outside finance must then decide between debt and equity, and they base that choice on the relative costs of the two instruments. Returns on debt to outside investors are bounded above and therefore depend less on the actions that firms take. Equity gains, in contrast, vary directly with firm valuation and thus hinge on the quality of managers and their investment opportunities. Moreover, firms have the incentive to issue new equity when insiders believe shares to be overpriced. Such information problems theoretically lead to the underpricing of equity and the rejection of worthwhile projects by existing shareholders. Consequently, if it is difficult to determine a firm's worth (either ex ante potential or actual outcomes), investors incur lower information-related costs from debt and prefer it over equity.[9] Likewise, when the potential for managerial perquisites and overinvestment is high, debt can increase managers' relative stake in the company and reduce the availability of funds available for overinvestment.

Debt itself comes in many forms, with varying degrees of maturity, liquidity, collateralization, intermediation, and monitoring. A firm's options among these alternatives are constrained by its inability to relay information

---

[8] Agency problems, as in Jensen and Meckling (1976), arise when firms are controlled by agents whose incentives are not bound to those of owners or financiers.

[9] Several well-known theoretical models are now available for comparing the costs of debt and equity finance. Problems of information about opportunities motivate Myers and Majluf (1984), while difficulties in ex post monitoring and state verification inspire Diamond (1984), Gale and Hellwig (1985), and Townsend (1979). See Calomiris (1993), Harris and Raviv (1991), and Hellwig (1991, 1998) for reviews of this and related literature. See Baskin and Miranti (1997) for discussion of the historical relevance of the pecking order hypothesis and other related theories of corporate finance.

credibly to securities markets. Bank loans, because they typically receive the closest monitoring, are usually seen as the first step to gaining a reputation for high quality and proper disposition of outside funds. Such monitoring is thought to alleviate asset substitution as well as under- and overinvestment.[10] Compared to bonds, however, bank debt may impose additional costs that result from monitoring, renegotiation, and the potential for rent extraction due to the banks' access to proprietary information.[11] Thus, firms may avoid bank financing when bond-issuance is feasible.[12]

The pecking-order hypothesis also suggests that financing decisions may change over a firm's lifecycle. Often, quality and availability of information grow with the development of the firm so that firms may experience fewer information-related problems as they age, grow, and establish track records. The fact that reputations take time to establish suggests that mature firms face lower relative costs of equity and often opt to reduce their exposure to fixed debt payments. That is, minimizing information problems reduces the cost gap between internal and external funding and between debt and equity securities and thus alters firms' trade-offs.[13] Thus, seasoned firms should tend toward more equity in their capital structure relative to immature firms.

FINANCIAL SYSTEM STRUCTURE AND THE OPTIMAL PROVISION OF FINANCE

The theoretical research on modes of financing raises the possibility that the efficiency of financial institutions may depend on the scope of their activities. Therefore, the structure of financial systems may affect the overall efficiency of corporate finance. While there are certainly physical costs involved in providing finance, recent research focuses on costs related to information transmittal. Each step between saver and investor adds costs, so, all else being equal, institutions that minimize the number of transactions or times which information needs to be transferred should gain a cost advantage.

Universal banking institutions simultaneously provide all three types of corporate financial claims (bank debt, bonds, and stocks) under one roof, whereas specialized systems typically distribute services across several types

---

[10] See Jensen and Meckling (1976), Myers (1977), and Stulz (1990).
[11] See Rajan (1992) on the possible monopoly rents accruing to banks due to private information about firms.
[12] Diamond (1991) models the choice between monitored bank debt and directly placed bonds. See also Chemmanur and Fulghieri (1994).
[13] In the Myers and Majluf (1984) model, in the absence of information problems, firms always fund investment with equity.

of intermediaries. Because firms' financing needs often vary over time, universal banking can arguably benefit from economies of scope. If information about a given firm may be reused for the provision of multiple services, universal banking will yield cost advantages over specialized systems. By similar arguments, reputations gained in one branch of financing may spill over into others and promote freer entry into all financial services.[14] Lower costs may translate into a higher volume of finance and therefore stronger investment by industrial firms. Access to information about the full range of financial assets may also enable universal banks to diversify their investments more optimally than could the equivalent set of several specialized intermediaries.

Universal banking may also encourage the creation of long-term relationships, because of the incentives for both bank and firm to do business with one another repeatedly. Time-inconsistency problems, however, may hamper multiperiod optimization of financial contracting. For example, having received relatively cheap finance when young, a seasoned firm may subsequently find itself able to procure outside funds more cheaply than it can through its original bank. Knowing of this possibility ex ante may discourage the bank from providing the start-up capital in the first instance. Thus, a number of explanations of creditor relationships underscore the possible need to enforce long-term relationships through formal institutions, such as equity stakes and bank representation on firm boards.[15]

Much of the theoretical work on the existence of financial intermediaries focuses on the need for supervision that arises due to asymmetric information between entrepreneurs and investors. The placement of bank directors on the boards of firms may facilitate the monitoring of firms' activities and outcomes; improved oversight, in turn, potentially benefits firms in a number of ways. Careful monitoring makes loans more secure and may enable a bank to extend credit to firms that it would otherwise ration for lack of information. Even when information problems would not prevent lending, oversight may substitute for collateral and may therefore allow the bank to finance firms with apparently good projects but with insufficient collateralizable assets. If monitoring is a crucial ingredient in intermediation, then systems that permit close, formal monitoring may perform better than

---

[14] Calomiris (1995) focuses on information reusability, while Rajan (1995) discusses both arguments. See Greenbaum, Kanatas, and Venezia (1989) on theoretical economies of scope resulting from information reusability.

[15] See Calomiris and Himmelberg (1993), James and Wier (1990), Mayer (1988), and Petersen and Rajan (1994) for theories and some evidence.

those that limit financial institutions' engagement in corporate ownership and control.

Beyond its potential role in enforcing commitment between banks and firms, relationship banking may create its own advantages quite apart from universal banking. Compared to systems in which banks do not take such active, direct roles in the firms that they finance, relationship systems, some have argued, promote stronger, more efficient investment. Formalized bank–firm relationships may engender a long-term perspective on investment programs, so that firms with bank monitors may engage in qualitatively different projects than they would in the absence of the relationship. If investments with the highest ex post returns sometimes take longer to bear fruit, then firms that have the leeway to make such investments may yield higher long-run returns than those forced to pay back loans quickly. More precise pinpointing of the causes of poor short-term performance allows remedying of underperformance without premature liquidation of projects with high long-run value.[16] Thus, relationship-based systems may raise firms' long-run returns.

In a related vein, it is often argued that relationship banking improves the allocation of corporate control. Arm's-length systems discipline management through market mechanisms, such as mergers and takeovers. The problem with market-based systems is that managerial failure may be difficult to detect from the outside: Poor performance alone does not conclusively imply managerial slack or incompetence. Relationship banking, in contrast, is often seen as obviating market mechanisms. As in the monitoring of investment projects, bank oversight and control may permit quicker, more accurate weeding out of poor managers without sacrificing good managers stuck in relatively adverse circumstances.[17] Thus, relationship banking may further boost firm efficiency and long-term value by both minimizing unnecessary turnover and expediting beneficial attrition.

From the perspective of securities underwriting, as well, relationship banking may improve the efficiency of financing. Banks offer important screening services, and close bank involvement with firms' management may create advantages in gathering the information necessary for successful

---

[16] Dewatripont and Maskin (1995), Narayanan (1985), Stein (1989), and von Thadden (1995) offer models of this problem.

[17] This idea is nearly the same as the previous, though the target of monitoring (projects or managers) is different. See Stiglitz (1985) for a clear discussion of the potential shortcomings of arm's-length mechanisms for insuring shareholder value maximization.

ex ante monitoring.[18] Access to information may allow more accurate valuation of share capital worth, and the good reputation of the underwriter may increase the market for firms' shares. Formalized bank relationships, for example through bank representation in firms' boards, may then signal firms' quality to potential investors. Together, these effects may lower the cost of securities issue and increase firms' access to capital markets.

These possible roles that combined universal-relationship banking may play in monitoring, signaling, and ameliorating conflicts of interest suggest that the behavior of financial intermediaries may also influence the capital structure of firms. In particular, institutions that facilitate access to firm information and coordination of diverse interests may temper the problems that lead to inefficient financing decisions. Bank oversight may lower the relative costs of and increase access to bank finance, so that bank-attached firms may have higher leverage (with greater reliance on bank debt) than independent firms on average. If bank relationships narrow information gaps and improve firms' chances of earning positive reputations in capital markets, then such involvement should also reduce the cost differential between debt and equity. In line with the pecking-order hypothesis, then, formal bank relations should speed firms' movement from debt to equity financing. Universal banks' provision of equity underwriting and brokerage, in addition to all kinds of debt services, should further facilitate adjustments in capital structure.

Much of the recent theoretical work deals with information problems that can arise between firms and potential investors. Relationship banking is seen, in theory, as a means of equalizing information and resolving to the extent possible the uncertainty that accompanies finance.[19] Even with the best possible information, outcomes are rarely certain. Thus, lenders and investors, as well as the firms themselves, also face some measure of risk. An important task of any financial system is to manage and distribute that risk. If relationship banking enables bankers to reveal true risks, then such practices may also improve the allocation of risk among investors. Moreover, the fact that universal banks engage in all types of financial transactions may allow these institutions a greater choice of instruments through which to diversify risk. Improved risk sharing will, theoretically, increase the public's willingness to invest and also reduce the costs of such investment.

---

[18] See, for example, Boyd and Prescott (1986) on the role of banks in channeling investment to highest return projects.

[19] Boot (2000) examines the theoretical contributions to relationship banking in depth and discusses some of the empirical evidence as well.

A principal upshot of the theoretical literature is the idea that the existence of financial intermediaries in general enhances both the quantity and the quality of investment in the economy. But it may also be argued on a theoretical basis that universal and relationship banking practices further raise the quantity of funds provided to industry and may also increase both the quality of projects undertaken and the long-term returns to investment.

Costs of Universal Banking and Relationship Banking

Not all work on universal banking supports the view that universal banking and relationship banking offer unequivocal improvements in the efficiency of corporate finance. Some have argued quite the opposite: that combining services into one institution and allowing shareholding and interlocking directorates between banks and their clients leads to several kinds of inefficiencies.

Though there is little theoretical work on the subject, universal banking has long been claimed to undermine the stability of the financial system. Instability may result from banks' equity stakes in firms – a position that exposes the banks to business downturns and the vicissitudes of the stock markets. In addition, the combination of lending and securities underwriting permits banks to float loans on the assumption that future securities issues can be used for repayment. Any subsequent difficulty with issuing the firms' securities can then endanger the bank and perhaps the financial system more generally.[20] Even if universal banking does not create financial fragility in practice, avoiding instability may lead to underinvestment in risky projects. Because a universal bank must protect depositors, it may be unable to finance high-risk sectors that may offer higher returns. If universal banks can prevent nondepository investment banks from entering the market, then the system may bias investment toward conservative, low-growth sectors of the economy.

Universal banking may also suffer from conflicts of interest. Such problems may arise because banks are able to underwrite securities for the firms to which they lend. In situations of asymmetric information between banks and customers, banks may be tempted to issue securities for distressed firms in order to liquefy doubtful debts. The bank could then sell the low-quality securities to customers. While a bank that repeatedly and consistently issues notably inferior securities would presumably lose its reputation and

---

[20] These hypotheses are discussed in Benston (1994), Kroszner and Rajan (1994), and White (1986). Of course, equity stakes are part of relationship banking and may be absent in a universal banking system.

potentially its business, occasional underperforming securities may not provoke flight.

Due to another form of possible conflict of interest, universal banking may theoretically discourage the development of active stock markets. Since universal banks often trade securities and also take deposits, they can potentially gain an advantage over specialized stockbrokers in attracting clients. Given sufficient size, banks themselves can make their own markets in securities. Such internalization of secondary securities trading within universal banks harms investors if it constrains the size or liquidity of markets or if it segments markets into multiple trading centers. Universal banks' trading of the securities that they underwrite (and potentially also hold on their own account) may undermine the banks' incentive to offer the optimal portfolio to investors. Moreover, the fact that universal banks often hold securities for a variety of reasons, including poor performance, lessens the signaling value of bank equity stakes and further subverts efficiency in the allocation of capital.

Two very different types of anticompetitive behavior may result from universal and relationship banking, particularly in the absence of competitive markets. First, the economies of scope that possibly motivate the combination of many services in one institution may also lead to concentration in financial services. If concentration is excessive, it may lead to market power, higher costs of finance, and poor service to depositors and borrowers. For example, if universal banks gain market power due to economies of scope in information – such as reusing information revealed through short-term lending experience in subsequent underwriting business with the same client – they may have less incentive to underwrite new securities than do pure investment banks.[21] Furthermore, the ability to compete in several different markets may facilitate limit pricing and enable universal banks to stave off competition from specialized intermediaries even in segments in which the universal bank is relatively inefficient. A second form of anticompetitive behavior can arise if the involvement of banks in the management of companies leads to cartelization of industry. In a relationship banking system, intermediaries may have access to important strategic information for several firms in the same sector, and such information may permit the bank to orchestrate mergers or enforce cooperation.

---

[21] Kanatas and Qi (2003). Their result is particularly interesting in light of the commonly cited *advantage* of universal banking due to economies of scope (the same institution providing both investment and commercial services and thereby saving on information-gathering costs). The savings, however, may be dissipated rather than passed on in lower cost or higher quantity or quality of finance.

These activities, while perhaps benefiting some firms, may harm others and may reduce competition and possibly consumer welfare more generally.

The effects of universal and relationship banking may create further disadvantages for individual firms and the economy as a whole. Banks can gain proprietary information about the firms they finance, either by providing multiple services over time or through direct access to company boards. When firm quality is difficult to observe from the outside, being an informed insider may permit an intermediary to extract rents in the form of high costs of finance. In such a system, costs of switching intermediaries are high, because other banks may interpret a firm's attempt to change banks as a sign that the original bank declined to provide further funding.[22] When the market for financial services is not competitive, the potential costs of holdup problems are even higher. As a result, firms may forgo many investment plans that would be profitable in a more competitive system.

Relationship banking tends to give financial institutions direct links to the management of affiliated companies. In the most extreme cases, banks own shares, take seats in firms' boards, and exercise proxy votes for shareholders. While such insight may be seen as beneficial to companies in need of entrepreneurial expertise, explicit control over investment decisions and firm strategy may not benefit all firms or all outside investors. For banker influence in firm decisions to be beneficial, bankers must both know better than industrialists and investors what would be the optimal choices to make and have incentives similar enough to those of the firms and their investors to see that the best decision is implemented. Equity stakes are one way to try to align the incentives of the bank with those of the firm and its other shareholders.

At least in the German system, however, banks are permitted to exercise proxy votes and take positions in firms' boards even in the absence of share ownership. Control without any ownership, when banks also hold firms' debt, may lead to excessive conservatism – that is, banks may allow their interest as debt holders to dominate their decisions. Banks' desire for future

---

[22] See Rajan (1992) and Sharpe (1990). On an important technical note, however, von Thadden (2004) contradicts Sharpe's finding that there exist pure strategy equilibria of the game. Von Thadden shows that no pure strategy equilibrium, only a unique mixed strategy equilibrium, exists. Using his corrected model, he predicts in equilibrium limited capture of borrowers in bank-firm relationships, above-market interest rates, and occasional switching of borrowers. In a related vein, Berglöf (1997) suggests that firms may maintain links with multiple banks in order to safeguard against holdup problems.

commission business, however, may mitigate these problems both directly and indirectly. Assuming that the banks will have a significant part in future issues, the fact that firms are more likely to issue new securities when they are growing and investing may restore the banks' incentive to take risks. Furthermore, the banks' need to maintain a good reputation with proxy owners may, in a sense, force the banks to internalize shareholders' preferences. Yet these kinds of guarantees work perfectly only in the absence of information problems and in the presence of competition. Asymmetric information, especially when the bank sector has monopoly power, may permit banks to subjugate small shareholders' interests to the banks' interests as debt holders. Furthermore, commissions on share trading and issuing may take a back seat to the banks' interest in insuring debt repayment. Thus, proxy voting and direct equity ownership may not provide equivalent incentives for banks.

Clearly, the literature on universal banking offers much theoretical fodder on the microlevel effects of financial system structure. The organization of financial institutions may partly determine the extent of competition among financial intermediaries, the quantity of financial capital drawn into the financial system, and the distribution of that capital to ultimate uses. The choice between universal and specialized banking may affect interest rates, underwriting costs, and the efficiency of secondary markets in securities. Furthermore, the existence or nonexistence of relationship banking may affect the quality of investments undertaken, strategic decision making, and even the competitiveness of industry. Financial systems may therefore influence the costs of finance in two distinct ways: general effects on the economy as a whole, and localized influences on individual firms and industries. At both levels, the structure of the financial system may have substantial influence on the real economy.

FINANCIAL STRUCTURE AND ECONOMIC GROWTH

Given the theoretical notion that the efficiency of different financial institutions may vary, it is reasonable to wonder whether the real effects of financial systems differ as a result. The idea that financial institutions can actively influence growth is quite old. Joseph Schumpeter (1912), for example, suggested that bankers, through their selection and funding of entrepreneurs, promote innovative activity and spur economic growth. The literature on economic growth has begun to grapple with this question, and progress in such research may help in understanding whether certain types of financial systems encourage higher rates of growth and greater welfare than others.

The question of causality remains a problem in the theoretical literature, though some models acknowledge that influences run in both directions.[23] Boyd and Smith (1996) and Greenwood and Smith (1997) offer a reasonable compromise: models in which financial markets arise after some period of real development, and the expansion of those markets fuels further real growth. A logical implication of these models is that, in the absence of some progress toward industrialization, the exogenous creation of a financial system with advanced features may not spur real growth.

These latter two models also provide some insight into the ramifications of financial system structure. Greenwood and Smith (1997) provide a first step toward thinking about such distinctions; showing that growth rates obtained in economies with either banks or equity markets exceed those of economies without financial intermediaries. This model indicates further that, with sufficient risk aversion on the part of the investing public, equity markets produce stronger growth than banks do. In a series of papers, Boyd and Smith (1994, 1995, 1996) introduce the changing roles of debt and equity in the development process and show that, though stock markets should develop after a period of intermediary dominance, both debt and equity remain viable and complementary sources of finance.

Still, most of the literature offers no comparison of the relative benefits of different types of financial systems, and even these models do not differentiate between universal and specialized banking and the possibly different outcomes that such systems promote. Variation in growth effects, however, might be inferred from other recent work. R. G. King and R. Levine (1993), for example, formalize the Schumpeterian view into the framework of an endogenous growth model. In their model, the financial system affects productivity growth through four channels: screening prospective entrepreneurs in order to select the most promising projects, mobilizing capital to fund investments, diversifying investors' portfolios to eliminate risk, and revealing the potential benefits of participating in productivity-enhancing activities.[24] A. V. Thakor (1996b), who is explicitly concerned with the question of financial system design, lays out six

---

[23] The more recent literature considering the causal relationship between finance and growth includes King and Levine (1993), Jappelli and Pagano (1993), Jayaratne and Strahan (1996), and Rajan and Zingales (1997). Lucas (1988), perhaps not surprisingly, expresses doubt about the importance of financial factors and excludes these considerations in his model of development.

[24] Galetovic (1996) and Pagano (1993) provide good reviews of the growth literature to that point. For a relatively up-to-date overview (mainly empirical), see the brief survey in Levine (2003) or the edited volume by Demirgüç-Kunt and Levine (2004).

partially overlapping links between the financial system and the real economy: screening by banks, credit rationing by banks, liquidity transformation and bank runs, loan commitments by banks, debt restructuring, and the feedback role of financial markets. In general, financial institutions may enhance economic growth by raising the total quantity of financial capital available to entrepreneurs, improving the quality (productivity) of investments, and increasing the efficiency of intermediation between the sources and uses of funds. Thus, the structure of financial systems may influence real variables, since different institutions may handle these tasks with varying efficiency.

While it is clear that financial systems vary in their real effects, it is not yet clear what kind of system offers the greatest net benefit to the real economy. Research so far suggests that trade-offs exist between banks and financial markets in the revelation and transmission of information necessary for making optimal real decisions; the desirability of one system over another depends on the context. Franklin Allen (1992) reasons that, because markets aggregate information from a wide range of disparate sources, but banks depend primarily on their own assessments, markets dominate banks when technologies are new, complex, or rapidly evolving.[25] Banks prevail when technologies are clearly understandable and optimal investment decisions are easy to make. Also, as Thakor (1996a) argues, bank-dominated systems exacerbate effort-aversion and overinvestment, while market-based systems lead to excessive reliance on borrower reputation as well as greater asset-substitution moral hazard.[26] Furthermore, the analyses of Ernst-Ludwig von Thadden (1990) and Mathias Dewatripont and Eric Maskin (1990) suggest that banks tend to prolong low-quality projects for too long, while markets often liquidate good projects prematurely. All of these problems can lead to suboptimal investment decisions and lower real economic growth.

The theoretical literature on the effects of various banking structures remains sparse.[27] One exception to the general pattern is Arnoud Boot and Thakor (2002), who examine the effect of banking scope on financial

---

[25] See also Allen and Gale (1999), who provide a comprehensive discussion of comparative financial systems.

[26] Thakor bases his argument on the predictions of Diamond (1991), Rajan (1992), and Wilson (1994).

[27] Works by Crane (1995) and Peters and Thakor (1995) show that variation in information availability and in incentives to monitor (both banks and borrowers) recommend functional separation between insured, deposit-financed banks to finance projects that require no monitoring and uninsured intermediaries to invest in projects associated with private information and a need for monitoring.

innovation. They find that in equilibrium financial innovation is less likely in universal banking systems than in functionally separated banking systems.[28] They also find that the more developed the financial system is, the greater the incentives for innovation. In other words, the development of financial systems is path-dependent – an idea that comes as little surprise to historians.

The tendency to conflate the questions of banking structure and more generally financial system structure (banks versus markets) stems from the perception that universal, relationship-based banks dominate the financial systems in which they operate and that financial markets prevail in systems in which financial intermediaries are specialized. Much of the variation in both banking structure and financial system structure, however, results from peculiarities of financial regulation. Thus, observed patterns may be fundamental traits of certain institutional designs or simply artifacts of government intervention. For example, it is unclear whether universal banking in itself constrains the development of financial markets, or if government intervention in the cases so far studied simultaneously promoted banks and hindered securities markets.[29] Likewise, it is difficult to tell whether limitations on bank operations spur financial market development, or if something else about the American and British economies or societies has led to market-oriented financial systems.[30] So far, theoretical research has not rationalized the endogenous development of distinct financial system designs and their persistence in the absence of regulation. Answers to such

---

[28] Similarly, Kanatas and Qi (2003) also find theoretically that integrated financial systems support less underwriting effort and will be less innovative than functionally specialized systems.

[29] See Boot, Dezelan, and Milbourn (2001) on regulation in a competitive environment of banking. They identify two dimensions that are key to optimal regulation design: competitiveness and the degree of development of the financial system. They find that in a highly competitive environment with well-developed financial markets, optimal regulation should take the form of setting minimum standards (certification requirements). Boot and Schmeits (2002) consider conglomeration in banking, examining the optimal design of organizational structure of bank activities. They argue that depending on whether bank divisions act as separate entities or as part of a conglomerate, the internal incentives and effectiveness of market discipline differ.

[30] Allen (1992) argues, in part, that the historical experiences of Britain and the United States support the idea that markets are preferable in situations of complex decision processes and rapidly advancing technology; whereas banks should dominate where optimal investments are agreed upon and primarily just need monitoring. The question of financial system structure and innovation is addressed in Boot and Thakor (1997b) and Thakor (1996b).

puzzles may hinge both on making advances in theoretical modeling and on assembling a wider range of empirical evidence.

THEORY MEETS EVIDENCE

The German financial system in the pre–World War I era represents the archetype of universal banking envisioned by the theoretical literature. Of particular importance, the original version of universal banking meant the combination of services within one institution, often in a single location, where the same small group of individuals could share information on the progression of their clients through successive stages of development. The political, economic, and legal upheaval of the two world wars and the intervening depression, followed by the challenges of postwar reconstruction, and the expected pursuit of expansion by banking institutions wrought myriad changes on the German corporate financial system – banks, firms, shareholders, and markets. The system that emerged in the second half of the twentieth century bore little resemblance to that built up by financial pioneers over the second half of the previous century. The modern incarnation of "universal" banking within a financial conglomerate, of course, portends a disintegration of services and increasing disjuncture among units within the so-called universal bank. Naturally, this increasing scale undermines much of the information advantage that plays such a prevalent role in the theory of universal banking. The events of the mid-twentieth century also eviscerated the German securities markets and relegated them to minor importance up to the present. Looking at the German financial system over the past half-century would therefore lead the researcher to conclude that universal banks somehow obviate vibrant securities markets; yet the longer history gives a markedly different view.

The theories laid out in this chapter offer a wide range of predictions about the structure of financial institutions, the shape of the banking industry, the impact of banking relationships on nonfinancial firms, and the overall effect of financial system architecture on aggregate-level industrial development, productivity, and economic growth. By studying the prewar universal banking system, we can isolate universal banking in its natural form and investigate its characteristic features, its place within the broader financial system, and its impact on the real economy. We can use this theoretical literature to guide and structure the evaluation of the system, and at the same time, we can use the historical study to assess the empirical validity of those theories. Using this approach will steer the analysis away from the more traditional economic history literature based on the Gerschenkron-inspired paradigm; but it will in fact shed more light on many of the most critical facets of the long-standing literature on the history of corporate finance during industrialization.

The next four chapters therefore set out on these dual paths to uncover the true shape and significance of the German financial system in the later stages of industrialization. The evidence ranges from the level of the individual loan all the way to the growth of aggregate output for the whole country. The real core of the analysis, however, focuses on the behavior of firms and their interactions with banks and financial markets, using a new database of company information gathered expressly for this purpose.

4

The Development and Impact of Universal Banking

Economic historians generally agree that wealth sufficient for industrialization existed in Western Europe by early in the nineteenth century and that mobilizing those funds presented the critical challenge for industrial development. Capital mobilization proceeds first through collection of idle funds from the public, and then via dispersion of the gathered funds to entrepreneurs in the form of loans, advances, or other types of credit. By repeating this process, the banking system multiply expands the money supply and effectively redistributes the economy's capital. These banking functions increase the share of the economy's resources directed to productive investment. To mobilize capital successfully on an ongoing basis, banks must continually induce savers to purchase deposits or shares and then locate borrowers to use the acquired funds. Such capital mobilization forms the core activity of most financial institutions, and, as a result, theories of economic growth indicate a role for banks in the expansion of the economy.

In the German context, the corporate commercial-investment banks – known interchangeably as universal, mixed, or credit banks – take the leading role in the story of industrial credit. As Chapter 2 pointed out, questions about the nature of the banks' involvement in matching savers and entrepreneurs persist. This chapter therefore takes up the problem of detailing, both quantitatively and qualitatively, the development of the German corporate financial system. The analysis focuses on characteristics of the German banks that are viewed as growth or efficiency enhancing, as laid out in the previous two chapters – most notably, combined services (universality), widespread deposit taking, and branching.[1]

---

[1] The next chapter investigates the relationship banking practices of the universal banks: active involvement in corporate governance of firms and equity stakes in industrial companies.

The findings suggest that many of these practices emerged only to a limited extent during industrialization, if at all. Moreover, universality existed independently of banks' involvement in branching. At the aggregate level, the chapter shows that the universal banking sector developed late in the industrialization process, expanding most rapidly in concert with the final push of industrialization in the 1890s and early-twentieth century. Statistical analysis further demonstrates the lack of a causal relationship between expansion of the universal banking system and growth of capital formation or gross domestic product (GDP) per capita. The findings of the chapter undermine the economic importance traditionally placed on the structure and practices of German institutions and suggest an alternative view: that immensely successful industrial development, even in a country that has trailed economically, can proceed with a fairly modest financial system. Moreover, development in the real sectors pushes development of financial institutions, so that highly advanced, nationally networked financial institutions may result from the demands raised by industrial development. In other words, the finance–growth nexus is complex and almost certainly bidirectional. Finally, the unique path of the German economic and financial system underscores the impact of political, social, and cultural environments, along with historical accident, in molding financial systems.

THE GROWTH AND STRUCTURE OF THE UNIVERSAL BANKING INDUSTRY

Up until the second wave of industrialization, the German financial system consisted primarily of private bankers. Taken together, these (primarily) small, atomistic institutions held far more assets than the central bank at the time and held nearly as much as the mortgage banks, savings banks, credit cooperatives, and mixed banks combined (see Table 4.1 and Figure 4.1).[2] The private bankers dominated the German financial system of the mid-nineteenth century and their assets far surpassed those of other banks in the 1860s. The banking industry underwent significant organizational change over the course of the nineteenth and early-twentieth centuries,

---

[2] Table 4.1 and Figure 4.1 give numerical and graphical breakdowns of financial system assets for 1860, 1880, 1900, and 1913 translated into billions of 1913 marks. These figures, based on Goldsmith's (1969) data, should be viewed as rough, since the sources are difficult to follow or judge for accuracy. Much of the data appears to come from Hoffman's (1965) calculations, which in themselves have suffered critiques. Deutsche Bundesbank (1976) provides similar series on an annual basis, but they start only in 1883 and cover fewer institutions.

Table 4.1. *Assets of German Financial Institutions: Goldsmith's Estimates*

	1860	1880	1900	1913
Panel A: Billions of 1913 marks				
Central bank	0.95	1.57	2.57	4.03
Large (nationwide) banks[a]	0.39	1.35	6.96	8.39
Regional (local) banks	–	–	–	13.65
Private bankers	1.50	2.50	3.50	4.00
Specialized commercial banks	–	–	–	0.98
Savings banks, local	0.51	2.78	9.45	20.80
Savings banks, central	–	–	–	1.76
Credit unions, local	0.01	0.59	1.68	5.73
Credit unions, central	–	–	–	0.47
Private mortgage banks	0.04	1.85	7.50	13.55
Public mortgage banks	0.68	1.76	4.05	7.20
Life insurance companies	0.07	0.44	2.42	5.64
Property insurance companies	–	0.35	0.83	2.05
Social insurance organizations	–	–	0.87	2.44
Total for all financial institutions	4.15	13.19	39.83	90.69
Panel B: Percent				
Joint-stock credit banks/total financial institutions	9.4	10.2	17.5	24.3
Joint-stock & private banks/total financial institutions	45.5	29.2	26.3	28.7
Assets of financial institutions/GNP	40.0	73.0	114.0	158.0
Joint-stock & private banks/GNP	18.2	21.3	29.9	45.4
Domestic securities (nongovernment)/total assets	1.0[b]	3.0[c]	n/a	4.0
Domestic securities (nongovernment)/financial institution assets	109.0[b]	80.0[c]	n/a	62.0

Notes:
[a] Includes regional banks until 1913.
[b] 1850.
[c] 1875.
Sources: Goldsmith (1985), Mitchell (1992), and author's calculations.

with the private bankers rapidly losing their share of the sector, especially toward the end of the period. By 1913, joint-stock banks took over the vast majority of the commercial banking business, relegating the private banks to a small segment of the banking market.[3] Some of the private banks

[3] By comparison, British commercial banks accounted for twice as much as their German counterparts over the same period. These figures are based on Goldsmith (1969). He almost certainly undercounted private-banking assets in Britain after 1891, since he used Sheppard's (1971) figures from The Economist. Unless the remaining financial institutions'

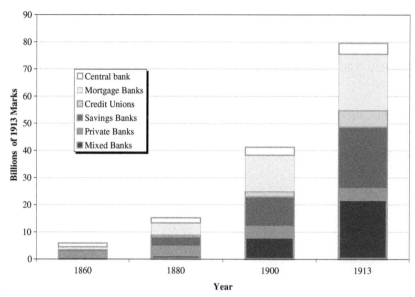

Figure 4.1. Financial Institution Assets by Type.

performed functions similar to the joint-stock universal banks, and some of them participated with relatively small shares in underwriting consortia. Still, it is inaccurate to equate even the largest private bankers with the joint-stock universal banks. Thus, because of the difficulty in measuring the assets and liabilities of private banks, and due to the lack of broad comparability in their services, this chapter focuses on the joint-stock banks.

In 1860, institutions dealing mostly with commercial business, the incorporated mixed banks, barely appear on the financial radar – accounting for less than 10 percent of financial institution assets and only 4 percent of the gross national product (GNP). These figures dramatize the real lack of development of the financial system even into the second half of the nineteenth century and also underscore the importance of other, probably informal forms of finance that played a role in the early steps toward industrialization.

assets are similarly underestimated, the ratio of commercial banks to total financial institutions in Britain should be higher, especially for 1880 (Capie and Webber's [1985] aggregate U.K. bank deposit series is 38 percent higher than Sheppard's). Goldsmith's sources for private banks in both Germany and Britain in the earlier years are unclear and are therefore difficult to assess.

It is important to keep in mind, however, that the earliest industrial firms took on noncorporate forms. Before the formation of railroad companies and joint-stock banks, few firms left the control of founding families, meaning a limited clientele for the underwriting and brokerage side of universal banks.[4] Moreover, whole regions of the country persisted in almost purely agricultural pursuits and had little use for universal banks well past the mid-nineteenth-century mark. Therefore, for the early stages of industrialization, evaluating the universal banks' size relative to the whole German economy does undervalue the impact of financial institutions within the very tiny and regionally concentrated corporate industrial sector that they served. Such was the point of Charles Kindleberger (see Chapter 2), and it is an assertion that is both difficult to deny and difficult to test rigorously.[5]

The main point of these figures, however, is to establish the timing of German financial expansion, and to demonstrate how late in the industrialization period the industrial banking sector developed. Total banking assets nearly tripled between 1860 and 1880 and between 1880 and 1900, and they increased almost as much annually between 1900 and 1913.[6] Part of the early growth, however, stemmed from the creation of the Reichsbank and the accompanying blossoming of central bank assets. So, in fact, total banking assets outside of the central bank grew fastest after 1900 and slowest between 1860 and 1880 (see Figure 4.1). The joint-stock universal banks made up a significant portion of these institutions and accounted for a substantial share of the growth. The sector's assets, of which the largest banks maintained a nearly constant share, increased more than sixfold between 1883 and 1913 (see Figure 4.2), with total bank assets growing at almost 7 percent per annum (see Table 4.2). Even considering population expansion, real bank assets per capita grew more than 5 percent per year on average. As a result, in the thirty years leading up to World War I, real bank assets per person more than quadrupled, growing from less than 100 marks

---

[4] And, of course, the converse could also be true: The absence of joint-stock banks may have kept firms from incorporating. The main roadblock, however, was the cumbersome concession process required to incorporate. Chapter 7 takes up this issue as well as the question of the development of markets to trade the resulting securities.

[5] See also Herrigel (1996) on small industrial firms, especially with respect to regional variation in the industrialization process.

[6] Figures here are calculated in real terms (1913 marks). The percentage growth in assets is essentially the same whether or not insurance company assets are included. Data come from Goldsmith (1969) and Deutsche Bundesbank (1976).

Table 4.2. *Estimated Annual Growth Rates*

Variable	Units of Underlying Variable	1883–1913	1895–1913
Assets of all commercial banks	Millions constant	0.068** *48.51* [0.99]	0.068** *25.69* [0.98]
Assets of largest commercial banks (great banks)	Millions constant	0.074** *36.15* [0.98]	0.066** *20.55* [0.96]
Assets of all commercial banks/NNP		0.043** *21.68* [0.94]	0.044** *11.17* [0.88]
Assets of all commercial banks per capita	Millions constant/ thousands at midyear	0.055** *40.04* [0.98]	0.051** *21.47* [0.96]
Cash/assets of largest commercial banks		−0.018** *−7.49* [0.67]	−0.021** *−8.07* [0.79]
Cash/deposits of largest commercial banks		−0.034** *−9.70* [0.77]	−0.047** *−15.00* [0.93]

Notes: Growth rates are estimated as the coefficient in an ordinary least squares (OLS) regression of the log of the given variable on a constant and a time trend. T-statistics are in italics below coefficient estimates, and R-squared statistics are given in brackets. ** indicates statistical significance at better than 1 percent.

Sources: Author's calculations, based on data from Deutsche Bundesbank (1976) and Mitchell (1992) (net national product [NNP]).

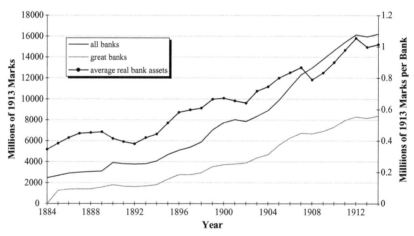

Figure 4.2. Total and Average Real Assets of Joint-Stock Universal Banks, 1884–1913. *Sources:* Calculated from Deutsche Bundesbank (1976), *Handbuch der deutschen Aktiengesellschaften* (various years), and *Saling's* (various years).

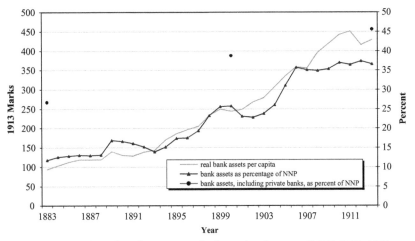

Figure 4.3. Universal Bank Assets per Capita and as Percent of NNP, 1883–1913.

to approximately 450 marks per person (see Figure 4.3).[7] Bank assets also grew relative to the overall economy, despite the fact that the economy also became more efficient during this time; output per person increased. Assets of the joint-stock universal banks increased nearly 4.5 percent per annum as a share of net national product (NNP) and tripled as a percentage of NNP over the period. Even when the much slower growing private banks are included, the assets of the two segments of commercial banking nearly doubled their share of NNP.

Industrial Organization of Universal Banking

A common perception about the German banking system, and about universal banking systems more generally, is that individual institutions must be large compared to those operating within specialized banking systems. The direction of causality is dual: Minimum efficient scale may be larger for a universal bank, or universality may simply offer greater opportunities for a bank to grow. Without some quantification of minimum efficient scale for specialized versus universal banks, we can only determine whether size is associated with universality. It is safe to say that many of the German banks, especially the great banks, were large institutions. The nine biggest

---

[7] Again, the figures are given in real terms (1913 marks). In comparison, the Italian universal banking sector amounted to 250,000 real marks per capita circa 1895 and reached just over 500,000 real marks per capita by World War I. Bank assets per capita grew at an average annual rate of 6.2 percent in Italy during the same period. See Fohlin (1999a).

banks held an average of 180 million (1913) marks of assets in 1884, and that figure had grown to nearly 900 million by the First World War (see Figure 4.2). Most banks, of course, remained much smaller, averaging one million marks on the eve of the war. To understand how large these numbers really are and to assess the connection between size and universality, it is necessary to compare the German universal banks with commercial banks operating within specialized banking systems. Such an exercise reveals some interesting and surprising results. While it is true – as expected – that average assets of the German universal banks far exceeded those of the specialized American commercial banks, the same cannot be said for the equally specialized deposit banks in the United Kingdom. U.K. banks averaged three times the assets of their German counterparts in 1890, 1900, and 1910 (see Table 4.3). Thus, size clearly does not beget universality, and one can at least reasonably argue that the German banks were not overly large at this time. To be sure, universality still could require size, but other pieces of evidence undermine such a claim: First, the German banks were very small at their inception in the 1850s and in 1910 were still smaller than the U.K. deposit banks had been in 1890. Second, many banks in the United States in this period held assets on par with the average German banks and held far more assets than the vast majority of other American banks. Finally, quite a few universal banks in Germany were smaller than many American banks; so, even if American banks were as large as they could be given existing restrictions, it appears that the minimum efficient scale for universal banking was not the crucial roadblock for at least some American banks to become universal.[8] Thus, universality is not inextricably linked to size, as either cause or effect.

Still, Germany clearly had fewer banks than the United States did, even counting the private banks. The figures for Germany vary substantially depending on the source and on the inclusion of private bankers. Official figures (Deutsche Bundesbank, 1976) put the count of joint-stock banks at seventy-one in the 1880s. Klaus Donaubauer (1988) estimates that over

---

[8] This point arises because economic historians have argued that size constraints prevented American banks from becoming universal. Calomiris (1995, 2000), for example, makes this point explicitly. If the German private banks are included (using the estimate of two thousand such banks in 1900, for example), the figures for Germany would drop dramatically – to about 1.5 million 1913 dollars average assets per bank (compared to just short of nine hundred thousand for the American commercial banks and 43 million 1913 dollars for the British banks). In addition, it is worth noting that Italian banks were also universal in many cases but were much smaller than the German universal banks. So, there were even more American banks that were the same size or larger than Italian universal banks.

Table 4.3. *Banking Industry Structure*

	1890			1900			1910		
	Germany	U.S.	U.K.	Germany	U.S.	U.K.	Germany	U.S.	U.K.
Thousands of people/bank[a]	302	6.3	115.5	268	6.1	204.4	221	3.8	374.4
Thousands of people/banking office[a]	211	6.3	7.5	45.1	6.1	6.3	14.8	3.7	5.5
Branches per bank[b]	0.98 (2.6)	0	14.3	1.01 (4.4)	0.01 (1.4)	31.5	4.3 (16.8)	0.02 (1.9)	67.5
Average assets/bank (millions 1913 dollars)	9.4	0.64	27.8	15.6	0.89	43.3	23.3	0.79	73.7
Five-firm concentration ratio[c]	19 (37.1)	3.2	21 (26.5)	22.5 (33.8)	6.5	25.5 (31)	29.3 (36.9)	6.23	35.5 (43)
Ten-firm concentration ratio[c]	28.8 (56.3)	5.6	32 (38)	33.3 (50)	9.8	41 (46.3)	43.5 (54.8)	9.06	56 (64.7)

Notes:

[a] Population per branch includes the main office. Number of banks and branches for the U.K. comes from Capie and Webber (1985). For Germany, 1890 figures are estimated based on joint-stock banks listed in Berlin (reported in *Saling's*, 1891); thus, population per branch and branches per bank are overestimated. Number of banks for Germany comes from Deutsche Bundesbank (1976), but those numbers are lower than the number of banks reported in the *Handbuch der deutschen Aktiengesellschaften* (HDAG) under credit banks. Branches per bank and population per branch for Germany in 1900 and 1910 come from HDAG. So, for Germany, people per bank and people per branch are not comparable. See discussion in the text.

[b] Branches per bank excludes the main office. For the United States and Germany, figures in parentheses are the number of branches per bank that owned branches (not including the main office itself).

[c] Figures in parentheses, for Germany, exclude estimated private bank assets; and, for the U.K., include only England and Wales. Available series exclude private banks for Germany. The concentration ratios estimated for the U.K. by Capie and Rodrik-Bali (1982) include private banks. The ratios for the United States are from 1908. Ratios for 1913 are 4.45 and 6.78. See discussion in the text.

2,000 private bankers operated in Germany in the 1890s, while the Deutsche Bundesbank (1976) estimates around 1,100 for 1913. In addition, Manfred Pohl (1982) suggests that there were about 1,500 such banks at the time of the formation of the German Empire in 1871. In the United States in 1900, by contrast, commercial banks numbered 12,427.[9] Population per bank provides a different perspective on the proliferation of financial institutions.[10] For example, in 1890, there were over two-and-a-half times as many people per bank in Germany as there were in the U.K., yet by 1910, the positions had reversed and there was over 50 percent more population per institution in the U.K. than in Germany.

Creation and Expansion of Branch Networks

The number and size of individual banks hinges on the extent of their branching networks. And the spread of universal banks' depository offices offers further, though indirect, clues to the expansion of the banking industry as well as to the degree of banks' mobilization efforts. Branches aid the direct collection of deposits from small savers and possibly also facilitate sales of banks' securities. To be sure, the number of deposit offices is not a necessary condition for the growth of deposits to the universal banking system, since it is possible for institutions in other areas to collect funds regionally and make deposits at one of the universal banks. In this way, associated banks in outlying regions function as branches to the larger universal banks. But branching across regions probably facilitates banks' matching of surpluses in some regions with deficits in others; and interregional expansion permits banks to diversify their short-term liabilities and possibly safeguard against systemic instability. Greater geographical diversification can therefore also lead to lower reserve ratios and greater mobilization of capital to productive uses.[11]

---

[9] Of these, 3,731 held national charters, and 8,696 held nonnational charters. See Board of Governors of the Federal Reserve (1959) and U.S. Bureau of the Census (1960).

[10] For the U.K., Sheppard (1971, based on *The Economist's* reports) estimates far fewer banks than do Capie and Webber (1985). The latter figures are almost certainly superior to the former and are therefore used where possible. Since Capie and Webber report only deposits, not total assets, for their banks, Table 4.3 uses the Sheppard figures to calculate average assets per bank. To the extent that the Sheppard data miss primarily the smallest banks, the resulting estimate will be too high. On the other hand, as previously noted, given the exclusion of what could be thousands of primarily very small private banks in Germany, those figures are also overestimated. Moreover, many more banks are reported in the Handbuch der deutschen Aktiengesellschaften in 1900 than in Deutsche Bundesbank (1976) – the source used for population per bank.

[11] Subsequent sections discuss banks' balance sheet ratios, riskiness, and capital mobilization in greater detail.

Table 4.4. *Deposit Offices of Large Banks*

Year	9 Berlin Banks		Deposit Offices in 1913	Number
	Deposit Offices	All Affiliates		
1885	10		Dresdner Bank	48
1894	22		Dresdner Bank	47
1895		59	Commerz- u. Disconto Bank	44
1896		63	Darmstädter Bank (BHI)	30
1900		99	Disconto-Gesellschaft	26
1901	73		Nationalbank fur Deutschland	26
1902		147	Schaaffhausen'scher BV	20
1905	124	241	Mitteldeutsche Creditbank	16
1908		442	Berliner Handelsgesellschaft	0
1912				
1913	252			

Sources: Deposit offices compiled from Motschmann (1915), pp. 54–9, and total institutions from Riesser (1910 [1911]), p. 1008.

Germany developed branching quite late, even though there were no legal restraints to doing so. Hardly any branches existed until the 1870s, at which point the newly founded Deutsche Bank began a campaign to build a network. In fact, Deutsche Bank was an outlier for decades, since (near) unit banking persisted in Germany until the turn of the twentieth century.[12] The number of offices for all of the Berlin banks totaled a mere ten in 1885, and, in 1890, fewer than a quarter of Berlin-listed banks maintained branches (see Table 4.4). Even the branching banks averaged only two subsidiary offices each. Furthermore, the new offices of the great banks were clumped in certain regions of the country. Almost all of Schaaffhausen's branches (twenty of twenty-two) and nearly half of Deutsche Bank's domestic branches (twenty-six of fifty-four), for example, were located in the heavily industrial Rhine Province. At the same time, four of the Berlin banks maintained no offices in the southern provinces, and one had only a single branch (in Alsace-Lorraine).[13]

By 1894 the great banks had opened seventy-three deposit offices altogether. But even by 1900, the joint-stock banks more generally averaged only one branch apiece, or four branches on average for just those that branched. The total number of branches quadrupled over the ensuing decade, and particularly strong growth came in the eight years leading up to World

---

[12] See Fohlin (1999a).

[13] The southern provinces include Bavaria, Württemberg, Baden and the Palatinate, Hessen, and Alsace-Lorraine.

War I. Yet by 1913, there were still only 252 great bank branches, and 22 of them were foreign. Given the comparatively early initiative shown by the Deutsche Bank in the 1870s, it comes as no surprise that this bank held the lead in branch formation (forty-eight branches). Dresdner and Commerz- und Disconto Bank followed close behind, however, with forty-seven and forty-four deposit offices respectively. With the exception of the Berliner Handelsgesellschaft (with no deposit offices), the other great banks maintained between sixteen and thirty branches in 1913 (see Table 4.4).[14] Of course, population grew over these decades, and many universal banks created branches by absorbing previously independent banks. Thus, the availability of banking offices to the population increased less than the figures on branching per institution might imply. The increased penetration of banking offices was dramatic nonetheless. Population per branch in Germany declined from forty-five thousand in 1900 to under fifteen thousand in 1910.[15]

One upshot of these findings on the German experience is that neither size nor universality requires branching in general. Comparison with the U.K. underscores the lack of a generalized connection between universality and branching: The German banks were universal before they branched, and the British banks branched very actively without becoming universal. Also, since many German unit banks grew larger than American banks, it is clear that the contrast in the sizes of American and German banks rests at least partially on factors other than branching restrictions.

Concentration in Universal Banking

The results on size and proliferation of banks and branching lead naturally to the question of industry concentration. From nearly the start of universal

---

[14] By comparison, in the U.K., the branch network covered the country much earlier than in Germany. Banks averaged thirty branches apiece in 1890, forty-five in 1900, and ninety-three in 1910. There were about 8,000 people per U.K. branch in 1890 and only 5,500 per branch by 1910. The top four Italian universal banks also opened branches earlier, and at a somewhat faster rate, than did the Germans. Banca Commerciale Italiana (Comit) led the Italian universal banks in branching, opening six offices in its first four years and maintaining thirty branches outside of its Milan headquarters by 1906 and fifty-eight branches – 20 percent more than the German leader, Deutsche Bank – by the First World War. See Confalonieri (1974). Of course, due to widespread limitations on branching, there was a negligible number of bank branches in the United States throughout the period. Some states, notably California, did permit intrastate branching, and banks increasingly took advantage of their freedom.

[15] If private banks are included, using a rough estimate of 1,500 single-office institutions, the figure for population per branch would fall to 9,200 people per office in 1910.

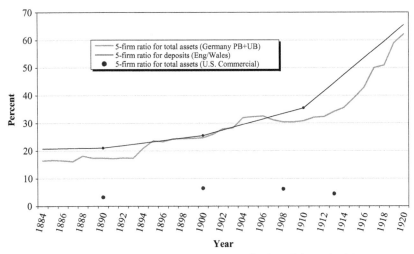

Figure 4.4. Banking Concentration in Germany, England, and the United States, 1884–1920. *Sources:* Calculated from Capie and Rodrik-Bali (1982), Deutsche Bundesbank (1976), Goldsmith (1969), *Handbuch der deutschen Aktiengesellschaften* (various years), *Saling's* (various years), and U.S. Comptroller of the Currency (various years).

banking in Germany, commentators have remarked, sometimes with great alarm, on the concentration of economic power within the great banks. In 1910, for example, the well-known great-banker Jakob Riesser proclaimed that "the movement toward concentration precipitates itself headlong like a flood and proceeds with awful violence, as if all contrivances for stemming the tide had been swept away and all dams had been destroyed by some natural catastrophe."[16] The truth, however, may be somewhat at odds with the lore. Concentration may be measured in a number of ways, and these different measures offer varying views of the universal banking industry over the 1884–1913 period.

Concentration ratios indicate little growth in the share of the largest banks in the banking industry (see Figure 4.4 and Table 4.3).[17] While the asset-based ratio increased 5 percentage points (to 39.6) between December 1892 and December 1894 and climbed just over 43 percent over the course of 1895, it had remained flat in the mid-1880s and declined steadily between

---

[16] Riesser (1910 [1911]), p. 614.

[17] The measures are five-firm ratios using two different balance sheet indicators (total assets and total share capital) and two different denominators (all joint-stock credit banks and the sum of such banks and private banks). The joint-stock credit banks are the Kreditbanken in the Deutsche Bundesbank (1976) series. Since private banks reported no consistent balance sheets, they are included only for total assets and then only at estimated values.

1896 and 1901 (back down to 37 percent). The ratio declined on net in the latter half of the 1880s and remained around 33 to 34 percent in the early 1890s. Putting these findings together, and still ignoring the private banks, the lack of a steady trend toward concentration over the period is evident. The top five banks began the period with 37 percent of joint-stock bank assets and ended it with just short of 42 percent.

Ratios using share capital show even less growth. Though the five-firm capital ratio increased from 34 to 39 percent over the course of 1895, the ratio had generally declined through 1894 and continued to drop steadily between 1895 and 1901 (to a low of just over 31 percent) and then between 1904 and 1912 (from 37 to under 31 percent). The difference in the two ratios sheds some light on the relative use of capital in the expansion of joint-stock universal banks. The fact that asset concentration ratios grew relative to share capital–based ratios suggests that the largest banks (by this time, all centered in the capital, Berlin) increased their assets more through deposits than through share capital, compared with the provincial banks. In other words, since a given volume of deposits very likely corresponds to a larger number of individual investors than an equal amount of share capital, the great banks appear to have been expanding their customer base rapidly at the expense of provincial universal banks.

In line with previous sections, the figures so far exclude the multitudes of private bankers. Because a few, but not all, private bankers can be viewed as competitors of the universal banks, the relevant measure of universal banking concentration may actually lie somewhere between those based on joint-stock banks alone and those computed with the sum of private and joint-stock institutions. Unfortunately, such a calculation proves to be essentially impossible, since there is no way to determine the assets or even the existence of all private banks, much less categorize them according to their clientele and lines of business. Including an estimate of the number of private banks does provide a lower bound on the true level of concentration. Such calculations yield a new concentration ratio for total assets of 16 percent in 1884 and 33 percent in 1913.[18] Because of the linear interpolation used in estimating private-bank assets, the inclusion of the private banks smooths the decline and then rebound of the concentration ratios between 1895 and 1905. The estimated figures probably exaggerate the steadiness of the increase, but, interestingly, the sharp rise of 1892–5 and the decline of

---

[18] The data come from Deutsche Bundesbank (1976) for the joint-stock banks and from Goldsmith (1969) for the private banks (using linear interpolation between his estimates for 1880, 1900, and 1913).

1906–8 both remain apparent in these new ratios. Nonetheless, if we consider the private bankers, it is clear that concentration in universal banking increased over the period in question; but it changed less than contemporaries and many historians perceived.

There are several possible explanations for such a trend toward growth and concentration: increasing demand for a few large banks to serve growing and merging industrial firms, increasing availability of scale and scope economies in the financial services business itself, or a simple progression toward a more rational structure in the banking sector (identifying and capturing existing economies of scale and scope or stability gains from branching). In fact, all three possibilities may have worked in concert.[19] Even if there is no direct connection between industrial and financial concentration in general, the possibility remains that banking is, or was becoming, a naturally oligopolistic business and was simply progressing toward a more ideal industry structure. Contrary to the popular concern over growing concentration, then, the process may have actually enhanced consumer welfare. Moreover, all types of banking institutions may benefit from branching and resulting industry consolidation because of economies of scale in advertising and marketing, greater opportunity for matching supply and demand for capital, or increased diversification and stability. Concentration that comes with increased branching may therefore raise the efficiency and stability of surviving banks while placing more banks in competition with one another. Small banks with local monopolies may become branches of larger banks, and multiple national banks may open small deposit offices in the same areas.

This point also suggests that industry concentration is unrelated to the form of banking institutions (universal versus specialized) in place. A comparison with England drives home this point. The German universal banking sector was actually less concentrated than the English deposit banking sector over the entire period from 1884 to 1913 (see Figure 4.3 and Table 4.3).[20] In both countries, the largest members of the commercial/universal banking sector built up significant nationwide branching

---

[19] There are also possible political explanations. Rajan and Zingales (1999), for example, argue that the preparation for and exigencies of war prompted many European governments to attempt to gain control over the financial system. By directly orchestrating concentration in banking, governments could direct financial matters with greater ease. In the German case, the government intervened in the banking sector to a far greater extent during the 1930s and World War II (see Chapter 8 for further details).

[20] Since the British ratios include private banks, the discussion here uses the analogous ratio for Germany. Because of the declining private-banking sector, the gap between the two ratios declines over time.

networks during this period. They often accomplished such branching by taking over a smaller bank (very often a private bank) in the location of a desired branch, and thereby contributed to the concentration increases in both England and Germany. Although branch networks grew even more rapidly after World War I, both countries achieved an essentially national banking system by 1913, if not earlier. As a result, while the top five banks held approximately one-fifth of the total bank assets in both Germany and the U.K. in 1890, the top five held 29 and 36 percent in the two countries, respectively, by 1910. In other words, the German universal banking sector was no more (and probably less) concentrated than the corresponding British sector, so there are no grounds here for the idea that universality led to banking industry concentration.[21]

These findings cannot prove that universality does not stimulate concentration; but the results indicate very clearly that sufficient conditions for concentration can arise in specialized systems, especially when they are unhampered by branching restrictions. Most important for the historical debates over German universal banking, the data reject the common notion that the disadvantage of the German universal banking system was its excessive concentration. It may well be that the historical literature has overemphasized the concentration movement in German banking, due to a presumption of anticompetitive behavior that did not materialize or that was at least not directly related to that concentration.[22]

DEVELOPMENT OF UNIVERSAL BANKING PRACTICES

So far, the discussion has focused on the overall growth of the credit banking sector and the organization of the industry as a whole. But it is also useful to examine the microstructure of the banks, both to better place the

---

[21] Since banks in the United States could not build a nationwide branching network due to regulatory restraints, the U.S. experience makes for a less useful comparison than does that of the U.K. See Fohlin (2000c) on concentration and competition in the U.S. banking market; also see Davis (1965) and Sylla (1969). The latter offers evidence that, around the turn of the last century, country banks acted as price discriminating monopolists in their respective markets.

[22] Industry efficiency is notoriously difficult to assess empirically, but future research should consider the impact of increasing concentration on market power and efficiency in banking. Fohlin (2000b) estimates structural supply and demand equations for the German universal system in the 1884–1913 period to estimate the markups taken by the universal banks and therefore their market power. The results constitute a weighted average for the country as a whole, and they indicate a low level of market power overall. By inference, the largest banks could not have held tremendous market power, since they make up such a large part of the average. The most likely monopolists would be the small banks located in more isolated areas with little penetration from the great banks or larger provincial banks.

institutional development of the banks within the industrialization period and to understand more precisely how institutional design did or did not influence capital mobilization and economic growth. By the start of World War I, the German joint-stock credit banks were full-fledged universal banks, combining the regular services of commercial banks (deposit taking, current accounts, bill discounting, acceptances, trade credits) with underwriting and brokerage of securities. But the banks, especially those founded in the first wave, started their existence with a much narrower focus. As the economy developed, financial instruments evolved, the customer base grew and changed, and entrepreneurs adjusted their demand for financial services. Thus, banks changed the composition of their services over the decades, and true universality became the norm only after some period of industrialization. Using an array of sources, this section studies the banks' provision of commercial and investment services and traces the evolution of those lines of business over the later industrialization era.

The View from Aggregate Bank Balance Sheets

Balance sheet and income data for the joint-stock banking sector allow us to draw inferences about the relative extent of different lines of business and thereby build a financial portrait of the German universal banks. The proportion of loans and advances in total assets indicates the magnitude of the banks' commercial business, and the breakdown between short-maturity liabilities (such as deposits) and net worth hints at the same. The ratio of interest and commissions on current accounts and loans to income from securities underwriting and participation – all reported in bank income statements – offers another measure of the relative importance to the universal banks of commercial and investment services.

Aggregate Bank Assets

The German banks' financial assets fall into six liquidity or maturity classes: cash, bills of exchange, government securities, other securities, current account loans or advances, and very short-term loans (see Figure 4.5).[23] In addition, of course, the banks held relatively small and stable amounts of fixed assets (approximately 2 percent). Cash is the most liquid of assets and naturally provides no income to banks. Lacking any minimum reserve requirements, the German universal banks kept cash holdings as low as

---

[23] The German bank data come from Deutsche Bundesbank (1976). Since German law required annual balance sheets of all joint-stock firms, reporting problems are mitigated, but the series necessarily omit the private banks.

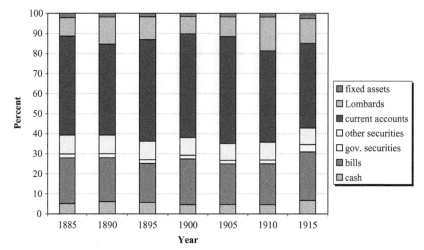

Figure 4.5. Bank Assets – Germany.

possible given their perceived need for immediate reserves. In practice, the banks as a group kept about 4.5 to 5 percent of their assets completely liquid, though they did raise the level in times of uncertainty. For example, they increased cash holdings to over 6.5 percent in the one war year represented in Figure 4.5 (1915).

Universal banks provided short-term capital through bills of exchange and short-maturity loans. Bills of exchange were essentially IOUs with government backing. These bills, in use long before the initiation of universal banking, financed short-term liquidity needs and represented about 20–25 percent of universal bank assets over the period – on the lower end in good years for the stock markets, and on the higher end in times of stress (1890, 1900, and 1915). Short-term loans, or call money (*täglisches Geld*), fell under the general category of Lombards and reports. Typically maturing within days or weeks, Lombard loans provided credit primarily for securities transactions and for covering lags between merchandise delivery and payment. The banks commonly made these short-term loans on collateral (usually bills of exchange and securities), though they certainly offered some unsecured credits.[24] These loans are considered a component of the commercial business, but they clearly related to the investment side of the business as

---

[24] See Riesser (1910 [1911]) for details of the specific conditions on Lombard loans made by one of the great banks, Berliner Handelsgesellschaft. Also see Weber (1915) on both Germany and Britain. In the British case, very short-term loans, termed "money at call," consisted primarily of loans to stockbrokers for transactions in the London discount market

well. Even more than with the banks' stocks of bills, the levels of Lombard loans varied from year to year. In 1900, for example, the universal banks as a whole held around 8 percent of their assets in Lombards; ten years later, they held nearly twice that amount.

Current account advances comprised the largest single component of the banks' assets: nearly half on average over the whole period, and well over half in some years. As described in Chapter 2, borrowers used current account advances for a range of financing needs, most of which required financing over longer periods than those covered by bills of exchange or by Lombards. The advances provided immediate returns from interest and fees, but they also represented a possible start to a long-term relationship that might subsequently bring in underwriting fees and commissions as well as possible proxy voting rights over equity shares held for customers. Adding these current accounts to the other types of lending, it is clear that the universal banks invested very significantly in the commercial lines of business. Over 80 percent of the sector's considerable assets went into commercial lending throughout the period, and even in 1915, the level fell only to just shy of 80 percent.

Much of the investment side of the universal banking business takes place off balance sheet. For example, underwriting and brokerage activities often result in asset holdings that remain in the portfolio too briefly to be booked on an annual balance sheet. To the extent that these services did yield longer-term holdings, they appeared in the banks' balance sheets in the form of securities. Securities can be divided into two types: nongovernment and government. The former category consists of equity and bonds of public firms or other banks, including subsidiaries; the latter comprises primarily government bonds or the securities of government-owned enterprises. While most of the government bonds constituted secondary reserves, the nongovernment securities usually represented either issues that the banks were unable to place or investments that the banks kept in order to earn income or to maintain direct control rights.[25] Nongovernment issues took up the lion's share of the banks' securities holdings, but the total amounted only to 11 percent of total bank assets over the years. Overall, in the late-nineteenth and early-twentieth centuries, the asset portfolios of the universal banks look more similar to those of the straight commercial banks of England and

---

or the London Stock Exchange. See Goodhart (1972) for further descriptions of English bank balance sheet items.

[25] Chapter 5, on corporate governance relationships, investigates banks' securities holdings in depth.

Wales rather than to those of a pure investment bank. The English banks held more cash and government-backed securities but far fewer bills; however, the three most liquid classes amounted to similar proportions of bank assets in the two countries. The other four classes of assets were nearly identical, even taken individually.

Aggregate Bank Liabilities

The choice among funding instruments hints both at the trade-off between investment and commercial banking and at the banks' methods of capital mobilization. The banks could have funded their business through either shares or deposits. Shares may have been more difficult to place with the public than deposits, since equity presents both diversifiable risk and (not diversifiable) uncertainty and may also be sold in denominations larger than the total amount of the average depositor's desired savings.[26] The average saver or businessperson would likely have preferred the greater security and liquidity of a deposit contract. And banks may have resisted expansion through share capital issues in order to limit the dilution of their control. At the same time, however, banks may have preferred equity financing, if they required long-term use of the funds they gathered, or the universal banks may have lacked access to depositors and needed to issue equity instead. Thus, deposits may be favored by both bank and investor, but equity may have been necessary if the universal banks were to fund risky ventures or simply could not attract depositors.[27]

The empirical evidence on deposit ratios over the period 1883–1912 is perhaps surprising but does underscore the changing policies of the banks (see Figure 4.6). At their inception, the German universal banks financed

---

[26] The face value of German joint-stock bank shares typically ranged from 400 to 1,200 marks in the nineteenth and early-twentieth century. Market value would normally have been higher. The Disconto-Gesellschaft grew from 1,163 members at its founding in 1852 to 1,675 four years later. The average stake of the members ranged from 3,000 Thaler (9,000 marks) to over 4,000 Thaler (12,000 marks) during these early years. See Däbritz (1931) for further details. Even by 1876, 95 percent of those counted in the census earned less than 2,000 marks (presumably per annum). See Sombart (1903). It is possible that groups of individuals may have purchased shares, but because joint-stock companies were not required to reveal the identities of their shareholders, virtually no data is available that would permit investigation of such a phenomenon.

[27] Having to finance with equity could result in the banks' focusing on investment banking activities in order to yield the comparatively higher returns required by equity owners. This point is emphasized by Verdier (1997). But the bank charters that have been discussed in the literature indicate that the early banks formed with the stated purpose of undertaking investment-banking type activities. Whether this choice was a matter of necessity is harder to determine.

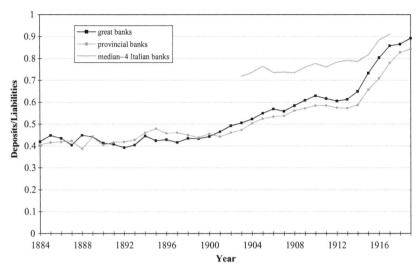

Figure 4.6. Deposits as a Share of Joint-Stock Bank Liabilities (1884–1919).

themselves almost entirely with equity and took only small amounts of deposits on current accounts. The situation certainly evolved, and eventually deposits were taken for short terms – three, six, or twelve months – and at low interest rates (averaging between 1 and 2 percent until 1906).[28] Deposit taking remained meager until 1894 but increased rapidly thereafter, as the universal banks built up the facilities for widespread deposit taking concurrent with the major upswing in the German economy.[29] By the 1880s, and until the turn of the twentieth century, deposit accounts amounted to 40 to 45 percent of liabilities. Universal banks pursued deposits much more actively after 1894, but levels remained below 50 percent of bank liabilities until after the turn of the century. Deposits reached at least 60 percent of liabilities in 1913 and 75 percent during the First World War.[30] One might expect the great banks and provincial banks to use different modes of

[28] See Motschmann (1915) for an exhaustive survey of the deposit business of the Berlin banks.

[29] This point is made in Fohlin (1994) as well as in Edwards and Ogilvie (1996). Deposits could be made on term or demand, but it is difficult to disaggregate the two types for certain; thus, the two categories must be considered together.

[30] The booking of acceptances deserves mention. The German banks appear to have booked acceptances (along with checks in many cases) under a separate heading in the liability side of the balance sheet, but apparently included them among other categories on the asset side. Given the level of aggregation on the asset side, it is difficult to determine how best to deduct acceptances from assets. Removing acceptances from liabilities increases the deposit/liability ratio by about 10 percentage points in the 1880–1913 period, but by almost

funding, particularly as time passed, yet they followed nearly identical paths throughout the period.[31]

Besides their use in measuring universality, the figures on deposits also provide an estimate of capital mobilization of the universal banks. Deposits include both funds provided by individual depositors as well as deposits created by the banks through their current account lending activities. Deposits alone (that is, not including current accounts) may therefore provide a more accurate picture of banks' contribution to mobilization. In Germany, in the period before 1900, reported current account credits ranged from four to five times deposits, and therefore pure deposits comprised less than 10 percent of bank liabilities. In line with the expansion of branch networks, credits fell to two times the amount of pure deposits in the five years following 1907 and to nearly equal levels after 1911. The expansion of both types of liabilities, in addition to the gradual shift from current account credits to deposits, meant that deposits alone nearly quadrupled as a share of liabilities between 1900 (10 percent) and 1919 (38 percent). Despite this burgeoning in the deposit business, Jakob Riesser (1910 [1911]) concluded that the level remained lower than that in Great Britain, France, and the United States.[32]

A second way to estimate deposit mobilization (as opposed to deposit creation) is to subtract loans and credits (debits on current accounts) from deposits and credits on current account. Since the numbers are aggregated, the results apply to the universal banking system as a whole. Thus, internal drain – the transfer of loaned funds of one bank to deposits in another – causes no problems of interpretation in this context. Aggregation, however, restricts to averages conclusions about how banks covered their assets. The numbers provide a striking result in the German case – namely, that loans and credits exceeded deposits and current account surpluses for the entire period through 1914. After 1914, the balance reversed, and the deposit surplus reached 25 billion marks by 1919 (equivalent to 45 percent of banks' liabilities).

---

nothing after that (given the drop-off in the use of acceptances during World War I). See Deutsche Bundesbank (1976), p. 55.

[31] A useful comparison can be made to the four largest Italian universal banks, which had already hit 70 percent deposits by 1903 and 91 percent by 1917. Thus, by World War I, the heavy use of equity to finance operations no longer distinguished the universal banks from pure commercial banks, such as those in England.

[32] For comparisons of British and German banks' financial structure, see Fohlin (1997c), and for comparisons of Italy and Germany, see Fohlin (1999a). The latter shows that the principal Italian universal banks began operations in 1894–5 with significantly greater deposit financing than the German universal banks had even by that time.

Individual Bank Income Statements

Income breakdowns for the universal banks are notable in two respects. First, as with the aggregate balance sheet data, they provide insight into the division of the banks' services on an annual basis. But unlike the aggregate data, these bank-level reports also reveal any disparities that may exist across banks. Reporting categories vary somewhat from bank to bank, but most banks report similar items to one another and over time. In the years from 1884 to 1898, it is possible to distinguish those income sources related to investment banking from those stemming from commercial activities. In particular, statements typically separate earnings on stocks or other securities on the one hand from fees and interest on loans and current account balances on the other. The former posts comprise the investment banking income, and dividing that income by the total revenues of the bank yields an investment banking income percentage. By 1913, the statements mostly aggregate fees and commissions from various lines of business, making it impossible to differentiate the sources and determine precisely the ratio of investment to commercial banking income within the banks.

Keeping in mind the standard warnings about the validity of reported incomes, the figures should be viewed as estimates and used as a rough guide to the breakdown of the banks' business. Overall, for the fifty to sixty domestic banks with Berlin stock market listings – and therefore reported on in *Saling's* – the percentage of income stemming from investment banking functions hovered in the 17–21 percent range during the 1880s and 1890s.[33] Involvement in investment banking varies more among the banks than it does over time. The average percentage of revenues from investment banking remained quite stable over the sampled years, but it varied substantially among the different banks within each year. Investment banking income averaged 17.5 percent in 1884 and 18.6 in 1897, for example; but it had a standard deviation of around 12 percent in both years. Over all of the years, investment banking income ranges from basically nothing for some banks to over 60 percent of total income for others. In every year, there are banks at both ends of the spectrum, but the low end is certainly more heavily populated than the high end. Half of the banks earned investment

---

[33] Investment banking revenues include posts such as profits on securities traded or fees on securities issued. The categories and level of aggregation vary from bank to bank, but commercial banking activities are excluded as much as possible. Brokerage activities are included, as they were linked intimately, even inextricably, to the universal banks' investment banking activities. *Saling's* refers to *Saling's Börsen-Jahrbuch,* a yearly collection of financial reports on German corporations.

banking income of 15 percent or less of their total revenues, and 60 percent of the banks earned between 5 and 25 percent. Consistent with perceptions of their relatively heavy involvement in investment banking operations, the great banks always land in the top half of the range – regularly around 25 percent. Investment banking services, however, do not depend on size; some of the smallest banks accrued some of the highest percentages of income from investment banking sources. Still, the largest handful of banks always ranges above some moderate level of investment banking income (usually the mean for all banks).[34]

Summing Up the Evidence on Universality of Services

German universal banking evolved considerably, shifting from a strong investment orientation to a relatively heavy commercial leaning, over the second-half of the nineteenth century. At the inception of joint-stock universal banking in Germany, the banks looked a lot more like investment banks than anything else. In the 1850s, some banks took essentially no deposits and held the vast majority of their assets in the form of a small number of equities.[35] In these cases, income flowed primarily from investment rather than commercial banking activities. It is also clear from individual bank statements that the mix of business varied considerably from bank to bank, and that by the turn of the twentieth century a large proportion of the so-called universal banks focused primarily on commercial business. Comparing the financial structure of the German and English commercial banks – the similarity in asset holdings, the comparable use of deposits toward the end of the period, and the low proportion of German bank income stemming from securities – highlights important similarities in the two banking systems more than it confirms stark contrasts that might be expected to emerge between universal and specialized institutions.

BANK PERFORMANCE: CAPITAL MOBILIZATION, RISK, COMPETITIVENESS, AND RETURNS

How the German universal banks performed – in terms of internal financial success, risk taking, and competitiveness, as well as in terms of serving the

---

[34] Because of the variable accounting practices, it is difficult to create a sufficiently detailed database of bank-level information to allow a sophisticated econometric analysis of the determinants of investment banking activities. It remains a possibility for future research to explore more detailed data sources.

[35] See the example of Disconto-Gesellschaft in the next chapter.

capital mobilization needs of the young industrial economy – remains a central and yet understudied question in the debates over financial system design and the role of the German banks during industrialization. The historical evidence cannot provide answers to all of these questions, but it can shed new light on many of them, particularly with the help of some conceptual structure from economics.

The basic mechanism of capital mobilization emerges from a simple model of a monetary economy with financial intermediaries and currency holding by the public: The total nominal money stock (M1) is a function of the nominal monetary base (currency plus reserves), the ratio of bank deposits to currency, and the cash reserve ratio.[36] That is, $(M1)_t = [(1 + H_t (1 - \gamma_t))/Q_t]M_t$, such that H_t is the real stock of inside money (deposits), Q_t is the real stock of currency balances, γ_t is the cash reserve ratio, and M_t is the nominal monetary base. The ultimate impact of the banks' activities on the economy depends directly on the amount of funds assembled by the financial system and inversely upon the proportion of the system's assets retained in the form of cash reserves. These variables, in turn, relate at least in part to the funding and lending policies pursued by the institutions involved. Financial intermediaries maintain partial control over both the reserve ratio and the deposit-to-currency ratio. For example, banks can raise the deposit-to-currency ratio by encouraging individuals to deposit their savings or buy equity shares in the bank. More directly, they can reduce their reserve ratios by increasing the proportion of funds lent out or otherwise invested in risky assets. These allocations, naturally resulting partly from the banks' responses to market forces in the banking industry, influence the riskiness of individual banks and the sector as a whole.

On-Balance-Sheet Activities: Asset and Liability Ratios

Banks determine when and how much to expand liabilities, and simultaneously their own liquidity and maturity risk, through their retention of liquid assets as reserves. Asset and liability ratios therefore offer detailed insight into the banks' methods and performance. The inverse relationship between a bank's reserve ratios, on the one hand, and multiple expansion of the bank's deposit base, on the other, forces bank managers to walk a fine line between providing a solid return to investors and safeguarding the stability of the bank. Changes in banks' reserve policies go hand in hand with

---

[36] See Champ and Freeman (1994) and sources cited there for a straightforward exposition of the theory.

developments in the industrial organization of banking – branching, mergers, and capital structure. At the same time, individual bank-level policies and practices go on to influence overall banking system stability, competitiveness, and profitability as well as economywide mobilization of financial resources. Bankers surely consider these larger consequences of their decisions, but they primarily take actions based on their first-order effects on the bank itself. Even if discrete events or choices create only minor effects, the collective impact of these actions is often marked.

Proportion and Riskiness of Various Liquid Assets

In the German case, as in most banking systems, reserves took the form of cash, call money, bills, or low-risk securities, often government issued. Total stocks of these short-term or liquid assets remained remarkably stable relative to total assets (36–42 percent) of the universal banks throughout the later industrialization period, but the proportions in the various subcategories fluctuated over time. Bills of exchange and government securities weigh quite differently in German bank portfolios, the former consistently exceeding the latter by a significant amount. Between 1883 and 1913, the universal banks booked around 20 percent of their assets under the category bills (*Wechsel*) and 2 percent in government securities.[37] The limited holdings of government paper likely stemmed at least in part from the use of such securities by the savings banks and other financial institutions requiring conservative investments.[38] The German government issued substantial and growing amounts of debt, but increases in that indebtedness lagged the banks' rapid expansion of assets. As the buildup to the war began in 1913,

---

[37] Disaggregation of the securities began only in 1912. The figures for prior years are estimated based on the lowest holdings of government securities between 1912 and 1920 as well as on the detailed account of one of the great banks between 1896 and 1899. The proportion for great banks ranged from 17.6 to 28.6 percent of total securities held between 1912 and 1920. Given that this period covers the First World War, it would be natural to expect that government securities might comprise a higher proportion of securities than they did in the preceding years. Bank für Handel und Industrie, a great bank, reported government securities between 24 and 55 percent of total securities in the period 1896–9. Thus, 17 percent is a conservative estimate of the proportion of all great bank securities held in government securities.

[38] By comparison, during the same period, both bills and government securities ranged between 5 and 10 percent of assets for the English and Welsh banks. Given the active use of government debt in the British Empire, it is not surprising that home banks held a substantial proportion of their investments in the form of British and colonial government and government-guaranteed assets.

the Reich debt exploded and began to take up a far greater proportion of bank assets.[39]

Assets with less liquidity – such as loans and advances or nongovernment securities – therefore also comprise steady shares of bank assets.[40] Aggregation over all joint-stock banks, of course, hides much of the variability among these assets. The quality of assets may differ systematically among the banks and even within one bank, giving varying degrees of risk to holdings that have ostensibly the same maturity. For example, offering credit with little or no collateral (or on the basis of the firm's own securities) and rolling over short-term loans repeatedly – as the German banks are reputed to have done – may be riskier than offering collateralized loans that are not rolled over. German banks may have offered less uncovered credit than is commonly supposed: The few available figures indicate unsecured loans usually amounted to one-fifth to one-third of the total.[41] Given the difficulty of assessing the quality of collateral, however, it is exceedingly difficult to draw direct conclusions about the relative quality or risk of the German lending business based only on the use of secured lending.

Comparing bills and securities presents essentially the same problems. Further complicating comparisons across banks, bills could be either directly discounted for the banks' own customers or bought on the open market, creating potentially significant differences in risk. Yet no distinction is made in the banks' accounts. A particular difference arises in the case of bills, in that some banks may have been more reluctant to rediscount bills or issue bills without collateral, while others apparently did so freely. The quality of German banks' bill holdings are often compared unfavorably to those of the British banks, who are commonly thought to have held an especially high-quality portfolio of bills. But this assessment is perhaps based on the perception that the British banks adhered closely to the Real Bills Doctrine.[42] Despite the many potential problems with accounting, it is likely that the asset breakdowns represent an accurate portrayal of the overall, long-term

---

[39] See Deutsche Bundesbank (1976) for data on German government debt (local, state, and national) from 1876 to 1974.

[40] Again, it is interesting to note that the British deposit banks booked nearly identical shares of assets under both categories (50 percent for loans and approximately 9 percent for nongovernment securities).

[41] Weber (1915), p. 142.

[42] See ibid., pp. 145–51, for a lengthy discussion of bill discounting in the two countries, and Warburg (1910) for an essay on the European discount system more generally. Interestingly, Warburg draws the main distinction between Europe and the United States, not between Britain and other European countries or the United States.

patterns of holdings by the universal banks. Both contemporary and historical accounts clearly indicate that banks presented as conservative an overall
financial picture as possible. Yet there is a limit to how far the banks could
manipulate their balances, especially over long periods, and such limits were
similar across banks.

When banks are financed by significant amounts of equity as well as
deposits, the cash/liabilities ratio becomes relevant as well as the cash/deposit
ratio. Among the German joint-stock universal banks, the cash/liability ratio
hovered in the 5–6 percent range in the late 1880s and early 1890s, but it
declined somewhat after 1893.[43] The decline in the banks' cash/liability
ratio coincides with the expansion of those same banks (see Figure 4.7).[44]
Banks' holdings of cash cannot be taken as completely exogenous, and the
heavy use of equity financing among German banks helps explain their
fairly low cash/liability ratios, particularly in contrast to their cash/deposit
ratios.

The cash/deposit ratio offers greater insight into the banks' participation
in changing short-term liabilities into longer-term assets (maturity transformation). Among the German universal banks, cash/deposit ratios followed
a similar, though more extreme, pattern as cash/liabilities ratios: rising over
the late 1880s and declining after 1893. By comparison, English and Welsh
banks reported smaller amounts of cash reserves, and the gap between the
two countries exceeded 6 percentage points around 1891 (even more when
excluding acceptances among the German bank liabilities). The London
joint-stock banks, as a group, appear to have maintained cash balances
between 10 and 15 percent of deposits. In contrast, the comparable set of

---

[43] Banks typically practice window dressing, holding more cash at balance sheet time, so it is
hard to know just how low cash balances fell throughout the year. The banks' bimonthly
balances, published starting in 1909, do show somewhat lower cash reserves than the annual
balances.

[44] Over the same period, the British banks seem to have maintained considerably higher
cash/liability ratios, and the gap appears to have widened after 1893. When acceptances
are subtracted from the German bank liabilities, the cash/liabilities ratio increases slightly
throughout the period (approximately 1.5 percentage points until the mid-1890s and gradually declining to 0.7 percentage point after 1907). Complaints of window dressing seem
somewhat less strenuous for the German banks than for the English deposit banks, yet
defenders of the German joint-stock banks claimed that the British banks held much slim-
mer reserves than the Germans. See Riesser (1910 [1911]) and sources cited there. For a
brief period, between 1888 and 1893, the English and German cash/liabilities ratios are
frequently less than 0.5 percentage point apart. Also of note, the German banks issued no
notes – the latter having been traded away for general limited liability during the formation
of the German central bank (the Reichsbank) in 1876.

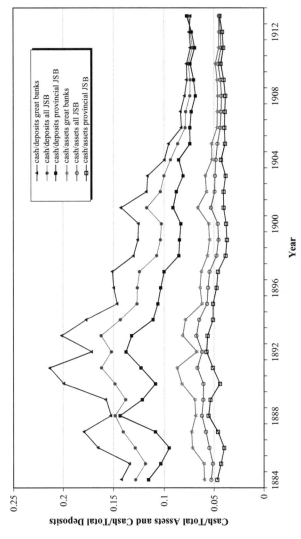

Figure 4.7. Cash/Asset and Cash/Deposit Ratios of German Joint-Stock Banks.

93

German banks kept aggregate ratios as low as 7 percent and as high as 22 percent.[45]

Reserve ratios hinge on the structure and activities of the banks. For example, demand deposits require higher cash ratios than term deposits, and risky, unsecured loans necessitate greater reserves than do conservative, well-collateralized loans. Because the German universal banks often took deposits for terms of three, six, or twelve months, they enjoyed greater latitude in investing these funds than they had with current account credits – deposit accounts that permitted withdrawal on sight. The change in the cash/deposit ratio resulted largely from the marked increase in the universal banks' use of deposits at the turn of the century; although the banks certainly expanded their liabilities through new issues of equity, from the 1890s they generally used deposits to a far greater extent. During this time, the banks expanded their personal deposits in particular, therefore raising their ratio of term-to-demand deposits and necessitating lower cash/deposit ratios.[46] By simultaneously holding cash at steady levels while increasing deposits, the ratio naturally fell precipitously.

The short-term coverage ratio – measuring the extent to which banks cover their short-term liabilities with short-term or liquid assets – gives a broader indication of the maturity transformation taking place and offers an interesting contrast to cash ratios. Among German joint-stock banks, the ratio of short-term assets to liabilities reached 71 percent in 1892 but had fallen to nearly 50 percent fifteen years later.[47] This coverage policy seems all the more conservative in light of the readily available lender of last resort facilities apparently provided by the Reichsbank.[48] Historians have

---

[45] Neither the British nor the German banks were bound by minimum reserve requirements in the pre–World War I period, and there appears to be no firm evidence that either country's central bank imposed implicit reserve requirements. In Germany, proposals for reserve requirements recommended cash holdings of 1–5 percent of the sum of deposits and current account balances to be held at the Reichsbank. The German Reichsbank, it is argued, both squeezed the universal banks out of much of the short-term commercial business and, by standing as lender of last resort, facilitated those banks' provision of riskier investment services. See Fohlin (2001a). For comparisons with Italian banks, see Fohlin (1999a).

[46] Unfortunately, the sources contain no detailed breakdowns of deposit maturities, so these hypotheses currently remain without solid evidence. Deutsche Bundesbank (1976) provides some information on reported breakdowns of current accounts versus deposits, but the detailed notes also indicate that reported breakdowns bore no consistent resemblance to reality.

[47] In rather surprising contrast, the English and Welsh banks' ratio remained in the 44 to 48 percent range for virtually the whole period.

[48] See Warburg (1910) and Weber (1915), especially with regard to bill rediscounting.

argued that the security provided by the central bank allowed the universal banks to offer sometimes large-scale, rolled-over credit to industry and more generally to have permitted greater risk taking. Financial records show, however, that the banks tied up moderate shares of assets in loans and advances – certainly not significantly more than their English counterparts.[49] To be sure, much qualitative variation escapes scrutiny when using such figures. German bills of exchange, for example, may have carried greater risks than those used in England. In addition, if the German banks' current account advances were rolled over more readily than the equivalent English and Welsh loans, thus making them relatively longer-term, then they would have possibly needed to hold higher ratios of true short-term assets to easily liquefied liabilities.[50]

Even within the German universal banking sector, disparities appear in operating policies of different banks. Most remarkable is the gap between the provincial network of universal banks – typically composed of smaller institutions, located outside of the capital – and the Berlin-centered great banks. The former maintained markedly lower cash ratios than the latter right up to the eve of World War I. Both segments of the industry lowered cash ratios steadily after 1890, but the great banks did so more rapidly, so as to converge with the provincial banks around 1910. The decline in cash ratios matches the expansion of the great banks into other regions of the country through branching and absorption of provincial and private banks and therefore coincides with the trend toward concentration in banking. Amalgamations in turn are thought to have stemmed not just from ever larger economies of scale and scope but from growing competition among banks for increasingly overlapping territories. As banks combined, they diversified, and probably became more able to lend a greater proportion of their capital. Moreover, an environment of competition may have necessitated less conservative policies in order to maintain profit rates.[51]

These patterns of cash and broader coverage ratios (as well as of branching and deposit taking) arrived on the heels of the economic expansion that

---

[49] Fohlin (2001a).

[50] Again, because accounting irregularities are possible, banks may have booked illiquid or risky assets under headings that seem to refer to quick assets. In addition, because the German balance sheet include acceptances among liabilities, the German ratio is not exactly comparable to the English ratio. If acceptances were booked under loans and advances on the asset side, then the current ratio is underestimated; if they were booked under bills, then the current ratio is overestimated. The English banks did roll over current accounts as well, according to Collins (1998).

[51] One can also infer risk of the overall portfolio from variability of returns and the magnitude of the estimated risk premium. Such an analysis is carried out subsequently.

began around 1894 and mushroomed just prior to World War I. The data therefore seem to indicate a puzzling lack of effort on the part of the German credit banks in fostering deposits for use in industrial enterprise until the very last years of the nineteenth century. If the banks' deposit policy was a response to industry requirements for external finance, demand for bank lending should have remained low until the mid-1890s and should have then risen continuously throughout the two decades before World War I.[52] Company balance sheets, however, show that German industrial firms were becoming more, not less, liquid after the turn of the century. As a share of fixed assets, German firms had higher stocks of liquid assets in the 1900–13 period than they did between 1882 and 1900. Among one sample of fifty long-lived German corporations, median stock liquidity as a share of fixed capital rose from approximately 20 percent in 1880 to 60 percent in 1912, yielding an average annual growth rate of 2 percent.[53] Internal funds of newly public German firms (IPO firms) grew quite a bit faster (8 percent per year on average) than those of the more established firms.[54] The IPO firms still lagged the long-lived firms in 1900 (36 percent versus 50 percent) but had caught up shortly thereafter. Even measuring from 1895 on, when deposit taking and branching were already under way, firms' stocks of liquid assets were growing relative to their other assets, and their cash flows were rising faster than investment.[55]

The picture that emerges of the German banks is one of moderate and sometimes high reserve ratios (compared with both English and Italian counterparts) and conservative participation in maturity transformation – changing short-term liabilities into longer-term assets. The relationship between cash/deposit ratios and total banking system assets is pronounced in the German case. While other factors external to bank policies must also play a role, cash/deposit ratios demonstrate a strong negative impact on

---

[52] Borchardt (1963) argues that the banks did not take deposits in their early years because of lack of demand for new funds from industry, but this explanation applies only to the first-half of the nineteenth century.

[53] See Fohlin (1994, 1999a).

[54] Part of the observed aggregate growth stems from the fact that the firms entering the sample in the later years held higher levels of liquidity than those entering earlier. Even counting from 1892, when at least half the sample had already entered, the liquidity ratio of the IPO firms (10 percent) fell significantly below that of the long-lived firms (32 percent).

[55] These results are based on the median values of these variables for a panel of 320 joint-stock firms from 1895 to 1912, randomly selected from the *Handbuch der Deutschen Aktiengesellschaften*. The data derive from the annual reports of each company. Fohlin (1997b) provides further details.

total assets mobilized by the universal banking system.[56] In line with the underlying theory, these results attest to the potential impact of the universal banking sector on the growth and fluctuation of the Germany economy. But since the composition of on-balance-sheet business represents only one facet of risk taking on the part of banks, it is difficult to say much about overall bank risk from this measure alone. The next section adds to the evidence with an examination of the banks' rates of return.

Bank Returns

Profit rates of banks provide some indication of the risk taking of those ventures, since investors demand a higher return, in general, when they place their capital at greater risk. Of course, other factors, such as monopoly rents, play into higher returns, but German universal banks appear to have priced at least their commercial banking services fairly competitively.[57] Despite their competition, on average, the German universal banks profited handsomely from their range of business. Rates of return on equity grew from just short of 8 percent to over 12 percent between 1882 and 1888, but then declined markedly – with a hiatus in the last half of the 1890s – until the stock market crisis of 1900–1 (see Figure 4.8). ROE then rebounded until the 1907 stock market crisis and then leveled off until World War I.[58] It is useful to compare these returns with those for specialized commercial banks in England and the United States in order to determine whether the universal banks were earning a particularly large return for their possibly riskier investment portfolio. Returns for U.S. banks, focused primarily on commercial business, also declined significantly over the late 1880s and early 1890s, but began a generally sustained, and sometimes dramatic, upturn until the same 1907 crisis. U.K. performance, based on Capie's (1988) figures,

---

[56] Total real assets in the universal system is modeled as a function of concurrent (t) and lagged (t − 1) cash ratios plus a trend variable to capture other determinants of assets (given the persistent growth of total assets over the period). For Germany, estimated coefficients on concurrent cash/deposit ratios are negative and significant at 5 percent or better. Despite the tight theoretical link between reserve ratios and total capital supply, the empirical connection is difficult to establish generally. For example, in Germany, decreasing cash/asset ratios do not increase overall system assets for the pre–World War I period. And for Italy, when total assets are modeled as a function of cash ratios, estimated coefficients are negative as expected, but are statistically insignificant. See Fohlin (1999a). Regression results are available from the author.

[57] See Fohlin (2000c).

[58] Ibid.

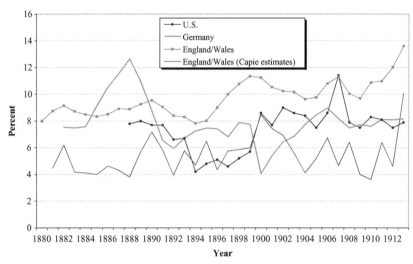

Figure 4.8. Return on Equity of Commercial Banks, 1880–1913.

fluctuate considerably over the period, and follow no perceptible trend. Between 1888 and 1913, average annual returns are nearly the same for the United States (7.4 percent) and Germany (7.7 percent), but are significantly lower for the U.K. (5.8 percent).[59] Thus, the universal banks' returns were healthy overall, but ROE was not necessarily higher in the universal system.

Returns on assets (ROA) tell a somewhat different story, because of the German banks' heavy reliance on net worth compared to the U.S. and U.K. deposit-oriented banks. Returns on assets follow a more stable and more noticeable trend than do returns on equity (ROE) (see Figure 4.9), the difference stemming primarily from the shift toward greater deposit taking by German banks. ROA declined in both the United States and Germany over this period, but the German banks' average ROA was slightly higher than American ROA in most years – overall averaging 2.4 percent in Germany and 1.7 percent in the United States. The mean annual differential was just over 0.75 percent. Though the disparity is statistically very significant, the magnitude of the difference is small. Indeed, such a small gap is really over

[59] British banks' reported returns averaged over 10 percent for the period – much higher than those computed by Capie (1988). Naturally, national data average over all areas of the countries and therefore mask what could be large regional variations or major disparities between rural (possibly monopolized) and urban (probably competitive) banking markets. The variation could be larger in the United States, where unit banking prevailed, regional differences may have been greater, and markets were possibly less integrated in the late-nineteenth century.

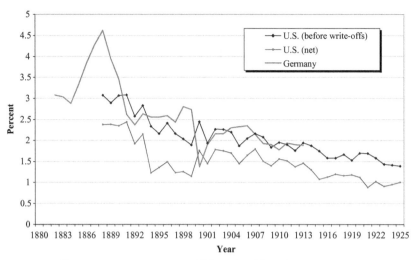

Figure 4.9. Return on Assets of Commercial Banks, 1880–1925.

explained by hypothetical superiority in efficiency or returns to risk taking on the part of the German banks. Moreover, the differential disappears altogether in the absence of the large write-offs on loans taken by the American banks.

Levels of development and economic growth rates, as well as the prevailing rates of return in other sectors of each economy, may differ considerably among countries and can therefore create disparity among returns in the respective banking sectors. Germany lagged the U.K. but followed a similar path to that of the United States. One might expect these structural differences to appear in prevailing rates of interest and returns; and clearly, the U.S. and German return figures are more similar to each other than to those of the U.K. One way to account for the contextual variation is to compute the return on investments in banking in excess of the given country's risk-free rate of return or some other indicator of local costs of finance. Federal government bonds – admittedly an imperfect proxy – is the best available and most comparable measure for the risk-free rate. Thus adjusted, ROA and ROE still follow very similar patterns as the original variables, but the levels are markedly different. U.S. banks led the German banks, while England and Wales trailed considerably (see Figure 4.10, using Capie's [1988] estimates). During the relatively quiet decade of the 1890s, adjusted ROE was actually very close among all three countries, but major divergences are apparent in the years before and after. The large swings are extremely pronounced for the United States and Germany, and the correlation with stock market

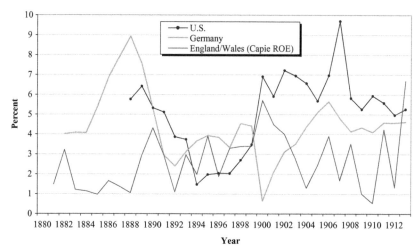

Figure 4.10. ROE in Excess of Risk-Free Rate of Commercial Banks, 1880–1912.

ups and downs are particularly noticeable for the latter – emphasizing, once again, the connections between universal banks and the domestic securities markets. Finally, subtracting estimated loan rates from ROE yields nearly identical adjusted ROE figures for the United States and Germany on average from 1888 to 1913: 1.51 percent and 1.58 percent, respectively. Loan-rate adjusted ROE figures for England and Wales are higher on average than for the other two countries (2.33 percent), but the differences fall just short of statistical significance for the period in which all data overlap.[60]

Given the various profitability measures, in their original and adjusted forms, it is clear that German returns are not significantly and consistently higher than both American and British returns over the period examined. While we can claim a slight absolute ROA advantage for the German universal banks compared to the American banks, there is no pronounced performance advantage for the German system. And, to the extent a premium exists, we cannot necessarily attribute it to superior efficiency or greater risk taking. The changing pattern of returns, particularly the marked drop in the early 1890s, bolsters the idea that the German universal banks encountered greater competition and transitioned largely to a lower-risk commercial banking structure as their national branching efforts expanded.[61]

[60] See Fohlin (2000c).
[61] Relative efficiency, risk taking, and returns are important topics that deserve more extensive future research but are beyond the scope of the current discussion.

UNIVERSAL BANKING DEVELOPMENT AND ECONOMIC GROWTH

This chapter began by discussing the hypothesized roles of financial institutions and systems in capital mobilization and economic development as well as the more specific claims that have been made about the importance of the German universal banks in the rapid economic growth of the late-nineteenth and early-twentieth centuries.[62] The first section of the chapter presented some figures on financial and economic development, but the majority of the chapter has focused on the institutional features of the universal banks and the returns they generated for investors. As a final note, therefore, it is helpful to bring the discussion back to the big picture: the contribution of the universal banking system to German industrial development.

Again, some conceptual structure from economics helps bring the issue into sharper focus. For decades, economists have searched for a link between financial and real development in an effort to understand how mobilization of financial resources influences investment in and expansion of the real sectors, if at all. The primary question in studies of the finance–growth nexus is whether the financial system is able to spur real per capita growth or whether the causation runs in the other direction.[63] Two strands of empirical investigations prevail. In the cross-country regression approach, subsequent growth rates of per capita GDP are regressed on initial income, other variables controlling for the steady state, and measures of financial development of the economy.[64] Using post–World War II data, R. G. King and Ross Levine (1993) and Levine and Sara Zervos (1998) find a prominent role for measures of financial development in predicting growth rates. Peter Rousseau and Richard Sylla (2001) use historical data for seventeen industrialized nations covering 1850–1997 to verify these findings. Like the results of preceding studies, they find a robust correlation between financial factors and real sector development leading to the conclusion that growth is "finance-led."

Some have argued that the cross-country approach suffers from statistical bias due to the endogeneity of the regressors and, in any case, can only uncover an "average" effect of financial development. Instead, these researchers promote the use of time-series–based evidence for individual countries. Given the richness of different financial institutions, it is likely that patterns of causation vary between countries or perhaps even within a

---

[62] See Chapter 2 for extensive discussion of the historical literature.
[63] See, for example, Levine (1997).
[64] See Barro (1991).

single country at different stages of its development. One might also be able to establish long-run relationships between real per capita GDP and measures of financial development and address the question of Granger causality. The results of these investigations are mixed. Philip Arestis, Panicos O. Demetriades, and Kul B. Luintel (2001), for example, find bidirectional causality between banking system development and the level of output for Germany, while a measure of stock market development is weakly exogenous to output in the long run. These findings contrast with their rather different findings for the United States, where they establish the weak exogeneity of real GDP. Far less analysis is available on historical patterns. Rousseau and Paul Wachtel (1998) investigate this question covering the time span 1870–1929 for the United States, U.K., Canada, Norway, and Sweden. They find a single cointegrating relationship between per capita levels of output, money, and intermediary assets as a measure of financial development, and unidirectional causation running from finance to growth.[65] Rousseau (2002) confirms these results in a recent study using time-series evidence for the Dutch Republic (1600–1794), England (1700–1850), the United States (1790–1850), and Japan (1880–1913).

In the context of the German industrialization, however, no such finance–growth nexus appears. Bank capital mobilization likely requires several years to produce results in the real economy, and contemporaneous relationships therefore probably represent the simultaneous effects of other influences on both bank assets and economic growth. The expansion of the German financial system is impressive, yet it did not clearly precede that of the real economy overall (see Table 4.5).[66] Contemporaneous correlations between GNP per capita and financial assets as a share of GNP are high (97 percent), but no systematic relationship emerges between lagged and current values of these variables, regardless of direction of causation. Regressions of NNP per capita, using both logged levels and annual growth rates, indicate statistically insignificant effects of bank liabilities (either in logged levels or logged levels as a share of GNP) out to five lags.[67] The relationship is especially weak

---

[65] However, the finding of a single cointegration relationship is significant only at the 15 percent level for Norway and 15 percent or less for Canada and Sweden, casting some doubts on the robustness of the results.

[66] Economists have debated the causal relationship between financial and real economic growth for decades, and the most recent research seems to favor the financial-to-real direction of causation. This issue is beyond the scope of the current investigation. See the review of recent work by Levine (1998).

[67] Table 4.5 reports several different estimators and lag structures, but none yields robust positive relationships between GNP growth and financial assets.

Table 4.5. *Bank Assets and Economic Growth, 1895–1913*

Variable	Differences	Logged Levels
(Bank assets/NNP)$_{t-1}$	−0.00	0.06
	−0.48	*0.40*
(Bank assets/NNP)$_{t-2}$	−0.01	−0.01
	−1.66	*−0.08*
(Bank assets/NNP)$_{t-3}$	−0.01	0.11
	−0.63	*0.67*
(Bank assets/NNP)$_{t-4}$	−0.02	−0.09
	−1.63	*−0.55*
(Bank assets/NNP)$_{t-5}$	–	0.12
		0.77
Intercept	0.00*	−4.08**
	2.43	*−31.19*
Adjusted R^2	0.06	−0.09
P-value of F-statistic	0.37	0.58
Durbin-Watson statistic	2.18	2.02
Rho	–	0.50
N	14	13
Corr (real NNP/cap, bank assets/NNP)	0.93	–

Notes: The dependent variable is real NNP (Germany) per thousand capita, using logged levels or first differences. Independent variables are also measured in logged levels or first differences, according to column headings. Bank assets are divided by NNP. Logged level regressions use a Hildreth-Lu estimator to correct for serially correlated residuals, and reported DW statistics for these regressions are corrected. T-statistics are in italics below coefficient estimates, and R-squared statistics are given in brackets. *,** indicate statistical significance at better than 5 percent and 1 percent (two-sided tests), respectively.
Sources: Deutsche Bundesbank (1976) (German bank figures), Maddison (1995) (population), and Mitchell (1992) (GNP, NNP).

using the Cochrane-Orcutt or Hildreth-Lu estimators to correct for serially correlated errors.

Hypothetically, it is more plausible that the effects would appear after two or more years; the first lag may simply continue to reflect contemporaneous influences. The fifth lag of bank assets, a more plausible period of time for financial institutions to make an impact on the economy, obtains a positive coefficient; however, the significance of the estimate is very weak (t-statistic of 0.77). The permanent effect of bank assets, measured as the sum of the estimated coefficients, is also quite small (0.19).

The findings here underscore a difficulty in the Gerschenkron-inspired version of German industrialization – namely, the late appearance of large-scale, universal banking relative to the growth of industry. The problem is twofold: that the biggest growth of the banking sector followed several bursts of industrial growth, and that, in any case, a consistent causal relationship between real and financial growth is difficult to establish. Thus, regardless of the reasons underlying the evolution and disposition of the universal banks' liabilities, the evidence casts some doubt on the traditional presumption that the universal banks played the most significant role in spurring real GNP growth by linking private savers with productive uses for their capital and thereby mobilizing large sums of capital. To be sure, the financial system provides a vital input to industrial development, but its importance cannot be encapsulated in a simple causal relationship based on the quantity of bank finance alone. The upshot of these findings is actually encouraging: Qualitative factors may contribute even more to industrial growth than do quantitative ones, and industry can thrive even with modest amounts of mobilized finance.

CONCLUSIONS

The common perception that German industrialization hinged on both a well-defined institutional design and overall growth of universal banking clearly finds little support in the historical record. At the macroeconomic level, the data reveal no causal relationship between banking and industrial growth. At the microeconomic level, the evidence demonstrates little support for the typical claims of heavy, widespread involvement in investment banking. To be sure, the universal banks, and the great banks among them, provided vital investment banking services to some portion of the population, but those services grew in step with industry. In the very first stages of corporate universal banking – in the 1850s – when there were few corporations, few entrepreneurs, and tiny markets for industrial securities, the banks acted largely as investment banks. At the same time, the few that existed were predominantly unit banks serving primarily a local clientele. The banking industry mirrored the political and economic changes of the time; with the formation of the Second Empire and the push for national unity, the evolution toward an integrated, national system of depository commercial banks began. And the organization of the banks themselves changed in step.

The path of the German universal banking industry, though impressive in some respects, differs hardly at all from that of the specialized commercial banking sector of the U.K. on a number of key measures. Industry concentration and institutional financial structure tracked each other with remarkable similarity, and even returns on bank equity matched closely over many years of the late industrialization period. In the pre–World War I era, universality translates to a joining of commercial and investment banking services, and while the German banks were pushing on the commercial banking side, the British banks began forays into investment banking services. Thus, by the onset of World War I, the two systems had started a long-run convergence toward industry concentration and conglomeration that would continue even more vigorously later in the century.

5

Corporate Governance Relationships

Patterns and Explanations

Perhaps more than universality of services, formal relationship building with nonfinancial firms constitutes both a keystone of the German commercial banking system and a fundamental point of divergence between the German and Anglo-American corporate financial systems. Three practices typically associated with the German universal banks fall under the heading of relationship banking: equity stakeholding, proxy voting of customers' shares, and representation in the supervisory boards of industrial firms. In other words, relationship banking relates to those bank activities that cede to them at least partial control over the decisions and actions of their client firms. In theory, corporate ownership and governance relationships between banks and firms discipline banks and firms to behave in each other's long-term interest. Thus, relationship banking is seen as an important advantage of the German system and is seen as integral to the operations of the universal banks, even though the two characteristics are theoretically and empirically distinct from one another.

BANK-HELD EQUITY STAKES IN NONFINANCIAL FIRMS

One of the most prevalent notions in the literature on German corporate finance is that the universal banks held significant equity stakes in firms and used those positions to exert influence over those firms' decisions. Long-term holdings of equities – or anything held over the close of a business year – should appear in the balance sheets of the banks. One measure of the importance of equity stakes relative to the other activities of the banks is their size and variety. Since accounting laws were weak and vague in the pre–World War I era, we have to contend with reporting problems. The banks did book their securities holdings if they existed, but according to such contemporaries as Jakob Riesser, banks undervalued and improperly categorized their securities in their financial statements. In his view:

> It would therefore be of but little value to give figures of securities held by the various banks, since the account "securities owned" in many cases appears understated, inasmuch as a certain portion of the securities, properly belonging under that head, is booked under the head of "syndicate participations." On the other hand, it is equally true that securities which properly belong under the head of "syndicate participations" are at times found booked under the head of "securities owned."[1]

Underreporting is most severe for industrial securities, since the banks feared that investors would view large holdings of nonfinancial shares as a signal of poor bank performance. Again, according to Riesser, "considerable security holdings are not regarded as a favorable sign, although during critical periods large holdings of this class may represent an increased proportion of particularly liquid assets, or a special reserve for deposits."[2] He goes on to explain that

> ... excessive holdings of securities will be interpreted to mean either that the times have not been propitious for the issue business of the bank, or that it maintains excessive speculative engagements, or that it is involved to an excessive extent in speculative transactions on its own account ... or, finally, that it has been unable to find sufficiently profitable employment for its funds. It is for these reasons that a large proportion of the writing off done by the banks occurs under the head of securities account.[3]

Thus, the banks' equity stakes are probably undervalued relative to other financial assets in their balance sheets, but the extent of the misreporting is uncertain and almost certainly highly variable. The very fact that banks attempted to downplay their stock holdings, along with Riesser's contention that the banks' investors frowned upon significant stakeholding, suggests that the banks did not pursue equity holdings as part of an active policy of direct control of nonfinancial enterprises. On the contrary, at least from the 1880s until World War I, the banks seem to have avoided holding large proportions of nongovernment securities over the long term.

Aggregate Patterns of Securities Holdings by Banks

Building on the earlier data for individual years, this section provides annual details of the banks' equity holdings, in order to investigate their use as a

---

[1] See Riesser (1910 [1911]), pp. 402–4.
[2] Ibid.
[3] Ibid.

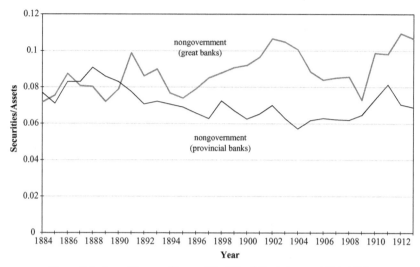

Figure 5.1. Securities as a Share of Real Total Bank Assets, 1884–1913.

relationship-banking device. Corporate securities make up a small proportion of universal bank assets. For the great banks, the holdings varied between 7 and 8 percent of (real) assets but did trend upward toward the end of the period (see Figure 5.1).[4] For the whole period, the great banks' nongovernment equity holdings never exceeded 11 percent. The denominators of these series are computed in real terms, since securities tended to be posted at book values. Loans and cash assets turn over frequently within any year and therefore increase or decrease in nominal value along with the general price level. Thus, as other assets inflate (deflate), the apparent proportion of securities declines (increases). To give a sense of the magnitude of the potential measurement error, Figure 5.2 compares the "great bank" series using the nominal and real denominators. The low levels of equity holdings are a bit surprising, especially considering the average contribution of the securities business to the overall revenues of the universal banks.

Because these figures aggregate all nongovernment securities holdings, they include many stakes that the banks did not intentionally take as part of their investment strategy. In fact, a significant portion of the universal banks' total investments arose out of their involvement in underwriting consortia

---

[4] Banks often held government securities as reserves. These assets are unrelated to industrial finance, so it is important to compare securities' net of government issues. Because the data source aggregates government and nongovernment securities until 1912, the figures here are estimated, as described in Chapter 4.

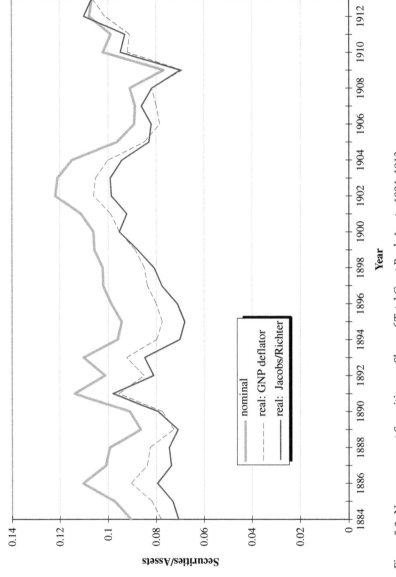

Figure 5.2. Nongovernment Securities as a Share of Total Great Bank Assets, 1884–1913.
Note: Nongovernment securities include Consortial-Beteiligung and Beteiligung accounts. Real figures are in 1993 marks.

(or syndicates). These participations therefore include some shares that remained on the banks' books only because of the banks' inability to place the shares or the fact that the underwriting process spanned the end of a business year. The subset of nongovernment securities *not* held as a result of underwriting syndicates gives an approximation of the proportion of assets that the universal banks may have held as purposeful investments in the absence of the underwriting business (see Figure 5.3).[5] Consortium-related holdings by the great banks increased steadily throughout the boom in joint-stock foundings of the late 1890s and reached a prewar peak in the years just after the stock market crisis of 1900–1.[6] The banks shed securities holdings as the market improved, though they increased holdings slightly after the 1907 stock market crisis. In 1909, syndicate securities holdings reached their lowest point in the twenty-five years of available data.[7]

Provincial banks, it seems, behaved quite differently from their Berlin-based counterparts throughout the period (see Figure 5.4). In line with the findings on their investment banking income streams, the great banks clearly held proportionately more corporate securities than did the provincial banks. While both sets of banks began the period with similar levels of overall stakeholding, the provincial banks steadily lowered those holdings, relative to their other assets, from the early 1890s until sometime around 1905. Relative to other assets, the provincial banks also held far smaller proportions of syndicate securities than did the great banks. In fact, the differential involvement in the underwriting syndicate business more than accounts for the excess of the great banks' total equity holdings over those of the provincial banks. As a result, the provincial banks' nonsyndicate holdings actually exceeded those of the great banks. The provincial banks never engaged very significantly in the syndicate business, but they did decrease

---

[5] Nonsyndicate securities were estimated using a similar method as that described for nongovernment securities (see Chapter 4). For the years in which disaggregated securities holdings were reported (1912 to 1919), syndicate-related securities amounted to 51 to 61 percent of total securities held. As with government securities, I used the lowest number during the period to estimate the proportion of securities due to syndicate participations.

[6] The rapid increase in joint-stock share capital following 1901 stemmed from an increase in the average nominal share capital of firms, while the upward trend of the 1890s related primarily to an expansion of the number of companies.

[7] In the leadup to World War I, universal banks markedly increased their holdings of syndicate securities. After the onset of the war, the great banks' syndicate holdings declined dramatically as a share of bank assets – from 8 percent in 1914 to 3 percent in 1919. Perhaps contrary to intuition, government securities crowding out such holdings does not primarily account for the decline. Government securities holdings did increase in the early years of the war, but all securities holdings declined steadily after the war.

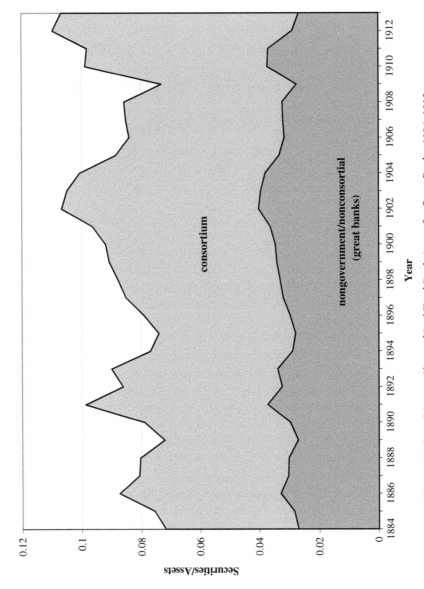

Figure 5.3. Securities as a Share of Real Total Bank Assets for Great Banks, 1884–1913.

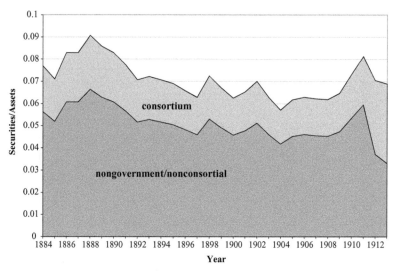

Figure 5.4. Securities as a Share of Real Total Bank Assets for Provincial Banks, 1884–1913.

their holdings noticeably after the 1891 crisis. Only in the couple of years before World War I did the smaller banks substantially raise their syndicate holdings, though it is impossible to say from aggregate data whether the increase stemmed from greater participation in underwriting or simply less success in placing underwritten securities.

It is worth emphasizing the disparities in holdings between the provincial banks and the great banks, as it underscores the significant differences in the business practices of universal banks, depending on their size or location. In the case of equity stakeholding, much of the difference likely stems from the proximity of the largest universal banks to the major securities markets (particularly Berlin) and – as the next chapter will argue – the relatively stronger involvement of the great banks in large firms with more dispersed ownership structures. Of particular note, the findings here suggest that the syndicate business of the largest banks crowded out other types of equity holdings. This finding reveals one important fact about the great banks' corporate relationships via equity stakes: Most of them were not exclusive. By definition, the consortium holdings represented participation within a larger group of banks. So, while the great banks likely engaged in long-term relationships with many of the firms whose shares they helped issue through syndicate participations, those relationships were clearly multilateral. Certainly, the great banks took a larger volume of equity stakes than their provincial counterparts did, but the provincial banks may have – and it is important to emphasize the uncertainty here – pursued more intimate relationships. The aggregate data obviously cannot speak to this hypothesis, but the subsequent investigations of board memberships can help.

Arnold's Panel of Large Universal Banks

In 1903, Anton Arnold published a compilation of balance sheets and income statements for thirty-two of the most important German universal banks, including all of the Berlin great banks, for 1894 through 1902. Those data provide insight into the variability of securities holdings among banks and even for individual banks over time. Securities could take up as much as a third or as little as 1 percent of a bank's total assets, averaging 12 percent during the period for all of the banks. These figures still permit only an extreme upper bound on industry equity stakes, since the categories combine a range of security types – industry stocks mixed with industry and government bonds, railroad securities, and participations in other banks.

A substantial portion of the banks' overall holdings represented "own securities." The asset shares of these holdings ranged widely from bank to bank, from less than 1 percent to over 11 percent, but averaged 6 percent for the sample during the period (see Table 5.1). About two-thirds of the sampled banks also held securities resulting from consortium business – typically, issuing stocks or bonds in concert with a group of banks assembled on an ad hoc basis for that purpose. As the previous section noted, these shares usually represented temporary stakes that were intended for sale to investors. In other words, the account could remain large and could absorb a sizeable portion of a bank's assets, but the specific securities in the account would have varied from year to year. Naturally, less successful issues might stay on a bank's books for several years, but they were not considered part of the bank's (intentional) investment portfolio. Some banks – Darmstädter Bank, Disconto-Gesellschaft, and Berliner Handelsgesellschaft, for example – held 12 to 14 percent of assets in consortium securities in certain years; but the proportion fluctuated from year to year, and holdings averaged 3 to 5 percent for the sampled banks throughout the period.

"Permanent participations" and "partner shares" make up the final category of securities reported in the balance sheet summaries.[8] One-third to one-half of the sampled banks reported no such holdings, and only five of them reported holdings of 5 percent of assets or more. A small handful of

---

[8] The category is *dauernde Beteiligungen und Kommanditen*. In other words, the two types of holdings were aggregated.

Table 5.1. *Panel A: Securities Holdings as a Share of Total Assets, Twenty-seven Large Universal Banks*

	Own Securities	Consortium Participations	Sum of Own and Consortium	Permanent Participations & Subsidiaries	Total
Averages for all banks					
1894	6.2	4.5	10.2	1.1	11.9
1895	5.7	2.9	9.0	1.6	10.7
1896	6.1	4.1	10.1	1.7	11.8
1897	5.5	4.2	9.7	1.9	11.6
1898	5.5	4.8	10.4	2.3	12.7
1899	5.4	4.9	10.4	2.4	12.7
1900	5.8	4.8	10.5	1.9	12.5
1901	6.3	3.9	9.9	1.9	12.0
1902	6.0	3.0	9.3	2.1	11.6
Averages for Berlin banks					
1894	6.9	4.3	11.6	2.1	13.0
1895	5.5	5.1	11.0	3.1	13.5
1896	5.6	6.8	12.9	3.1	15.4
1897	4.3	6.4	11.3	3.4	14.2
1898	4.0	6.9	11.7	4.0	15.3
1899	5.1	7.4	13.0	3.1	15.3
1900	5.0	7.6	12.8	3.4	15.5
1901	6.3	8.2	14.8	2.9	17.2
1902	6.1	6.1	13.1	2.4	15.5
Averages for provincial banks					
1894	5.7	4.7	9.4	0.6	11.2
1895	5.8	1.8	7.9	0.8	9.0
1896	6.3	2.7	8.6	1.0	9.7
1897	6.1	3.2	9.3	1.3	10.7
1898	6.3	3.9	9.6	1.4	11.2
1899	6.0	3.7	9.2	1.6	11.0
1900	6.2	3.6	9.3	1.2	10.7
1901	6.3	2.0	7.3	1.3	9.0
1902	6.0	1.5	7.1	1.9	9.2

banks, among them Darmstädter Bank, Disconto-Gesellschaft, and Rheinische Diskontogesellschaft, held so-called permanent participations of more than 10 percent of assets.

On average, securities holdings grew in line with the banks' overall expansion. At first, this pattern might appear counterintuitive given the banks' significant move toward deposit taking during these years. The two phenomena

Table 5.1. *(continued)*
Panel B: Individual Banks in 1899, Ranked by Total Securities as a Percent of Total Assets of the Bank

1899	Own Securities	Consortium Participations	Sum of Own and Consortium	Permanent Participations & Subsidiaries	Total
Bank fur Handel und Industrie	7.01	12.91	19.92	11.55	31.48
Creditanstalt fur Industrie und Handel	11.47	13.96	25.44	0.00	25.44
Diskontogesellshaft	n/a	n/a	12.90	11.70	24.60
Berliner Handelsgesellschaft	2.56	11.56	14.12	5.53	19.66
Rheinische Diskontogesellschaft	1.14	4.38	5.52	13.33	18.86
Berliner Bank	n/a	n/a	14.94	1.62	16.56
Norddeutsche Bank	10.22	0.00	10.22	4.98	15.20
A. Schaaffhausen'scher Bankverein	7.43	6.80	14.22	0.35	14.57
Deutsche Effekten und Wechselbank	8.18	6.31	14.49	0.00	14.49
Dresdner Bank	5.01	6.78	11.79	2.57	14.36
Commerz und Diskontobank	6.41	4.31	10.72	2.84	13.56
Breslauer Diskontobank	5.97	6.84	12.80	0.37	13.18
Rheinische Bank	9.06	4.09	13.16	0.00	13.16
Deutsche Vereinsbank	3.64	7.63	11.27	1.04	12.31
Nationalbanlk fur Deutschland	3.30	8.95	12.26	0.00	12.26
Pfälzische Bank	7.42	2.64	10.05	1.11	11.17
Rheinische Kreditbank	4.26	5.02	9.28	1.67	10.96
Leipziger Bank	6.34	4.23	10.57	0.00	10.57
Mitteldeutsche Kreditbank	2.33	7.06	9.39	0.64	10.03
Magdeburger Privat-Bank	6.62	0.00	6.62	1.43	8.05
Deutsche Genossenschaftsbank	2.70	n/a	n/a	n/a	7.43
Niederrheinische Kreditanstalt	5.60	0.00	5.60	0.00	5.60
Vereinsbank	n/a	n/a	4.62	0.92	5.54
Deutsche Nationalbank	4.05	0.00	4.05	0.00	4.05
Barmer Bankverein Hinsberg	3.57	0.00	3.57	0.00	3.57
Dresdner Bankverein	3.33	0.00	0.00	0.00	3.33
Essener Kreditanstalt	2.41	0.34	2.75	0.00	2.75

Source: Computed from data reported in Arnold (1903).

do make sense, however, since the fastest growing category of securities holdings, those held as permanent participations, most likely in other banks, represents the beginnings of the merger movement in the banking industry. Quite often, larger banks would buy up stakes in smaller banks in order to establish a foothold in the new territory. If the banks ultimately merged, of course, the balance sheets would as well. But so long as a bank kept up its takeover process, new stakes in other banks would continually enter the balance sheet.

Compared to their smaller, provincial counterparts, the Berlin great banks tended to hold substantially larger securities portfolios, even controlling for their larger asset base. The volume multiplied remarkably over time, increasing in percentage of assets, even as those assets ballooned. For the four so-called D-banks, total securities increased from 17 to 19 percent of assets on average, which in turn doubled from 313 to 665 million marks per bank. Yet even these four arguably quite similar institutions pursued different strategies. Deutsche and Dresdner, for example, both more than doubled in size between 1894 and 1902; but while Deutsche still doubled (from 2.4 to 4.9 percent) the proportion of assets held in permanent participations and partnerships, the latter liquidated those holdings (from 1.3 percent). On the other hand, Disconto-Gesellschaft reported just short of 2 percent of assets in these sorts of holdings in 1894, but 10 percent in 1902. Because of caveats about the banks' bookkeeping practices, it is perhaps best to draw modest conclusions from individual accounts and years. Still, some general patterns appear, such as the relatively strong correlation (approximately 35 percent) between the size of the institution in terms of total assets and the proportion of those assets held as securities. The strongest relationship appears between total assets and asset shares devoted to permanent participations and partnerships. In line with what we know about this pivotal period of the merger and branching movement, the largest banks tended to hold the largest stakes in other banks (*Kommanditen*).

Detailed Securities Holdings for Two Great Banks

The data so far reveal nothing about the magnitude or duration of specific bank–firm relationships, since balance sheet posts, even at the bank level, provide no clue to the identity of the firms, the value of shares, or the length of their inclusion in the banks' portfolios. To gain this sort of insight, we need to look at the specific holdings of individual banks; that exercise presents its own myriad difficulties. At least in the German context, details of securities held and records of any kind for the pre-1913 period, especially

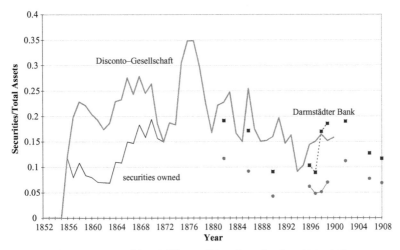

Figure 5.5. Securities Holdings of Two Great Banks, 1852–1908.

pre-1880, are generally unavailable.[9] Nonetheless, some details are available for two of the earliest German joint-stock universal banks. Walther Däbritz presented a sketch of the activities of the Disconto-Gesellschaft (DG) in its early years, and an earlier *Festschrift* published the annual accounts of the bank through 1900. Additionally, *Saling's Börsen-Jahrbuch*, sheds light on the holdings of the Darmstädter Bank. Pulling together the available data allows a rough tracing of the movements in the ratio of total securities to assets for these two banks (see Figure 5.5). For the DG, the sum of all securities held ranged between 0 and 35 percent of assets over the period 1852 to 1900. While the bank's holdings fluctuated markedly throughout the last half of the nineteenth century, the proportion of securities followed a generally downward trend toward the end of the period.

From its founding in 1852 through 1855, DG held no securities among its assets. Thereafter, the bank acquired a substantial interest in securities, but a breakdown of securities from 1856 to 1865 indicates that two mining companies accounted for the major share of DG's industrial holdings. Shares in the two firms, Heinrichshütte and Bleialf, amounted to around 11 percent of assets for most of the period in which the bank held the shares. Däbritz provides an account of the bank's involvement with these firms

---

[9] The Dresdner Bank archives from before World War I were inaccessible to anyone until recently and are still unavailable to the public as the organization effort continues. The Deutsche Bank archive is difficult to gain access to for other reasons, but inquiries there have turned up the answer that no such details exist in their materials (which would include the predecessor banks that the Deutsche Bank took over).

and indicates that such direct participation arose out of the bank's intention to convert the firms into joint-stock companies. Having bought up Heinrichshütte in 1857, the bank invested heavily (equivalent to 25 percent of the firm's capital) in the expansion of production capacity. The timing was inopportune; immediately the firm faced rapidly falling prices of iron and questions about the profitability of ironworks in general. In the six years following the bank's investment in the ironworks, the enlarged firm averaged earnings of approximately 2 percent of the total capital invested by the bank (50,000 thaler per year on an investment of 2.5 million thaler). During these years, according to Däbritz, "hardly a general meeting passed in which the bank's management did not have to defend against sharp criticisms about the purchase of Heinrichshütte."[10] The other two firms presented similar problems for DG, and the bank was forced to hold their shares until they could extricate themselves in the more favorable market of the late 1860s and early 1870s.

Other than Bleialf and Heinrichshütte, DG held relatively conservative investments: government debt, railway shares and bonds, and other priority bonds and shares (represented by the solid line in Figure 5.5). And with the exception of a few minor holdings of shares, the DG confined its participation in industry to three companies (the two already discussed plus another mining concern). Indeed, the bank's holdings of industry stocks amounted to between 0 and 3 percent of its assets for the years in which disaggregated data are available (1852–65). Thus, even the early activities of the great banks involved direct involvement in only a few industrial companies, and it appears that the larger the stake held by the bank, the less attractive the firm was as an investment. At least based on this one prominent bank, then, the idea that the universal banks' holdings served purposes similar to modern venture capital holdings appears misplaced.

Though the disaggregated data for DG run out before the second wave of the German industrialization hit its peak, the story can be picked up in the 1880s using evidence from another of the great banks. Darmstädter Bank (BHI) published unusually detailed accounts of its securities holdings, and *Saling's* reproduced the information in its series on Berlin-listed companies (see Table 5.2).[11] It is clear from the available data that holdings of industrial shares amounted to less than 1 percent of BHI's assets for most of the

---

[10] Däbritz (1931), p. 105.
[11] Unfortunately, *Saling's* only began publishing in 1876, and the volumes before 1882 are scarce. Also unfortunately for this analysis, *Saling's* stopped publishing details of securities holdings in 1899.

Table 5.2. *Securities Held by Darmstädter Bank (1882–99)*

Securities by Type (Percent of Total Assets)	1882	1886	1890	1896	1897	1898	1899
German and Prussian bonds				0.89	0.69	0.49	2.51
Foreign government and railroad debt				0.69	0.47	2.06	1.37
Railway, industry, and land shares	4.10	2.43	2.75	2.47	2.09	1.44	2.01
Bank shares				1.24	1.03	0.82	0.72
Miscellaneous				0.50	0.51	0.29	0.41
Total securities				5.79	4.79	5.11	7.02
Total assets (millions of marks)	146.5	169.5	181.1	206.8	188.9	232.8	235.4
Rail, industry, land shares (% of securities)				51.25	54.23	33.86	34.46
Government securities (% of securities)				15.41	14.38	9.63	35.75
Industrial shares owned (thousands of marks)							
Württembergische Kattunmanufaktur	303	158	14	0	0		
Dessauer Wollengarn-Spinnerei	720	690	690	690	690		
Deutsche Gold- u. Silberscheide-Anstalt	420	0	0	0	0		
Frankfurter Hotel-AG	152	0	0	0	0		
Deutsche Wasserwerke	96	96	96	96	96		
Rheinische Wasserwerke	90	0	0	0	0		
Heilbronner Maschinenbau-Gesellschaft	86	86	0	0	0		
Wetterauer Zuckerfabrik	0	150	150	150	150		
Gross-Gerauer Zuckerfabrik	0	121	121	121	121		
Franken Compania Metalurgica de Mazarron	0	0	113	113	113		
Heilbronner Salzwerks	0	0	288	73	73		
Maschinenanstalt Venulath & Ellenberger	0	0	0	100	100		
Miscellaneous	36	52					
Total industrial shares (% of total assets)	1.3	0.8	0.8	0.6	0.7		

Source: Computed from *Saling's Börsen-Jahrbuch*, various years.

1880s and 1890s, and that, even at its peak, the ratio of industrial shares to assets only reached 1.3 percent (in 1882). Including railway and real estate shares, the total of nonbank equity shares probably reached only 4 percent of assets. When bank shares are included, the total rises to no more than 6.5 percent.[12] These data provide further support for the notion that the great banks invested a relatively small portion of their portfolios in the equity of industrial firms.

Bank Stakes in the Larger Context

From at least the 1880s until World War I, the banks clearly owned few major, long-term, direct stakes in nonfinancial firms. If their total holdings of securities measured low compared to their own assets, they also amounted to a relatively small proportion of total nominal capital of joint-stock companies (see Figure 5.6). Overall, the universal banks never held more than 9 percent of total equity of German AGs (share companies). And this figure represents a conservative upper bound on the figure. Surely, for some firms, bank stakes comprised a significant portion of equity, but those cases must have been rare and most likely temporary.

We can also assess bank shareholding relative to the size of the overall economy. Nongovernment securities holdings of the universal banks ranged between 2 and 4 percent of GNP for the three decades preceding World War I.[13] Even if the estimates are only approximately correct, the banks' holdings of nongovernment securities accounted for a very small share of the economy. The German banks' share did increase between 1880 and 1913, but their holdings of nongovernment securities still amounted to only 4 percent of GNP by World War I. The biggest part of the increase came after 1900.

In sum, the wide-ranging evidence on corporate ownership suggests that banks' stakes in German firms were small relative both to the banks' assets and to the total pool of share capital in Germany. In this regard, the universal banks acted in accordance with the traditional investment banking business of the time – quite like that of the English investment banks, for example.

---

[12] It should be underscored that the earlier numbers are estimated based on the ratio of industrial shares to total securities for the period in which both types of data are reported (1896 and 1897). The proportion of assets held in industrial, railway, or bank shares for those years peaked at 3.7 percent. Thus, only if BHI held a significantly greater part of its securities in the form of bank shares in the 1880s than in the 1890s (unlikely, given that the concentration of banking accelerated in the 1890s) would 6.5 percent be an underestimate.

[13] Calculated from Deutsche Bundesbank (1976) and Goldsmith (1969).

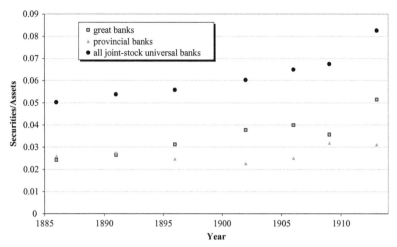

Figure 5.6. Bank-Held Nongovernment Securities as a Share of Total Nominal Share Capital of German Joint-Stock Corporations (*Aktiengesellschaften*), 1886–1913.

In other words, significant, long-term equity stakes appear not to have constituted the kind of theoretically appealing method of tying banks to the fortunes of their client firms and vice versa, thereby enforcing long-term relationships and a long-term perspective on firm investments. The possibility remains, however, that the banks wielded substantial control over corporations, either through proxy voting of shares or through seats on supervisory boards (Aufsichtsrat).

PROXY VOTING

In the prewar era, the institution of proxy voting by banks manifested itself in two principal forms: First, a shareholder could give his bank a *Stimmrechtsvollmacht*, allowing the bank to cast the votes in the shareholder's name but also forcing shareholders to reveal their identity. Second, and more important in practice, the *Stimmrechtsermächtigung* ceded the shareholder's voting rights to the bank.[14] This form of proxy voting was later called *Bankenstimmrecht* or *Depotstimmrecht*, due to the heavy use of banks as the proxyholder.[15] Many banks required customers to turn over

---

[14] See Hüffer (2002), p. 694. Though similar, the *Stimmrechtsermächtigung* gave banks much more power. See also von Falkenhausen (1966), p. 69

[15] Hopt (1996) calls the *Depotstimmrecht* a misnomer for that reason. The correct word is *Vollmachtsstimmrecht*, but these words are now used synonymously.

Stimmrechtsermächtigungen automatically upon opening securities accounts, granting the bank widespread access to control rights of equity stakes they did not own. Banks could still do more or less whatever they wished with the voting rights that shareholders ceded to them.[16]

Given their involvement with the placement of new issues, their provision of safe deposit services, and their lending secured by stocks, the universal banks – especially the largest ones – were the logical parties to take an investor's proxy votes. Indeed, many investors would have seen the banks' proxy voting as a valuable service, particularly when the individual stake was small compared to the investor's overall portfolio. Having acquired voting power in the general assembly (*Generalversammlung*), the bank could directly influence the voting on issues before that body, which could include long-term strategic decisions along with the selection of supervisory board members. Thus, even without any equity ownership, the banks could affect firm management and strategy.

Unfortunately, it is virtually impossible to know exactly how prevalent proxy voting has been in Germany until quite recently. Because companies have traditionally issued bearer shares, shareholders have remained largely anonymous. Those with the highest likelihood of turning over uninstructed proxy control to their banks – the small stakeholders – are the most likely to stay anonymous. At the same time, larger shareholders, those who eventually fell under reporting laws, usually must reveal their identities but are simultaneously more likely to retain their voting rights. Statistical inquiries for the recent past show that the universal banks hold overwhelming majorities of votes in the general meetings of the largest, listed firms with relatively dispersed ownership structures – typically without holding direct stakes themselves.

The extant records prohibit confirmation of the same patterns for the prewar era, but one study for the early 1900s offers some relevant insights into share representation at annual meetings of three of the largest banks. The figures show that typically less than 20 percent of the share capital, and closer to 5 percent in the case of the Darmstädter Bank, was represented at annual general meetings of shareholders (see Table 5.3).[17] These small percentages were represented by a limited number of shareholders and shareholder representatives, giving a great deal of power to those who did appear at the meetings. In the most extreme case presented, seventy-one participants at the 1905 general meeting of the Darmstädter Bank represented 4.5 percent

[16] See von Falkenhausen (1966), p. 71.
[17] See Passow (1922).

Table 5.3. *Voting at General Meeting of Shareholders: Three Banks, 1903–6*

Bank/Meeting Type	Year	Percentage of the Capital Stock Voted at Meeting	Number of Shareholders and Representatives Attending	Average Face Value of Shares Per Participant (Marks)	Average Stake of Shares Registered Per Participant (%)	Average Voting Power Per Participant (%)	Average Voting Power/Average Stake
Deutsche Bank							
Regular general meeting	1903	18.32					
Regular	1904	20.75					
Regular	1905	21.39					
Extraordinary	1904[1]	19.78					
Dresdner Bank							
Regular general meeting	1903	9.59	41	304,000	0.23	2.44	10.43
Regular	1904	12.13	42	375,000	0.29	2.38	8.24
Regular	1905	14.59	46	508,000	0.32	2.17	6.85
Extraordinary	1903[2]	19.55	53	479,000	0.37	1.89	5.12
Extraordinary	1904[3]	18.81	44	556,000	0.43	2.27	5.32
Darmstädter Bank							
Regular general meeting	1903	5.42	47	152,000	0.12	2.13	18.45
Regular	1904	5.42	29	207,000	0.19	3.45	18.45
Regular	1905	4.55	71	178,000	0.06	1.41	21.98
Regular	1906	8.15	39	377,000	0.21	2.56	12.27

Notes: [1] June 25 meeting; increase capital stock by 20 million marks.
[2] December 10 meeting; community of interest with the Schaffhausen'schen Bankverein.
[3] June 25 meeting; acquisition of Deutsche Genossenschaftsbank, increase capital stock by 30 million marks.

Source: Calculated from Passow (1922, chapter 21).

of the company's share capital. On average, then, each participant voted 178,000 marks worth of shares (at par value) or 1.4 percent of the capital. Since the actual represented ownership stakes averaged a little more than 0.006 percent, the participants voted an average of twenty-two times their average stake. Across the board, participants held voting power many times their actual ownership stake, ranging from 7 to 10 percent at Dresdner and 12 to 22 percent at Darmstädter. Even at the Dresdner's extraordinary meetings held in 1903 and 1904, capital representation was only 19 percent of all shares, and only a handful more people turned out for the extraordinary meetings than attended the general meetings (fifty-three rather than forty-one in 1903 and forty-four rather than forty-two in 1904). So, even when special meetings were called to vote on such major issues as creating a community of interest with another large bank (1903) or undertaking a corporate takeover accompanied by a significant capital increase (1904), the vast majority of shareholders stayed home and left the decision making to the larger shareholders and to the proxy holders.

Interestingly, Richard Passow (1922) lists a number of explanations for the low attendance rate at shareholder meetings, most of which boil down, in current parlance, to "rational apathy" among small shareholders: costs of traveling the distances to meeting locations, insufficient time to attend, the sense that news coverage provided enough information for the small shareholders, and, of course, the presumption that as a small shareholder, one's influence was very limited.

In addition, Passow mentions that women shareholders would not have attended meetings, since they were not believed to be able to handle them. The extremely low turnout rates meant that interested parties could gain pluralities and even majorities in the general meeting with very small ownership stakes. In fact, given the rules on proxy votes, voting shares at the general meeting required no direct ownership stake at all. And when a majority of the shares were diffusely held, banks needed to gather very few proxy voting rights from shareholders in order to exercise significant influence over the votes at the general meetings.[18] Armed with this level of voting power, a

---

[18] This statement assumes that shareholders holding significant stakes would have appeared at shareholder meetings. If not, then the small minority of shares represented at meetings does not imply anything about ownership dispersion. Passow (1922) himself bemoans the lack of data on shareholding, proxy voting, and participation at shareholder meetings, thus suggesting that the problem is that few records were kept at the time, not just that they were subsequently destroyed during World War II (as was the case for many historical archives in Germany). Passow's data came from newspaper articles surrounding the meetings, making it a hit-or-miss proposition to locate additional cases.

bank would have significant say over the makeup of the firm's supervisory board and therefore firm management. The analysis of firm-level data later in this chapter lends broader-based support to the impressionistic accounts that indicate a connection between ownership dispersion and firms' participation in bank-related networks of interlocking directorates.

INTERLOCKING DIRECTORATES

The practice of interlocking directorates – the placement of individuals on multiple boards of directors – has always played a prominent role in the historical accounts of the German industrialization. While cross-memberships appeared to some degree early on, the institution became widespread in the last quarter of the nineteenth century. Before midcentury, when few share companies existed, there were too few firms with formal boards of directors to permit substantial interlocking. As restrictions on chartering stock companies relaxed around 1870, however, and after the 1884 promulgation of regulations requiring stock companies to form supervisory boards, the foundation was set for formalized governance relations among firms and between banks and firms.

The Makeup of Corporate Boards

For corporations, most top-level decision-making power lies in the hands of their boards of directors. These organs of corporate governance may affect everything from day-to-day operations to long-term company strategy. At the same time, the structure and influence of corporate boards vary significantly across firms, among countries, and over time. In the German case, formal governance of stock corporations is divided into two boards: the executive board (*Vorstand*) and the supervisory board (*Aufsichtsrat*). The former is made up of top firm managers, while the latter is comprised of shareholder representatives. Shareholders or their representatives elect supervisory board members at the general meeting, which typically takes place annually. The supervisory board is responsible for appointing the executive board. While all companies have some form of directorship or management, only certain types of companies are required by German law to maintain separate executive and supervisory boards. These regulations developed over the latter half of the nineteenth century, particularly with the company laws of 1870 and 1884.

Prior to 1870, corporate charters were approved individually via a concession system, and regulations regarding their governance were lax. The company law that appeared in 1870 coincided with the general slackening of restrictions on corporate charters. In promulgating this new legislation, the government conceded a large measure of control over incorporation but demanded, in return, greater uniformity and consistency in corporate accounting, reporting, and governance.[19]

The company law that appeared during the early stages of the new empire applied to the two main types of German stock corporations, the *Aktiengesellschaft* and the *Kommanditgesellschaft auf Aktien*. The law stipulated the dual board structure, in part as a means of protecting shareholder and public interest, independently of the management of the company.

Responding to the corruption, scandals, and severe losses in stock values of the 1870s, the 1884 law was put forth as a major reform of corporate law with the specific intent to create legal protections for shareholder interests. Among several other stipulations, the 1884 law required a complete split between the supervisory and executive boards (*Aufsichtsrat* and *Vorstand*, respectively). Specifically, the law prohibited any individual from sitting on the two boards simultaneously. Former company directors could, and often did, enter the supervisory board, as long they had been officially discharged from the executive board (Art. 225a HGB). The law did not forbid cooperation between the executive and supervisory boards, and the two bodies naturally did work in concert in many cases. The 1884 law also strengthened the role of the supervisory board, particularly the fiduciary responsibilities of its members. Prior to the 1884 law, most supervisory board members took little responsibility for supervising company operations; the position was often seen as sinecure, despite the controlling function outlined in the 1870 law. Whereas the 1870 law granted supervisory board members the right to obtain information about the company, the 1884 law made such oversight a duty.[20] The legislators enacted this change in order to guarantee greater protection of shareholders, particularly those unable to ensure that their representatives served them sufficiently well.

The voting rights of shareholders and their representation by supervisory boards also evolved over time. German legal scholars and politicians weighed in on these questions from early on in the development of the joint-stock company, well before the movement toward free incorporation and the laws concerning executive and supervisory boards. In the 1840s and 1850s, scholars wrote on the distribution of voting rights according to

---

[19] Hopt (1998).
[20] Interestingly, though the 1870 law stipulated that supervisory board members must own shares of the firm on whose board they sat, the 1884 law made such equity stakes optional.

share ownership.[21] Many were concerned about the ability of the smallest shareholders to be heard and the potential for excessive control by a small number of large shareholders. Early on, the smallest shareholders were often disenfranchised, but representation became more democratic as the century wore on.

Executive Boards

Over the two decades preceding World War I, executive boards of joint-stock companies remained rather small. The boards averaged just two members, though they comprised a dozen or more in some cases. Mean board size varied little across industrial branches, but extremely large boards tended to appear in specific sectors – diversified heavy industrials and sugar manufacturers stand out (see Table 5.4).[22] Executive boards also grew only slightly over the two pre–World War I decades. While the median number of directors remained constant at two, the largest board size nearly doubled from nine in 1895 to seventeen in 1912. Most of the growth came in two jumps, one in 1901 and the other in 1907 – perhaps not coincidentally the years of the two major stock market declines.

Executive board size correlates with the size of a company. In a multivariate statistical model, firm size (measured by total assets or, equivalently, liabilities) also clearly predicts executive board size, but the coefficient is rather small (see Table 5.5). According to the coefficient estimates, every additional 50 million marks of assets above the mean implies one more director on the executive board. Since mean assets in the sample are approximately 5 million (median of 1.6 million), there is a very flat, albeit statistically strong, relationship between the two variables. Size of assets naturally represents a number of characteristics for which direct observation is difficult in the data, such as the number of product markets and the complexity of the organization. Even without quantifiable data to include in the statistical models, qualitative evidence supports the idea that large firms tend to have more highly diversified organization and production than smaller firms. Thus, larger firms tend to have more divisions at every level of the hierarchy and therefore have more top-level managers to seat on the executive board.

Size also tends to vary with the branch of industry, but the latter enters the calculation directly, via fifteen sector indicator variables. The indicator variable coefficients measure the effect of membership in the given sector

---

[21] See Dunlavy (1998).
[22] The data for this analysis come from a panel of 320 nonfinancial firms randomly sampled from the *Handbuch der Deutschen Aktiengesellschaft*.

Table 5.4. *Examples of German Joint-Stock Corporations*
with Large Boards

Firm	Sector	Number of Members	Total Liabilities (Millions of Marks)
Panel A: Executive Board (*Vorstand*)			
Fried. Krupp AG	Mining	13	389.88
Schultheiss' Brauerei AG	Brewing	11	31.18
AG des Altonaer Schauspielhauses	Theater	10	0.48
Felten & Guilleaume-Lahmeyer Werke AG	Electrical	10	53.64
Aktien Zuckerfabrik Niederndodeleben	Sugar	6	0.45
Steinhuder Meer-Bahn	Light rail	6	2.93
Zucker Fabrik Pelplin	Sugar	6	1.43
Zuckerfabrik Markranstaedt	Sugar	6	0.66
Aktien Zuckerfabrik Mattierzoll	Sugar	5	0.58
Aktien Zuckerfabrik zu Barum	Sugar	5	1.02
Deutsche Waffen u. Munitionsfabriken	Metal	5	28.16
Israelitische Religionsges. Karlsruhe	Religious	5	0.17
Kaliwerke Aschersleben	Salt	5	18.65
Kleinbahn AG Bismark-Gardelegen-Diesdorf	Light rail	5	3.99
Petroleum Producte AG	Petroleum	5	20.96
Zuckerfabrik Gross-Düngen	Sugar	5	0.81
Zuckerfabrik Salzwedel	Sugar	5	1.68
Zuckerfabrik Schwetz	Sugar	5	1.63
Zuckerfabrik Unislaw	Sugar	5	0.95
Aktien Zuckerfabrik Büdingen	Sugar	4	1.53
Flensburger Export Brauerei	Brewing	4	1.60
Kulmbacher Rizzibräu AG	Brewing	4	5.61
Vereinigte Berlin-Frankfurter Gummiwaren-Fabriken	Rubber	4	3.96
Mean/median		1.91/2.00	5.09/1.61
Panel B: Supervisory Boards (*Aufsichtsrat*)			
Palmengarten-Gesellschaft	Entertainment (garden)	21	2.23
Stuttgarter Badgesellschaft AG	Baths	21	1.75
Deutsche Waffen u. Munitionsfabriken	Metal	20	28.16
Oberschlesiche Eisenbahn-Bedarfs AG	Mining	19	39.53
Felten & Guilleaume-Lahmeyer Werke AG	Electrical	13	53.64

Firm	Sector	Number of Members	Total Liabilities (Millions of Marks)
Ostdeutsche Eisenbahn-Gesellschaft	Railroad	13	7.67
AG Vereinsbrauerei zu Zwickau i. S.	Brewing	12	1.88
Aktien Zuckerfabrik Büdingen	Sugar	12	1.53
Gesellschaft f. elektrische Unternehmungen	Electrical	12	78.25
Kleinbahn AG Bismark-Gardelegen-Diesdrf	Light rail	12	3.99
Kraftübertragungswerke Rheinfelden	Electrical	12	11.62
Rheinisch-Westfälische Sprengstoff AG	Chemical (explosives)	12	7.60
Steinhuder Meer-Bahn	Light rail	12	2.93
Zoologische Gesellschaft	Entertainment (zoo)	12	1.23
Kleinbahn AG Selters-Hachenburg	Electrical rail	11	1.77
Klosterbrauerei	Brewing	11	3.51
Salzwerk Heilbronn	Salt	11	4.71
Zuckerfabrik Markranstaedt	Sugar	11	0.66
Zuckerfabrik Salzwedel	Sugar	11	1.68
Mean/median		5.39/5.00	5.09/1.61

Note: The firms are those among the random panel database that have the largest boards.

compared to the excluded category, mining. The multivariate analysis makes it clear that only food processing companies (primarily sugar and water) had unusually large boards, after controlling for firm size. In other words, the fact that the largest boards typically appear in firms such as Krupp (mining), Felten & Guilleaume (electrotechnical), or Schultheiss (brewing) has more to do with their size or diversification than with their branch of industry.

The statistical results indicate an upward trend in the size of executive boards, but the coefficient estimates are extremely small. Because firm age correlates significantly with the trend variable, one might wonder whether the trend variable actually proxies for age effects. Perhaps older firms tend to maintain larger executive boards, because it is difficult to eliminate older directors, even when new directors are brought in. Such a scenario would lead to a positive relationship between firm age and board size. But cross-sectional regressions including the same variables used in the panel

Table 5.5. *Models of Corporate Board Size*

	Supervisory Board			Executive Board		
	Fixed Effects	XTGEE		XTGEE		
Private banker	**0.91**	**0.92**		−0.05	−0.06	
	0.00	*0.00*		*0.38*	*0.33*	
Provincial banker	**0.94**	**0.94**		−0.03	−0.04	
	0.00	*0.00*		*0.62*	*0.51*	
Great banker	**1.10**	**1.11**		0.19	0.18	
	0.00	*0.00*		*0.11*	*0.14*	
Mixed banks	**1.61**	**1.63**		0.01	0.00	
	0.00	*0.00*		*0.91*	*0.98*	
Number of AR members					0.01	0.01
					0.59	*0.60*
Liabilities (millions)	**0.03**	**0.03**	**0.03**	**0.02**	**0.02**	**0.02**
	0.00	*0.00*	*0.00*	*0.07*	*0.08*	*0.08*
Number of shares	**0.20**	**0.19**	**0.20**	0.01	0.01	0.01
	0.00	*0.00*	*0.00*	*0.76*	*0.81*	*0.76*
Listed in province	0.06	0.06	0.05	0.04	0.04	0.04
	0.64	*0.82*	*0.87*	*0.54*	*0.54*	*0.57*
Listed in Berlin	**0.74**	**0.72**	**0.80**	−0.11	−0.12	−0.14
	0.00	*0.05*	*0.04*	*0.44*	*0.41*	*0.34*
Age (incorporation)	0.02	0.00	0.00	0.00	0.00	0.00
	0.28	*0.74*	*0.83*	*0.43*	*0.44*	*0.47*
Trend	0.03	**0.04**	**0.05**	0.00	0.00	0.00
	0.17	*0.00*	*0.00*	*0.85*	*0.92*	*0.82*
Machinery, metalworking		−0.67	−0.73	0.04	0.04	0.02
		0.19	*0.17*	*0.86*	*0.83*	*0.93*
Printing, woodworking		−1.00	**−1.31**	0.06	0.07	0.04
		0.06	*0.02*	*0.80*	*0.77*	*0.88*
Rail transport		**1.95**	**1.66**	0.32	0.30	0.27
		0.02	*0.04*	*0.36*	*0.39*	*0.43*
Ship transport		0.02	−0.25	−0.28	−0.28	−0.32
		0.97	*0.67*	*0.20*	*0.20*	*0.16*
Electrical		−1.12	−1.17	0.21	0.22	0.22
		0.26	*0.28*	*0.63*	*0.61*	*0.61*
Gas, petroleum		0.11	−0.44	−0.34	−0.35	**−0.38**
		0.84	*0.44*	*0.11*	*0.11*	*0.09*
Water		−0.62	−1.13	**0.84**	**0.85**	**0.83**
		0.68	*0.45*	*0.04*	*0.04*	*0.05*
Chemicals		−0.03	−0.26	0.06	0.06	0.04
		0.96	*0.62*	*0.79*	*0.79*	*0.87*
Stones, cement, earthenware		−0.52	**−0.87**	−0.14	−0.13	−0.17
		0.30	*0.10*	*0.51*	*0.53*	*0.44*

	Supervisory Board			Executive Board		
	Fixed Effects	XTGEE	XTGEE	XTGEE	XTGEE	XTGEE
Textiles		**−0.83**	**−1.11**	−0.20	−0.20	−0.21
		0.10	*0.05*	*0.33*	*0.35*	*0.32*
Food processing, milling		**1.49**	1.02	0.56	0.54	0.51
		0.10	*0.26*	*0.16*	*0.17*	*0.20*
Brewing		−0.12	−0.41	0.07	0.07	0.03
		0.80	*0.42*	*0.80*	*0.80*	*0.91*
Schools, charities		−0.25	−0.90	0.60	0.60	0.58
	0.78	*0.32*	*0.26*	*0.26*	*0.28*	
Hospitality, entertainment		**4.01**	3.65	**−0.47**	**−0.51**	**−0.53**
		0.04	*0.08*	*0.05*	*0.03*	*0.04*
Constant	**3.52**	**3.62**	**4.36**	**1.62**	**1.58**	**1.60**
	0.00	*0.00*	*0.00*	*0.00*	*0.00*	*0.00*
Sigma_u	2.35					
Sigma_e	1.16					
Rho	0.80					
F test that all u_i = 0						
F(312, 4343)	6.00					
Prob > F	0.00					
Number of observations (obs)	4,666	4,666	4,666	4,685	4,685	4,685
Number of groups	313	313	313	313	313	313
Obs per group						
Min	2	2	2	2	2	2
Avg	14.9	14.9	14.9	15	15	15
Max	18	18	18	18	18	18
Wald chi2(24)		195.47	133.89	51.17	54.15	47.32
Prob > chi2		0.00	0.00	0.00	0.00	0.00
F(10,4343)	109.52					
Prob > F	0.00					
corr(u_i, Xb)	−0.168					

Note: The dependent variables are VORNUM and ARNUM, the number of individuals seated on the executive and supervisory boards, respectively. Total assets are in millions of marks. Models are estimated using the Huber-White sandwich method for estimating robust standard errors and assuming that observations are clustered by firm. P-values of t-tests are in italics below coefficient estimates. Boldface indicates statistically significant coefficient estimates.

models (except trend, of course) indicate that firm age is not associated with board size in any way. Moreover, looking closely at the pattern over time, it is obvious that the vast majority of firms maintained virtually constant board size, and that only a couple of firms increased their boards markedly after the turn of the century.

Supervisory Boards

Executive board size correlates with supervisory board size among German nonfinancial corporations, and the story of the *Aufsichtsrat* roughly parallels that of the *Vorstand*. As with executive boards, German supervisory boards generally remained moderate in size – averaging five members throughout the period 1895–1912. Supervisory board size also varied little among firms, though some companies maintained boards with upwards of twenty members (see Table 5.4). Firms with the largest supervisory boards appeared in a number of different sectors and were not necessarily those with the largest executive boards. For example, Oberschlesische Eisenbahnbedarfs AG, a mining products firm, had nineteen supervisory board members but only two executive board members. Similarly, Deutsche Waffen und Munitionsfabriken, a heavy metal (weapons) manufacturer, had a twenty-person supervisory board with a five-person executive board. Conversely, Friedrich Krupp AG, with thirteen directors, and Schultheiss' brewery, with eleven directors, both had only five supervisory board members. The fact that all of these firms were at least an order of magnitude larger than the median firm highlights the point that firm size may not directly determine supervisory board size. Dispersion of ownership typically provides the underlying motivation for larger supervisory boards, since a closely held firm has few outside shareholders in need of representation. Firm size may simply relate statistically to ownership dispersion and thereby enter the regression as a proxy for dispersion. Certainly, in the case of Krupp, the firm was owned almost outright by one person, and a supervisory board was hardly called for at all.

In the multivariate analysis of supervisory board size, the firm size effect is statistically significant and positive, but its magnitude is only slightly larger than it was for executive board size (see Table 5.5). In the models of supervisory board size, two additional proxies for ownership dispersion arise: the number of shares outstanding and a binary variable for listing on a stock exchange (either in Berlin or in any German exchange). Such proxies are useful, since ownership information is not generally available (and was not recorded). Because the model also includes total liabilities, the number of shares outstanding reflects the upper bound on the number of owners, for a given firm size. Listing on a stock exchange proxies for ownership dispersion inasmuch as shares with an active market prove more attractive to outside investors. And exchange listings, particularly in Berlin, offered firms greater access to potential purchasers. Despite their lack of precision, both of these proxies provide additional predictive power for supervisory board size – even controlling for firm size. The listing variable is particularly strong, and in line with expectations, obtains larger coefficients for Berlin listings than for listings overall. Indeed, listing only on a provincial exchange is unrelated to supervisory board size. These findings raise a number of interesting issues about the purposes of the various German stock exchanges, but these questions are reserved for Chapter 7. The results do suggest, however, that compared to provincial exchange listing, Berlin listings better describe the set of firm characteristics – presumably including ownership dispersion – that led to larger supervisory boards.

The regression models for supervisory board size also include industrial sector and trend. As in the earlier models, these variables have relatively strong predictive power, but the trend is more pronounced than in the models of executive board size. The patterns are similar, in that median supervisory board size was essentially constant throughout, and that only a few of the largest boards grew substantially. Clearly, both kinds of boards were growing on average over time, but the pattern was not one of general expansion.

Defining Interlocking Directorates

Against this backdrop of executive and supervisory board structure, it is possible to paint a more detailed picture of the makeup of corporate boards. In particular, we can examine the interrelationships between banks and non-financial firms through shared positions in corporate governance bodies. German universal banks are thought to have used interlocking directorates to maintain close, long-term relationships with the firms they financed.

Given the dual nature of German corporate boards, there are four hypothetical types of relationships or links: bank director on a firm supervisory board, firm director on a bank supervisory board, joint membership in bank and firm executive boards, and joint membership in bank and firm supervisory boards. As shorthand in the subsequent discussion, the relationships are sometimes denoted as V2AR, AR2V, V2V, and ARAR, respectively. That is, the V (*Vorstand*) or AR (*Aufsichtsrat*) in the first position refers to the bank, and in the second position, it refers to the firm. Since the supervisory and executive boards perform very different functions, the four types of linkages carry with them possibly very different meanings – for bank–firm relationships generally and for the ability of bankers to alter firms' behavior in particular. A bank director sitting on a firm supervisory board holds the greatest potential to influence a firm. In contrast, concurrent supervisory board memberships may not indicate much or any direct relationship between the given bank and firm. Indeed, most such joint members were third parties with independent interests in both entities. Similarly, representation by a firm director in a bank supervisory board would not afford the bank any opportunity to intervene in the business of the firm represented. Such a relationship might, however, facilitate information flows or give the firm increased access to bank funding and other kinds of support.

Patterns of Interlocking Directorates

Since comprehensive data on corporate supervisory boards was not gathered until the very end of the nineteenth century, it is nearly impossible to measure exactly the extent of bank representation in the corporate population as a whole for the earlier years. The available figures do, however, capture bank representation at least in the chair and vice-chair position.[23] German corporate governance forms changed considerably during industrialization – particularly during the last twenty years of the nineteenth century. Banks and firms enlarged their boards and expanded formal interaction after 1882.[24] In 1882, directors of Berlin-listed universal banks served as the chair or vice-chair of the supervisory board in approximately 12 percent of sampled companies, all of which were also listed on the Berlin exchange. That number rose to 18 to 24 percent in 1894. By 1898 as many as 56 percent of firms (in a random cross section) had some form of interlocking directorates with at least one bank. Such representation leveled off in the decade after 1900. These interactions involved many third-party relationships, in which one individual, quite often an industrialist, sat on the supervisory boards of both a bank and a firm. Positions of bank directors on nonfinancial firm supervisory boards were considerably less common and likely did not grow substantially over the period, and may have even declined between 1898 and 1913. Thus, the phenomenon of interlocking directorates grew apace with industrial development and became widespread among Berlin-listed companies during the last stages of industrialization.

By the time the industrial economy began its new phase of growth in the mid-1890s, interlocking directorates had become a common institutional arrangement. But even in this later part of the industrialization process, the phenomenon was not as prevalent as the traditional accounts suggest (see Table 5.6). Casting the broadest possible net – that is, combining the four types of bank links and including even small private bankers in the

---

[23] The main source for data on stock companies before 1895 is *Saling's Börsen-Jahrbuch*, and that publication often reports only part of the supervisory board – in some cases, just the chair and vice-chair. Some firms, particularly in the years before the 1884 law requiring joint-stock firms to have supervisory boards, may have had little more than a chair and vice-chair.

[24] The estimates presented here come from Fohlin (1999b).

Table 5.6. *Interlocking Directorates between Nonfinancial Firms and Universal Banks, 1895–1912*

Variable	Definition	Number	Percent of Sample
Panel A. Percentage of Firms with Specific Types of Interlocking Directorates			
ATT	Any type of attachment	3,347	67.07
V2AR	Bank director sits on firm supervisory board	2,684	52.56
GBV2AR	Great-bank director sits on firm supervisory board	612	11.98
ARAR	Joint member of bank and firm supervisory boards	2,268	44.41
ARAR only	Joint supervisory board member and no bank directors on firm board	584	11.40
AR2V	Firm director sits on a bank supervisory board	265	5.19
V2V	Firm director is also bank director	107	2.10

Panel B. Tabulation of Interlocking Directorates by Bank Type

	Bank Director on Firm Supervisory Board		Firm Director on Bank Supervisory Board		Joint Bank and Firm (Supervisory Board Member)		Joint Bank and Firm (Executive Board Member)	
	Frequency	Percent	Frequency	Percent	Frequency	Percent	Frequency	Percent
No bank	2,423	47.44	4,842	94.81	2,839	55.59	5,000	97.9
Private bank	981	19.21	n/a	n/a	n/a	n/a	19	0.37
Provincial bank	1,091	21.36	228	4.46	1,453	28.45	58	1.14
Great bank	337	6.6	26	0.51	104	2.04	28	0.55
Provincial bank and great bank	275	5.38	11	0.22	711	13.92	2	0.04
TOTAL	5,107	100	5,107	100	5,107	100	5,107	100

Note: There are 5,107 observations (firm-years) for all variables except "ATT," for which there are 4,990. Private banks do not have a supervisory board, so they do not appear in the second and third categories of interlocking directorates. Private bankers are treated as bank directors.

135

measure – two-thirds of the sampled firm-years fall into the "attached" category.[25] In other words, one in three stock corporations had no governance relationship with a commercial banker at all – even indirectly, via some other nonfinancial firm. Closer to half of the firms had a bank director or private banker sitting on their supervisory boards, and 40 percent of these positions (19 percent of the sample overall) were held solely by private bankers – in other words, not by joint-stock universal banks. A slightly larger number of firms had provincial-bank directors, and no other bankers, on their supervisory boards. Only 12 percent of joint-stock firms received representation from a great bank (one of the top nine banks), and that number is even smaller if attention is constrained to the top four banks – the so-called D-banks – Deutsche, Dresdner, Darmstädter, and Disconto. In his 1910 treatise on the German universal banks, Jakob Riesser listed all joint-stock companies with great bank directors on their supervisory boards as of 1909. That list contained 171 industrial firms (that is, not counting railroads and commerce), which would have amounted to fewer than 5 percent of all joint-stock firms in the relevant sectors in that year.

The numbers decline further when considering bank control of the leading positions in nonfinancial firm supervisory boards. The chair (*Vorsitzender*) and vice-chair (*stellvertretender Vorsitzender*) of the supervisory board typically maintained the most control over the policy agenda of a firm. Thus, a banker in such a post might have wielded more power than he could as an ordinary member. Fewer than 22 percent of firms had a bank director as chair or vice-chair of their supervisory boards – fewer than 14 percent of firms when we consider only chairmanships (see Table 5.7). In other words, in fewer than half of the cases in which a banker sat on a firm supervisory board was the banker in one of the top two posts. The provincial banks held the most chair- or vice-chairmanships (10 percent of the sample), but the private bankers were close behind (7 percent of the sample). The great banks held relatively few chair or vice-chair positions, amounting to fewer than 5 percent of the full sample and fewer than 2.5 percent when considering only chairmanships. Compared to the smaller banks, the great banks were also less likely to hold the top positions among the firms on whose boards they sat: 26 percent of board seats for the great banks, compared with 48 and 37 percent of board seats for provincial and private bankers, respectively. In cases in which both provincial and great-bank directors sat on the

---

[25] The set of banks considered in the four measures include all joint-stock universal banks as well as all private bankers that could be identified. The measures exclude other types of financial institutions, such as mortgage banks or state-sponsored banks, since they are not considered universal banks and were not generally engaged in the corporate financing business.

Table 5.7. *Bank Directors as Supervisory Board Chair or Vice-Chair of Nonfinancial Firms, 1895–1912*

	Chair		Vice-Chair		Chair or Vice-Chair		Firms with Bank Chair/V.C. as Percent of All Firms with Bank Directors
	Frequency	Percent	Frequency	Percent	Frequency	Percent	
No bank	5,050	86.31	5,258	89.86	4,582	78.31	
Private bank	253	4.32	178	3.04	410	7.01	36.5
Provincial bank	414	7.08	264	4.51	603	10.31	48.3
Great bank	48	0.82	54	0.92	100	1.71	25.9
Provincial and great bank	86	1.47	97	1.66	156	2.67	49.6
TOTAL	5,851	100	5,851	100	5,851	100	

137

supervisory board, bankers were chairs or vice-chairs about half of the time – similar to the rates for provincial banks alone.

Extrapolating to the full population of German industrial firms, these figures indicate that great-bank directors chaired the supervisory boards of fewer than one hundred German nonfinancial firms in the last two decades before World War I. Riesser's analysis from 1910 gives sixty-one firms (again, as in the current sample, excluding railroads and commercial firms) with great-bank chairs or vice-chairs. Thus, ironically, the findings here suggest that Riesser – or his sources – missed a number of firms with great-bank directors on their boards, and that he therefore understated the extent of great-banker presence in nonfinancial firm governance.[26]

One fact becomes evident even with a cursory look at the firms involved in formal bank relationships: The firms with great bankers on their boards tend to cluster in certain sectors (see Table 5.8). This concentration of the largest banks on a few sectors meant that their relatively small number of positions translated into control rights over a significant proportion of certain industries. For the most part, the banks also sat on the boards of the largest firms in these industries, so that the proportion of industry assets under their partial control typically exceeded the proportion of firms in the given sector. Three sectors stand out: metalworking (including machinery and shipbuilding), light rail, and electrotechnicals. In 1910, firms with great-bank representation accounted for nearly 70 percent of total assets of joint-stock firms in each of the first two sectors and over 98 percent in the latter. The bank positions involved a much smaller proportion of the firms in those sectors: only 21 percent of firms in metalworking, 18 percent in light rail, and 64 percent in electrotechnicals (still a hefty percentage, but far lower than the percentage of assets in the sector). This last sector is the most striking, since it is the only branch of industry in which the great banks held positions in more than half the firms, representing such an enormous proportion of total assets. While the prevalence of the great banks in this sector is impressive, it is worth keeping in mind that electrotechnicals accounted for less than 3.5 percent of all industrial joint-stock firms and 15 percent of the total joint-stock assets.

The traditional view holds that the great banks dominated most of heavy industry, and the perception is understandable based solely on the

---

[26] Ideas about the power of the great banks, right up to the present, have rested, at least indirectly, on Riesser's (1910 [1911]) accounts. Riesser's list, along with a list of firms from the current sample with bank directors on their supervisory boards as of 1910, are given in an appendix to this chapter.

Table 5.8. *Percentage of Firms and Assets Controlled by Supervisory Boards with Bank Representation, by Sector*

Sector	Great Bank or Combined Provincial and Great Bank				Percentage of Assets			
	Number of Firms	1910 % of Assets	1910 % of Firms	Overall % of Obs.	Prov. Banks only	Prov. & GB	Sum	% of Firms
Mining	26	25.5	38.5	35.5	4.2	19.0	23.2	38.5
Machinery, metalworking	43	69.1	20.9	16.1	7.6	24.6	32.2	27.9
Printing, woodworking	21	26.8	14.3	12.6	13.1	26.8	39.9	28.6
Rail transport	17	68.5	17.6	17.1	5.6	18.7	24.3	23.5
Ship transport	11	0	0	2.5	50.1	0	50.1	36.4
Electrical	11	98.3	63.6	59.3	0	78.0	78.0	45.5
Gas, petroleum	12	1.9	8.3	2.1	69.8	0	69.8	8.3
Water	7	0	0	0	42.2	0	42.2	14.3
Chemicals	32	7.1	6.3	10.8	56.3	0	56.3	37.5
Stones, cement, earthenware	29	5.7	6.9	4.0	11.3	2.6	13.9	24.1
Textiles	15	15.0	6.7	14.5	25.1	0	25.1	20.0
Food processing, milling	23	10.5	4.3	2.7	52.9	0	52.9	21.7
Brewing	47	2.0	2.1	2.1	21.6	0	21.6	23.4
Schools, charities	7	0	0	0	12.9	0	12.9	14.3
Hospitality, entertainment	8	53.7	12.5	11.5	0	0	0	0

appearance of bankers on the boards of some of the largest firms. But even this superficial measure of "domination" suggests a more moderate view of bank involvement. The top nine banks, for example, held supervisory board positions in fewer than 40 percent of mining sector firms, representing about one-quarter of assets in the sector in 1910. It is therefore safe to say that the banks had substantial interest in the sector, but the facts do not support any kind of bank domination theory. This broader evidence lends quantitative support to doubts raised about the qualitative influence of the great banks over some of the largest German firms of this time.[27]

At the same time, the provincial and private banks played a far greater role in the governance of stock companies than the historical literature acknowledges. These smaller banks held positions in nearly every sector of the corporate economy and took partial control over a substantial share of the assets in several industries. For example, private bankers sat on the supervisory boards of approximately one-quarter of mining corporations, making up over 68 percent of total assets in that sector. Firms with provincial-bank directors on their supervisory boards owned over half of the assets in shipping, electrotechnicals, lighting (gas and petroleum), chemicals, and food (primarily sugar refining); they owned between a quarter and a half of the assets in metalworking, manufacturing, water, and textiles; and they owned just short of a quarter of the assets in mining, light rail, and brewing. These results do not necessarily indicate that individual provincial banks maintained links with diverse sets of firms, just that provincial banks as a group did so.

While certainly not as prevalent as the converse relationship, firm directors did periodically gain access to joint-stock bank supervisory boards (AR2V positions, as shown in Table 5.6). Private banks are excluded from this measure, naturally, since they did not maintain supervisory boards. The vast majority of banks with firm directors on their boards were provincial banks, so that of the 265 firm-years falling into this category, only thirty-seven observations, representing eight individual firms, involved the nine great banks. In contrast, dual positions in bank and firm supervisory boards appeared with relative frequency (44 percent of firm-years), especially considering that private banks are excluded by definition from the ARAR measure. Almost two-thirds of these relationships, representing about 28 percent of the full sample, involved only provincial banks. Only 2 percent of the population maintained such relationships only with a great

---

[27] See Wellhöner (1989), in particular.

bank. That is, when a firm had a supervisory board member who also sat on the supervisory board of a great bank, it almost always had the same sort of link with a provincial bank as well. Also, three-quarters of the firms with bank supervisors on their supervisory boards also had at least one bank director on their supervisory boards.

In contrast to dual supervisory board positions, joint directorships (V2V) were extremely rare – 2 percent of the full sample. Continuing the previous patterns, more than half such relationships involved only provincial banks. One would expect concurrent executive board positions to be virtually nonexistent, given the level of responsibility and time commitment typically associated with the job. Moreover, the overlap in expertise between financial and nonfinancial firms could be limited. Thus, in a sense, one might be surprised to find even the five to ten cases of such relationships that appeared in each year. And while some of the cases likely arose because a bank had taken control of the firm management during liquidation proceedings, the majority did not. More likely were cases in which a successful industrialist began offering industrial credit and ultimately found it useful or profitable to incorporate his financial services business into a separate firm.

As the preceding several tables suggest, there were many cases in which great banks, provincial banks, and private bankers all occupied seats on the same supervisory board. These findings raise questions about the exclusivity of banking relationships. Many of the theoretical models of financing relationships, as well as the traditional historical view of the German corporate financing system, emphasize the benefits of a "house–bank" relationship. In a theoretical framework in which a firm engages in a long-term relationship with a bank, and in which board representation ensures that the firm continues to do business with the bank even as the firm develops, multiple relationships would appear infrequently. The reality in the German case, however, diverges quite a bit from the idealized view – at least with formal relationships. On average, when a firm had at least one bank link, it had more than one (see Table 5.9).[28] Indeed, for firms with great-bank directors sitting on their boards, it was typical to have three to five bank connections, taking up 45 to 62 percent of all supervisory board positions. Most of these

---

[28] The term "links" includes both direct (bank directors) and indirect (bank supervisors) connections between a firm and bank. The first two rows of Table 5.9 exclude private bankers, but the subsequent two include them. The set of rows considers only private banks, bank directors, or the number of different banks represented directly on a firm supervisory board.

Table 5.9. *Bank Representation in Levels and as Percent of Supervisory Board Members*

Variable	Private Banks (PB) Only			Provincial Banks Only			Great Banks Only			Provincial and Great Banks		
	Mean	Std. Dev.	Max	Mean	Std. Dev.	Max	Mean	Std. Dev.	Max	Mean	Std. Dev.	Max
Number of linked members	0.91	1.19	8	1.84	0.99	8	3.24	2.34	14	5.42	3.40	16
Percent of board with links	16.73	20.11	100	35.98	19.65	100	44.54	24.32	100	61.53	19.08	100
Number of linked members (including PB)	1.97	1.12	9	2.07	1.15	10	3.59	2.46	14	5.75	3.41	16
Percent of board with links (including PB)	38.25	19.77	100	39.75	20.36	100	49.33	24.76	100	66.26	18.00	100
Number of bank directors with seats	1.43	0.61	4	1.20	0.47	3	1.32	0.71	5	2.66	1.27	6
Number of banks represented	n/a	n/a	n/a	1.19	0.45	4	1.14	0.47	4	2.73	1.35	6
Observations	473			518			166			136		

positions were indirect, and the average number of bank directors on firm boards was far lower – between 1.3 and 2.7 for firms with either great-bank directors alone or both provincial and great-bank directors on their boards. Still, 43 percent of the firms with great bankers on their boards had more than one joint-stock bank represented, and overall, joint-stock bank directors made up one-fifth to one-third of board seats in the two great-bank categories. While certainly not the norm, some firms had as many as six bank directors on their boards, sometimes representing as many different banks. About 60 percent of these firms also counted private bankers among their supervisory board members, bringing the average number of bankers up to almost three (38 percent of the board) for firms with great bankers. Counting private bankers, nearly three-quarters of these firms had more than one bank represented on their supervisory boards.

For firms with provincial-bank directors – but no great-bank directors – on their boards, the figures are lower. On average, these firms maintained about two provincial-bank links (35 to 40 percent of their boards), and about 1.2 provincial-bank directors (24 percent of their boards). Compared to great-bank firms, these firms had much less formal connection to private bankers. Just over a third of the provincial-bank firms had private-bank representation, and those that did averaged between one and two such members. Thus, including private-bank links, the total number of directors for provincial-bank firms averaged just short of two, and nearly half (47 percent) of these firms had more than one bank represented on their boards.

It is more difficult to assess the exclusivity of relationships for firms that had no joint-stock bank representation but that did have private bankers sitting on their supervisory boards. Private bankers (principals in private-banking firms, as opposed to directors of incorporated universal banks) are only identifiable by their title (*Bankier*). There are no exhaustive lists of private bankers for the period, so, hypothetically, the source could omit the title for a particular banker, and then that connection would be missed. It is clear that more than one-third of the firms in this category had at least two private bankers on their boards, but it is often uncertain whether these bankers represented multiple banking houses. Still, when private banks were the only type of bank represented, relationships were more likely to be exclusive; only a handful of firms had more than two private bankers on their boards. These firms also tended to have smaller boards, so private bankers took up a relatively large proportion of seats (29 percent).

Finally, it is important to view these bank–firm interlocking directorates in their larger context. Over half of the firms sampled in 1904 had at least one board member (either supervisory or executive) in common with a

Berlin-listed nonfinancial firm. Nearly 22 percent of these "firm-linked" companies had no board interlocks, either direct or indirect, with a bank; and a third had no banker sitting on their supervisory boards. Of those with bank representation, almost half had only a private banker – not one of the joint-stock universal banks – on their boards. In other words, the practice of interlocking directorates extended well beyond the placement of bank directors on company supervisory boards and intertwined the governance structures of many nonfinancial firms. To be sure, the universal banks played a key role in these networks, but they were just one part of an overall system of shared corporate governance.

EXPLAINING BANK AFFILIATIONS

Although historians and contemporaries clearly underscore the pervasiveness of bank–firm relationships through interlocking directorates, the older literature does not reveal how or why bankers gained access to firm boards or vice versa. Formally, the supervisory board is elected by shareholders, and since "one share, one vote" was the norm at this time, those holding larger stakes in the firm received more votes than those with small holdings. Although the most direct way to gain board seats was through share ownership, membership in the supervisory board did not require an equity stake. In practice, banks or firms could initiate interlocking directorates in several ways. The bank may have ended up holding shares from new issues of securities or from bailouts of troubled firms (via debt-equity swaps), but the bank also may have exerted equivalent control through proxy votes conferred by depositors. Alternatively, firms may have pursued bankers as board members for their expertise or simply for prestige, or, less commonly during this period, the parties could have swapped shares and formed communities of interest (*Interessengemeinschaften*).

Direct Comparison of Firms with and without Bank Affiliations

From the analysis in the previous section, it appears that bank presence varied considerably among the different branches of the German economy. While it is plausible that banks focused their attention on particular industries in order to reap gains from scale or possibly from interfirm coordination, it is also possible that branch of industry simply proxies for other firm characteristics that provide the true, underlying explanation for the development of banking relationships. Firm characteristics, particularly financial ones, do seem to vary depending on the presence of bank directors in their supervisory boards, but much of the apparent divergence hinges on extreme outliers in one subset or another (see Table 5.10).[29]

One of the most obvious distinctions between attached and independent firms is their size. Firms with bankers on their boards are significantly larger than those with no director representation, and the effect is particularly noticeable for firms with great bankers sitting on their boards. Size differences emerge for all relevant measures, such as share capital, net worth, and total assets (and equally, liabilities). Total assets reached over 8 million marks on average for attached firms but amounted to less than 2.5 million for independents. Average total assets for great-bank–attached firms doubled that of attached firms more generally. Nearly identical patterns appear for share capital and net worth. Age, however, varies little with bank attachment. While the statistical significance is relatively strong (p-values of 0.05 and 0.11), average age differs by less than a year between attached and independent firms or between great-bank–attached and all other firms. The small differences that appear stem from a handful of very old firms with bank directors on their boards. The oldest attached firm is eighty-six years old, while the oldest independent firm is fifty-four. Overall, however, the distribution of ages is similar among categories: The 5th percentile is consistently zero or one years, the 25th percentile is six or seven years, the median is thirteen years in all cases, and the 75th percentile is twenty-two or twenty-three years. Even the 95th percentile ranges only between thirty-seven and forty-four years.

Other disparities arise in the structuring of firm assets. Attached firms, particularly those with great bankers on their supervisory boards, tend to

---

[29] The descriptive variables are defined as follows. Share capital is the sum of all types of capital, including ordinary and preference shares, as reported in the balance sheet (at book values). Net worth is share capital plus reserves. Net investment is the first difference of fixed capital, while gross investment is the sum of net investment and depreciation. Fixed capital includes land, property, plant, equipment, patents, and permits and excludes inventories. Short-term financial assets are the sum of assets available on short notice, such as cash, notes, bank deposits, and accounts receivable; long-term financial assets include less liquid financial wealth such as securities and participations in other firms; and total financial assets are the sum of short-term and long-term financial assets. Sales, gross income, costs, depreciation, and gross profits are as reported in the profit and loss statements of the firms. Gross profits are gross income less total costs. All variables in levels are reported in thousands of current marks. Listed and Berlin are binary variables, taking values of 1 for exchange listing (any exchange and Berlin only, respectively) and 0 otherwise. In other words, the Berlin variable takes the value 0 for firms with only provincial exchange listings. For simplicity, the firms with bank directors on their boards are designated as "attached," while those with no directors on their boards are denominated as "independent." P-values of one-sided t-tests are given next to each pair of means.

Table 5.10. *Summary Statistics*

	Bank Director on Firm Supervisory Board			Great-Bank Director on Supervisory Board		
	0	1	P(t)	0	1	P(t)
Age	15.63	16.45	0.05	15.94	16.89	0.11
	11.24	*13.50*		*12.24*	*14.01*	
Sum of assets or	2,975.66	9,435.06	0.00	4,573.86	17,237.66	0.00
liabilities	*22,617.61*	*32,519.89*		*29,294.51*	*24,189.33*	
(reported)						
Total assets	2,442.23	8,265.40	0.00	3,902.90	16,668.35	0.00
(computed)	*17,858.50*	*28,813.37*		*24,024.58*	*23,818.19*	
Share capital	1,136.77	3,778.64	0.00	1,769.59	7,801.24	0.00
	5,592.53	*11,507.64*		*8,768.81*	*10,794.83*	
Net worth	1,605.22	5,110.77	0.00	2,425.10	10,593.06	0.00
	8,784.45	*14,642.01*		*11,640.46*	*14,441.8*	
Fixed assets/total	0.62	0.58	0.00	0.61	0.53	0.00
assets	*0.24*	*0.23*		*0.23*	*0.26*	
Short-term	1.67	2.56	0.22	2.06	2.64	0.37
financial	*14.42*	*36.75*		*29.52*	*17.85*	
assets/fixed						
assets						
Long-term	0.54	4.81	0.03	1.07	14.88	0.00
financial	*5.41*	*74.07*		*32.53*	*125.59*	
assets/fixed						
assets						
Total financial	2.21	7.37	0.05	3.14	17.52	0.00
assets/fixed	*16.52*	*102.25*		*59.06*	*143.08*	
assets						
Debt/equity ratio	0.61	0.65	0.13	0.63	0.67	0.22
	0.80	*0.77*		*0.80*	*0.70*	
Net investment	1.50	4.82	0.05	2.78	6.71	0.00
(percent)	*14.33*	*18.23*		*15.22*	*23.94*	
Gross investment	7.00	10.95	0.03	8.27	14.87	0.00
(percent)	*16.96*	*19.45*		*17.00*	*25.67*	
Depreciation	5.29	6.35	0.00	5.39	9.03	0.00
(percent of	*6.60*	*7.26*		*6.29*	*9.99*	
lagged fixed						
assets)						
Revenues/total	0.28	0.21	0.00	0.25	0.17	0.00
assets	*0.36*	*0.17*		*0.30*	*0.14*	
Income/total assets	0.30	0.22	0.00	0.27	0.18	0.00
	0.49	*0.18*		*0.38*	*0.14*	
Cost /total assets	0.25	0.17	0.00	0.22	0.12	0.00
	0.34	*0.16*		*0.28*	*0.13*	

	Bank Director on Firm Supervisory Board			Great-Bank Director on Supervisory Board		
	0	1	P(t)	0	1	P(t)
Sales growth rate	6.71	6.93	0.45	6.48	9.29	0.16
(percent)	*41.56*	*41.58*		*39.54*	*53.58*	
Income growth	8.07	8.72	0.37	7.98	11.51	0.12
rate (percent)	*44.82*	*44.65*		*43.50*	*52.35*	
Costs growth rate	8.20	9.39	0.27	7.90	15.34	0.00
(percent)	*44.24*	*43.74*		*41.13*	*59.58*	
Gross profits/total	0.05	0.05	0.41	0.05	0.06	0.38
assets	*0.30*	*0.07*		*0.23*	*0.07*	
Return on equity	0.07	0.07	0.41	0.07	0.07	0.28
(ROE)	*0.31*	*0.11*		*0.24*	*0.10*	
Annual dividend	5.59	6.92	0.00	6.01	8.34	0.00
	6.60	*5.74*		*6.10*	*6.60*	
Share price on	180.68	162.70	0.01	158.48	200.33	0.00
December 31	*96.00*	*78.37*		*77.86*	*94.99*	
(percent of par)						
Increase in share	3.23	8.54	0.13	7.35	6.60	0.44
price (percent/year)	*29.12*	*48.99*		*44.53*	*46.02*	
Increase in share	11.39	14.59	0.25	13.76	13.80	0.50
price plus dividends	*31.59*	*50.91*		*45.80*	*50.32*	
(percent/year)						
Listed on some	0.19	0.51	0.00	0.32	0.65	0.00
German exchange	*0.39*	*0.50*		*0.47*	*0.48*	
Listed in Berlin	0.07	0.23	0.00	0.12	0.39	0.00
	0.25	*0.42*		*0.32*	*0.49*	

Note: Standard deviations are in italics below the sample means. P-values are from one-sided t-tests. "0" means there was no director, and "1" means there was a director. Investment and depreciation variables exclude extreme outliers, as discussed in the text.

have lower ratios of fixed to total assets compared to independents. While the differences are highly significant statistically, they are small in magnitude – 53 percent for great-bank firms compared to 62 percent for independents. Much larger is the percentage gap in long-term or less liquid financial assets between great-bank and other firms. Firms with great bankers on their boards average 11 percent, yet the other firms average 4.5 percent. There is virtually no difference in long-term asset ratios between independents and firms with only private bankers on their boards, but those with only provincial bankers on their boards have lower ratios of long-term assets (3.9 percent). Average short-term assets (such as cash, credit balances with banks, and receivables) are more similar across categories, all of which range between 18 and 22 percent. Again, great-bank firms are on the high end of the distribution and differ notably from provincial-bank firms.

Despite the differences in asset structure, capital structure varies little across subpopulations. Regardless of the presence or absence of bank directors on company boards, the ratio of outside to inside capital (all liabilities other than net worth divided by net worth) ranges between 0.61 and 0.67. Great-bank firms have the highest debt ratios, and independents the lowest, but the differences are statistically and economically insignificant. The flip side of this coin is capitalization ratio, or the ratio of net worth to total liabilities. Here the range is 67 to 70 percent – obviously with great-bank firms on the lower end, and independents on the higher end. The differences turn out to be statistically significant, reflecting the low variance across firms and years. The 95 percent confidence interval for firms with great-bank directors on their boards is 65 to 69 percent, while the corresponding range for unattached firms is 69 to 71.5 percent. Such small differences suggest little diversity in the use of debt versus equity and are unlikely to affect a firm's subsequent financing options. Relative to modern firms, these figures also indicate markedly higher capitalization and imply that firms, or perhaps their bankers, pursued far more conservative debt policies than they do currently.

Investment in fixed capital is another story. A great divergence in mean investment appears between attached and independent firms, with the former appearing to invest far more heavily than the latter. Investment measures are notoriously noisy, however, and there are extreme outlier values in the current samples. If the variables are restricted to plausible ranges, even very broad ones, the results become much more economically sensible and statistically significant.[30] In the sample overall, gross investment averages 9 percent, while net investment averages just over 3 percent. After eliminating the extreme values, the altered distribution retains its asymmetry, since the imposed constraints still leave substantially more room in the right tail than the left. The median values are markedly lower than the means – 4.5 percent for gross investment and exactly zero for net investment. It is certainly notable that at the height of the heavy industrialization period, the median joint-stock firm invested nothing in fixed capital beyond depreciation.

Once extreme outliers are cleaned from the data, significant and meaningful differences appear among the subsamples, depending on type of bank

---

[30] Firms cannot lose more than 100 percent of their assets, and even losing half of fixed assets in one year would be highly unusual. On the upper end, a tripling of fixed assets in one year would seem extraordinary. By constraining the sample of firms to those with investment between –50 and 200 percent, the descriptive statistics omit fewer than 1 percent of observations (18 out of a total of 2,033).

attachment. There is some disparity between firms with no bank directors on their boards and firms with some type of bank director on their boards (the V2AR variable). The former have mean (median) net investment of 1.5 (0.0) percent, while the latter have mean (median) rates of 4.8 (0.3) percent. Mean (median) gross investment is correspondingly higher at 7 (3.5) percent for unattached firms and 11 (5.8) percent for those with bankers on their boards. Dividing the sample by great-bank attachment yields even more divergence between the subsamples. Firms with great-bank directors on their boards invest on average at 6.7 percent (median of 1 percent) after depreciation and 14.9 percent (median of 10.6 percent) before. At the same time, firms without a great banker on board invest on average (median) at 2.8 (0) percent net and 8.3 (4.3) percent gross. Statistically speaking, the subsample means are all significantly different at high levels – less than 1 percent, based on a one-sided t-test.

Looking at the distribution of investment rates in graphical form drives home the differences among the subpopulations and reaffirms the descriptive statistics and t-test results: Compared to all other firms, the great-bank firms clearly have a flatter investment density function with higher mean and median (see Figure 5.7).[31] Independents have the narrowest distribution, with the smallest upper tail. Provincial- and private-bank firms fall in between, but appear more similar to the unattached/private-bank category than to the great-bank category. Statistical tests such as the Shapiro-Wilk, Kruskal-Wallis, and Kolmogorov-Smirnov tests all yield very low p-values. The tests, respectively, confirm the facts that investment is not normally distributed, that the samples appear to come from different populations, and that the underlying distributions differ significantly from one another. The Kruskal-Wallis test also supports the pooling of the private- and provincial-bank firms as well as the great-bank and combined-bank firms.[32] At this stage, these findings are primarily important for what they indicate about general patterns of investment. The results obviously do not permit causal inferences – bank presence on boards does not necessarily promote stronger

---

[31] Figure 5.7 uses a kernel density estimator for each of three subsamples of the dataset. The graphed samples exclude the extreme outliers on the far ends of the distribution. Because it turns out that firms with private bankers on their boards invest at rates very similar to those with provincial bankers on board, the graph shows the private bank and provincial-bank categories together. The same is true for great-bank firms and combined (great- and provincial-) bank firms.

[32] The test yields p-values of 0.24 for the great- versus combined-bank comparison and 0.42 for the provincial- versus private-bank comparison. In other words, we cannot reject the hypothesis that the relevant sub-samples are drawn from the same population. Other subsample pairs yield p-values of less than 0.001, suggesting that those subsamples are drawn from significantly different populations.

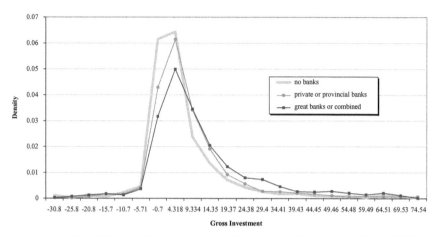

Figure 5.7. Kernel Density Estimate of Gross Investment, Nonfinancial Firms, 1895–1912.
Note: Density is estimated over the range (−50 percent, 200 percent), and the graph depicts the portion of the density function falling in the range (−31 percent, 75 percent). "Combined" indicates the presence of both provincial- and great-bank directors on the company supervisory boards.

investment – but they do point to possible differences among firms with and without close bank involvement. The results also raise the possibility that the causes or consequences of bank attachments differ depending on the size and type of bank involved – an empirical twist that fits poorly with the theoretical role of bank relationships.

The divergence between gross and net investment indicates that firms typically took substantial deductions for depreciation. Unconstrained averages are indeed high. But the values are implausible, and extreme outliers once again influence these results. If just the eight observations of depreciation exceeding the logical limit of 100 percent are excluded, the mean depreciation in the sample overall drops to 5.8 percent – a very believable figure. The differences among subpopulations now also attain statistical significance. Firms with no bank directors on their boards claimed an average of 5.3 percent annual depreciation, while those with bank directors claimed 1 percentage point more. Firms with great-bank directors on their boards generally took the greatest depreciation of all, averaging 9 percent annually. Depreciation allowances were not regulated at this time, and the amounts taken could vary considerably. Ten percent of firms reported no depreciation in their profit and loss (P&L) statements, while an equivalent number took 10 to 20 percent – or far more – in any given year.

The rest of the P&L statement provides additional insights into the similarities and differences among firms with varying types of bank affiliations. In the population as a whole, sales revenues averaged around 24 percent of total assets, and total income averaged about 26 percent. Both variables demonstrate significant variation among the subsamples, particularly when great-bank firms are singled out. On average, as a share of total assets, firms with great-bank directors on their boards reported less than two-thirds the income and revenues of the remaining firms in the sample. Revenues and income for private- and provincial-bank firms fall between those of great-bank firms and independents. The differences among all three categories are significant. Among the subsamples, costs follow a very similar pattern as income and revenues. On average, all three measures grew at essentially the same rates for all types of firms, with costs increasing somewhat faster than income or revenues.

Not surprisingly, given the forgoing results, gross profits end up approximately the same for all subsamples on average. In the population as a whole, gross profits average slightly more than 5 percent of total assets. Relative to net worth, profits are closer to 6.5 percent on average. There are no statistical differences among the three categories (see Table 5.10); however, firms with only a provincial-bank director sitting on the board do show lower returns. On average, their gross profits are 4.5 percent of total assets and 6 percent of net worth. The remaining firms average nearly 1 percentage point higher on both measures. Despite the fact that gross profit rates do not vary significantly among the categories of bank attachment, dividend payout rates do differ. Firms with bankers on their boards averaged 6.9 percent dividends, or 1.3 percentage points higher than firms with no bankers on board. Averaging 8.3 percent, firms with great banks on their boards paid the highest dividends of all. Combining all firms with bankers on their boards masks some marked variations among subcategories. Firms with only private bankers on their boards also paid high dividends – 7.5 percent on average, compared to 5.5 percent for provincial-bank firms and independents. Thus, the dividends for firms with only provincial bankers on their boards were more similar to those of independents than to companies with other types of bankers on their boards.

For the subset of firms with stock market listings, share prices and returns offer additional measures of firm performance and value. The market-to-book ratio is often used as a marginal Tobin's Q, to gauge the desirability of new investment by a firm. Overall, firms with bankers on their boards have significantly lower market-to-book ratios than do independents. But firms with great bankers on their boards have very high ratios.

Once again, examining the types of bank attachments separately uncovers apparent variation. Great-bank firms are at the high end of the range, but independents have the next highest average ratios. Firms with private or provincial banks on their boards fall at the low end of the spectrum.

Stock returns also appear to differ widely among the categories of firms. Because of rather large variance and small subsamples of listed firms, however, these differences are not statistically significant. Still, it is interesting to note the disparities among certain subcategories of bank attachments. Provincial-bank firms' stock prices grew the most rapidly on average (11.2 percent per annum). Even adjusting for dividends, average provincial-bank returns were second only to firms with combined-bank board memberships (15.9 percent and 17.7 percent, respectively). Firms with only private bankers on board were next at 14.2 percent on average, while independents and firms with great-bank directors on board made the lowest average returns – both 11.4 percent per year on average. Overall, attached firms have higher average returns, but the differences between those with and without great bankers on their boards are extremely small.

The results on stock prices and returns raises the issue of stock market listings. Stock markets sprouted up in many German regions in the mid- to late-nineteenth century. All of the major cities, and many minor ones, supported some form of exchange. Often, the exchanges focused on particular commodities or securities, and those specialties usually corresponded to the emphasis of the local economy. By the period covered in the current database, the Berlin exchange held the lead in securities business, so Berlin listings are differentiated from provincial listings. The results are quite striking: Compared to attached firms, independents are far less likely to have a stock market listing, and are especially unlikely to be listed in Berlin. Firms with great-bank directors on their boards are the most likely to be listed (65 percent) and have the highest proportions of Berlin listings (39 percent). Interestingly, 55 percent of firms with private bankers on their boards had listings, while only 39 percent of firms with provincial bankers on board did so. Similarly, nearly a quarter of private-bank–attached firms listed their shares in Berlin, while fewer than 13 percent of provincial-bank–attached firms listed at the top exchange. These findings hint at a potentially strong tie between the securities underwriting and brokerage business and the presence of bankers on firm supervisory boards. This connection resurfaces later on in the analysis and plays a prevalent role in the larger story of firm performance.

For stock market listings, as well as a number of other variables, firms with provincial-bank representatives on their boards appear more similar to firms with no bank directors on their boards than to firms with private banks or great banks on board. This variation within the bank-attached population suggests that bank attachments in themselves do not cause the differences that appear. Instead, other characteristics that may be closely associated with the presence of certain types of banks on the supervisory board – being part of the industrial sector, for example – may explain the disparities. Multivariate analysis is required to control for the range of firm characteristics and their interactions with bank relationships.

Multivariate Models: Connections between Proxy Voting and Interlocking Directorates

As the forgoing section hinted, multivariate models provide a more complete, and also more complex, picture of bank relationships than do simple comparisons of means for individual variables. There are several ways to approach the problem of explaining bank attachments. The method here is to use discrete-choice analysis, with a dependent variable that categorizes firms by the type of bank with a director on the supervisory board. In the framework of asymmetric information theory, discussed in Chapter 3, all bank relationships are considered essentially the same. There is no a priori reason to assume that smaller, provincial universal banks resolve information problems differently from their larger, Berlin counterparts, or that certain banks do ameliorate information asymmetries while others do not. Yet given the differences among the five categories of attachment laid out previously (no bank, private bank, provincial bank, great bank, and joint provincial and great bank), it is quite likely that the multivariate analysis would also reveal some variation. Thus, instead of comparing attached and independent firms in binary fashion, the empirical analysis differentiates among the types of banks represented on firm boards.

To develop a cogent statistical model of the bank-attachment decision, and to determine which specific firm characteristics should be examined as predictors of bank board memberships, I turn to several commonly cited hypotheses from the theoretical literature on formalized banking relationships. Over the years, researchers have posited a number of means by which formalized relationships between universal banks and industrial firms might have benefited the German economy during the later stages of industrialization. The now standard explanations of bank–firm relationships, interpreted in terms of the modern theoretical literature, emphasize the resolution of information problems that often beset industrial undertakings. A financial intermediary might help equalize information by screening firms before providing finance (ex ante monitoring). After funding, banks could have – and are argued to have in the historical literature – employed formalized relationships in order to keep watch over firms' activities and results (interim and ex post monitoring).[33] Improving bank oversight capacity is assumed to decrease the potential for and severity of moral hazard problems in the financing of firms' investment. In the most direct sense, interlocking directorates between banks and firms should lower the cost of debt finance and should reduce the banks' incentive to ration credit.[34]

The universality of banks, in the German case, means that banks underwrite new issues of securities for firms in addition to lending to them. Interlocking directorates might thus also be viewed as means by which well-known banks affixed their seal of approval to investment-worthy firms. The firm may be willing to pay otherwise unnecessary costs in order to maintain a banker on its supervisory board, if the mere presence of that individual sends a message to the capital market that the firm is a good risk.[35] Participating in interlocking directorates may lower the cost (raise the benefits) of issuing securities by increasing the size and liquidity of the potential market. The effect should be the strongest for equity issues, since returns depend on improving firm valuation rather than on the mere ability to service debt. There is good reason to question, however, whether a signaling hypothesis can logically hold simultaneously with a monitoring explanation. Since banks are likely to demand the closest oversight for the weakest or riskiest firms, board representation by banks may send mixed signals to capital markets. The possibility that interlocking directorates might reflect poor firm quality would seriously undermine the credibility of banks' signals and would weaken the appeal of interlocking directorates for the healthiest firms.

Finally, the historical literature has also characterized universal bankers as consultants of sorts, and interlocking directorates have been seen as solidifying the links between banks and firms. Traditionally, universal banks are seen as substitutes for missing entrepreneurship in industry. Positions on firm supervisory boards are thought to have allowed banks access to and influence on firms' strategic planning and investment decision making. According to this line of reasoning, having such control facilitated the banks' funneling capital into industrial enterprises and thereby promoting stronger, more efficient investment.

In testing these hypotheses, it is important to distinguish between the direct and indirect oversight provided by interlocking directorates. Recall

---

[33] See Aoki (1988) on various types of monitoring.
[34] On credit rationing, see Stiglitz and Weiss (1981). On delegated monitoring, see Diamond (1984).
[35] The classic signaling model is developed in Spence (1974).

that bank directors could gain seats for themselves and thus appear very obviously in the firms' supervisory board (V2AR connections), but that many bank connections to firms were indirect and involved the joint representation by the same individual in the supervisory boards of both bank and firm (ARAR connections). P. B. Whale warned of this confusion: "Particularly misleading results are obtained when the industrialists sitting on bank Aufsichtsräte are regarded as bank directors and then all their connections represented as ramifications of the banks' interests."[36] Direct representation might be the clearest means of signaling firm value or gaining access to information, but it would not have been the only way. Thus, indirect involvement may still relate to the traditional idea of bank control, or its modern interpretation based on problems of asymmetric information. Joint representatives might have signaled membership in a network of banks and firms that interacted with one another repeatedly. Involvement in such a group might have indicated ex ante firm quality as well as improved access to the consultancy services of knowledgeable bankers. Moreover, indirect representation may have provided conduits for the transmission of information among entrepreneurs and bankers. Thus, it is useful to examine the factors that influence membership in these looser networks as well as the narrower ones.

Expected Coefficients and Results

The monitoring, signaling, and consultancy hypotheses yield a variety of implications about the characteristics of bank-attached firms. These characteristics can then be used as explanatory variables in the multinomial logit model of the bank attachment decision. If bank monitoring provides easier access to external finance, it should lessen firms' need to hold liquid assets in reserve, instead of investing them for greater returns. In addition, less liquid firms may require greater external funding. These same firms may have greater need for the quality signal provided by bank representation. Thus, the monitoring and signaling hypotheses suggest that liquid assets, normalized by total firm assets, should negatively predict bank representation. If such representation were costly, then firms that were growing or planning on growing would be the most likely to purchase such services. Even if bank attachment is seen as a debt-monitoring device imposed by banks, it is likely that affiliated companies would be those wishing to invest. Thus, regardless of the direction of causality between investment and bank attachment, all three hypotheses predict that the sign should be positive. Likewise, a primary goal of bank advice would arguably be to increase market share and thus to

[36] Whale (1930), p. 51.

spur income growth. High rates of income growth may also signal a potential for future investment and thus a need for bank monitoring and signaling services. Thus, income growth, under any of the three theories, should positively predict bank representation. In a related vein, successful consultancy services should yield higher firm profitability and thus a positive relationship. Profitability may also be reflected in dividend-adjusted stock returns for those firms listed on an exchange. Signaling and monitoring offer less clear conclusions about the sign of profits or stock returns.

The signaling and monitoring hypotheses imply possibly conflicting incentives concerning the choice of outside finance. If interlocking directorates were employed primarily to monitor debt, and if such involvement lowered the relative cost of debt for attached firms, then debt/equity ratios should positively predict bank attachment. In contrast, if the purpose of a bank affiliation is to provide a positive signal (or a seal of approval) to the equity markets, then bank-attached firms should favor equity and debt/equity ratios should negatively predict attachment. If both effects exist and have equal weight, then debt/equity ratios may be indistinguishable between attached and independent firms – though attached firms should still grow faster overall than unattached firms. As noted, however, it is difficult to rationalize the usefulness of a signal that can have widely varying interpretations; thus, the two hypotheses may be logically inconsistent.

Firm age may provide further insights, since younger firms have shorter track records and may require more bank services. Signaling is likely to be most fruitful when relevant information is scarce, and debt monitoring and entrepreneurial advice is likely to be needed most when firms are inexperienced and unproven. Thus, young firms likely have the greatest need for bank attachments. Thus, to the extent that reputations can mitigate information or agency problems associated with external finance, firm age should correlate negatively with bank representation.

For the subset of listed firms, stock returns may be included. Given the strong univariate significance of stock market listings, the analysis also includes a binary listing variable. In general, it is often thought that larger firms grow and invest less. If so, firm size may relate negatively with bank relationships. If there are economies of scale in financing, however, then firm size (measured here by total assets) may be expected to correlate positively with attachment to large banks. It is useful, therefore to control for size in estimating other effects. In addition, since bank involvement varies so clearly by branch of industry, the model controls for the sector in which each firm operates. The analysis also controls for possible trends in bank involvement over time.

Table 5.11. *Multinomial Logit Model of Bank Board Membership Type*

	Private Bank	Provincial Bank	Great Bank	Great Bank and Provincial Bank
Total fixed assets (millions)	0.10	0.10	0.07	0.11
	0.64	*0.59*	*0.78*	*0.65*
Number of shares (millions)	**0.39**	0.22	**0.79**	**0.86**
	0.08	*0.31*	**0.00**	**0.01**
Gross investment	−0.00	0.01	**0.03**	−0.00
	0.86	*0.20*	**0.00**	0.85
Debt/equity	−0.09	**0.50**	**0.85**	**1.15**
	0.79	**0.04**	**0.06**	**0.01**
Listed	**1.22**	**0.87**	**1.57**	0.74
	0.00	**0.01**	**0.02**	0.20
Gross profits	1.13	2.70	3.55	**12.94**
	0.63	*0.22*	*0.46*	**0.00**
Age	−0.01	**−0.03**	−0.02	**−0.03**
	0.69	**0.03**	0.43	**0.10**
Income growth	−0.20	**−0.45**	**−1.60**	**−0.99**
	0.45	**0.05**	**0.02**	**0.06**
Financial assets	**−1.77**	−1.16	−0.56	−0.24
	0.05	0.17	0.71	0.92
Trend	−0.01	0.01	0.04	0.04
	0.68	0.53	0.31	0.48
Constant	−1.15	−0.97	**−4.67**	**−5.16**
	0.13	0.18	**0.00**	**0.00**
Observations	1,605			
Wald chi2 (92)	92,173.12			
Prob>chi2	0.00			
Pseudo R2	0.17			
Log likelihood	1,694.75			

Note: The dependent variable, v2ar, takes the value 0 if the firm has no bank directors on its supervisory board, 1 for a private bank, 2 for a provincial bank, 3 for a great bank, and 4 for a combination of provincial and great banks. Models are estimated using the Huber-White sandwich method for estimating robust standard errors and assuming that observations are clustered by firm. Total fixed assets are in millions of marks; gross investment and income growth are in percent; gross profits and financial assets are normalized by total assets. Sectoral indicator variables are included in the model. Italics indicate p-values of t-statistics. Boldface indicates statistical significance of the coefficient estimates.

It is immediately clear, and by now hardly surprising, that the firm characteristics that help explain bank affiliations vary markedly by the type of bank considered (see Table 5.11).[37] This finding, in itself, indicates a lack of general

[37] Table 5.11 reports multinomial logit coefficient estimates, but relative risk ratios – the estimated change in probability of being in the given category due to a one-unit increase in

validity of the traditional hypotheses. Even within specific bank categories, the results demonstrate little support for the three hypotheses. In particular, investment and profits – both of which are expected to predict positively bank board memberships – provide explanatory power for only one bank type each. And income growth, also considered a positive predictor of board memberships, is actually negatively related to all forms of joint-stock bank representation. Among listed firms, dividend-adjusted stock returns are also statistically insignificant.[38] The insignificance of investment and the negative signs on income growth cast doubt on all three hypotheses, while the results for profitability undermine the consultancy hypotheses most specifically.[39] Certain other variables are significant in some cases but not others. For example, financial assets (normalized by total assets) negatively predicts board participation by private banks as anticipated but provides no statistical power for joint-stock bank attachment. Age, also expected to relate negatively to attachment, is significant and negative only for firms attached to provincial banks – either with or without a great-bank director also on board. The sign on debt/equity ratios was more difficult to forecast due to conflicting implications of the hypotheses. Curiously, high levels of debt finance positively predict supervisory board membership by a joint-stock bank, but not for private banks alone. Thus, while it is not a general predictor of attachment, debt finance is clearly one of the more consistent factors.

The level of fixed assets is included as a control variable, and it strongly predicts board membership by all but the provincial banks when the number of shares outstanding is omitted. This latter variable supercedes fixed assets as a valid attachment predictor when the two variables are included simultaneously. While both variables give a sense of firm size, the number of shares also relates to the feasible number of shareholders in the firm and therefore the potential for ownership dispersion. It is not surprising that the largest banks should attract the largest customers, so one would expect that

---

the explanatory variable – can be calculated as the exponential of the given logit coefficient estimates (e^b, where b is the estimated logit coefficient). The dependent variable in the reported model refers to bank directors sitting on firm supervisory boards – the narrow definition of bank affiliation (V2AR).

[38] This model is not reported, since the variable of interest is insignificant, and the other results are qualitatively unaltered. The inclusion of stock returns obviously limits the sample to listed firms, and therefore reduces the number of observations by about two-thirds to three-quarters.

[39] It is not very plausible, given the rest of the results, that bank consultancy services increased profitability of firms with bank attachments, but that those firms started at a lower profit level than unattached firms.

among attached firms, the largest ones affiliate with the great banks and the smaller ones with the provincial banks. It is less clear, however, that size should be closely tied to attachment in general or to the private banks (in most cases much smaller than their joint-stock counterparts) in particular. Ownership dispersion would logically relate to all forms of bank involvement as so-called delegated monitors, and yet the variable is insignificant for provincial-bank firms.

These findings do point out the connection between many of the private bankers appearing in corporate boards and the great banks. As the forerunners, and often founders, of the universal banks, an important subset of private banks was intimately tied to various joint-stock universal banks. Some clearly maintained those links, often sitting on incorporated banks' supervisory boards for many years. The most powerful of the private bankers were likely those associated with the largest banks, primarily the Berlin-centered great banks. Such an explanation for the connection between size and private-bank board memberships therefore hints at the importance of location, personal connections, and prestige – in addition to bank size – in determining which banks gained board memberships. So, for example, though private banks on their own were too small to underwrite securities issues fully for the largest firms, several of them participated in underwriting syndicates with other banks and gained access to corporate boards in this manner.

The findings on size and ownership dispersion therefore lead naturally to the question of stock market listings and the role of universal banks in the securities markets. Stock market listing provides nearly consistent, significant prediction of board membership for all four categories of bank affiliations. The magnitude of the effect does vary depending on the type of bank considered, but the probability of bank board membership increases dramatically with the existence of a stock market listing (see Table 5.12). Controlling for all the other factors included in the multinomial regression analysis permits calculation of adjusted probabilities. The difference between the "listed" and "unlisted" probabilities yields the change in probability of falling into the given bank category when moving from unlisted to listed. For example, unattached firms comprise nearly half (48 percent) of the overall sample of firms, but among unlisted firms that share is 61 percent. After controlling for the multiple factors that relate to interlocking directorates (in Table 5.8), however, the adjusted probability of being independent given that the firm is unlisted is 52 percent. In contrast, listed firms have a 31 percent adjusted probability of being unattached, compared to a 26 percent unadjusted probability. These figures mean that, even when

Table 5.12. *Probabilities of Bank Attachment*

	Overall	Unadjusted		Adjusted	
		Unlisted	Listed	Unlisted	Listed
No banks	0.48	0.61	0.26	0.52	0.31
Private bank	0.19	0.13	0.29	0.15	0.26
Provincial banks	0.21	0.20	0.23	0.19	0.25
Great banks	0.07	0.03	0.13	0.06	0.11
Combined	0.05	0.03	0.09	0.08	0.07

Note: "Unadjusted" refers to the probability of bank affiliation in the given category without controlling for other factors that influence the attachment decision. "Adjusted" refers to the predicted probability of bank affiliation in the given category resulting from the multinomial logit model reported in Table 5.11 – that is, controlling for several other factors expected to influence the attachment decision.

we control for other firm characteristics, the chance of being unattached is 21 percentage points lower for firms with a stock market listing than those without (about a 75 percent reduction in the likelihood of independent status). In contrast, the probability of attachment rises between 3 and 9 percentage points, depending on bank type, when a hypothetical firm changes from unlisted to listed. Given the relatively low likelihood of having a great bank on an unlisted firm's board (about 6 percent, controlling for other factors and excluding those with combined attachment), the increase due to stock market listing represents a near doubling of the probability. In comparison, the adjusted probabilities of private-bank or provincial-bank board membership rise less with listing status, but still increase substantially (15 to 26 percent for private-bank attachment, and 19 to 25 percent for provincial-bank attachment).[40]

The strong significance of listings suggests that bank board memberships were at least partly related to securities issue and trading. Such an explanation is very plausible for a number of reasons. By the end of the nineteenth century, companies wishing to gain admission to a German stock market were subject to several preliminary requirements, not least of which was the stipulation that the firm's share capital be fully paid up.[41] This regulation alone likely necessitated the engagement of a universal bank, and, having

---

[40] The one curiosity is the firms with both great bankers and provincial bankers on their boards. The probability of attachment is actually 1 percentage point lower for listed firms than for unlisted firms (8 percent versus 7 percent).

[41] See Chapter 7 on the stock markets and their place in the overall corporate financial system in Germany.

underwritten the new securities, that bank would have acquired some portion of the issued shares (and sometimes more than the bank could place with investors). Banks often joined forces to underwrite large issues, and larger offerings naturally would have required a greater number of banks in order to keep each individual bank's stake constant. Under such circumstances, firms with the highest share capital would be the most likely to end up with supervisory board representation from large banks and from multiple banks. In addition, universal banks actively engaged in the brokerage business. The extensive trading of securities through the banking system likely provided further opportunities for banks to hold firms' shares. Furthermore, since the universal banks maintained extensive networks of commercial clients, retaining a universal bank may have allowed firms to reap the benefits of network externalities. Bankers not only created their own secondary markets in listed shares, but they also became fully ensconced in the governing bodies of the stock exchanges. As the gatekeepers of the German capital market, therefore, the universal banks gained easy access to a broad range of securities – particularly those that were listed.

Finally, it is also possible that firms made their way into bank networks because they were already listed or about to become so. One line of reasoning runs as follows. Since the Reichsbank accepted as collateral only securities listed at a German bourse, such issues may in turn have been more likely to be accepted as collateral by universal banks.[42] A bank may have then exercised influence in the choice of supervisory board members of the firms whose shares the bank held as collateral, particularly when shares were owned by small, outside stakeholders.

Proxy Voting

The connection between stock market listings and board memberships leads naturally to the issue of proxy voting. Direct ownership of shares accounts for only part of the networking between universal banks and industrial firms. As the first part of this chapter indicates, universal banks owned significant stakes in relatively few firms at this time – quite clearly a smaller set of firms than those on whose supervisory boards they held seats. Bankers must have entered boards by other means, and one important avenue for such bank access is proxy votes – votes entrusted to the bank by the actual owner of the share. Given their involvement with the placement of new issues, their

---

[42] See Engberg (1981).

provision of safe deposit services, and their lending secured by stocks, the universal banks would have been the logical parties to take an investor's proxy votes. Indeed, many investors would have seen the banks' proxy voting as a valuable service.

Unfortunately, it is difficult to test such a hypothesis. It may be possible to provide insights into the matter with the current data, but several assumptions must be made. One argument runs as follows: If small stakeholders felt less compelled to vote their own shares than did those with large stakes, then small shareholders would have been more likely to deposit their shares with and turn over their voting rights to a universal bank. According to this reasoning, closely held firms – firms whose capital was held by a small number of large shareholders – would experience less proxy voting than would widely held firms. As a result, the dispersion of capital ownership may increase the likelihood of accumulation of board seats by universal bankers. The same network of customers who facilitated a firm's securities issues, therefore, may have been the main suppliers of proxy votes to universal banks.

Since firms were not required to report the identities of shareholders or their holdings (in the prewar period), no comprehensive data on ownership structure and proxy voting exist. Data on the number of shares issued are available, and they are used here as a proxy for dispersion of ownership. While it is hardly a perfect measure of dispersion, the number of shares outstanding does offer valuable information. For a given share capital, as the number of shares declines, the value of each share relative to total capital increases. If shares are indivisible, the number of shares outstanding represents the maximum number of shareholders in a firm.[43] Clearly, it is possible that firms with large numbers of shares were closely held, yet firms with relatively few shares outstanding are more likely to have been closely held. In the current sample, share prices fall in a narrow range, regardless of attachment status, and therefore the number of shares issued is highly correlated with total assets, share capital, and net worth (96 to 98 percent). The stock of fixed assets is slightly less highly correlated with the number of shares (90 percent), making it the best available control for firm size. This measure does also correlate positively with private- and great-bank attachment.

---

[43] It may have been possible for several people to own a single share, but I have no evidence for or against such a practice.

Repeating the previous multinomial logit model of narrow attachment but replacing the attachment variable with the broadly defined bank affiliation variable yields completely different results (see Table 5.13). The number of shares outstanding is the only variable that strongly predicts broadly defined bank affiliations of all types.[44] Several other variables (stock market listing, debt/equity ratio, and age) also help explain combined broad attachment, and leverage also correlates positively with broadly defined great-bank association. Beyond industry sector, however, only the number of shares helps predict broad attachment with just a provincial bank. The strong, positive relationship between the number of shares in circulation and broadly defined bank affiliation suggests that ownership dispersion is positively associated with at least loose involvement in a joint-stock bank network. Given the limitations on the data, this is the most compelling evidence available that proxy voting constituted an important factor in the involvement of firms in interlocking directorates with banks.

Clearly, these arguments about proxy voting and ownership structure are largely hypothetical. Because the necessary evidence probably never existed for the prewar period, it is unlikely that we can resolve definitively the remaining uncertainty about the importance of proxy voting.[45] Clearly, the available data point in favor of the role of securities issues, market listings, and proxy voting in the linking of the governing bodies of banks and nonfinancial firms.

Gaining and Losing Bank Board Members

One further approach to uncovering motivations for bank board memberships is to examine the characteristics of switchers – firms that started or ended relationships in the sample period. In general, banking relationships appear to be stable; firms changed status infrequently. But even though fewer than 5 percent of the sampled firm-years gained or lost attachment, the 197 episodes of switching represent 91 different firms or more than one-quarter of the sample. Of 113 incidents of gaining attachments, 94 gained private or provincial bank attachments (46 and 48, respectively).

---

[44] In the broad definition of bank involvement, firms with private bankers only on their boards are considered unattached, since the private banks do not generally have supervisory boards whose members can concurrently sit on firms' supervisory boards.

[45] Having searched unsuccessfully for evidence of ownership structure and proxy voting in Germany, I have become pessimistic about the possibility of finding sufficient data to test the proxy-voting hypothesis in any direct or conclusive manner for the prewar period.

Table 5.13. *Multinomial Logit Model of Broadly Defined Bank Affiliations*

	Provincial Bank	Great Bank	Great Bank and Provincial Bank
Fixed assets	0.11	−0.07	0.24
	0.44	*0.75*	*0.18*
Number of shares (millions)	**0.32**	**0.99**	**0.58**
	0.08	***0.00***	***0.02***
Gross investment	0.00	0.1	0.01
	0.82	*0.24*	*0.36*
Debt/equity	−0.08	**0.93**	0.70
	0.78	***0.00***	*0.04*
Listed	0.29	−0.19	0.84
	0.27	*0.71*	*0.08*
Gross profits	−2.92	5.85	2.34
	0.16	*0.46*	*0.53*
Age	0.00	0.03	**0.05**
	0.69	*0.21*	***0.01***
Income growth	−0.07	−0.37	0.01
	0.78	*0.54*	*0.97*
Financial assets	0.85	−1.72	0.44
	0.27	*0.33*	*0.76*
Trend	**−0.04**	−0.06	−0.02
	0.05	*0.22*	*0.50*
Sectors			
Machinery, metalworking	−0.20	0.12	0.21
	0.75	*0.92*	*0.79*
Printing, woodworking	−0.56	0.17	0.40
	0.43	*0.90*	*0.67*
Rail transport	**−1.78**	−0.03	−0.59
	0.02	*0.99*	*0.63*
Ship transport	−0.24	−0.83	−0.89
	0.75	*0.52*	*0.43*
Electrical	0.24	**−35.43**	1.82
	0.84	***0.00***	*0.25*
Gas, petroleum	−1.25	0.86	−1.25
	0.23	*0.49*	*0.53*
Water	−0.55	**−35.39**	**−34.54**
	0.66	***0.00***	***0.00***
Chemicals	−0.13	0.40	0.79
	0.85	*0.73*	*0.31*
Stones, cement, earthenware	0.02	**−35.19**	−2.27
	0.97	***0.00***	*0.14*
Textiles	**−1.76**	−0.77	−0.27
	0.02	*0.59*	*0.78*

	Provincial Bank	Great Bank	Great Bank and Provincial Bank
Food processing, milling	−0.96	**−35.64**	−0.82
	0.17	*0.00*	*0.44*
Brewing	−0.61	−2.94	**−1.82**
	0.30	*0.05*	*0.02*
Schools, charities	0.02	**−34.97**	1.99
	0.98	*0.00*	*0.11*
Hospitality, entertainment	−0.84	**−36.48**	0.87
	0.35	*0.00*	*0.50*
Constant	−0.44	**−4.28**	**−4.53**
	0.49	*0.00*	*0.00*
Observations	1605		
Wald chi2	39,322.15		
p > chi2	0.00		
Pseudo R2	0.152		
Log likelihood	1,341.26		

Note: The dependent variable, ARAR, takes the value 0 if the firm has no private-bank directors or only private-bank directors on its supervisory board, 2 if it is a provincial bank, 3 if it is a great bank, and 4 if it is a combination of provincial and great banks. Models are estimated using the Huber-White sandwich method for estimating robust standard errors and assuming that observations are clustered by firm. Fixed assets are in millions of marks; gross investment and income growth are in percent; and gross profits and financial assets are normalized by total assets. The excluded sector is mining and smelting. Italics indicates p-values of t-statistics. Boldface indicates statistical significance of the coefficient estimates.

The multinomial logit model uses a three-choice indicator as the dependent variable, taking the values 1 for firms that lost their bank affiliation, 1 for firms that gained a bank affiliation, and 0 for firms that made no change. In other words, the variable does not register changes from one attachment type to another. Since this variable can also be seen as ordinal, the model is also analyzed using ordered logit. The findings thus far suggest that ownership structure and stock market activities relate closely to the positioning of bankers on company boards. The results provide additional support for the previous findings (see Table 5.14). For example, share capital growth and acquisition of a stock market listing relate negatively to losing a bank attachment. In addition, share capital expansion and growth in the number of shares issued are positively associated with gaining a bank attachment. The ordered model yields similar results. In other words, capital market operations appear as significant factors in decisions about bank

Table 5.14. *Multinomial Logit Analysis of Change in Attachment Status*

Change in Attachment Status	Multinomial Logit		Ordered Logit
Lose bank director			
Income growth	**0.02**	**0.02**	
	0.00	*0.00*	
Share capital growth	**−1.26**	**−1.48**	
	0.00	*0.06*	
Age	**−0.03**	**−0.03**	
	0.02	*0.01*	
Trend	0.01	0.01	
	0.59	*0.69*	
Change in listing status		**−0.62**	
		0.00	
Growth of number of shares		0.71	
		0.63	
Constant	**−4.22**	**−4.50**	
	0.00	*0.00*	
Gain bank director			
Income growth	−0.05	−0.06	**−0.02**
	0.49	*0.59*	*0.00*
Share capital growth	0.40	0.29	**0.43**
	0.16	*0.38*	*0.06*
Age	0.00	0.00	**0.01**
	0.64	*0.57*	*0.01*
Trend	**−0.17**	**−0.17**	**−0.10**
	0.00	*0.00*	*0.00*
Change in listing status		−0.41	0.01
		0.56	*0.98*
Growth of number of shares		**1.75**	1.04
		0.10	*0.24*
Constant	**−2.98**	**−2.97**	
	0.00	*0.00*	
Number of observations	4,288	4,085	4,085
Wald chi2	18,331.28	20,354.18	83.05
Prob > chi2	0.00	0.00	0.00
Pseudo R2	0.07	0.07	0.03
Log likelihood	−768.97	−724.87	−753.53

Note: The dependent variable takes the value −1 if the firm had a bank director in the previous period but not in the given period, 1 if the firm had no bank director in the previous period but did in the given period, and 0 if there was no change in the firm's status. The final column eliminates thirty-seven observations with extreme rates of growth in the number of shares (exceeding 100 percent). Italics indicates p-values of t-statistics. Boldface indicates statistical significance of the coefficient estimates.

relationships – whether to keep an existing relationship or to acquire a bank board member anew.

Other factors are also significant. Interestingly, growing income is associated with loss of bank attachment, and age is negatively related to losing bank attachment. In the ordered model, these results translate into a negative relationship between income growth and attachment change and a positive relationship between age and attachment change. Thus, firms that eliminated bankers from their boards tended to perform well. At the same time, older firms were less likely to shed attachment. The two effects may be connected, given the slight negative correlation between age and income growth. Finally, trend is negatively related to gaining a bank board member. So, the slight expansion in board positions that emerged in the earlier results is apparently explained by changes in firm characteristics. This is a particularly interesting result, as it clarifies the cause for the seeming trend toward more bank attachment.

CHAPTER SUMMARY AND CONCLUSIONS

This chapter has provided a wide-ranging account of German corporate governance relationships in the two decades preceding World War I. The discussion raises several key points that will be useful to bear in mind in reading succeeding chapters. Most fundamental, universal banks owned few stakes in nonfinancial firms, particularly after the major industrialization push of the 1870s. Equity stakes comprised a small part of bank portfolios, and constituted a minor portion of total corporate capital at the time. Corporate governance institutions, executive and supervisory boards, remained quite underdeveloped in Germany until the last quarter of the nineteenth century. Boards were generally small and grew little over the prewar period.

The universal banks had a significant but not overwhelming presence in the governance of German corporations during this period of rapid heavy industrialization and economic expansion. These bank affiliations appear to have arisen largely out of the banks' close involvement with securities markets. The combination of commercial, investment, and brokerage services within individual banking institutions may have perpetuated the networking of bank and firm supervisory boards through the practice of depositing equity shares at one's bank and transferring the associated proxy votes to that bank. In addition, attachments are associated with firm size and with industrial sector.

The findings in this chapter therefore suggest only spotty empirical support for traditional explanations of German bank–firm relationships that focus on banks' intervention in or advising on investment decisions, direct monitoring of debt contracts, or even the signaling of quality in equity markets. Thus, we must also systematically reconsider the impact of formalized banking relationships on firms' financing and performance.

6

Firm Financing and Performance

The historical and theoretical literature offers many hypotheses about the potential advantages of corporate banking systems that provide a wide range of services and build formal relationships with clients.[1] The historical literature on Germany places particular emphasis on the representation of bankers in corporate supervisory boards, and the theoretical literature rationalizes such relationships. Indeed, from a theoretical perspective, the existence of relationship banking may affect firm financing in myriad ways. The preceding two chapters, however, raise a number of doubts about both the traditional emphasis on formalized banking relationships and some of the theoretical explanations for these links. Bank board memberships could not have been prevalent until the last quarter of the nineteenth century, when the joint-stock form (and therefore the institution of the supervisory board) began to spread. Informal precursors to interlocking directorates, while possibly important, are neither unique to the German system nor traceable in any comprehensive or quantitative way. Even once interlocking directorates became more common, the majority of firms had no representation from the joint-stock universal banks, and the largest of those banks – the great banks – were nearly absent from many sectors of the economy. In addition, the reasons typically proffered for the formation of bank relationships – especially those having to do with monitoring debt, signaling firm quality, or providing consultancy services – find little support in the historical record.

If the causes of interlocking directorates differ from the received wisdom, perhaps the consequences do as well. Thus, the findings in earlier chapters raise additional questions about the impact of formalized banking

---

[1] I discuss the historical literature in Chapter 2 and the theoretical literature in Chapter 3.

relationships in the later stages of industrialization, once banks and firms had built up their governance networks. Inspired by the modern corporate finance literature, therefore, the current chapter focuses on six broad areas of possible influence: access to and costs of capital, firm capital structure, credit rationing and liquidity constraints, rates of growth in industry, firm survival, and managerial turnover. These issues represent some of the most critical factors in the functioning of a corporate financing system and therefore bear directly on industrial investment and performance. Investment provides the seeds of industrial growth, which, in turn, fuels economic growth and prosperity. The greater the returns to investment, the greater the financial benefit to investors. To invest and grow rapidly, however, most firms need at least some outside financing. Corporate finance theory suggests that information asymmetries and conflicts of interest systematically influence firms' investment and financing decisions. For example, conflicts between debt and equity holders may alter the relative extent of debt and equity financing used by firms as well as the balance between bank debt and bonds. Different forms of finance present varying costs to the firm, affecting returns to investment and possibly the decision to invest at all. Firm capital structure may reveal information about the presence of information asymmetry and conflicts of interest, and therefore also allows clearer insights into the costs of finance as well as potential financial constraints faced by individual firms and the economy as a whole.

Institutions that facilitate access to information about firms or ameliorate conflicts may temper the problems that lead to inefficient financing decisions. The older historical literature depicts Germany's joint-stock universal banks as such an institution, under the assumption that they resolved problems of moral hazard (for example, improper or suboptimal use of funds) on the part of firms as well as conflicts of interest between equity and debt holders. It is also plausible, at least on the surface, that the German system's integration of universal and relationship-based corporate finance may have given some firms greater access to external finance and may have altered their decisions (perhaps even unwillingly) about the various sources of funds to tap as they grew and matured. At the same time, a significant strand of the historical literature has continually probed the less desirable side of banking relationships – emphasizing excessive control, abuses of power, and anticompetitive behavior. This *bankenmacht* debate raises the possibility that formal banking relationships forced firms into decisions they would not have otherwise made and that may even have been deleterious to firm performance.

In fact, the results here lead to quite different conclusions. Given the results of the previous chapters, it should be unsurprising to find that the empirical evidence continues to cast doubt on certain hypotheses and suppositions that stem from the orthodox paradigm of German universal banking. Indeed, this chapter shows that formal bank involvement alters firms' decisions in no systematic, theoretically predicted way. To be sure, banks influenced some firms some of the time, perhaps even in extreme ways. The point here, however, is that such influence was too uneven to turn up general patterns of consistently different behavior in a large, randomly chosen group of firms. Thus, we cannot infer a significant or definitive role for formal bank relationships in resolving information problems or conflicts.

ACCESS TO FINANCE AND COSTS OF CAPITAL

Firms finance their activities in several ways, ranging from plowed-back earnings to bank funding to debt and equity securities of various types. While new instruments have certainly been developed in the past century, the primary methods of financing appeared before or during the industrialization period. As noted in Chapter 2, some methods were developed for one purpose, such as government debt or commercial trade credit, and then adapted and applied to joint-stock companies in industrial sectors. The pecking-order hypothesis, described in Chapter 3, provides a theoretical motivation for the different choices firms make in financing their activities. Information asymmetries about firms' prospects and performance account for most of the hypothetical cost differential among financing instruments. The more sensitive the investors' return is to unobservable firm information, the more the firm must pay to acquire the funding. Outside funding also usually brings nonpecuniary costs, such as dilution of control or constraints on owners' or managers' decision making. As a result, internal sources of funds, whether the resources of insider owners or cash flows from operations, typically comprise the cheapest and therefore most prevalent source of capital for small and emerging firms. Even more advanced firms with easy access to capital markets may prefer internal finance, depending on their assessment of the various costs involved.

Overall, German corporations maintained relatively high stocks of financial assets, much of which could be easily marketed to provide liquid capital. Total financial assets averaged between 20 and 30 percent of firm assets between 1895 and 1912, the great majority of which took the form of liquid assets (cash and bank deposits) and receivables. On average, firms held only 4 to 6 percent of assets in the form of securities. All financial assets followed a noticeable upward trend relative to total assets, particularly in the prosperous years after 1901. Cash flows are harder to measure precisely with historical accounting data, since the level of aggregation varies substantially from firm to firm. Gross profits less dividend payments provide a close substitute for cash flow, and that measure yields sample averages between 0.5 percent and slightly more than 5 percent of total firm assets throughout the period.

Debt funding, particularly through banks, is often perceived as the most important type of external capital for German firms, both historically and more recently. The universal banks provided short-term capital through bills of exchange and very short maturity loans. Universal banks usually included call money (*täglisches Geld*) under the more general heading of Lombards and reports.[2] The universal banks are widely believed to have offered significant medium- and even long-term credit through their current account lending. Thus, despite the ostensibly short maturity of these loans, they may have actually been quite illiquid. The banks collateralized their loans primarily with bills of exchange and securities, but also made many unsecured loans.[3] Short-term debt also came from other firms and included advances on goods from suppliers. Short maturity financing grew from 9 percent of liabilities on average in 1895 to 16 percent in 1912. German corporations also accessed a range of longer-term debt, including various types of bonds and loans. Long-term loans primarily comprised mortgage loans for real estate purchases, frequently funded through mortgage banks (*Hypothekenbanken*) rather than universal banks. Long-term loans and bonds averaged between 15 and 18 percent of total liabilities between 1895 and 1912.

The cost of debt finance varied quite a bit over the industrialization period. Estimated nominal current account rates ranged between 5 and 8 percent and trended up, albeit with great variability, from 1895 to 1913 (see Figure 6.1a). But since inflation rates fluctuated widely during this time, real interest rates were highly volatile. While the largest swings followed the great foundation boom of the 1870s, firms still faced large year-to-year changes in their real interest rates throughout the period. Real rates fell below 1 percent – notably still positive – in the most inflationary years, but they increased to 8 and even 10 percent in the deflationary years of the early 1890s, 1903, and 1908. In contrast to the U.K., where nominal loan rates ranged between 2 and 5 percent during the same time, Germans paid dearly for debt. The German rates are more in line with the U.S. rates of the time, typically in the upper 5 to low 6 percent range (see Figure 6.1b). Similar comparative

---

[2] See Chapter 4 for additional discussion of the banks' loan and asset types.
[3] See Riesser (1910 [1911]) for details of the specific conditions on Lombard loans made by one of the great banks, Berliner Handelsgesellschaft. Also see Weber (1915) on both Germany and Britain.

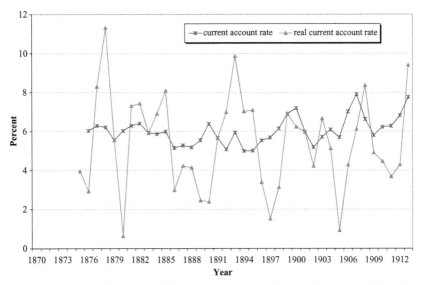

Figure 6.1a. Nominal versus Real Current Account Loan Rates in Germany, 1870–1913. *Note:* See discussion in the text.

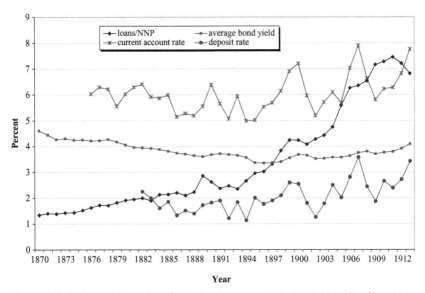

Figure 6.1b. Price and Quantity of Debt in Germany, 1870–1913. *Note:* See discussion in the text.

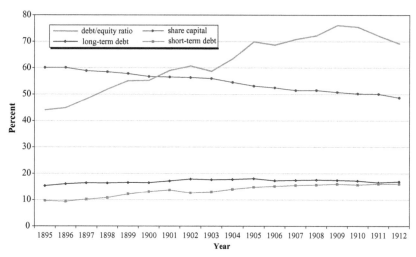

Figure 6.2. Average Liability Shares and Debt/Equity Ratios of German Corporations, 1895–1912. *Note:* See discussion in the text.

patterns among the three countries emerge for bond rates of various types.[4]

The use of debt is perhaps most relevantly evaluated relative to the available alternatives, primarily internally generated funds or equity shares. Naturally, all of the firms considered in the current database are joint-stock firms and therefore funded some portion of their activities with equity shares. Equity could take the form of ordinary shares (*Stammaktien*), preferred shares (*Vorzugsaktien*), or sometimes a hybrid (*Prioritäts-stammaktien*). Some older mining firms issued shares known as *Kuxen*, and *Kommanditgesellschaften auf Aktien* issued equity shares with slightly different rights from normal joint-stock companies. The vast majority of share companies were *Aktiengesellschaften* with mostly ordinary shares. Indeed, nearly all shares issued were ordinary shares, and only 15 percent of firms issued any preference shares in this period. As the previous chapter described, equity shares and the markets in which they traded played an important role in the financing of German corporations. And despite the perception that German firms have typically depended heavily on debt financing, the debt/equity ratios of corporate firms averaged between 44 and 76 percent over the period (see Figure 6.2). Thus, net worth, the majority of which was

---

[4] See Fohlin (2000c) and sources cited there on the banking industries of the United States, the U.K., and Germany between 1880 and 1920.

share capital, comprised two-thirds to three-quarters of total liabilities in the period studied here.

CAPITAL STRUCTURE AND FINANCING DECISIONS

The choice of financing instrument is one of the most obvious arenas in which banking relationships might have influenced firms' decision making. The historical and theoretical literature motivates the following set of hypotheses to be tested[5]:

1. Firms with banking relationships, formalized through board memberships, used more debt than independent firms. Moreover, higher leverage arose mainly in the form of short-term debt (predominantly from banks). Banks may have gained access to board seats in return for funding new projects or younger firms for which sufficient equity funding may have been difficult to find (the venture capital role). Less plausibly, the banks may have used their existing votes to force overborrowing in order to earn more interest from attached firms.

2. Leverage, and particularly bank debt, declined as firms aged. The corporate finance literature suggests that firms' choices about financing sources may change as firms mature. Young firms may have too short a track record to convince relatively less-informed outside investors to purchase shares. If so, these newer firms may be more dependent on banks to provide funding. As more information becomes available, though, a firm should find a larger set of attractive financing options. On the whole, firms should gain greater access to securities markets and use less bank debt as they mature.

3. Bank-attached firms decreased their leverage – primarily reducing bank debt – faster than independents. This effect would appear if information asymmetries that produce the pecking order are resolved faster for attached firms than for independents. This dynamic impact implicitly assumes that bank board memberships require some period of time to take effect. In other words, a firm's information problems do not disappear immediately upon placing a banker on the supervisory board. The hypothesized decline in leverage might be all the greater, since banks stood to gain from underwriting fees, commissions, and issuing spreads on stocks.

---

[5] These literatures are surveyed at length in Chapters 2 and 3, respectively.

If the venture capital function or lending motivation of banks dominates, then the first hypothesis will prove correct. That is, a strong connection between formal bank relationships and a bank's provision of funds should reveal itself in a tendency toward high leverage, particularly short-term debt, for bank-affiliated firms. Similarly, if lack of information inhibited access to equity markets, and if age (years since initial public offering) relates positively to information availability or transparency, then the second hypothesis will hold. If banks removed barriers to equity markets, then the third proposition should hold as well.

Clearly, hypotheses one and three partially countervail each other. They remain mutually consistent, if bank-affiliated firms carry particularly high leverage when young but transition faster than average to lower leverage. In other words, the first hypothesis relates to levels, while the third relates to rates of change over time. As discussed in Chapter 5, however, universal banks may have gained many of their supervisory board positions as a result of equity underwriting, since the banks often captured voting rights as a consequence of their indirect (proxy) and direct (usually temporary) equity stakes. If so, no unusual pattern of decline in leverage would appear for affiliated firms, but static comparisons might reveal high levels of equity finance for some bank-attached firms. In this case, mean leverage may not differ significantly depending on attachment status, but distributions of leverage ratios may vary between the two populations. In particular, firms with bankers on their boards may fall at the two ends of the overall leverage spectrum and therefore exhibit a bimodal leverage distribution. The remaining, unattached firms, would then naturally cluster toward the middle.

If the lending and issuing motivations of universal banks exactly offset each other for all firms, or if bank relationships do not consistently affect either lending or issuing decisions, then hypotheses one and three should prove false. Hypothesis two should still hold, assuming that asymmetric information models apply in general. Note that the three hypotheses are all phrased as correlations, since the qualitative literature proposes bidirectional causal links.

Testing Capital Structure Theories

Theoretical models of capital structure decisions provide the framework for testing these three hypotheses. The literature also suggests several particular firm characteristics that, if related to leverage, either support or undermine the theories.[6] First, tangibility of assets (fixed divided by total assets) proxies

---

[6] See Harris and Raviv (1991) and Rajan and Zingales (1995).

for the availability of collateralizable assets. In the theoretical literature, the existence of liquifiable assets makes banks and bondholders more willing to provide credit, and associates positively with leverage. Second, because larger firms tend to be more highly diversified and therefore present lower risks of bankruptcy than small ones, firm size (natural log of income) may relate positively to leverage.[7] If size reduces the investigation costs of debt, then conflicts of interest between debt and equity holders will be mitigated in larger firms, and debt may be preferred. However, to the extent that size proxies for availability and transparency of information about the firm or for the company's reputation in equity markets – and thus the firm's ability to access additional equity financing – the size effect may be smaller or even turn negative. A third factor, free cash flow, may also influence capital structure, but available theories yield conflicting results. On the one hand, cash flow may increase banks' desire to lend to a firm, thereby producing a positive correlation with leverage; on the other hand, free cash flow may result from a lack of debt, indicating a negative connection. Either way, the analysis should control for this characteristic when searching for other relationships. Leverage may also relate to a fourth factor, equity share price. Market-to-book value of equity is often used to measure the quality of investment prospects, and under some theories strong growth opportunities are hypothesized to relate negatively to leverage. At the same time, though, market-to-book value may relate to a firm's reputation in equity markets, and strong past performance may encourage share issuing rather than debt financing. Thus, the underlying reason for the negative correlation is ambiguous.[8]

These effects may appear both in the makeup of debt and in the overall debt/equity ratio. Moreover, firm characteristics and bank relationships may influence both the static structure of firms' liabilities or changes in that structure over time. Thus, empirical analysis investigates a range of possible models, and uncovers several consistent patterns (see Tables 6.1 and 6.2). First, while debt overall is positively associated with tangibility of assets, short-term debt is negatively related. At the same time, tangibility of assets tends to predict declining leverage overall but no change in short-term debt ratios. Thus, it appears that tangible collateral was not generally a limiting factor in the provision of short-maturity financing. This finding would not be surprising, given the typical use of short-term funds as a means of bridging gaps between production costs and sales receipts. Yet many economic historians have suggested that short-term credits from the universal banks

---

[7] The literature tends to use income to measure size. Income is highly correlated with total assets in the current sample. Using natural logarithms helps control heteroskedasticity.

[8] Bossaerts and Fohlin (2000) find that market-to-book ratio relates positively to stock value.

Table 6.1. *Correlates of Firm Leverage*

Variable	Leverage (Outliers Removed)	Leverage	Leverage (Outliers Removed)	Debt Maturity	Short-Term Debt Ratio (Outliers Removed)
Fixed assets/total assets	0.25	0.52	0.34	−0.36	−0.06
	0.05	*0.00*	*0.00*	*0.00*	*0.01*
Natural log of income	0.05	0.03	0.07	−0.02	0.02
	0.07	*0.20*	*0.00*	*0.11*	*0.00*
Net profits/total assets	−1.85	−0.08	−2.10	0.05	−0.63
	0.00	*0.22*	*0.00*	*0.60*	*0.00*
Market-to-face value of shares	−0.06	–	–	–	–
	0.04				
Age of firm	−0.004	−0.01	−0.01	0.00	−0.002
	0.15	*0.00*	*0.00*	*0.52*	*0.01*
Trend	0.01	0.02	0.02	0.00	0.004
	0.00	*0.00*	*0.00*	*0.29*	*0.00*
Listed on Berlin stock exchange	–	−0.11	−0.11	−0.06	−0.04
		0.08	*0.03*	*0.07*	*0.02*
Constant	0.10	0.09	0.00	0.80	0.06
	0.57	*0.50*	*0.99*	*0.00*	*0.06*
P(chi-squared statistic)	0.00	0.00	0.00	0.00	0.00
Number of firms/ observations	99 1,240	321 4,668	320 4,547	320 4,458	320 4,582

Notes: Leverage is the ratio of book values of debt to equity. Debt maturity is short-term debt divided by total debt. Short-term debt ratio is short-term debt divided by total assets. Estimated standard errors are semirobust. P-values of t-statistics (two-sided tests) are given in italics. Where indicated, outliers are removed using the Hadi multivariate outlier test at the $p = 0.05$ level. Age of firm is number of years since registration as a joint-stock company. The listing variable takes the value 1 for true and 0 for false.

were often rolled over for many periods and actually financed longer-term fixed investments. If so, such lending would be inherently riskier than, for example, trade credits. To the extent that short-term lending provides the lender with greater control over funds, a negative relationship between tangible assets and short-term debt makes sense. That is, firms with fewer tangible assets may have turned to short-term credit rather than bonds. The dynamic effect seems to indicate that firms with a lot of tangible assets, and typically high leverage, sought to alleviate the debt burden. Examining the relationship between fixed assets and share capital growth, however, shows that tangibility also relates negatively with changes in equity. Thus,

Table 6.2. *Correlates of Changes in Capital Structure*

Variable	Leverage	Debt Maturity	Short-Term Debt Ratio	Share Capital Growth	Discrete Share Capital Change
Fixed assets/	−0.10	0.03	0.06	−0.03	−0.32
total assets	*0.00*	*0.26*	*0.15*	*0.02*	*0.35*
Natural log of	0.02	0.02	0.02	0.01	0.30
income	*0.00*	*0.00*	*0.00*	*0.05*	*0.00*
Net profits/	−0.86	−0.23	−0.28	0.01	0.13
total assets	*0.00*	*0.12*	*0.10*	*0.46*	*0.29*
Age of firm	−0.001	−0.001	−0.001	−0.00	−0.02
	0.10	*0.03*	*0.05*	*0.39*	*0.01*
Trend	−0.00	0.003	0.00	−0.002	−0.03
	0.36	*0.06*	*0.55*	*0.00*	*0.02*
Listed on Berlin	−0.03	−0.04	−0.05	0.01	0.43
stock exchange	*0.10*	*0.01*	*0.01*	*0.25*	*0.00*
Constant	0.06	−0.10	0.04	0.03	−
	0.12	*0.01*	*0.51*	*0.12*	
P(chi-squared statistic)	0.00	0.00	0.00	0.00	0.00
Number of firms/	319	315	318	320	320
observations	4,040	3,836	3,867	4,381	4,381

Notes: Leverage is the ratio of book values of debt to equity. Debt maturity is short-term debt divided by total debt. Short-term debt ratio is short-term debt divided by total assets. Dependent variables are calculated as the percentage growth in the given variable over the preceding year. The discrete variable for share capital change takes the values −1 for a reduction, 0 for no change, and 1 for an increase. That model is estimated using ordered logit. The listing variable takes the value 1 for true and 0 for false. Age of firm is number of years since registration as a joint-stock company. Estimated standard errors are semirobust. P-values of t-statistics (two-sided tests) are given in italics below coefficient estimates. The first three columns exclude outlier observations according to the Hadi multivariate test (p = 0.05). Leverage outliers = 168. Debt maturity outliers = 139 (1 whole firm). Short-term debt ratio outliers = 131 (1 whole firm).

these firms were less likely to take out either new debt or new equity. Not surprisingly, debt decreased faster or increased even less than equity.

Both levels and growth rates of leverage relate positively to size, supporting the idea that larger, more diversified firms pose less bankruptcy risk to lenders. Thus, the fact that short-term debt is also higher relative to total liabilities for larger firms – and grows faster – suggests that large size (measured by income) of an enterprise offsets some of the risk associated with lending to low-collateral firms. Large, or high-income, firms are also more likely to issue equity and to do so at a faster rate than smaller firms. Still, in net, large firms prefer debt, supporting the idea that conflicts of interest are mitigated. But they also appear to access more equity capital, indicating that the reputation or information availability effect is also important.

In general, age relates negatively to both debt and equity use, but the effect is stronger for debt than for equity. That is, age is also associated with lower leverage and short-term debt ratios as well as with lower growth rates of all three debt ratios. While the static trade-off between short-term and long-term debt appears essentially constant over the firm lifecycle, the growth of short- relative to long-term debt diminishes with age. Short-term debt relative to total liabilities relates weakly to age as well. Older firms are also less likely to float new issues of shares, but equity capital appears to grow independently of age. These results generally support the pecking-order hypothesis, assuming that age proxies for information availability and transparency. But the results are not completely in accordance with the theory. Most capital structure theories based on asymmetric information differentiate sharply between bank debt and bonds. Pecking-order theories in particular indicate that bank debt is the first line of funding and is usually deemphasized as firms create a track record. Thus, the firms sampled here clearly follow the expected pattern for debt versus equity, but do so less obviously in choosing between the two maturity categories of debt.

The analysis also allows insight into the key role that stock exchange listings played in firms' financing choices. Firms with Berlin listings carried significantly lower leverage than unlisted firms and also tended to have lower ratios of short- to long-term debt than did unlisted firms. These firms increased their debt ratios less than unlisted firms, at least in part because they were much more likely to raise equity. Moreover, from a statistical standpoint, listing on the Berlin exchange provides one of the strongest predictors of all of the capital structure variables – the three debt ratios and their growth rates on the one hand (negative), and the likelihood of issuing equity shares on the other (positive). All of these findings underscore the potential information and liquidity benefits of stock markets. Requirements imposed on firms wishing to list shares likely improve investor confidence and facilitate placement among relatively uninformed outside investors. Market size and liquidity expand the possibilities for secondary trading and therefore attract investors. It is quite natural that firms with the most share capital or securitized debt would be the most likely to seek outside investors and therefore benefit from listing. The findings also differentiate between Berlin and the provincial markets: Listing outside of Berlin is mostly insignificant in the econometric models. While there were surely a few other

Table 6.3. *Debt Ratios by Bank-Attachment Category*

Percentile	No. of Banks	Private Banks	Provincial Banks	Great Banks	Combined
Leverage (debt/net worth)					
1	0.00	0.00	0.00	0.00	0.01
5	0.00	0.00	0.03	0.06	0.04
10	0.01	0.03	0.09	0.14	0.06
25	0.13	0.15	0.25	0.26	0.22
50	0.41	0.39	0.53	0.48	0.44
75	0.79	0.67	1.02	0.82	0.79
90	1.43	1.10	1.54	1.70	1.37
95	1.81	1.40	2.09	2.26	1.52
99	3.37	2.30	5.42	4.03	2.43
Mean	0.61	0.51	0.77	0.73	0.59
Std. dev.	0.80	0.53	0.96	0.77	0.60
Debt maturity (short-term/long-term debt)					
1	0.00	0.00	0.00	0.00	0.00
5	0.00	0.01	0.02	0.02	0.02
10	0.02	0.02	0.05	0.06	0.05
25	0.15	0.12	0.20	0.16	0.14
50	0.49	0.33	0.47	0.50	0.41
75	1.00	0.75	0.78	0.86	0.93
90	1.00	1.00	1.00	1.00	1.00
95	1.00	1.00	1.00	1.00	1.00
99	1.00	1.00	1.00	1.00	1.00
Mean	0.53	0.43	0.50	0.51	0.48
Std. dev.	0.39	0.36	0.34	0.35	0.37
Short-term debt ratio (short-term debt/total liabilities)					
1	0.00	0.00	0.00	0.00	0.00
5	0.00	0.00	0.00	0.00	0.00
10	0.00	0.00	0.01	0.01	0.01
25	0.02	0.01	0.04	0.03	0.03
50	0.09	0.07	0.12	0.12	0.08
75	0.22	0.15	0.24	0.27	0.21
90	0.35	0.24	0.38	0.46	0.35
95	0.43	0.32	0.47	0.62	0.53
99	0.59	0.53	0.82	0.70	0.62
Mean	0.14	0.10	0.16	0.18	0.14
Std. dev.	0.14	0.11	0.16	0.18	0.16

important markets, such as Frankfurt or Hamburg, the findings speak to the dominance of the capital city's market in the prewar era.

Impact of Banking Relationships

The historical literature places much emphasis on the influence of banking relationships on the financing of industrial corporations. If prevalent, this influence should appear in the choices firms make about funding sources. It is useful to begin with a simple comparison of means and leverage distributions in order to appreciate the impact of the control variables in a multivariate analysis. The previous chapter already noted that mean leverage varies little across bank-attachment category, but that the variable provides some positive prediction of bank board memberships by some types of universal banks (see Table 6.3). Debt ratios vary significantly among firms, yet there is no obvious ordering of the ratios depending on the type of bank sitting on company boards (see Figures 6.3 through 6.5). For example, firms with provincial-bank attachment fall at the high end of the leverage spectrum, while those with private-bank attachments fall at the low end. And firms with no bank directors on their boards have leverage ratios in the same range as those with both provincial and great bankers on board. A similar lack of consistency appears for the two short-term debt ratios. Unattached firms have higher median short-term debt than many bank-attached firms, but they fall in the middle of the distribution overall.

Unlike the other two ratios, debt maturity (short-term debt/total debt) appears to follow a bimodal distribution. This phenomenon probably results from the lumpy nature of bond debt. Some firms use little or no bond debt, making their debt maturity ratio very high and producing a concentration of firms in the 80 to 100 percent range. Firms that do use bond debt have low maturity ratios in the first years following an issue, particularly if they use some of the bond issue to pay off shorter-term debt, but typically amortize the bonds over time. These firms create the bulge in the distribution around 5 to 20 percent. In the middle is a large range of debt maturity ratios over which firms appear in declining percentages. Again, the various subcategories follow little discernable pattern, but in this case there is one noticeable anomaly for the firms with no bank attachments. These firms fall disproportionately at the very high end of the maturity spectrum. In other words, far more unattached firms use little or no bond debt than do attached firms. At the low end of the distribution, however, there is at least as high a concentration of bond users among independent firms as there is among firms with joint-stock banks on their boards. Interestingly, firms

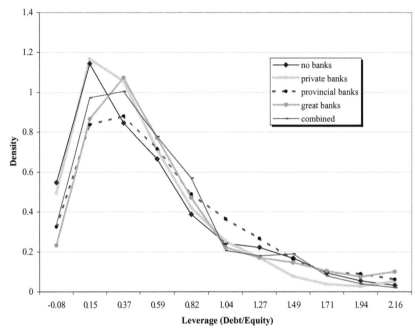

Figure 6.3. Kernel Density Estimates of Leverage by Bank-Attachment Status. *Note:* Combined attachment means the presence of at least one great bank and at least one provincial bank in the company's supervisory board.

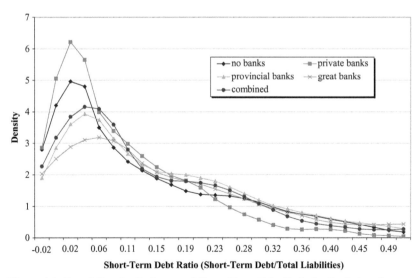

Figure 6.4. Kernel Density Estimates of Short-Term Debt Ratio by Bank-Attachment Status.

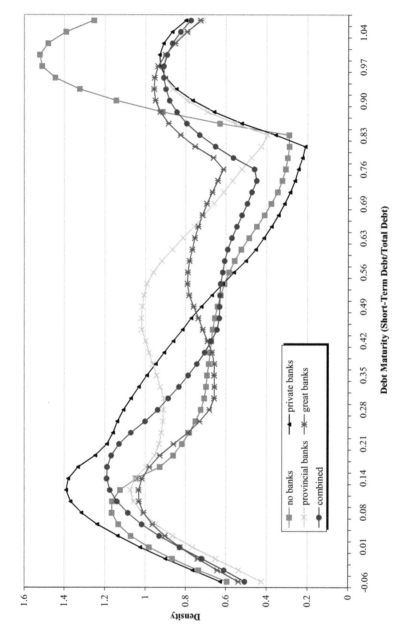

Figure 6.5. Kernel Density Estimates of Debt Maturity by Bank-Attachment Status.

with private-bank links held the least short-term debt, relative to both total debt and total liabilities, as well as the least debt overall. These findings add to the evidence in Chapter 5 indicating that private-bank affiliations differ substantively from joint-stock bank affiliations.

While the figures are useful for gaining an idea of capital structure differences within the firm population, it is important to acknowledge the other characteristics that influence financing decisions. The econometric models reported here consider all bank-attached firms together, so the variations among subpopulations are not apparent. The theoretical literature, however, offers no motivation for disaggregating bank attachment or for including certain types of attached firms with the independents. Given the apparent differences among bank-attachment categories, we might expect to find no significant impact of bank relationships overall. In fact, the multivariate analysis indicates that bank relationships do have some systematic connection with capital structure choices, but the effects run counter to the debt-monitoring hypothesis laid out previously.

Bank oversight actually relates negatively to static leverage and short-term debt ratios, so controlling for other factors, firms with bank attachments are not more likely to use debt. This result at first seems to conflict with the finding in the previous chapter that leverage positively predicts bank attachment. That finding, however, probably stems from the fact that listed firms have generally lower leverage and bank-attached firms are much more likely to be listed. Putting these facts together suggests that leverage is high for bank-attached firms, controlling for the fact that attached firms are more likely to have a listing – not that attached firms have particularly high leverage in the sample overall. Bank board memberships also appear to exert no influence on the growth rate of overall leverage. The only positive effect of bank board positions comes with the growth in short-term debt ratios. Bank-attached firms tend to have lower short-term debt ratios at any given time, but those ratios grow faster than average over time. Tables 6.4 and 6.5 also include the interaction effect of age and bank affiliation – an influence that the theory suggests would be negative. Contrary to the stated hypothesis, bank attachment is not associated with faster, but rather slower, reductions in leverage as firms mature. The flip side of this finding can be seen in the impact of bank relationships on equity issuance. Compared with unattached firms, those with bankers on their boards have a significantly lower propensity to slow their issuing of shares as they age. Still, bank relationships appear to have little effect on the static level of share capital or the decision to increase equity.

The addition of the bank relationship variable alters the other results only very slightly. Because of the close association between bank attachments and

Table 6.4. *Correlates of Firm Leverage and the Effects of Bank Relationships*

Variable	Leverage	Debt Maturity	Short-Term Debt Ratio
Bank attachment	−0.08	−0.04	−0.04
	0.06	*0.13*	*0.00*
Fixed assets/	0.31	−0.34	−0.07
total assets	*0.01*	*0.00*	*0.00*
Natural log of income	0.07	−0.01	0.02
	0.00	*0.19*	*0.00*
Net profits/	−2.17	−0.01	−0.64
total assets	*0.00*	*0.95*	*0.00*
Age of firm	−0.01	0.00	−0.003
	0.00	*0.71*	*0.00*
Bank attachment × age	0.004	0.00	0.001
	0.08	*0.56*	*0.01*
Listed on Berlin stock	−0.10	−0.06	−0.04
exchange	*0.04*	*0.09*	*0.03*
Trend	0.02	0.00	0.004
	0.00	*0.34*	*0.00*
Constant	0.06	0.80	0.08
	0.55	*0.00*	*0.01*
P (chi-squared statistic)	0.00	−0.00	0.00
Number of	320	320	320
firms/observations	4,510	4,359	4,546

Notes: Leverage is the ratio of book values of debt to equity. Debt maturity is short-term debt divided by total debt. Short-term debt ratio is short-term debt divided by total assets. Estimated standard errors are semirobust. P-values of t-statistics (two-sided tests) are given in italics. Outliers are removed using the Hadi multivariate outlier test at the $p = 0.05$ level. Age of firm is number of years since registration as a joint-stock company. The listing variable takes the value 1 for true and 0 for false.

stock market listings, it is particularly interesting to note that the latter variable still attains great statistical significance in the new regressions. That is, even controlling for the bank effect, the (negative) listing effect remains. The findings generally fall in line with predictions of recent capital structure theories but offer little support for the idea that formal bank–firm relationships markedly altered the financing options or choices of German firms. These results suggest the need for further investigation of credit provision and firm liquidity, particularly as these conditions influence investment and growth in the industrial sector.

Table 6.5. *Correlates of Changes in Capital Structure and the Effects of Bank Relationships*

Variable	Leverage	Debt Maturity	Short-Term Debt Ratio	Share Capital	Discrete Share Capital
Fixed assets/	−0.11	0.04	0.06	−0.04	−0.36
total assets	0.00	0.21	0.17	0.01	0.31
Natural log of	0.02	0.02	0.02	0.01	0.28
income	0.00	0.00	0.02	0.19	0.00
Net profits/	−0.83	−0.22	−0.23	0.01	0.18
total assets	0.00	0.13	0.17	0.34	0.15
Age of firm	0.00	0.00	0.00	−0.00	−0.04
	0.20	0.77	0.88	0.13	0.02
Bank attachment	−0.02	0.04	0.08	0.02	−0.09
	0.34	0.06	0.01	0.16	0.73
Bank attachment	0.00	0.00	0.00	0.00	0.03
×age	0.56	0.39	0.23	0.55	0.09
Trend	0.00	0.003	0.00	−0.002	−0.03
	0.40	0.05	0.49	0.01	0.02
Listed on Berlin	−0.03	−0.04	−0.06	0.01	0.36
stock exchange	0.12	0.00	0.00	0.45	0.02
Constant	0.17	−0.11	−0.05	0.04	–
	0.03	0.01	0.39	0.15	
P (chi-squared statistic)	0.00	0.00	0.00	0.00	0.00
Number of	319	315	318	320	320
firms/observations	4,013	3,813	3,840	4,348	4,348

Notes: The dependent variables are calculated as the percentage change in the given variable. Leverage is the ratio of book values of debt to equity. Debt maturity is short-term debt divided by total debt. Short-term debt ratio is short-term debt divided by total assets. The first three columns exclude outlier observations according to the Hadi multivariate test ($p = 0.05$). The discrete variable for share capital change takes the values −1 for a reduction, 0 for no change, and 1 for an increase in company share capital, either ordinary or preferred. That model is estimated using ordered logit. The listing variable takes the value 1 for true and 0 for false. Age of firm is number of years since registration as a joint-stock company. P-values of t-statistics (two-sided tests) are given in italics below coefficient estimates.

CREDIT RATIONING AND LIQUIDITY CONSTRAINTS

Chapter 3 raised the problem of asymmetric information between entrepreneurs and their potential financiers. Poor information often leads to difficulties in estimating expected returns on investment; incomplete or imperfect information may also enable firms to misuse funds or misreport returns.

With or without moral hazard, then, asymmetric information may limit the availability of outside funding of any type. In extreme cases of credit rationing, firm investment therefore hinges on internal funding – primarily taken from cash flows generated on a year-to-year basis. These theoretical discussions have led some researchers to hypothesize a generally positive relationship between firm investment and cash flow. Credit rationing diminishes as the ability to estimate returns improves. Thus, if bank relationships improve information flows between firms and investors, then firms with bankers on their boards may be rationed less and may therefore invest more on average. These relationships may also loosen the hypothetical link between investment and cash flow. That is, because of the attenuation of asymmetric information problems, a firm's investment will depend on the existence of new projects and not on the availability of internal funds. In contrast, firms without formal board representation, who arguably have more difficulty defending or advocating their projects to individual investors, must time investments according to their liquidity. According to this logic, investment should respond more to internal funds for unattached firms than it does for attached firms.

Hypotheses such as these have led to empirical tests of the disparity in liquidity sensitivity of investment according to a priori assumptions about the difference in information problems faced by individual firms. Some, but not all, previous studies have found higher cash-flow sensitivity for the group of firms considered to be unattached to a bank than for firms with bank connections. Such findings have been taken as evidence of the role of relationship banking in reducing information asymmetries between investors and savers. Investment–cash flow relationships usually appear within a more general model of the determinants of investment, such as Tobin's Q theory.[9] Of course, in these models that assume perfect competition and complete markets, internal funds play no role in firms' investment decisions; only expected future profitability of investment enters consideration. The violation of these assumptions and the resulting possibility of firm liquidity constraints motivate the inclusion of inside funds in the investment regression equation. Subsequent work has questioned this approach, suggesting that a simple test of the sensitivity of investment to internal funds does not fully capture the effects of liquidity constraints faced by industrial firms. Indeed, according to Steven Kaplan and Luigi Zingales (1997), liquidity sensitivity of investment

---

[9] See also Kuh (1963), and Meyer and Kuh (1957). Some tests use Hayashi's (1982) interpretation of Q theory.

bears no consistent relationship to financing constraints. Such doubts are worth bearing in mind, particularly in light of the results in the current case.

Empirical Evidence

The empirical implementation of Tobin's Q model requires some adjustments and proxy variables. Most importantly, Tobin's Q itself is notoriously difficult to measure and is often represented by a marginal measure of the market-to-book value of common equity. Such a proxy proves necessary in the current analysis as well. Another potential difficulty arises from the possibility that liquidity proxies for production. High levels of production in one period may lead to the need for more capacity in the next period. To control for this accelerator effect, lagged production or production growth is often included among the exogenous variables – despite the lack of strong theoretical motivation. In the absence of production data for the current sample, revenue growth is the nearest alternative. Thus, the basic reduced-form approach models gross investment as a function of liquidity, revenue growth, and common-equity Q. Additional models also include lagged (beginning of period) investment and annual indicator variables. Liquidity is represented by net profits and, in some models, by the stock of liquid assets. All level variables are normalized by the beginning-of-period stock of fixed capital to reduce the possibility of heteroskedasticity and to control for size effects. This basic specification is essentially the same as those used in other recent studies. Stock liquidity appears in some models since it provides an idea of a firm's available internal finance. Cash flow includes only funds newly entering the firm's accounts, while stock liquidity accounts for the accumulated wealth of the firm.

Overall, not controlling for stocks of financial assets, investment is sensitive to cash flows (see Table 6.6).[10] According to the common interpretation of these coefficients, then, German corporations on average were liquidity constrained. Of note, however, investment potential – as measured by marginal, common-equity Q – does not help predict investment. Higher stock valuations, relative to book value, did not spur firms to invest.[11] Eliminating this variable permits the inclusion of an additional 2,300 observations

---

[10] The investment equations are estimated using both the standard within-groups (fixed-effects) method and, in certain cases, a generalized estimating equation. The within-groups estimation runs OLS on the variables minus their time averages and is equivalent to a pooled regression in which indicator variables are included for each firm.

[11] This conclusion is based on a fixed-effects model of investment, the results of which are reported in Table 6.6.

Table 6.6. *Investment and Liquidity, Baseline*

	Fixed Effects (FE)			GEE
Lagged investment	0.21	0.18	0.14	0.31
	0.00	0.00	0.00	0.00
Cash flow	0.05	0.19	0.15	0.06
	0.40	0.00	0.00	0.31
Financial assets	0.04	–	–	0.01
	0.00			0.06
Market-to-book ratio	0.01	0.01	–	0.01
(common-equity Q)	0.19	0.21		0.06
Revenue growth	0.00	0.00	0.00	0.00
	0.08	0.04	0.06	0.02
1898	−0.01	−0.01	0.01	0.00
	0.56	0.60	0.38	0.93
1899	−0.01	−0.01	0.00	0.00
	0.61	0.77	0.71	0.89
1900	−0.03	−0.03	0.00	−0.02
	0.12	0.16	0.96	0.25
1901	−0.03	−0.03	−0.02	−0.02
	0.10	0.14	0.16	0.27
1902	−0.04	−0.04	−0.02	−0.02
	0.04	0.05	0.18	0.22
1903	−0.04	−0.04	−0.01	−0.02
	0.04	0.07	0.22	0.27
1904	−0.03	−0.03	−0.01	−0.01
	0.15	0.14	0.36	0.51
1905	−0.01	−0.01	0.01	0.01
	0.69	0.71	0.57	0.72
1906	0.00	0.00	0.01	0.01
	0.92	0.84	0.37	0.61
1907	−0.02	−0.01	0.00	−0.01
	0.28	0.66	0.78	0.61
1908	−0.04	−0.03	−0.01	−0.03
	0.03	0.07	0.28	0.24
1909	−0.03	−0.02	−0.01	−0.01
	0.13	0.28	0.42	0.64
1910	−0.01	−0.01	0.00	0.00
	0.55	0.78	0.90	0.85
1911	−0.02	−0.01	0.00	−0.01
	0.22	0.43	0.94	0.78

	Fixed Effects (FE)			GEE
1912	−0.01	0.00	0.00	0.01
	0.52	*0.95*	*0.83*	*0.78*
Constant	0.03	0.05	0.05	0.03
	0.14	*0.03*	*0.00*	*0.11*
Rho	0.29	0.24	0.25	–
Number of observations	977.00	999.00	3300.00	977.00
Number of groups	95.00	95.00	300.00	95.00
Prob > F	0.00	0.00	0.00	–
R-sq: within	0.13	0.11	0.05	–
Prob > chi2	–	–	–	0.00

Note: The first three columns employ a fixed-effects regression, whereas the final column uses general estimating equations. Investment, cash flow, and financial assets are all normalized by lagged fixed assets. P-values of t-statistics (two-sided tests) are given in italics below coefficient estimates.

(205 firms), but doing so makes only a modest impact on the estimated cash-flow sensitivities (they decline from 19 to 15 percent). Much more dramatic is the effect of including the level of liquidity, in addition to the annual addition to that stock. When both measures are included, the stock of financial assets is the stronger predictor; cash flows do not enter the equation significantly. Thus, firms with greater reserves of internal finance invest more than those with lesser reserves, and controlling for the level of financial assets, firms' investment is insensitive to single-period cash flows.[12] In all models, revenue growth provides small, but statistically strong, positive indication of investment. So, overall, growing revenues and large stocks of financial assets are the strongest factors associated with investment among German corporations in the later stages of industrialization.

The Impact of Banking Relationships

Banking relationships, particularly the placement of bank directors on company supervisory boards, may alter firms' investment programs. The impact of relationships can be direct, in that the bankers actually cause the firms to

[12] Moving from the fixed-effects model to the XTGEE (generalized estimating equations) model produces essentially no change in the cash-flow sensitivities. While the coefficient of financial assets is markedly decreased, that variable remains statistically significant.

take different actions than they otherwise would. In particular, the banker's presence may encourage or at least permit the firm to obtain more or cheaper external financing for investment and thereby allow more rapid investment. The changes may also be indirect or may actually provide the impetus for banking relationships: Bankers may appear on boards because of the changes that firms have already decided to undertake. To test for the importance of banking relationships, as in previous sections, the new models include indicator variables for bank attachment on its own and in interaction with each exogenous variable. The interaction terms allow a comparison of various coefficients between bank-attached and independent firms within the same regression equation. Because of the apparent disparities among the categories of banks, the analysis uses three versions of the binary bank representation variables: all banks, all joint-stock banks (excluding private banks), and great banks only.

Of prime importance, bank board membership – regardless of type – causes no increase in investment rates (see Table 6.7). Indeed, to the extent that bank representation enters the investment equation significantly, it does so negatively. Similarly, cash-flow sensitivities differ between bank-attached and independent firms, but not in the manner typically hypothesized in the literature. Firms with bankers on their boards actually invest much more in reaction to increased cash flows than do other firms. Such a finding would, according to many researchers, imply that bank relationships are associated with more severe liquidity constraints. The effect is particularly robust when great-bank firms are compared to all others, suggesting that firms with private or provincial bankers on their boards are more similar to unattached firms than to great-bank firms. As in the baseline models, stocks of liquid assets and revenue growth positively predict investment, but the effects vary inconsequentially between great-bank firms and others. Curiously, when the sample is split between those with any bank attachment and those with none, the coefficient of stock liquidity loses its statistical significance, but its interaction with bank attachment is significantly positive. Hence, it appears that the firms with provincial or private bankers on their boards are the ones driving the significance of stock liquidity.

Even if we adhere to the common interpretation and argue that firms with bankers on their boards experienced greater liquidity constraints than unaffiliated firms, we cannot accurately draw a causal interpretation; bank representation does not necessarily cause firms to invest, if they otherwise would not have, simply because they have more financial resources at their disposal. Moreover, the fact that firms with banks on board differ markedly from those without raises concerns about selection bias and the need to control for such influences in interpreting the evidence on investment. The

Table 6.7. *Correlates of Investment and the Impact of Bank Relationships*

	V2AR				V2ARJSB				GBV2AR		
	XTGEE	XTGEE	FE	FE	XTGEE	XTGEE	FE	FE	XTGEE	XTGEE	XTGEE
Bank attachment	-0.01	-0.02	-0.01	-0.02	-0.01	0.01	0.01	0.00	0.00	-0.05	0.00
	0.42	*0.26*	*0.38*	*0.03*	*0.71*	*0.29*	*0.06*	*0.86*	*0.93*	*0.04*	*0.62*
Lagged investment	0.24	0.17	0.11	0.12	0.24	0.20	0.20	0.24	0.21	0.26	0.21
	0.00	*0.00*	*0.00*	*0.00*	*0.00*	*0.00*	*0.00*	*0.00*	*0.00*	*0.00*	*0.00*
Bank × investment	0.11	0.16	0.06	0.06	0.16	0.08	0.07	0.16	0.19	0.16	0.17
	0.13	*0.02*	*0.07*	*0.08*	*0.02*	*0.06*	*0.09*	*0.01*	*0.00*	*0.01*	*0.01*
Cash flow	0.07	-0.04	0.09	0.03	0.04	0.04	0.10	0.11	0.05	0.00	0.09
	0.23	*0.62*	*0.03*	*0.40*	*0.48*	*0.24*	*0.00*	*0.01*	*0.12*	*0.95*	*0.00*
Bank × cash flow	0.04	0.09	0.11	0.07	-0.01	0.05	0.05	-0.03	0.12	0.16	0.12
	0.60	*0.29*	*0.03*	*0.25*	*0.95*	*0.40*	*0.35*	*0.73*	*0.09*	*0.10*	*0.08*
Financial assets		0.01		0.02	0.02	0.02			0.02	0.02	
		0.20		*0.02*	*0.03*	*0.00*			*0.00*	*0.05*	
Bank × financial assets	0.01			0.03	0.00	0.00			0.00	0.00	
	0.35			*0.00*	*0.81*	*0.55*			*0.73*	*0.98*	
Market-to-book ratio of common equity	0.01	0.02			0.01			0.01	0.00		
	0.20	*0.07*			*0.16*			*0.10*	*0.58*		
Bank × market-to-book ratio	0.00	0.00			0.01			0.01	0.00	0.02	
	0.71	*0.80*			*0.64*			*0.16*	*0.81*	*0.16*	

(continued)

Table 6.7 (continued)

	V2AR XTGEE	XTGEE	FE	FE	V2ARJSB XTGEE	XTGEE	FE	FE	GBV2AR XTGEE	XTGEE	XTGEE
Revenue growth	0.00 *0.07*	0.00 *0.38*	0.00 *0.08*	0.00 *0.11*	0.00 *0.12*	0.00 *0.00*	0.00 *0.01*	0.00 *0.10*	0.00 *0.01*	0.00 *0.02*	0.00 *0.02*
Bank × revenue growth	0.00 *0.68*	0.00 *0.48*	0.00 *0.50*	0.00 *0.45*	0.00 *0.53*	0.00 *0.59*	0.00 *0.62*	0.00 *0.54*	0.00 *0.77*	0.00 *0.90*	0.00 *0.53*
1896											
1897	0.00 *0.93*			-0.01 *0.57*			-0.01 *0.36*	0.01 *0.81*	-0.01 *0.46*	0.00 *0.90*	-0.01 *0.33*
1898		0.00 *0.88*	0.01 *0.37*		-0.01 *0.80*	0.01 *0.42*					
1899	0.00 *0.97*	-0.01 *0.68*	0.01 *0.42*	0.00 *0.77*	-0.01 *0.67*	0.00 *0.97*	-0.01 *0.48*	0.00 *0.98*	-0.01 *0.53*	0.00 *0.80*	-0.01 *0.49*
1900	-0.02 *0.14*	-0.03 *0.19*	0.00 *0.94*	-0.01 *0.36*	-0.03 *0.18*	-0.01 *0.60*	-0.01 *0.25*	-0.02 *0.15*	-0.02 *0.20*	-0.02 *0.09*	-0.02 *0.18*
1901	-0.02 *0.27*	-0.02 *0.25*	-0.01 *0.19*	-0.02 *0.02*	-0.02 *0.22*	-0.02 *0.07*	-0.03 *0.02*	-0.02 *0.24*	-0.03 *0.03*	-0.02 *0.13*	-0.03 *0.02*
1902	-0.02 *0.09*	-0.03 *0.19*	-0.01 *0.23*	-0.02 *0.02*	-0.03 *0.19*	-0.02 *0.12*	-0.02 *0.03*	-0.02 *0.11*	-0.02 *0.05*	-0.03 *0.06*	-0.02 *0.03*
1903	-0.02 *0.27*	-0.03 *0.21*	-0.01 *0.28*	-0.02 *0.02*	-0.03 *0.19*	-0.02 *0.10*	-0.02 *0.05*	-0.02 *0.28*	-0.02 *0.04*	-0.03 *0.12*	-0.02 *0.04*
1904	-0.02 *0.30*	-0.02 *0.46*	-0.01 *0.39*	-0.02 *0.05*	-0.02 *0.27*	-0.01 *0.31*	-0.02 *0.15*	-0.02 *0.30*	-0.02 *0.14*	-0.02 *0.17*	-0.02 *0.14*
1905	0.01 *0.39*	0.01 *0.8*	0.01 *0.44*	-0.01 *0.56*	0.01 *0.80*	0.00 *0.81*	0.00 *0.84*	0.01 *0.36*	-0.01 *0.61*	0.00 *0.77*	0.00 *0.77*

1906	0.02	0.01	0.01	0.00	0.01	0.01	0.00	0.02	0.00	0.01	0.00
	0.39	*0.74*	*0.30*	*0.96*	*0.80*	*0.48*	*0.94*	*0.40*	*0.91*	*0.76*	*0.85*
1907	0.00	–0.01	0.00	–0.01	–0.01	0.00	–0.01	0.00	–0.01	–0.01	–0.01
	0.98	*0.56*	*0.70*	*0.37*	*0.52*	*0.83*	*0.43*	*0.96*	*0.41*	*0.45*	*0.33*
1908	–0.02	–0.03	–0.01	–0.03	–0.03	–0.02	–0.03	–0.02	–0.03	–0.03	–0.03
	0.20	*0.20*	*0.38*	*0.01*	*0.18*	*0.08*	*0.04*	*0.18*	*0.04*	*0.11*	*0.04*
1909	–0.01	–0.02	–0.01	–0.02	–0.01	–0.01	–0.02	0.00	–0.02	–0.01	–0.02
	0.65	*0.49*	*0.52*	*0.02*	*0.52*	*0.22*	*0.10*	*0.74*	*0.09*	*0.36*	*0.08*
1910	0.01	0.00	0.00	–0.01	0.00	0.00	–0.01	0.01	–0.01	0.00	–0.01
	0.57	*0.91*	*0.93*	*0.22*	*0.97*	*0.78*	*0.37*	*0.68*	*0.41*	*0.95*	*0.34*
1911	0.00	–0.01	0.00	–0.01	0.00	0.00	–0.01	0.00	–0.01	0.00	–0.01
	0.87	*0.77*	*0.87*	*0.27*	*0.83*	*0.87*	*0.36*	*0.77*	*0.44*	*0.80*	*0.51*
1912	0.01	0.00	0.00	–0.01	0.00	0.00	–0.01	0.01	–0.01	0.00	–0.01
	0.72	*0.93*	*0.98*	*0.19*	*0.93*	*0.72*	*0.37*	*0.68*	*0.28*	*0.96*	*0.26*
Constant	0.04	0.05	0.05	0.06	0.04	0.04	0.05	0.04	0.05	0.05	0.06
	0.01	*0.62*	*0.00*	*0.00*	*0.06*	*0.00*	*0.00*	*0.01*	*0.00*	*0.00*	*0.00*
Rho (fraction of variance due to u_I)			0.24	0.23							
Number of obs	999	1,098	3,297	3,261	973	3,248	3,293	999	3,740	975	3,287
Number of groups	95	98	300	298	95	298	300	95	298	95	300
Prob> F	0.00	0.00	0.00	0.00	0.00	0.00	0.00	0.00	0.00	0.00	0.00
R-sq: within			0.05	0.12					0.16	0.06	0.13

Note: The column heads indicate estimation methods and type of banking relationship. Investment, cash flow, and financial assets are all normalized by lagged fixed assets. P-values of t-statistics (two-sided tests) are given in italics below coefficient estimates.

statistical methods used – particularly the fixed-effects regression models – eliminate firm-specific effects and therefore mitigate but may not eliminate selection bias. If biases systematically relate to characteristics other than firm identity, then additional statistical remedies may be recommended. Selection bias becomes a concern, in particular, if the same factors that predict investment play some role in the decision to place a banker on a corporate supervisory board.

Hypothetically, these selection biases can be positive or negative, depending on the reasons for bank relationships.[13] For example, if bank memberships represent attempts by banks to improve oversight of borrowing firms, then attached firms may be predisposed to liquidity constraints. On the converse, if firms gain attachments to signal creditworthiness to investors, then attached firms may be naturally less constrained on average. The conclusions of the last chapter, however, develop yet a different interpretation of bank board memberships – one that sees these bank positions as a logical outcome of the organization of German financial markets at the time. This explanation, focusing on the transfer of control rights from shareholders to banks via proxy voting and the engagement of universal banks in the underwriting process, shifts the attention away from bank monitoring and advice and thereby diminishes the hypothetical position of bank board members as an impetus for firm decisions or outcomes.

This line of reasoning still leaves open the possibility of selection bias: If banks disproportionately gain voting rights of large, dispersed firms, with listings on the stock exchanges, then these firms could simultaneously have particularly active and liquid securities markets and generally good access to credit. Their unattached counterparts may simply represent an alternative form of corporate governance, in which ownership was more concentrated, control more closely held, and both stock market listings and bank board memberships less desirable or frequent. There is no compelling evidence that the attached firms borrowed particularly heavily, and that suggests that attached firms were not using bank connections to access unusual amounts of debt funding to finance investment instead of waiting for internal liquidity – the latter being the behavior that has been interpreted as evidence of liquidity constraints. Moreover, if these firms tended to face softer financial constraints, then it would be all the more surprising that their investment responded more readily to internal funds.

Controls for selection bias, based on the analysis of bank board positions in the previous chapter, leave the previous results essentially unchanged.

---

[13] As the previous chapter considered at length, the historical literature raises a number of plausible explanations for banks' seats on company supervisory boards.

The firms with bankers sitting on their boards differ in some important respects from those without bank affiliations. Yet, even when those factors are accounted for, firms with bank attachments still experience greater liquidity sensitivity than those with no bankers on their boards.[14]

FIRM PERFORMANCE: GROWTH, SURVIVAL, AND PROFITABILITY

Firm Growth

The problem of investment leads naturally to more general questions about performance of firms and the factors that promote their growth. Researchers have long debated the causes of growth, and a number of consistent patterns have eventually emerged. To start with, the distribution of firm size – the basis for calculating growth rates – tends to be right-skewed; that is, in most cases, more firms fall in the small end of the distribution than in the large end. The smallest and youngest firms typically grow fastest, but their growth rates vary more than those of larger, older firms. Overall, however, average growth rates do fall as firms grow and age.[15]

The majority of the extant evidence rejects the theoretical propositions put forth by Robert Gibrat (1931): that the rate of growth of firms is drawn from the same distribution regardless of size. This hypothesis, known somewhat falsely as Gibrat's Law, yields a lognormal distribution of growth rates. The weak version of the law indicates that the mean growth rate remains constant across all firms; the strong version holds that the distribution of growth rates is the same for all firms. Jovanovic (1982) argues that the failure of Gibrat's Law might be explained by both statistical bias and theoretical reasons. For small or young firms, only the positive growth rate is observed, because there is probably a threshold below which firms disappear. Since small firms are more likely to reach that lower bound, and therefore exit any given sample of firms, statistical analysis overestimates the growth rate of the small firms. Jovanovic also argues that the vintage of a firm could impact the growth rate of the firm. In this hypothetical explanation, firms learn about the random components of their cost structure at each period, and they

[14] The investment equations are estimated using a two-stage procedure, essentially a "treatment-effects" model, in which the results of a first-stage discrete-choice model of bank attachment (from the previous chapter) feed into the second-stage investment equations. Like the standard panel models of investment, these models control for autocorrelation within firms.

[15] Empirical studies include Dunne, Roberts, and Samuelson (1989); Demirguc-Kunt and Maksimovic (1998); and Utrero (2002). Most studies have examined the manufacturing sector only.

update their calculations of profits based on these realizations as well as on their cost of entry. As a result, small firms are more likely to exit due to lower expectations of profits, growth is positively correlated with profits and with past growth rates, and small firms as a group experience greater variance in growth rates than do bigger firms. In support of these hypotheses, Timothy Dunne, Mark Roberts, and Larry Samuelson (1989) find that plant size, age, and ownership type predict growth and failure of plants.

In the historical context, little or no work has been done on firm growth. This deficiency has left open many questions about the determinants of growth during industrialization – one of the more important periods of firm development.[16] One might think that the rising tide of a rapidly developing economy would bring prosperity to an unusually wide range of firms. On the other hand, the notion of creative destruction and new technology replacing old might lead one to expect differential growth according to certain characteristics, such as technology or industry. Moreover, industrialization brought new risks associated with innovation, price decreases resulting from efficiency gains, and reorganization of firms and industries. Domestic industrial development progressed irregularly, and international trade and finance fluctuated as well. All of these factors raised potential difficulties for individual businesses and for the corporate economy as a whole.

By and large, German firms grew at moderate rates over the later stages of industrialization, with ups and downs, but with only a weak upward trend, over the period studied here.[17] Median growth rates ranged between 6 and 7 percent in the strong recovery years of the mid-to-late-1890s.[18] By 1899

---

[16] While there is little theoretical literature on which to base empirical studies, Lucas's (1988) model explains a mechanism by which firm size is determined by technology: Industry-specific technology determines optimal firm size. In a related vein, Ericson and Pakes (1995) and Hopenhayn (1992) explain firm growth by stochastic shocks in technology adoption and employment respectively.

[17] Firm growth, in this examination, refers to the expansion of revenues or sales. This variable provides the best available proxy for production growth and, in itself, represents a primary goal of industrial enterprises. Several recent studies have used sales and sales growth as measures of size and size growth, respectively. This approach makes the most sense in the German context, not only because of the nature of production, but also because of the availability of data. The main alternative is employment, but such data are available for very few firms.

[18] These and subsequent figures are median percentage growth rates of reported revenues calculated from the corporate database. Annual figures cover all firms for the given year, while industry medians include the firms in the given sector over all of the years in the sample. Medians reflect industry tendencies better than average rates, since the distribution is heavily skewed by small numbers of extremely high growth rates. Since revenues must be at least zero, the growth rate of revenues from one year to the next is bounded below by −100 percent.

and 1900, those rates had slackened to 3 to 4 percent per annum; and in 1901, the year of the stock market crash, growth fell to almost −4 percent. By 1903, a new turnaround materialized, bringing the growth rate back to 6 percent. Growth remained around those levels (5 to 8 percent) for three more years, before the 1907 crash and recession put a damper on the corporate economy. The declines of 1908 (−2 percent median) were short-lived, and firm growth rebounded (3 to 7 percent median rates) during the remaining prewar years.

Not surprisingly, the sectors on the forefront of the then-current stage of industrialization – electrical technology, gas production, and utilities distribution – typically experienced the strongest corporate revenue growth: 9 percent per year between 1895 and 1912. These high rates are all the more impressive given that they capture not just the prosperous years but some major down years as well and that they mix together leading-edge firms with those that might be better classified as old-technology firms. These older industrial sectors – textiles, sugar refining, and milling – grew less than 2 percent per year over the entire period. Even in the generally prosperous years leading up to the war, many textile firms, especially those in cotton, lost revenues. In between these extremes, corporate firms in brewing, stones and earthenware industries, metalworking, machinery, printing, woodworking, steam transport (primarily inland waterways), and chemicals grew at median rates of 3 to 4 percent, while light rail companies (predominantly electric streetcars) and mining firms grew at 6 percent or slightly more.

These median figures mask considerable variability within years and within sectors. Moreover, multiple other factors play a role in corporate growth, and those factors may relate partly, but not wholly, to the industry in which firms operate and the time period examined. To identify these effects, it is important to analyze growth in a multivariate model, in line with studies of more recent corporate populations. Given the obvious differences in institutions and historical context, the similarities with recent findings are remarkable: Controlling for annual ups and down as well as for unobservable characteristics wrapped up in firm identity, small, young firms tend to grow faster than large, old firms (see Table 6.8).

The Impact of Banking Relationships

The German banks have been likened to management consultants or venture capitalists; their positions in firm supervisory boards have been characterized as a benefit to incumbent managers, who seek bankers' advice

Table 6.8. *Firm Growth (Revenues)*

		V2AR	v2arjsb	gbv2ar
Revenues	0.02	0.02	0.02	0.02	0.02
	0.03	0.03	0.03	0.03	0.03
Lagged revenues	−0.03	−0.03	−0.03	−0.03	−0.03
	0.02	0.02	0.02	0.02	0.02
Age	−0.26	−0.27	−0.26	−0.27	−0.26
	0.02	0.01	0.01	0.01	0.01
Age squared	0.00	0.00	0.00	0.00	0.00
	0.02	0.02	0.02	0.02	0.02
Cash flow	33.62	33.47	33.23	33.24	32.99
	0.00	0.00	0.00	0.00	0.00
Negative cash flow (0/1)	−17.66	−17.63	−17.64	−17.64	−17.67
	0.00	0.00	0.00	0.00	0.00
Berlin listed	–	0.73	0.56	0.67	0.42
		0.46	0.57	0.50	0.68
Bank attachment	–	–	0.57	0.40	1.68
			0.56	0.68	0.27
1897	–	2.72	2.77	–	2.72
		0.33	0.33		0.33
1898	−2.69	–	–	−2.76	–
	0.34			0.33	
1899	−8.33	−5.61	−5.63	−8.38	−5.64
	0.01	0.02	0.02	0.01	0.02
1900	−9.54	−6.82	−6.84	−9.59	−6.85
	0.00	0.00	0.00	0.00	0.00
1901	−11.45	−8.72	−8.73	−11.49	−8.77
	0.00	0.00	0.00	0.00	0.00
1902	−6.51	−3.78	−3.79	−6.54	−3.80
	0.03	0.08	0.08	0.03	0.08
1903	−2.40	0.34	0.32	−2.44	0.22
	0.41	0.88	0.88	0.40	0.92
1904	−4.00	−1.27	−1.29	−4.04	−Z1.38
	0.19	0.53	0.52	0.18	0.49
1905	−2.39	0.35	0.32	−2.43	0.25
	0.42	0.88	0.89	0.42	0.91
1906	−3.17	−0.42	−0.45	−3.20	−0.49
	0.27	0.84	0.83	0.27	0.81
1907	−8.61	−5.86	−5.88	−8.64	−5.89
	0.00	0.00	0.00	0.00	0.00

		V2AR	v2arjsb	gbv2ar
1908	−13.92	−11.16	−11.19	−13.95	−11.20
	0.00	*0.00*	*0.00*	*0.00*	*0.00*
1909	−4.72	−1.97	−1.98	−4.76	−2.07
	0.09	*0.35*	*0.34*	*0.09*	*0.32*
1910	−4.61	−1.84	−1.85	−4.63	−1.95
	0.13	*0.42*	*0.42*	*0.13*	*0.39*
1911	−7.81	−5.03	−5.03	−7.81	−5.17
	0.01	*0.02*	*0.02*	*0.01*	*0.02*
1912	−5.52	−2.75	−2.75	−5.54	−2.88
	0.07	*0.23*	*0.23*	*0.07*	*0.21*
Constant	13.74	11.00	10.71	13.64	10.89
	0.00	*0.00*	*0.00*	*0.00*	*0.00*
Number of obs	3,249	3,249	3,249	3,249	3,249
Number of groups	298	298	298	298	298
Wald chi2(21)	216.63	219.55	220.24	221.43	224.73
Prob > chi2	0.00	0.00	0.00	0.00	0.00

Note: Cash flow is normalized by lagged fixed assets. For the last three columns, the column head indicates the type of banking relationship. P-values of t-statistics (two-sided tests) are given in italics below coefficient estimates.

and perhaps more importantly, their business connections. One way to determine how important a consultancy role the bankers played is to look for their impact on firms' expansion, particularly their sales or revenue growth. Such growth represents one measure of a firm's success in gaining access to new customers and markets and possibly its ability to increase market share. The traditional emphasis on the role of the universal banks leads to the hypothesis that bank-affiliated companies should grow faster than their independent counterparts, controlling for the possibility that certain types of firms choose the bank relationship.[19]

The bank-relationship hypothesis can be tested by adding measures of banking relationships to the previous analysis, in order to control simultaneously for the various factors in firm growth (see Table 6.8). Regardless of the type of bank involved with the firm, however, board memberships play no consistent role in firm growth, whichever direction one might posit causality.[20] Because of the close association with stock market listing,

---

[19] This choice would create a selection bias and potentially invalidate a causal interpretation.
[20] Selection bias is also ruled out by use of a two-stage model, as described in the section "Credit Rationing and Liquidity Constraints."

especially in Berlin, that possibility enters as a control variable as well. But listings have no apparent impact either. In other words, the financial characteristics of firms are clearly the most important factors in determining their rates of revenue growth.

Firm Survival Patterns

Firm growth and profitability differ markedly from firm to firm and industry to industry. Some firms survive for very long periods, while others, possibly in similar lines of business, fail to grow and prosper at all. Understanding company survival requires a closer examination of the performance of firms and an investigation of repeated patterns among firms that fail. Economists have studied this issue for many years and have converged on a statistical methodology, if not a theoretically based structural model, to identify the firm characteristics that help predict corporate bankruptcy.[21] Such methods build on the premise that the success or failure of firms depends on a number of factors: working capital, leverage, profitability and cash flows, volatility of stock returns, industrial sector, investment in research and development, firm size and age, and value of intangible assets. Economywide shocks, of course, put more firms at greater risk. Some have suggested that profits are not linearly related to failure: Decreasing profits over the positive range does not necessarily increase the likelihood of liquidation. Yet losses may increase a firm's chance of failing. Thus, it is informative to include a dummy variable taking the value 1 for negative profitability in order to control for this nonlinearity effect.[22] Other controls include firm size and age (including a squared age term to account for the lack of mobility of older firms) and industry indicators to capture interindustry differences.

Institutional arrangements, particularly those relating to corporate finance and governance, can play a significant part in determining the lifecycle of industrial enterprises. Naturally, in the German context, the universal banks could have played some role in firm survival. Long-term banking relationships, the famed cradle-to-grave financing, can be construed in many ways; some interpretations would imply that banks aid firms through difficult periods – by restructuring their financial obligations, providing managerial guidance, or assisting them in networking with other firms. These lines of reasoning suggest that firms with bankers on their boards may survive longer than their unattached counterparts, particularly if bank connections

---

[21] See the summary in Altman (1991). The appendix to this chapter discusses the econometric models used for these tests.

[22] This addition is suggested by Astebro and Winter (2001). See Dietrich and Kaplan (1982) for a detailed exposition of this effect.

allow firms to weather severe downturns or crises that they would otherwise not survive. Thus, when studying corporate survival, in addition to the standard financial variables, it is important to take account of firms' involvement with universal banks. Certainly, the historical literature provides examples of company bailouts, in which universal bankers took an active role. Whether or not a firm should be rescued is another question that is more difficult to answer. A bailout may preserve a fundamentally good firm that experiences temporary problems. But the rescue operation may also create inefficiencies: Those resources may possibly be better directed to other uses. Hence, the mere fact of financial restructuring, while undoubtedly appreciated by the managers who escape crises with their jobs, does not in itself represent a benefit to the economy.

While the German industrial economy expanded quite rapidly during the later stages of industrialization, the firms that operated still varied in their individual levels of success. Of the joint-stock corporations in existence in 1902, approximately 13 percent entered liquidation in the subsequent decade. Failure rates rose and fell, with relatively high rates in 1902, 1905–6, and 1909–10. None of the sampled firms failed in 1903, and only four failed in the last two years (two per year). On the whole, even the bad years were not extreme: No more than 2 percent of the sampled firms failed in any one year. Translated over the full population of about 5,500 German joint-stock corporations at the time, we can therefore estimate that something on the order of 120 firms failed in the worst year (1906) and far fewer failed in most years. Naturally, because of the small numbers of failures in this sample, and the even smaller numbers in each year, it is hard to know how well the percentages replicate themselves in the full population. Taking the overall rate of 13 percent, however, would suggest that somewhere between five hundred and seven hundred joint-stock firms failed in the decade before World War I. Since the corporate population was growing, births clearly outweighed these deaths.

Failed firms represented essentially the full range of sectors, though some industries certainly fared better than others (see Table 6.9). Relative to their share of the sample, firms in the light industries – small machinery and metalworking, inland steamship transport, textiles, and food processing (water, milling, sugar refining) – along with nonprofits and charitable groups were most likely to fail. Firms in heavy industry (mining and smelting), electrotechnicals, chemicals, and brewing were particularly likely to succeed. In between fell light rail and electric streetcar companies, gas and petroleum companies, and stones and earthenware firms.

Somewhat contrary to intuition, but not unique in the empirical literature, older firms were more likely to fail than were younger ones (see

Table 6.9. *Firm Failures, by Sector and by Year*

	% of Failures in Sample	% of Firms in Sample	Failure Rate / Prevalence in Sample
Panel A: Sectors			
Mining	2.38	8.07	0.30
Metal, machinery, shipbuilding	19.05	14.29	1.33
Printing, woodworking	14.29	6.83	2.09
Rail, streetcars, electric streetcars	4.76	5.59	0.85
Steam ships (mostly inland waterways)	7.14	3.42	2.09
Electrotechnical	2.38	3.42	0.70
Gas, petroleum, sterno (denatured alcohol)	4.76	4.35	1.09
Water, ice, baths	7.14	2.17	3.29
Chemicals	2.38	10.56	0.23
Stones, earths, cement	9.52	9.32	1.02
Textiles	7.14	4.66	1.53
Food processing (primarily milling and sugar)	9.52	7.45	1.28
Breweries	4.76	14.91	0.32
Nonprofits, coops, community, charity, academic/student houses	7.14	2.48	2.88
Entertainment (zoos, parks, theaters, concert houses, etc.)	0.00	2.48	0.00

Year	% of Failures	Relative Chance of Failure in Given Year	% of All AGs	Estimated Total # of Failures of AGs
Panel B: Years				
1902	11.9	1.31	1.55	85.40
1903	0.00	0.00	0.00	0.00
1904	7.14	0.79	0.93	51.24
1905	14.29	1.57	1.86	102.48
1906	16.67	1.83	2.17	119.57
1907	7.14	0.79	0.93	51.24
1908	7.14	0.79	0.93	51.24
1909	14.29	1.57	1.86	102.48
1910	11.9	1.31	1.55	85.40
1911	4.76	0.52	0.62	34.16
1912	4.76	0.52	0.62	34.16

Table 6.10).[23] Looking at the ages of the individual firms that failed in this sample (see Table 6.9), it is clear that half of the failed firms were at least fifteen years past their incorporation date, and three-quarters of them made it at least ten years. None of the liquidated companies had been around for less than three years as a joint-stock firm, and well over a third were at least twenty years old. As old as these firms were, there were quite a few survivor firms that lived even longer. Thus, the oldest of the old tended not to fail, so "middle-aged" is a more apt descriptor of the age profile of firms at greatest risk of failure.[24]

Despite the positive connection between age and failure, large firms (measured by revenues) are less likely to fail than are small firms. Though the analysis does control for industry branch, these combined characteristics may pick up some specific characteristics of the high-tech sector of the late industrialization period. Large, (relatively) young firms are most likely to represent the vanguard of the second industrial revolution – those that are most likely to prosper, and thus least likely to fail.

Financial conditions also affect firms' chance of success. Those with negative or zero cash flows fail much more readily, close to five times the rate, than those with positive cash flows.[25] But the difference between having some cash flow and having none is more important for determining failure than the difference between having high cash flows and having low (positive) cash flows. The firms with the highest cash flows survive, but more general increases in cash flow lessen a firm's likelihood of failure insignificantly. Low leverage (total indebtedness/total assets) and high liquidity (short-term assets relative to short-term debt) seem to help safeguard against failure, but again, the factors are weak in a statistical sense.

The data do not reveal the precise reasons for corporate liquidations, but one can discern quite a bit from this quantitative analysis. Putting all the risk factors together, one might conjecture that small, old firms, in

---

[23] The firms here are all joint-stock companies, and the ages therefore refer to the time since incorporation. So, a firm that appears to be young may or may not have a substantial track record. Krupp is an extreme example, having existed for nearly a century before incorporating in 1903. Nonetheless, firms that are old in terms of incorporation life span are certainly old.

[24] The squared age variable controls for the possible quadratic shape of the age effect and is negative, as these impressionistic results suggest. Thus age has diminishing predictive value as it passes a certain point. But the squared age term turns out to be statistically insignificant, meaning that the oldest firms are insufficient in numbers to have strong statistical meaning.

[25] The regressions control for industrial branch and other firm characteristics, so these rates are conditional.

Table 6.10. *Correlates of Firm Failure*

	Baseline	V2AR	V2AR	V2ARJSB
Age	1.17	1.17	1.03	1.12
	0.07	*0.07*	*0.76*	*0.28*
Age-squared / 100	0.79	0.78	1.05	0.89
	0.19	*0.20*	*0.83*	*0.61*
Lagged revenues	1.00	1.00	1.00	1.00
	0.03	*0.03*	*0.04*	*0.04*
Lagged short-term financial assets	3.79	3.52	16.18	2.97
	0.49	*0.52*	*0.22*	*0.62*
Lagged leverage	2.19	2.32	3.91	4.44
	0.53	*0.50*	*0.40*	*0.31*
Lagged total financial assets	0.84	0.84	0.77	0.87
	0.18	*0.20*	*0.33*	*0.28*
Lagged cash flow	0.09	0.07	0.27	0.02
	0.60	*0.56*	*0.81*	*0.48*
Lagged negative cash flow (0/1)	4.73	4.60	5.45	4.15
	0.00	*0.00*	*0.01*	*0.02*
Bank attachment		0.83	0.02	0.02
		0.64	*0.22*	*0.31*
Interaction terms with "bank attachment"				
Age			1.67	1.74
			1.10	*0.19*
Age-squared / 100			0.27	0.20
			0.12	*0.18*
Lagged revenues			1.00	1.00
			0.28	*0.58*
Lagged liquid assets			0.01	17.00
			0.31	*0.58*
Lagged leverage			0.33	0.12
			0.65	*0.45*
Lagged liquidity			1.17	0.75
			0.59	*0.51*
Lagged cash flow			0.47	170.40
			0.94	*0.64*
Lagged negative cash flow (0/1)			0.90	1.50
			0.92	*0.74*
Number of observations	2,423	2,434	2,383	2,387
Number of outliers (10%)	300	289	340	336

Notes: The dependent variable is a binary variable that takes the value 1 if the firm goes into liquidation in that year and 0 otherwise. Once a firm enters liquidation, it is dropped from the sample for subsequent years. Liquidity is the ratio of short-term liquid assets to short-maturity liabilities. Leverage is the ratio of debt to total assets. Financial assets and cash flow are normalized by total assets. The models use random-effects logit with robust standard errors and clustering on firms; resulting odds ratios are reported. Sector indicators are included but not reported. P-values of Z-statistics are entered in italics below coefficient estimates.

old-technology sectors, with significant debt burden may simply find it more economical to direct resources to other ventures. The period of study does, after all, comprise the later stages of heavy industrialization. The failure pattern uncovered here looks like the "creative destruction" process that Schumpeterians would expect.

The Impact of Banking Relationships

The observable performance of firms may differ depending on the existence of formalized bank relationships. When it comes to the very survival of firms, one could reasonably create two sets of hypotheses. In the first, banker board positions are associated with *greater* survival rates because bankers help firms through liquidity crises: The bank either gains board membership through that activity or was compelled to provide the rescue services because of its preexisting relationship. In the second story, bank board positions are associated with *lower* survival rates, because bankers gain entry into the boards of firms they are helping to liquidate. Nothing in the two lines of reasoning prevents them from pertaining simultaneously; making it difficult to disentangle the effects empirically.

At the most basic level of comparison, simply calculating the percentages of attached firms among those that failed, it appears that banks are less likely to be on the boards of liquidating firms: One-third of failed firms had bankers on their supervisory boards versus more than half of survivors. Such a comparison naturally overlooks the characteristics that jointly determine the presence of bank representatives and the relative success of firms. After controlling for such factors as sector, size, and financial strength, it becomes clear that bank attachment is neither positively nor negatively associated with firm survival; the impact is neutral (see Table 6.10). This new round of analysis, though, indicates that the age effect that appeared in the baseline results relates primarily to the firms with bankers on their boards. Given the small number of failures and even smaller number of failed firms with bankers on their boards, it is unwise to draw strong conclusions from this result. It does hint at the possibility, however, that bankers may have helped sustain troubled firms for a while longer than they might otherwise have lasted.

Firm Profitability

Discussions of firm growth and survival naturally raise questions about other measures of corporate performance: productivity, stock returns, and accounting profitability. Total factor productivity measures the extra production capability not accounted for by changes in capital and labor inputs.[26] But because German firms reported only spotty information on labor inputs, it is difficult to say much about that sort of performance. On the other extreme, it is possible to measure accounting profits and dividends for virtually all corporate firms and stock returns for all listed companies.

Return on assets (ROA) or on equity (ROE) is typically calculated as earnings before interest and taxes as a fraction of total assets or of total equity, respectively. Naturally, accounting measures of profitability must be taken with a grain of salt, particularly before the formalization of accounting standards. German firms notoriously used depreciation as a means of accumulating so-called silent reserves, and all firms can be prone to exaggerate costs and thereby depress apparent profitability in prosperous years. These practices tend to smooth the year-to-year fluctuations in profits and permit firms to keep dividend payments flowing in a more even stream. To inoculate measures against the depreciation problem, at least, returns are typically measured before depreciation. Measured by accounting returns, Germany's corporate firms performed well during the last years of the nineteenth century and the first decade or so of the twentieth. Average return on assets ranged between 1 and 5 percent between 1895 and 1912, with a samplewide average of 3 percent over the full period (see Table 6.11). Profits varied considerably from firm to firm and year to year, with at least 7 percent and up to 22 percent of firms showing negative returns for the year (the high coming in 1901, the year of a major stock market decline).[27]

Stock returns, defined as the dividend-adjusted annual return on common stocks, offer a completely different measure of corporate profitability, focusing as they do on shareholders' equity. Like other measures, a stock's return has its pros and cons as a portrayer of firm performance. Firms cannot misrepresent profits calculated on the basis of actual market prices for their shares, though firms and their representatives might possibly attempt to manipulate those market prices. At the same time, those who held shares over the long term might never realize the portion of dividend-adjusted stock returns accounted for by the appreciation of the share price.

---

[26] Specifically, it is the residual from ordinary least-squares regression estimation of a Cobb-Douglas production function, $y - ak - Bl$, s.t. $y = \ln(\text{total sales})$, $k = \ln(\text{replacement cost of tangible assets})$, and $l = \ln(\text{total number of employees})$. Sales and capital stock are deflated by price index.

[27] Cash flow on equity, a measure that adds depreciation and interest to cash flow and normalizes by the book value of equity, is another useful alternative. Because interest payments are not generally disaggregated in the firms' income statements, and because of the lack of standards on depreciation, it is difficult to measure this variable precisely for this sample.

Table 6.11. *ROA, Dividends, and Stock Returns*

		ROA (Percent)			Negative ROA (Percent of Sample)			Dividends (Percent)			Dividend-Adjusted Stock Return (Percent)		
		Obs.	Mean	Std. Dev.	Obs.	Mean	Std. Dev.	Obs.	Mean	Std. Dev.	Obs.	Mean	Std. Dev.
Berlin	0	3,891	2.90	23	4,414	17.00	38	4,414	3.53	5.33	548	11.91	40.83
	1	699	3.40	5	712	5.00	23	712	7.04	6.89	444	14.78	45.02
	Total	4,590	2.90	21	5,126	15.00	36	5,126	4.02	5.70	992	13.19	42.76
V2AR	0	2,104	3.20	30	2,293	18.00	39	2,293	3.78	5.96	228	13.89	34.58
	1	2,446	2.70	6	2,591	14.00	34	2,591	4.56	5.58	753	13.05	45.15
	Total	4,550	3.00	21	4,884	16.00	37	4,884	4.19	5.77	981	13.25	42.91
v2ar	0	2,104	3.20	30	2,292	18.00	39	2,292	3.78	5.96	228	13.89	34.58
	1	891	2.80	5	939	12.00	33	939	5.29	5.55	314	14.38	42.58
	2	986	2.70	6	1,061	15.00	36	1,061	3.50	4.86	218	10.21	47.56
	3	310	3.30	5	323	16.00	37	323	4.42	6.25	138	11.84	42.52
	4	259	2.00	6	266	13.00	33	266	6.38	6.54	83	17.49	52.13
	Total	4,550	3.00	21	4,881	16.00	37	4,881	4.19	5.77	981	13.25	42.91

Notes: Berlin indicates a listing on the Berlin stock exchange. For ROA and dividends, the firms without Berlin listings may be listed on a provincial exchange or may be unlisted; for stock returns, firms without a Berlin listing are listed on a provincial exchange (otherwise, there would be no stock price quote for them). V2AR indicates the presence of some banker (joint-stock or private) on the company supervisory board; v2ar indicates the type of bank: 0 = no banks, 1 = private bankers.

These returns averaged more than 13 percent annually over the period (equally weighted), but the highs and lows made stock investing quite risky. Excluding dividends, half of the firms made negative stock returns in most years. Even in bull markets, and even adding in dividends, 20 percent of firms made negative stock returns for the year. Still, the median firm produced positive dividend-adjusted returns in all but one year (1902).

While Berlin-listed firms averaged higher returns than their provincial counterparts, the difference was statistically insignificant. In other words, an investor who had invested equal shares in the exact firms in this sample would have done better on those listed in Berlin. But the results would not necessarily be reproduced in some other random sample of firms at the time. Even less dependable differences appear for bank affiliations. Firms with bankers on their boards actually made lower dividend-adjusted returns than independents overall, though the finer breakdown by bank type indicates marked variation. Firms with multiple bank attachments yielded the highest returns; those with just provincial banks or just great banks performed the worst of all (but still over 10 percent per annum). In this case, simply taking the presence of a banker on the board as a quality signal would have produced no relative gain to the uninformed investor, and possibly a relative loss. Since the results are statistically indistinguishable from category to category, an investment in any random selection of bank-attached firms would be expected to offer the same returns as an investment in some random assortment of any other firms.

These favorable returns stem partly from dividend payouts, and those amounts are essentially immune to creative accounting or manipulation. During the late-nineteenth and early-twentieth centuries, German corporations often distributed dividends. In any given year, at least half of the firms paid no dividends at all, but dividends still averaged around 3.5 percent over all firms and years in the sample. Among dividend-paying firms only, the average is more than double (8.4 percent). And some firms paid out very high dividends: Almost a third of the dividend-paying sample distributed at least 10 percent payouts, and sixteen different firms paid dividends of more than 20 percent. Asphalt-Fabrik F. Schlesing Nachfolger, for example, reported dividends between 22 and 36 percent in every year between 1900 and 1912. Oberschlesische AG für Fabrikation von Lignose claims the top-payer position, with dividends of 20 percent or more in thirteen of the eighteen sample years and payouts of 60 and 80 percent in 1906 and 1905, respectively.[28] By modern Standard and Poor (S&P) 500 standards, prewar

---

[28] According to the 1913 Webster's Dictionary, courtesy of hyperdictionary.com, lignose is an explosive compound of wood fiber and nitroglycerin.

German firms paid very generous dividends on average, particularly for the more comparable Berlin-listed firms, despite those firms' higher propensity to hold back on payouts altogether.[29]

Highly concentrated ownership, particularly family ownership, suppresses the motive ever to show profits or to distribute dividends, since there are few or even no shareholders to please and significant taxes to pay.[30] While we cannot say who owned the firms in general, we can surmise that firms with listings on a stock exchange, especially the main equity market in Berlin, were more widely held than firms without listings or even provincial listings. And a simple comparison of means backs up this hypothesis. By all available measures, the Berlin listed firms performed better than the rest: They averaged higher ROA, were less prone to showing negative accounting profits, distributed far more generous dividends on average, and yielded much higher dividend-adjusted stock returns (in Berlin compared to the provinces).

These apparent differences between Berlin firms and the rest and among the categories of bank attachment recommend taking a more systematic look at profitability and the factors that influence it, in order to control simultaneously for multiple factors. Doing so tells a more complex story about profitability. Berlin listing is clearly still an important predictor of profitability, but other factors enter as well. The number of shares outstanding, a rough proxy for ownership dispersion, is also positive but statistically weak. Still, the finding lends credence to the idea that closely held firms – most likely unlisted – had an incentive to minimize accounting profits. Strong sales growth and high concentration (measured by sales) in the industry in which a firm operates relates very markedly to profitability, and market concentration is all the more important among listed firms.[31] While these findings certainly do not constitute an incontrovertible test of market power, it is not surprising that rapid sales growth and a relatively small number of competitors correlate positively with company profits.

A number of negative influences also emerge. Controlling for the other factors, large firms with high equity ratios and strong capital intensity yield

---

[29] For specifics, see, for example, the data on S&P 500 dividend payouts compiled by indexarb.com at http://www.indexarb.com/dividendYieldSortedsp.html. Also, see the discussion in Carlson (2001) of declining U.S. dividend yields since the 1870s.

[30] See Fear (2005) on the industrialist August Thyssen, representing perhaps an extreme example of this practice. Thyssen distributed no dividends and took large depreciation expenses to build reserves. He also engaged in other interesting financial accounting practices.

[31] Since the models are estimated using fixed effects, the identity of the sector (which is constant over the period) cannot be included. Concentration ratios (Herfindahl index) for the various sectors can enter the analysis, since the ratios change over time, and they offer a specific example of why profits might vary by sector.

Table 6.12. *Determinants of Firm Profit Rates (ROA)*

	Baseline	V2AR	V2ARJSB
Number of shares outstanding	0.002	0.00	0.00
(ownership dispersion)	*0.48*	*0.54*	*0.57*
Size	−0.02	−0.02	−0.02
	0.00	*0.00*	*0.00*
Capital intensity	−0.04	−0.03	−0.04
	0.00	*0.00*	*0.01*
Lagged capital structure	−0.02	−0.01	−0.01
	0.03	*0.06*	*0.06*
Growth	0.02	0.03	0.02
	0.00	*0.00*	*0.00*
Market concentration	4.46	4.33	4.37
	0.00	*0.00*	*0.00*
Bank attachment		0.00	−0.003
		0.72	*0.16*
Constant	0.13	0.14	0.13
	0.00	*0.00*	*0.00*
Berlin listing	0.12	0.11	0.11
	0.03	*0.06*	*0.05*
Interaction terms with "Berlin listing"			
Number of shares outstanding	0.00	0.00	0.00
(ownership dispersion)	*0.90*	*0.97*	*0.95*
Size	−0.01	−0.01	−0.01
	0.03	*0.05*	*0.04*
Capital intensity	−0.001	−0.01	0.00
	0.95	*0.72*	*0.98*
Lagged capital structure	−0.01	−0.01	−0.01
	0.58	*0.58*	*0.57*
Growth	0.003	0.003	0.004
	0.61	*0.56*	*0.49*
Market concentration	3.00	2.82	2.73
	0.03	*0.04*	*0.04*
Bank attachment		0.01	0.01
		0.34	*0.25*
1896	−0.01	−0.01	
	0.03	*0.05*	
1897			0.01
			0.05
1898	0.00	0.00	0.01
	0.25	*0.22*	*0.00*

	Baseline	V2AR	V2ARJSB
1899	0.00	0.00	0.01
	0.50	*0.24*	*0.01*
1900	0.00	0.00	0.01
	0.83	*0.77*	*0.02*
1901	−0.01	−0.01	0.00
	0.02	*0.03*	*0.74*
1902	0.00	0.00	0.01
	0.29	*0.34*	*0.17*
1903	0.00	0.00	0.01
	0.68	*0.89*	*0.04*
1904	0.00	0.00	0.01
	0.78	*0.69*	*0.01*
1905	0.01	0.01	0.01
	0.12	*0.08*	*0.00*
1906	0.01	0.01	0.02
	0.09	*0.05*	*0.00*
1907	0.01	0.01	0.01
	0.11	*0.12*	*0.00*
1908	0.00	0.00	0.01
	0.45	*0.32*	*0.00*
1909	0.00	0.00	0.01
	0.58	*0.43*	*0.01*
1910	0.01	0.01	0.01
	0.17	*0.08*	*0.00*
1911	0.01	0.01	0.02
	0.01	*0.00*	*0.00*
1912	0.01	0.01	0.02
	0.02	*0.00*	*0.00*
Observations	3,205	3,225	3,229
Number of outliers	786	742	738
Prob > F	0.00	0.00	0.00
Within R2	0.15	0.15	0.15
Rho	0.71	0.71	0.72

Notes: Size is ln(total assets); capital intensity is fixed assets/total assets; growth (sales growth) is revenues/lagged revenues; capital structure is net worth (share capital plus reserves)/total assets; market concentration is the Herfindahl index for sales shares within sector. In columns 2 and 3, the bank attachment variables refer, respectively, to all banks (joint-stock or private) or just joint-stock banks (excluding private banks). P-values of t-statistics are entered in italics below coefficient estimates.

lower profits. As with market concentration, Berlin listing magnifies the negative influence of size. These indicators may represent conservatism of management, diversification of the firm's assets or markets, or stability of product markets and sales – all factors that tend to produce lower returns.

This more complete picture also demonstrates that bank affiliations exert essentially no influence on firm profitability. Since bank attachment does not cause growth (see Table 6.8), it is also unlikely that the banks caused any profitability gain via their indirect influence. Even stepping away from the question of causality, the results confirm the idea that using a bank affiliation as a signal of quality – in other words, strong returns to the investor – would have been a useless strategy for the uninformed outsider. The presence of bank directors in firm supervisory boards simply offered no consistent signal of superior performance.

Finally, the annual differences in profit rates reflect the vicissitudes of the economy and the stock market (see Figure 6.12). Firms showed high returns in the first year of the sample, 1895, and exceeded that performance only in 1906, 1911, and 1912. The relatively poor showing in 1896 (and the lack thereof following the crisis of 1907) is a bit surprising, but the significant decline of 1901 is exactly what one would expect.

MANAGERIAL TURNOVER AND FIRM PERFORMANCE

Firm performance and survival depend heavily on the actions and decisions of its leaders, and in joint-stock corporations, those leaders are often salaried managers. Thus, when firms perform badly, owners hold managers at least partly accountable. In a largely market-oriented financial system, as most would classify the United States and Great Britain, investors sell their stakes when they perceive a problem with a firm's profitability. And because asymmetric information prevents investors from knowing the true quality of managers, the shareholder uses stock price, accounting profits, or other quantitative performance measures to proxy for the manager's effectiveness. Thus, when investors begin to lose stock value, they pressure top executives and may even fire them. Observers often bemoan the myopia evidenced in these firings and suggest that the process inefficiently removes many managers who are truly performing as well as one could but who are simply caught in difficult situations beyond their control. At the same time, owners may retain bad managers who happen to preside over successful times.

In contrast, the common view of the German corporate governance system, with its focus on the information advantages of universal banks sitting in the governing boards of companies, suggests that these inefficient firings should be avoided. Formal relationships hypothetically allow banks to pinpoint the source of firm performance, and thereby eliminate only bad managers, regardless of firm-level outcomes. The implication is that managerial turnover will bear a negative relationship to firm performance (dividend-adjusted stock returns or profits) in general, but that the correlation will weaken for firms with bank relationships. That is, if bank overseers have better information or skills than firm owners in perceiving the need (or lack of need) for new management, then managerial turnover should be less tightly linked to observable firm performance when bankers are on the board.

Ownership patterns may also influence the relationship between managerial turnover and firm performance. When a firm is closely held, especially if it is largely family-owned, eliminating management – members of which may well be the owners themselves or close relatives – proves delicate and maybe even impossible. Since ownership structure is generally unknown for German firms at this time, the number of shares outstanding or the presence of stock market listings provides the next-best alternative. These proxy variables at least help distinguish very roughly between insider-dominated companies and those with markets for outsider equity stakes. If the German stock exchanges, especially the main equity market in Berlin, provided shareholders with a market for corporate control, then the fate of the management of firms listed on those exchanges should be tied more closely to the performance of their companies compared to unlisted firms.

Empirical Evidence on Managerial Turnover and Firm Performance

Board turnover is the proportion of board members who leave from one year to the next.[32] In the dual board structure of German corporations during the period studied here, the top managers made up the executive board, or the *Vorstand*, and were explicitly excluded from the supervisory board. Thus, the two boards turn over independently and often at different rates. These turnover variables permit a thorough investigation of the hypothesis that managers (or supervisory board members, for that matter) tended to depart when firms performed poorly. Just as expected, poor profit showing (ROA) increases managerial turnover very significantly (see Table 6.13). The connection is even tighter for particularly poor performers – those yielding negative ROA.

---

[32] This variable was created by entering into a spreadsheet the names of every company director and every supervisory board member in each sampled year, and then identifying changes in those lists from year to year.

Table 6.13. *Firm Performance and Executive Board Turnover, 1895–1913*

	1	2	3
ROA	0.43	−0.37	−0.37
	0.00	*0.00*	*0.00*
Loss-making (ROA < 0)	0.06	0.05	0.05
	0.00	*0.01*	*0.01*
Supervisory board turnover (%)	0.05	0.05	0.05
	0.00	*0.00*	*0.00*
Total number of executive board (VOR) members	−0.002	−0.002	−0.001
	0.78	*0.78*	*0.91*
Total liabilities (millions)	0.00	0.00	0.00
	0.84	*0.80*	*0.70*
Bank attachment (any kind of bank)		−0.01	
		0.50	
Interaction terms with "bank attachment"			
Return on assets		−0.10	
		0.54	
Loss-making (binary)		0.02	
		0.47	
Bank attachment – private banker			−0.02
			0.39
Bank attachment – provincial banker (only)			0.02
			0.45
Bank attachment – great banker (only)			−0.01
			0.75
Bank attachment – great and provincial bankers			−0.17
			0.00
Interaction terms with "bank attachment, by type"			
private banker × ROA			0.23
			0.30
provincial banker (only) × ROA			−0.58
			0.01
great banker (only) × ROA			−0.94
			0.05
great and provincial bankers × ROA			0.98
			0.00
private banker × loss-making			0.001
			0.98
provincial banker (only) × loss-making			0.02
			0.56
great banker (only) × loss-making			−0.07
			0.22

	1	2	3
great and provincial bankers loss-making			0.12 0.04
Berlin listing	−0.002 0.93	0.02 0.71	0.01 0.83
Interaction terms with "Berlin listing"			
ROA	−0.22 0.41	−0.23 0.39	−0.47 0.09
Loss-making	−0.04 0.43	−0.05 0.33	−0.07 0.18
Bank attachment (any)		−0.02 0.63	
Bank attachment – private banker			−0.005 0.92
Bank attachment – provincial banker (only)			−0.03 0.52
Bank attachment – great banker (only)			−0.001 0.98
Bank attachment – great and provincial bankers			0.06 0.33
Year indicators			
1901	−0.07 0.00	−0.07 0.00	−0.07 0.00
1908	−0.04 0.05	−0.04 0.05	−0.04 0.06
1909	−0.04 0.06	−0.04 0.06	−0.04 0.08
Observations	4,274	4,274	4,274
Prob > F	0.00	0.00	0.00
R2 (within)	0.06	0.06	0.07

Notes: The analysis uses fixed-effects regression, including a constant term (not reported). P-values of t-statistics are entered in italics below coefficient estimates. Only the statistically significant year indicators are reported, though all but the comparison year (1895) are included in the regressions.

Precisely in line with the institutional arrangements for hiring and firing top executives, managerial turnover responds positively to supervisory board turnover: When the general meeting of shareholders votes in new representatives to the *Aufsichtsrat*, those members in turn change the makeup of the executive board. Berlin listings also strengthen the relationship between firm performance and managerial turnover, so that those firms change even more board members for a given drop in earnings. Overall, though, listed firms have essentially the same rates of turnover as their unlisted counterparts. Moreover, among listed firms, stock returns provide much weaker prediction of turnover than do accounting measures of profits. Also, firm size and executive board size do not influence turnover rates, and that allays any fear that the turnover percentage might relate to turnover simply as a statistical artifact.

While managerial turnover varied some from year to year, there were only three years in which there was a significantly different proportion of managers leaving – compared to the first year of the sample. Those years, 1901, 1908, and 1909, had particularly low rates of turnover. At first, one might be surprised, thinking that the stock market crises of 1900–1 and of 1907 should have actually increased managerial turnover. The opposite turns out to be the case, and the explanation may be the following: In particularly bad years for the economy or the stock market, many firms perform poorly, and stakeholders are less likely to penalize their firm's directors when everyone else is doing badly as well. This finding alone says much about the German market for corporate control in the late-nineteenth and early-twentieth centuries. When combined with the other findings, the results suggest a system that functioned a lot like modern U.S. markets.

The Impact of Banking Relationships on Profits and Managerial Turnover

On the face of it, the presence of bankers on many company boards does differentiate the prewar German system from the more recent American system. The impact of those positions is less clear. In and of itself, a bank director sitting on the supervisory boards causes no change to the other relationships already discussed. In particular, the link between turnover and performance remains unchanged. But certain types of banks do seem to have some impact. Firms with a mix of great banks and provincial banks experience lower managerial turnover than everyone else. And they produce a positive relationship between performance and turnover (instead of the baseline negative effect). High profit firms have higher turnover in this case.[33] Private-bank attachment, on the other hand, produces no differences in the performance–turnover link.

---

[33] This result could indicate a missing piece of the story: that high performance of multiply attached firms relates temporally to changes that affect or stem from management changes.

Two categories of bank attachment do seem to matter. Compared to other firms, turnover is even more negatively related to profits for firms with great banks only or provincial banks only on their supervisory boards. This effect runs just the opposite of the posited result, under the assumption that bankers, because of their oversight, dampen the overreaction to bad results. A different take on the apparent effect might suggest that these bankers were actually correcting an underreaction to poor performance, perhaps because firms without bank board members had shareholders who could not effectively exercise their ownership rights. It is difficult to put too much credence in such an argument, however, given all the other findings: Turnover is very closely tied to performance even when a banker is not on board, and the other bank-attached firms have no such effects on their turnover–performance link.

SUMMARY AND CONCLUSIONS

This chapter presents a wide range of evidence on the financing and performance of German firms during the later stages of industrialization and offers several key findings. On the financing front, debt was costly in Germany relative to the U.K. but was comparable in price to that offered in the United States. Still, joint-stock firms gradually decreased their equity capitalization over the period, transitioning slowly to more debt financing. The financing behavior of German corporations falls generally in line with much of the theoretical literature on capital structure, in that firms structure their liabilities according to the relative costs and benefits and within the constraints of availability of collateral and desire to maintain control over decision making. Firms also seem to rely considerably upon internal funds to finance new investment in fixed capital, but the evidence of binding liquidity constraints is weak. Particularly in light of the apparent pattern of paying off debt with newly generated income, the sensitivity of investment to internal funds is less justifiable as a sign of credit rationing.

As a rule, small, young firms grew faster than large, old firms; and firms in the frontier technology sectors of the time grew faster than those in the "old-economy" sectors of the era. On the flip side, failures appeared most among small, old firms, in old-technology sectors, particularly those with significant debt burdens and poor profitability. Financial returns to corporate firms varied widely but measured up well on average. A large proportion of firms paid out no dividends at all, but average dividends still far exceeded modern rates. Similar patterns emerge for ROA and stock returns; a significant segment of firms did not perform well, but the strong showing of the rest tended to produce handsome rewards overall.

Managerial turnover responded very strongly to firm performance and to the reconfiguration of supervisory boards (the body that appoints and dismisses the executive board), suggesting that Germany had active markets for corporate control at the time. Accounting measures of profits relate the most significantly, indicating that stakeholders or their representatives took action when they perceived signs of poor long-range performance. Shareholders' representatives reacted less severely to low dividends or stock returns; and managers were much less likely to leave during times of widespread downturns in profitability.

Bank board memberships may have served important purposes – if only providing better than average entrepreneurial or strategic advice to managers – but they did not generally alter or respond to the behavior or performance of firms involved with them. The skepticism raised in earlier chapters about the ability of banks to influence firms in fundamental and consistent ways finds further support in this chapter. In particular, the relevance of bank board memberships almost always depends on the category of bank involved. In other words, some as yet unidentified correlates of certain types of bank relationships may matter (and then only in some situations), but bank board memberships themselves generally do not. At the same time, and perhaps a corollary, bank board memberships have no demonstrable downsides for firm financing or performance either.

Perhaps even more surprising, stock market listings appear as a key correlate of most of the financing and performance measures investigated here. Firms with Berlin listings used much less debt, especially short-term debt, than unlisted firms or those listed on provincial exchanges; instead, they were much more likely to raise equity. Firms with Berlin listings performed better on average and turned over management more readily in the face of poor performance. These findings underscore the potential information and liquidity benefits of stock markets and suggest that the German version of markets provided much more of these services than might be expected based on the traditional view of German financial history. The role of the stock markets receives much further investigation in the next chapter.

APPENDIX: SURVIVAL MODELS

To avoid the possibility of survivorship bias, given the fact that the sample was chosen from firms existing in 1903, the models of firm survival drop all observations before 1902, and include only firms that were not already in liquidation before 1902. Each failing firm contributes only one observation to the sample, corresponding to the year in which it failed. Following Tyler Shumway (2001), values from the previous year replace any missing observations of the financial variables, and all explanatory variables take lagged values in order to ensure that the data were observable at the beginning of the given year. Finally, multivariate outliers at a 10 percent level of significance were excluded prior to any estimation, using the method introduced by Hadi (1992, 1994).

The typical method for forecasting bankruptcy is a hazard model, which Shumway (2001) shows to be superior to a single-period model. The same author also shows that the hazard model is equivalent to a multiperiod logit model, in which the most restrictive assumption is the independence of the error term across observations. A relaxation of this assumption is a panel regression, as suggested by Thomas Astebro and Joachim Winter (2001). The same authors argue in favor of a multinomial logit instead of a binary method, differentiating between failure and mergers. Such a distinction is infeasible given the sample at hand, where the number of acquired firms is insignificant. Hence, the estimation methods are a pooled and a random-effects logit, allowing for a quick assessment of the independence assumption. In all equations, the dependent variable takes the value 1 if the firm is in liquidation and 0 otherwise.

The results given are odds ratios, defined as the exponential of the logit coefficient. For the binary variable differentiating positive and nonpositive values of cash flow, for example, the ratio is defined as follows:

$$[P(\text{inliquid} == 1 \mid \text{cash flow} \le 0) / P(\text{inliquid} == 0 \mid \text{cash flow} \le 0)] / < P(\text{inliquid}==1 \mid \text{cash flow} > 0) / P(\text{inliquid} == 0 \mid \text{cash flow} > 0)]$$

Since the odds ratio in this example is 4.73, the odds of failing when having negative profits are nearly five times higher than when having positive profits. In the sample, the following patterns appear: When cash flow is negative or zero, 23 observations have failures and 427 survive, so the empirical odds would be 0.054. When positive cash flows exist, 19 observations fail and 2,730 survive, so the empirical odds would be 0.007. Thus, the empirical odds ratio is even higher than that estimated in the model – primarily because extreme outliers identified by the multivariate outlier test are dropped.

7

Securities Markets

Existing work on the German financial system pays little attention to the securities markets in the pre–World War I era, in large part due to an assumption that these markets played hardly any role in the development of German industry at that time. Moreover, most modern research on comparative financial systems has viewed markets and banks as substitutes rather than complements and has assumed that markets embedded in universal systems naturally languish or perform poorly. This chapter sets the record straight by examining the origins of German securities markets, as well as their regulation, microstructure, and efficiency in the pre–World War I era. The results indicate that the German financial system of that era supported large and vibrant securities markets that performed very well, even by contemporary American standards. Supporting the previous chapters' findings on the close connections between bank relationships and stock market listings, this chapter argues that the universal banks and stock markets maintained a symbiotic relationship, producing a corporate financial system that combined large, universal banks with active markets. This prominent historical example casts significant doubt on the traditional dichotomy drawn between banks and markets.

BACKGROUND ON STOCK MARKET REGULATION AND COMPANY LAW

The German financial system has frequently been described as fundamentally bank-centered; one in which the financing of industry flows primarily through banks, to the exclusion of securities markets. This perception stems primarily from the post–World War II experience, when the banks did indeed play an unusually significant role in corporate finance, and securities markets lagged those of some other highly industrialized economies.

This chapter takes a longer perspective on the growth and evolution of the German securities markets, looking back well before World War I, and demonstrates the strength, size, and vitality of those markets before and during the second industrial revolution. The record of the German markets in the nineteenth and early-twentieth centuries resoundingly rejects the notion of the dichotomy of banks versus markets, showing instead a great interdependence of the two main components of corporate financial systems. This retrospective pays particular attention to the regulation and taxation of the German stock exchanges in order to link the political and economic developments closely together.

A Brief History of the German Stock Exchanges

As did many medieval European trading cities, Hamburg and Cologne developed formal securities exchanges in the middle of the sixteenth century. The Cologne exchange, founded in 1553, was originally the work of a group of local businessmen; formal regulation, however minimal, began before the end of the century. In the first two centuries of operation, the exchanges served only regional business, trading largely commercial paper, and laying idle for extended periods. As the Enlightenment built, business leaders in several German cities created new securities markets, and trading began at more regular intervals. But the more significant push for securities markets arrived with the first sparks of industrialization, around the turn of the nineteenth century.[1] By then, securities and commodities exchanges had appeared throughout Germany, dealing in a varying combination of securities and commodities.[2]

The securities exchanges listed mostly debt securities in the early years of their active development; equity securities played little role. Tight government controls over incorporation and limited liability rights kept entrepreneurs from using the joint-stock form, thus severely limiting the number of shares in circulation or available for public trading. Few proto-industrial undertakings warranted the formation of share corporations, but

---

[1] The primary American market, the New York Stock Exchange, began around the same time: "The New York Stock Exchange traces its origins back more than 200 years, to the signing of the Buttonwood Agreement by 24 New York City stockbrokers and merchants in 1792." See the historical review by the New York Stock Exchange, www.nyse.com.

[2] See Chapter 2 as well as Taeuber (1911). Such was the situation in 1911, although several of the exchanges began operations in the late-nineteenth or early-twentieth centuries. Another eight to ten exchanges dealt only in commodities (such as the shipping exchange in Ruhrort and the agricultural product exchange in Stuttgart).

those that did faced a difficult government concession process. As early as 1757, recorded prices indicate that at least two companies, the Asiatischen Compagne and the Bengalischen Compagne, traded on the Berlin exchange. Still, in 1800, only four joint-stock companies operated in all of Prussia, and in 1835, only twenty-five such companies functioned. Even by 1870, a cumulative total of approximately two hundred share corporations (*Aktiengesellschaften*) had formed in Prussia.[3]

The year 1870 brought German victory in the Franco–Prussian War, an enormous war indemnity payment, and the subsequent formation of the Second German Empire (the *Kaisserreich*). These events coincided with a new wave of industrialization – a time of great scientific innovation and discovery, rapid technological change in many branches of production, and burgeoning growth of heavy industries. The inherent risk of investments, coupled in many cases with a large minimum-efficient plant scale, encouraged entrepreneurs to seek outside equity investors and to limit their personal liability. With the enactment of a national company law and the loosening of incorporation restrictions in 1870, the government lifted the age-old roadblocks to the formation of joint-stock corporations. As business owners took advantage of their new liberty, hundreds of companies incorporated – over nine hundred between 1871 and 1873, more than half of which formed in 1872 alone (see Figure 7.1). The ranks of joint-stock companies swelled to over one thousand in 1873. The numbers exceeded three thousand by 1890 and stayed well over five thousand from the late 1890s until after World War I.[4]

Finally, share companies had begun to play a major role in the economy, and a substantial pool of equity securities gained admission for trading on the exchanges. The growing prevalence of the joint-stock form altered the balance of exchange business, especially at the larger bourses. Berlin, for example, traded mainly state bonds and other government paper until 1870 but shifted toward industrial securities once they became more widely used. Smaller, provincial exchanges retained their focus on local issues, though joint-stock companies gained ground across Germany. As Chapter 2 noted, Frankfurt and Hamburg maintained the leading exchanges in Germany until the formation of the Empire, when Berlin took over as the national

---

[3] See Wehler (1987), p. 103, for 1800, and Pohl (1982), p. 171, for 1835. See Horn (1979), p. 136, for 1870.

[4] Fohlin (2005) chronicles the post–World War I development of the German stock exchanges. Listings continued to increase rapidly during and shortly after the war. Chapter 8 also discusses the stock exchanges following the First World War.

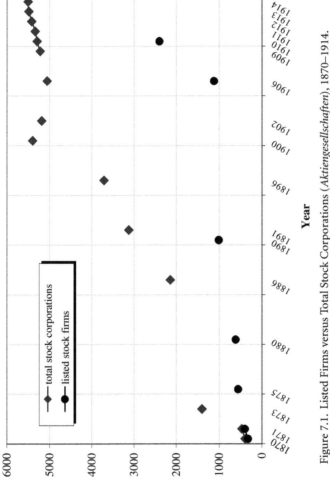

Figure 7.1. Listed Firms versus Total Stock Corporations (*Aktiengesellschaften*), 1870–1914.

Table 7.1. *Shares of Stock Exchanges in Tax Receipts, 1882–1893 and 1901–1913 (Percent)*

	1882–93			1901–13		
	Share Issue Tax (*Effektenstempel*)	Turnover Tax (*Umsatzsteuer*)	Total	Share Issue Tax (*Effektenstempel*)	Turnover Tax (*Umsatzsteuer*)	Total
Berlin		73.0	66.0		65.0	
Bremen			0.8			
Breslau			1.7			
Dresden			1.6			
Frankfurt/ Main	16.0	12.0	12.0	5.9	5.3	
Hamburg			9.0	5.3	5.3	5.3
Hanover	1.0	0.4				
Cologne		0.6	1.3	3.5		
Königsberg		0.2				
Leipzig			1.6			
Stuttgart		(0.6)	0.8	(1.5)		

Source: Calculated from Gömmel (1992). Empty cells indicate that the data are missing. Parentheses indicate estimates.

center of both politics and finance.[5] Turnover on the Berlin exchange averaged an estimated nine and twelve times that of Frankfurt and Hamburg, respectively, in the period between 1885 and 1913.[6] Berlin also far outpaced the other exchanges in tax receipts (for both new issues and turnover) and numbers of shares listed (see Tables 7.1 and 7.2).[7] Even before Berlin took over as the primary exchange, virtually all of the registered *Aktiengesellschaften* listed their shares there (see Table 7.1). As the use of the joint-stock form grew, a smaller proportion of new AGs listed their shares. Even by the early 1870s, the percentage listed in Berlin fell by almost half. Still, almost a third of joint-stock firms were listed in Berlin for most of the 1890s and early 1900s.

The quick drop in the percentage of firms with stock market listings coincided with an even larger decline in the average capitalization of firms. The firms incorporating in the first three years of general incorporation issued a total of 2.8 billion marks of share capital, for an average of 3 million marks apiece. The peak came sometime in 1872, when average share capital

---

[5] See Gömmel (1992), Marx (1913), and Pohl (1982).

[6] Wetzel (1996), p. 431 (Appendix VI).

[7] Note that Frankfurt listed nearly as many foreign securities as did Berlin. See also Wormser (1919), p. 229, for tax receipts in Berlin, Frankfurt, and Hamburg between 1900 and 1913.

Table 7.2. *Number of Shares* (Dividendenpapiere) *Listed on German Exchanges, circa 1910*

	Domestic Securities		Foreign Securities		Total Listed Securities	
	Entities	Issues	Entities	Issues	Entities	Issues
Augsburg	52	53	4	4	56	57
Berlin	914	996	56	62	970	1058
Bremen	55	57	2	2	57	59
Breslau	63	66	–	–	63	66
Dresden	211	223	2	2	213	225
Düsseldorf	78	78	–	–	78	78
Essen	68	68	–	–	68	68
Frankfurt	269	291	45	51	314	342
Hamburg	131	143	17	17	148	160
Hanover	39	41	–	–	39	41
Cologne	121	122	8	8	129	130
Königsberg	15	15	–	–	15	15
Leipzig	134	151	1	1	135	152
Magdeburg	31	33	–	–	31	33
Mannheim	62	63	–	–	62	63
Munich	95	99	4	4	99	103
Stettin	29	32	–	–	29	32
Stuttgart	43	44	–	–	43	44
Zwickau	23	28	–	–	23	28

Sources: Calculated from Krupke (1910–12) and Wormser (1919, from official price quotation pages [*Kursblätter*] of the respective exchanges), p. 221.

hit 3.85 million marks. The mid- to late-1870s would become the worst market for new issues in the following half-century. By 1875, the average share capital fell below 1 million, and the next year, that figure dropped below 0.5 million marks. The declining average size of issues likely indicates the greater relative benefits of incorporation to larger firms compared to small ones. Larger firms are more likely to seek a market for shares, though obvious counterexamples to the pattern (such as Krupp) certainly exist. As incorporation became more common, and as founders aged, smaller firms became more likely to go public or at least take on a corporate form. The year 1878 marked the ebb tide of the first incorporation cycle: Only forty-two new companies (AGs) formed with a total of 18 million marks of share capital (average of 320,000 marks). The numbers and sizes of new firms waxed and waned through the rest of the prewar period, but the highs and lows of the *Gründerjahre* remained unmatched (see Figure 7.2).

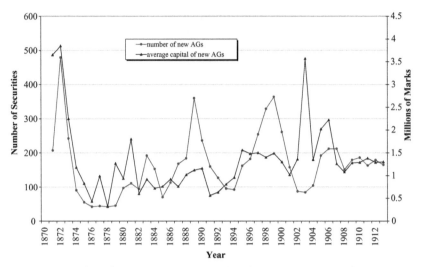

Figure 7.2. Number of New Corporations (AGs) and Average Share Capital, 1870–1913. *Sources: Handbuch der deutschen Aktiengesellschaften* (various years), Liefmann (1921), Riesser (1910 [1911]).

Regulating the Exchanges

Private chambers of commerce (*Handelskammern*) or similar trade organizations provided the sole regulation of the stock exhanges well into the nineteenth century and continued their extensive involvement even after government intervention intensified following the crisis of the 1870s.[8] The agricultural sector maintained a powerful voice in exchange regulation due to their strong interest in commodities trading. And naturally, the bankers, as the main providers of underwriting services, played a singificant role as well. As Chapter 2 noted, bankers became involved in the exchanges from their inception, and the linkages increased over time, as both universal banks and joint-stock companies grew and issued more and more new securities.

Though the universal banks remained virtually unregulated except by laws applying to all joint-stock companies, regulations and taxes on both joint-stock companies and stock exchanges influenced the operations of the banks. Indeed, tightening regulations on securities markets but not on the activities of universal banks may have actually encouraged growth of the

---

[8] See also Chapter 2 on securities market development.

banking sector at the expense of the exchanges.[9] Thus, company law and stock market regulations, according to both contemporaries and subsequent observers, made a variety of impressions on the German financial system as it developed over the last decades of the nineteenth century and the first decade of the twentieth.

Underwriting New Issues and Admission of Shares to Official Trading

Most of the issuing of new securities in Germany proceeded through the universal banks. Flotations could be performed in two ways: by direct subscription of shares (*Zeichnungsgründung* or successive founding) or by the taking over of shares by a promoter or underwriter and subsequent sale of the shares to the public (*Übernahmegründung* or simultaneous founding). The latter method prevailed in Germany during this period. Some have argued that the German method of underwriting arose because successive subscription was infeasible: The investing public in Germany required a seal of approval on individual securities and, more fundamentally, needed a role model for investing in general.[10] While investor naiveté might partially explain the need for simultaneous issuing, particularly early in the nineteenth century, there is also strong reason to believe that legal stipulations on new issues played a major part in determining the manner in which new securities were floated and possibly also helped shape the universal banking system. Indeed, Robert Liefmann (1921) attributed the form of the German universal banks to the regulations imposed on company promotions:

> Although of course other factors have contributed, and it has also to be recognized that the legal processes of promotion have themselves been shaped by special economic circumstances, none the less it can be asserted that it is the "simultaneous" German method of promotion, in opposition to the "successive" method of English law, which has given the German banks their special character.[11]

The 1870 company law nationally unified the regulation of share companies (*Aktiengesellschaften* and *Kommanditgesellschaften auf Aktien*).[12] Both

---

[9] This question comes to the fore later in this chapter.

[10] It is not clear why the German public would be more in need of a role model for investing than would the people of other countries at similar stages of development. Moreover, the German railroad boom, which preceded that for industrial companies, was largely financed by successive issue. So, arguments based on investor naiveté probably fail to hold up under closer scrutiny. The direct subscription method predominated in Britain.

[11] Liefmann (1921), p. 476, cited in Whale (1930), p. 40.

[12] See Whale (1930), pp. 331–3, for a discussion of different company forms in Germany. Briefly, an *Aktiengesellschaft* is a straight joint-stock company with limited liability, directed by an executive board (*Vorstand*). The *Kommanditgesellschaft auf Aktien* combines

the 1870 law and its 1884 revision required the full amount of an issue to be subscribed and at least 25 percent to be paid up before a new joint-stock company could be founded; for shares issued at higher than nominal value, 50 percent payment was required.[13] Moreover, a prospectus, specifying a time period within which the subscriptions would take place, was required; and the opening general meeting of shareholders had to attract attendance of a minimum percentage. Underwriting issues on the basis of subscriptions, for either new or transformed firms, could therefore cause long delays and possibly failure of an issue to meet regulations and deadlines. Thus, having an informed intermediary take over the full capital to be floated provided insurance to the company that the issue would succeed. In the German financial system, the logical providers of simultaneous underwriting services were the universal banks and, for large issues, the Berlin-based great banks in particular.

Through their stipulations on underwriting new issues, the 1870 and 1884 company laws solidified the position of the universal banks as industrial firms' main conduit to the securities markets. In particular, the need to pay up and, in some cases, hold shares in advance of operations and trading required substantial resources on the part of underwriters and therefore encouraged banks to expand both their capital and their customer networks. These incentives grew in line with the volume of new share issues – whether resulting from flotations of new companies, conversions of old private firms into share companies, or mergers and acquisitions activities of existing firms. Although the universal banks, and the private banks before them, arranged most company flotations even before the 1884 law, Whale (1930, p. 43), noted that the new law "can be held to have influenced the situation, in the sense that it provided new reasons for the intervention of the banks at a time when the original reasons were losing some of their force." This conclusion may overstate the impact of the 1884 law: If the need for simultaneous foundings, and therefore for large, universal banks, stemmed from stipulations on paying up shares, then the initial 1870 law should have provided the necessary impetus long before the 1880s.

managing partners with unlimited liability (*Geschäftsinhaber*) with limited liability shareholders. Both types of firms were required to have a general meeting (*Generalversammlung*) and a supervisory board (*Aufsichtsrat*). This latter body selects the *Vorstand* in the case of an AG. The discussion here addresses the AG form, since it dominated the KG; but regulations and de facto rights of shareholders were very similar.

[13] Text of share company law of 1884 (Gesetz, betreffend die Kommanditgesellschaft auf Aktien und die Aktiengesellschaften), Articles 209e and 210.

Regulations did change somewhat in the 1880s. The 1884 company law, as well as stock exchange regulations of 1881 and 1884, tightened up requirements on both underwriting and stock exchange listing. The 1884 law also strengthened the supervisory board (*Aufsichtsrat*). Prior to the 1884 law, most supervisory board members took little responsibility for supervising company operations; the position was often seen as sinecure, despite the controlling function outlined in the 1870 law. The 1884 law also required a complete split between the supervisory and executive boards. Whereas the 1870 law granted supervisory board members the right to obtain information about the company, the 1884 law made such oversight a duty.[14]

Tighter control of stock companies could not and did not prevent either the increase in stock prices in the late 1880s or the crash that followed in the early 1890s, especially in 1891. In the wake of these severe price declines, as well as several sensational trials over embezzlement and other abuses relating to stock market transactions, the public began to decry the rampant speculation and corruption. Although the bourses were ostensibly already regulated by the government by this time, many called for stricter protections for shareholders.[15] Moreover, farmers, blaming futures trading for low grain prices, demanded curtailment of stock exchange operations and of the forward market in particular. Thus, economic circumstances begot political pressure, and in 1892 the legislature formed a stock exchange enquiry commission (*Börsenenquetekommission*) to investigate charges and recommend remedies.

The law that resulted, the 1896 *Börsengesetz*, contained a number of measures that affected the issuing and listing of securities. For joint-stock firms transformed out of existing private companies, the new law stipulated a waiting period of one year after entry into the commercial registry, as well as a published balance sheet and profit and loss statement for that year, before the shares could be admitted to official trading.[16] In addition, only fully paid issues could be officially traded. Given that most shareholders wanted an active market for their shares, these new regulations meant that most firms would encounter difficulty in attracting outside investors if left to their own devices. It is commonly believed that these restrictions, while perhaps protecting shareholders, created a need for greater bank credit, pushed more

---

[14] Interestingly, though the 1870 law stipulated that supervisory board members must own shares of the firm on whose board they sat, the 1884 law made such equity stakes optional.

[15] Buss (1913), Meier (1993), Schulz (1994), and Wiener (1905).

[16] Conversions (*Umwandlungen*) far outpaced new creations (*Neugründungen*) by the early years of the twentieth century and ran about equal by the end of the nineteenth century. Weber (1915), pp. 224–5, and Whale (1930), pp. 41–2.

securities trading from the exchanges to the banks, and compounded the incentives for growth and concentration of universal banking stimulated by the earlier company laws.

The 1896 law also created new governing institutions for the stock exchanges – the *Staatskommissar*, the *Ehrengericht* (a judiciary body), and the *Börsenausschuss* (a committee of experts) – in order to ensure closer scrutiny of new issues. In addition, the law stipulated tighter enforcement of regulations and legal recourse to injured parties. Moreover, the law provided for greater independence in the body admitting securities to the exchanges (the *Zulassungstelle*); for example, the law dictated that half the members must not be listed in the stock exchange register, a third must not be involved in securities trading, and nobody involved in a new issue be permitted any say in the acceptance of that issue to trading.[17] The legislation reinforced the liability clauses of the 1884 law, making underwriters specifically responsible for damages to investors stemming from false or misleading information provided in the required prospectus for new securities (unless investors could reasonably have known that the information was incorrect). Together, these stipulations were intended to assure investors of a minimum level of quality of securities traded at the exchanges and to ameliorate the natural information asymmetries between firms and outside investors as well as between underwriters and securities purchasers. If effective, then, the law should have improved confidence in the exchanges and promoted greater use of securities and of equities in particular.

The influence of these protective provisions, however, may well have been offset by the restrictions on new issues and by the most contentious measure in the new law: the prohibition on futures trading in the securities of mining and factory enterprises as well as in a wide range of commodities (grain and mill products). The ban on futures essentially closed down the Berlin commodities exchange, and, it has been argued, hampered the operations of the spot securities market and further increased demands for bank services as well. The popular view held that forward dealing increased volatility, but it was also argued that speculation in futures actually stabilized prices.[18] It should be noted, however, that the law left some uncertainty about what exact business was prohibited, and enforcement by the courts varied.[19] Thus, even for restricted securities, some futures trading probably persisted after 1896.

---

[17] Wiener (1905).
[18] Meier (1993) and Prion (1910, 1929).
[19] Bund der Landwirte (1908) and Buss (1913).

The ban is also argued to have pushed more securities trading into the universal banking system, as those institutions attempted to simulate futures contracts. Naturally, centralized banks with larger clienteles and dealings in wider ranges of securities – in this case, the great banks – would have gained an advantage over smaller, provincial banks and private bankers. The lack of futures trading may have increased the demand for cash, and therefore for bank credit, for securities transactions. According to this line of thinking, the futures prohibition would have spurred further banking concentration. It is thought that these effects on securities markets and banking concentration proved difficult to reverse and lingered even after the 1908 amendment (*Aktiennovelle*) rescinded the blanket prohibition of futures trading.

Taxation of Bourse Transactions

Legislative intervention in the stock exchanges extended also to the realm of taxes; and several measures between 1880 and 1913 imposed a variety of duties. After four unsuccessful attempts in 1869, a tax on exchange transactions was finally introduced in 1881. The tax consisted of two parts: a stamp tax on final certificates of transfer (*Schlussnotenstempel*) and a tax on all new issues of securities (*Emissionsstempel*). The former amounted to a flat 20 pfennig per trade (one mark for forward trades), while the latter required a 1 to 5 per thousand pfennig fee on the face value of all new issues, depending on the type of security involved. Agitation for a percentage tax on bourse transactions continued, and, in 1885, a one-tenth per thousand pfennig tax replaced the flat tax. Nine years later, this tax was doubled to two-tenths per thousand pfennig and was imposed on all amounts, not just on every thousand marks. Very small transactions, those less than 600 marks, remained exempt. The 1900 stamp tax law eliminated this exception, increased all rates further, and initiated a tax on the issue and transfer of mining stocks (*Kuxe*). Thus, as the exchanges grew in importance over the last twenty years of the nineteenth century and beyond, their use as a tax revenue generator did as well (see Table 7.3).

At the time of the 1885 tax legislation, some policy makers, economists, and businessmen recognized that the tax might create an incentive for concentration in banking. Since banks could balance purchase and sale orders outside of the bourse and pay the tax only on the net transaction, large banks benefited from a network externality of sorts: Larger clienteles meant a broader market for securities and therefore more untaxed commissions on internal trades. Thus, the tax spurred banks to increase their customer base, and such growth meant encroachment on provincial-bank territory.

Table 7.3. *Rates of Stock Exchange Issuance Tax* (Effektenemissionssteuersätze) *and Turnover Tax* (Börsenumsatzsteuersätze), *1881–1909*

| | Shares (%) | | Debt Securities (%) | | | | Acquisitions (%) | |
| | | | Domestic | | Foreign | | | |
	Domestic	Foreign	Private	Public	Private	State	Securities	Goods
1881	0.5	0.5	0.2	0.1	0.2	0.2	0.01	0.02
1885	0.5	0.5	0.2	0.1	0.2	0.2	0.01	0.02
1894	1.0	0.15	0.4	0.1	0.6	0.6	0.02	0.04
1900	2.0	0.25	0.6	0.2	1.0	0.6	0.02/0.03/0.1	0.04
1909	3.0	3.0	2.0	0.5	2.0	1.0		

Sources: Calculated from Gömmel (1992), p. 168, and Warschauer (1905), p. 61.

The tax savings allowed larger banks to decrease commission rates to rates well below those charged by smaller, provincial banks. As tax rates increased, so did the savings from internal trading. This situation persisted until June 1900, when the new tax law eliminated the exemption on internal, or compensatory, transactions.

Jakob Riesser argued that compensatory transactions gave the great banks an insuperable advantage over the provincial banks:

[Compensatory transactions] remained untaxed until the extensive increases in bank capital, which had been made as a result of the stock exchange legislation, and the large number of branches and deposit offices which had meanwhile been established, made it seem hopeless for the smaller provincial bankers ever to overcome the lead which the banks in the meantime had gained on them.[20]

For a time, the advantage of the large, Berlin banks was magnified due to the double taxation of provincial banks executing orders through their Berlin correspondents.[21] That is, a provincial banker, having passed a security transaction to a banker on the exchange in Berlin, could turn over the original transfer certificate (*Schlussnote*) only if the provincial banker revealed the name of the bank performing the transaction in Berlin. Otherwise, the provincial banker must provide his own seal and pay the tax again. Until this system was amended by the 1894 stamp act, the extra tax burden added to the commission and brokerage costs borne by the provincial bankers, and therefore by their customers.

[20] Riesser (1910 [1911]), p. 620.
[21] Schumacher (1911), pp. 195–7, Riesser (1910 [1911]), p. 619, and Whale (1930), p. 34.

Price Setting on the Exchanges

A final set of institutions, those relating to price setting for traded securities, includes both rules set by the exchanges themselves and regulations imposed by the government. German exchanges were call markets throughout the period studied here, and price setting changed comparatively little over the period between 1880 and 1913, though the 1884 and 1896 stock exchange laws formalized certain institutions that were already common practice, at least in Berlin. The exchanges employed two sets of brokers for much of the nineteenth century: private brokers and official brokers (*vereidigte Maklern*). According to the 1884 law, the latter were appointed for life terms and were legally prohibited from trading on their own accounts (but apparently often did so nonetheless) or joining with other brokers. The official brokers were responsible for setting securities prices based on the unified price system. Under this procedure, brokers balanced purchase and sale orders and determined, after a round of price announcements and recalculations, the final binding price for all orders placed that day. The unified price system arguably ensured a significant level of transparency and therefore confidence in securities transactions on the Berlin exchange.[22] On the other hand, contemporary observers claimed that price setting was not exact or reliable enough and that, in setting the market price, the brokers often followed the wishes of interested bankers, especially when a deal could not be executed on the given day.[23] Indeed, such critics joined the voices calling for reform in the early 1890s.

The 1896 law instituted the official brokers (*Kursmaklern*) and established the unified price system as the national norm. To the extent that these institutions existed informally prior to the 1896 law, little change in behavior would be expected. The new regulations also stipulated that the exchange directors officially set prices in the absence of outsiders. That is, only the commissioner, secretary, brokers, directors, and representatives of other trades prescribed by exchange regulations were permitted to be present. To the extent that these prescriptions minimized opportunities for tampering with independent price setting, the law may have improved transparency and public confidence in the exchanges. At the same time, however, if bank intervention limited price volatility, and if the law hampered such involvement, then these measures on their own might have increased volatility. The general use of the unified price system eliminated one major reason

---

[22] Schulz (1994) and Tilly (1995).
[23] Wiener (1905).

for price differences among the various exchanges on which individual securities were multiply listed. Thus, a further result of the new law was the loss of many arbitrage opportunities and a significant source of income for the banks.[24]

STOCK MARKET DEVELOPMENT AND PERFORMANCE WITHIN THE UNIVERSAL BANKING SYSTEM

Previous chapters have hinted at the significance of the German stock markets in the financing of industrial companies before World War I and have identified an apparent link between these markets and the universal banks. These firm-level effects are manifest in the active use of new share capital to finance investment and, even more directly, in the listing of these equities on the stock exchanges. The following sections study a range of issues relating to the stock markets and their connections with the universal banking system: the impact of regulatory change on the development of both the markets and the banks; the influence of universal bank underwriting on the pricing of new share issues; the factors affecting firms' decisions about listing shares on the exchanges; cross-sectional firm characteristics predicting market returns; and the influence of market microstructure on pricing.

The Measurable Impact of Regulation and Taxation

The forgoing discussion identifies a number of possible effects of the various regulations enacted between 1880 and 1913. The brief overview gives a sense of the rapid succession and the often contradictory nature of potential influences. Laying out the important measures in chronological order along with the hypothesized impact on the financial system allows some disentanglement of the influences of legal and regulatory changes (see Table 7.4). There are at least three discernable ways in which regulations enacted between 1884 and 1913 might have influenced the various components of the financial system – growth of the universal banking sector, concentration among universal banks, and the expansion of commercial banking at the expense of securities markets.

---

[24] For example, according to Schulz (1994), Deutsche Bank earned 404 million marks on arbitrage business in 1895. The bank's arbitrage returns fell to 247.1 million in 1896, 155.2 million in 1897, 119.4 million in 1898, and to 94.3 million in 1900.

Table 7.4. *Chronology of Economic and Legislative Events*

Year	Date	Event	Concentration in Universal Banking	Expansion of Universal Banks	Use of Banks Over Securities Exchanges
					Hypothesized Effect on
1870		Company law (requirements on issuing shares)	+	+	+
1884	July 18	New company law: requirements on issuing shares, protections for shareholders	+	+	+
1885	May 24	Institution of percentage tax on stock transfers	+	+	+
1891		Fall in share prices			
1892	Feb. 6	Formation of stock exchange inquiry commission		+	
1893		Formation of Rhenish-Westphalian Coal Syndicate	+		
1894	April 27	Imperial Stamp Act; doubling of stock transfer tax	+	+	+
1896	June 22	Stock exchange law: prohibition on futures trading, waiting period	+	+	+
		Formalization of unified price system, tighter requirements and broader liability on new issues	+		−
1897		Formation of Rhenish-Westphalian Pig Iron Syndicate	+		
1900	June 14	Imperial Stamp Act; further tax increases	+	+	+
		Closing of tax loopholes on compensatory transactions	−		−
1901		Fall in share prices			
1907		Fall in share prices			
1908		New stock exchange law reinstating futures trading		−	−
1909		Increase in stock market issue tax	+	+	+

Notes: Blank cells indicate that the effect is indeterminate or the information is unknown.
Sources: Discussion in text and in Fohlin (2002b).

237

The first task in analyzing the impact of legislation is to create quantitative measures of the possible effects, recognize general patterns in these variables over time, and identify regulatory influences while controlling for other relevant factors. It is difficult, however, to isolate the influences of individual pieces of legislation. Of the legislative and economic events that took place between 1884 and 1900, seven plausibly could have spurred universal banking concentration, and six may have encouraged overall growth of the universal banking sector. No events before 1900 had effects that could be seen as slowing either growth or concentration, but such effects appear in both 1900 (for concentration) and 1908 (for growth overall). Effects of regulatory changes can also be difficult to pin down, when legislation is anticipated or is enforced gradually. For example, the 1896 stock exchange law is widely claimed to have significantly boosted universal banking growth and concentration. Yet the inquiry commission's deliberations began in 1892, and most of the law's provisions were not implemented until January 1, 1897. Most banks were likely aware of the impending need for greater capital well before the implementation of the law. Even in the case of tax increases, effects may be seen over the course of more than one year, particularly when the legislation appears midyear (as in the three major tax laws of 1885, 1894, and 1900). As a result, even disregarding nonregulatory forces, we might find a general trend toward growth and concentration in the universal banking industry, rather than large, discrete shifts in the two variables.

For the third category, the use of universal banks relative to securities exchanges, the hypothesized influences are split: three positive effects and three negative from 1884 to 1908. In two separate cases – the 1896 stock exchange law and the 1900 stamp act – the same piece of legislation contains clauses with countervailing hypothesized influences. At the same time, however, all three of the effects that might plausibly retard a shift of trading business from markets into universal banks are thought to have been minor compared to the forces pushing in the opposite direction. Thus, here too we ought to expect a positive trend over the period. But the wider spacing between the events thought to influence the relative use of banks and markets may permit discrete changes to appear more prominently. At the same time, one should keep in mind that tax increases may even result in higher measured turnover, because prices may rise even though quantities fall. For the 1896 law, since effects on the business of the exchanges would likely have been delayed until the provisions were in force, we should expect a significant change immediately following implementation, or, given the annual frequency of the data, by the end of 1897. The law left some uncertainty about what exact business was prohibited, and some have claimed that enforcement by the courts varied.[25] Thus, even for restricted securities, some futures trading probably persisted after 1897, and this delay might have spread the effects over a number of years.

Unfortunately, since most of the necessary data series begin in 1884, it is impossible to provide a baseline against which post-1884 data can be compared. Given the imposition of the percentage tax on stock transfers in 1885, it would be difficult in any case to disentangle the influences of the new company law and the increased taxes. The following analyses therefore restrict attention to legislative and economic events after 1884. The remaining data series still permit investigation of the regulatory changes of the 1890s. Even if the 1884 law set the processes of growth and concentration into motion, the later laws are commonly viewed as even more influential on the German economy. If so, their effects should compound existing trends. From a historical point of view, this marginal impact is of the greatest interest.

The first hypothesis is that the universal banking industry became significantly more concentrated between 1884 and 1913, and that this tendency increased after the tax and regulatory changes of 1894 and 1896. Chapter 4 traced the increasing concentration in the banking industry up to World War I and demonstrated the varying degrees of concentration over the period. Concentration ratios showed little growth in the market share of the largest banks (recall Figure 4.4 and Table 4.3).[26] If legislative changes had the supposed impact, banking industry concentration should have increased after 1885, 1893, 1894, 1896, 1897, and possibly 1900, and the data should exhibit a general trend toward concentration over the period. According to this first measure, the prediction turns out to be correct only for 1893–4. The asset-based concentration ratio increased from 34 to 39 percent in 1893 and 1894 and reached 43 percent in 1895. Though this development at first would seem to correspond to the legislative changes of 1892–6, the patterns outside of this short period undermine any causal interpretation: The ratio declined steadily between 1896 and 1901 and remained flat in the mid-1880s. While the largest banks did increase their share of assets between the beginning and end of the period, the increase was small – about 5 percentage points. The ratio declined on net in the latter half of the 1880s and remained around 33 to 34 percent in the early 1890s.

---

[25] Bund der Landwirte (1908) and Buss (1913).

[26] Figure 4.4 plots five-firm ratios for total assets and share capital as well as great-bank ratios for total assets and deposits for 1884–1913. Table 4.3 reports estimated five- and ten-firm ratios for total assets for 1890, 1900, and 1910.

Ratios using share capital further undermine the link between stock market regulations and banking concentration. The five-firm capital ratio increased 5 percentage points in 1895, but the largest banks had lost market share up through 1894, between 1895 and 1901, and again between 1904 and 1912. The divergence of capital and asset ratios, as Chapter 4 detailed, stemmed from the focus of the largest banks on deposit accumulation rather than on share issues. These findings also corroborate the claims of A. Weber (1915), regarding the concentration of German deposits within the Berlin joint-stock banks. The point raises a subsidiary but closely related issue: the ability of the largest banks to foster their brokerage and investment banking business through the development of deposit networks throughout the country. By increasing their presence outside Berlin, the great banks not only expanded their funds for lending, but they also created demand for securities, both new and old. Thus, since the hypothesized incentives for banking concentration stem from provisions regarding the securities business, we should expect that the greatest increases in concentration appear in measures based on deposits.

So far, these measures exclude an important component of the German industrial banking system: the private bankers.[27] Private-bank assets, by their nature, are difficult to count, but R. Goldsmith's (1969) estimates suggest that they amounted to at least that of joint-stock banks in the 1880s but only half between 1900 and 1913. When private banks are included, the concentration ratio for total assets falls to 16 percent in 1884 but reaches over 33 percent by 1913. Advanced statistics are unnecessary to spot the positive trend here, and this trend also swamps some of the yearly changes that appear in the joint-stock–only ratios. Most notably, the smoothing induced by the interpolated private-bank figures gives the appearance of a steady increase between 1895 and 1905. One should consider, however, whether private banks ought to be included in full in the denominator of these concentration ratios. Only a small percentage of these banks – albeit mainly the largest – competed with the joint-stock universal banks in commercial banking, brokerage, deposit taking, or underwriting. Many served a clientele that never dealt with joint-stock universal banks. Since private banks were not compelled to report any financial information, particularly not on an annual basis, it is exceedingly difficult to determine the size of the sector.[28] Including

---

[27] See Chapter 4 on the structure of the banking sector.

[28] The figures calculated here differ slightly from those presented in Tilly (1995), in which Figure 1 shows the equity capital of the six largest Berlin banks accounting for under 13 percent of the total in 1883 and just under 40 percent by 1913 (and peaking at 44 percent in 1905). The data in this chapter come from Deutsche Bundesbank (1976), *Saling's*

all private banks provides a lower bound on banking concentration in the early years and an upper bound on the rate of increase of concentration over the period. Even considering this upper bound, concentration in universal banking rose less than might be assumed. Clearly, concentration did not "precipitate itself headlong like a flood," as Riesser had so vividly described.[29]

The question remains, however, whether the observed increases in universal banking concentration resulted from regulation of the stock exchanges, from changes in the economy (such as growing concentration in industry), or from some combination of these two factors. It is therefore preferable to model the concentration ratio as a function of explanatory variables, some of which are related to regulatory changes, rather than simply to compare concentration before and after a legislative event. Regulatory changes are typically qualitative and are therefore represented by the timing of their enactment. One notable exception is taxes – a variable that may be measured simply by its percentage rate. Universal banking concentration can be seen as a function of a number of variables: regulatory dates, tax rates, and variables representing economic influences on concentration. Analyzing the impact of regulations presents problems of interpretation. The difficulty of identifying unique causes for the observed changes in the current case is particularly severe, especially in the period from 1892–1900. The few studies that have attempted a quantitative assessment of legal changes have focused exclusively on the 1896 stock exchange law, including an indicator variable only for the post-1896 period.[30] Other events in the mid-1890s also encouraged capital increases and greater bank concentration, especially the 1893 formation of the Rhenish-Westphalian Coal Syndicate and the 1894 doubling of the stock transfer tax (and other tax increases). Thus, models of banking concentration need to include variables for post-1892 and post-1894 subperiods, as well as the post-1896 period, and should also control for the overall trend. The post-1892 variable represents the formation of the stock exchange inquiry commission, while the 1894 variable represents the doubling of the stock transfer tax. These indicator variables may yield

---

Börsen-Jahrbuch, and *Handbuch der deutschen Aktiengesellschaften* for the joint-stock banks, and from Goldsmith (1969) for the private banks (using linear interpolation between his estimates for 1880, 1900, and 1913). Tilly uses figures from Bosenick (1912) and the *Deutschen Ökonomist* for the Berlin banks. The source of the discrepancy is unclear, but it may be the calculation of private-bank assets. If the Tilly figures use total assets of private banks but only equity capital for the joint-stock banks, then the concentration ratio would appear to be lower throughout the period, but this difference should be offset by the fact that he uses six banks rather than the five used here. While the differences in individual years are rather small, they yield obviously disparate trends in concentration overall.

[29] Riesser (1910 [1911]), p. 614. See Chapter 4 for the full quotation.

[30] See Tilly (1995).

significant coefficients simply because future changes are large enough to influence the average over the whole subperiod. To help determine whether there was any upward shift in the trend after a certain point, the analysis also investigates whether the trend changed significantly in each subperiod.

Riesser claimed that "concentration in banking, which had been greatly influenced both in the extent and rapidity of its progress by developments in industry, and particularly by the formation of cartels, in turn helped to bring about concentration in industry."[31] Given the lack of necessary data, economywide changes in industrial organization are not directly accounted for in the regression. Nonetheless, some reasonable variables are available to proxy for economic influences – such as availability of economies of scale and scope – that may lead larger banks to increase market shares at the expense of smaller banks. I include real net national product (NNP), total volume of new domestic share issues (in 1913 marks), average face value of new domestic shares (in 1913 marks), and an index of stock prices.[32]

Volume of share issues represents demand for underwriting and placement services. Increases in share volume should correlate positively with concentration, since larger banks located near securities markets are able to produce these services more readily than smaller banks located in the provinces. The average face value of new shares provides a measure of the scale of individual issues. Even more than the overall volume of issues, this variable captures the need for large intermediaries that could take share issues to market. Real net national product and the annual stock price index control for other economic influences on universal banking concentration. Given their stronger orientation toward the securities business, especially in Berlin, the largest universal banks benefited disproportionately from upswings in the stock market. Thus, universal banking concentration should increase during bull markets.

Concentration increased at an annual average rate between 1 and 3 percent from 1884 to 1913 (see Table 7.5). The lower bound, of course, reflects the exclusion of private banks, and the upper bound their inclusion.[33] These

---

[31] Riesser (1910 [1911]), p. 618.

[32] Some of these variables are suggested by Tilly (1995).

[33] The strong apparent serial correlation in the error is adjusted using a Cochrane-Orcutt regression. This procedure improves the Durbin-Watson statistics noticeably but also results in lower R-squared and F statistics. Hildreth-Lu and Prais-Winston corrections yield similar results. Concentration is measured by the five-firm ratio for total assets, including private banks. Because of the potential smoothing problem stemming from the interpolation of private-bank assets, Table 7.5 also reports regression results for the five-firm ratio based only on joint-stock bank assets.

Table 7.5. *Determinants of Concentration in German Universal Banking*

	Top 5 Bank Assets as a Share of Total Universal- and Private-Bank Assets				Top 5 Bank Assets as a Share of Total Universal-Bank Assets	
Real NNP	0.01	0.02	0.16	0.03	0.03	0.03
	0.35	*0.28*	*0.29*	*0.11*	*0.29*	*0.29*
Average face value of new domestic shares in Berlin (millions of 1913 marks)	38.52	34.63	36.92	35.32	55.99	55.99
	0.08	*0.08*	*0.07*	*0.08*	*0.16*	*0.16*
Annual stock exchange index	0.06	0.05	0.06	0.08	−0.03	−0.03
	0.10	*0.21*	*0.11*	*0.08*	*0.65*	*0.65*
Subperiod indicator variable	0.22	1.65	0.45	0.03	3.92	0.002
	0.87	*0.17*	*0.71*	*0.03*	*0.08*	*0.08*
	(post-1892)	*(post-1894)*	*(post-1896)*		*(post-1894)*	*(post-1894*yr)*
Turnover tax rate				70.29		
				0.09		
Year	0.52	0.47	0.50	0.25	−0.20	−0.20
	0.01	*0.01*	*0.01*	*0.25*	*0.54*	*0.53*
Constant	−977.16	−875.53	−931.06	−476.18	397.24	400.61
	0.01	*0.01*	*0.01*	*0.25*	*0.50*	*0.50*
Number of observations	29	29	29	29	29	29
F (Prob > F)	18.80	20.94	19.29	29.02	3.40	3.40
	0.00	*0.00*	*0.00*	*0.00*	*0.02*	*0.02*
Adj. R^2	0.77	0.78	0.77	0.83	0.30	0.30
D-W statistic (transformed)	1.60	1.60	1.54	1.64	1.70	1.70
Rho	0.70	0.70	0.79	0.65	0.54	0.54
	0.00	*0.00*	*0.00*	*0.00*	*0.00*	*0.00*

Notes: P-values of t-tests (two-sided) are entered in italics below coefficient estimates. Models are estimated using Cochrane-Orcutt regression. The final row of the table gives the resulting serial correlation estimate.

Sources: Concentration ratios calculated from Deutsche Bundesbank (1976), *Saling's* (various years), Goldsmith (1969), *Handbuch der deutschen Aktiengesellschaften* (various years); NNP from Hoffmann (1965); stock issues from Wetzel (1996); tax rates from Gömmel (1992); stock price index from Gielen (1994).

statistical results simply bear out the situation that is rather obvious from Figure 4.4, but they also serve as a reminder that one's understanding of banking concentration depends on one's views about the relevance of private banks in the concentration measure. Less obvious from visual inspection, there was no marked increase in concentration – as measured by the share of the great banks in total universal bank assets – after 1892, 1894, or 1896. The interaction of these subperiod indicators with the trend variable produces similarly insignificant coefficient estimates for this concentration measure. The joint-stock five-firm concentration measure, however, is significantly higher and increased faster after 1894 than before. Neither effect emerges for the post-1892 or post-1896 indicators. These findings suggest that the tax increase of 1894 was the most significant of the regulations imposed during this period, and that indeed the much-discussed stock exchange law of 1896 created no apparent effect. Such an inference is further bolstered by the significance of the turnover tax variable in explaining the movement of the first concentration variable (including private banks). Moreover, in this specification (column four of Table 7.5), the tax variable renders the trend insignificant. A somewhat puzzling finding, however, is that taxes produce no statistically significant effect on concentration among universal banks only.

The lack of response to the formation of the 1892 stock exchange inquiry commission may indicate that bankers only gradually determined the ramifications of the impending legislation, expected the law to be weak, or calculated that the provisions did not warrant early reaction. Indeed, Knut Borchardt's (1999, 2000) discussion of Weber's (1915) work on the inquiry commission suggests that the promulgation of a stock exchange law by 1896 took many observers by surprise. It is also possible that the universal banks saw the merit of increasing their capital in 1892 but were unable to do so until the improvement of economic conditions beginning in 1894 – at which point there were other reasons to expand.

Economic variables do provide further explanatory power. The size of new equity offerings, measured by the average face value of new domestic share issues (in real terms), obtains significant, positive coefficient estimates, particularly for the measure including private banks. In addition, the stock index is moderately significant in some models.[34] Both measures may capture the effects of growing industrial cartelization and concentration as well.

---

[34] The stock index is highly correlated with both net national product (NNP) and the volume of new domestic stock issues (80 and 87 percent, respectively) but is less correlated with average face value of new issues (38 percent).

Average face value of new stock issues, likely the closer proxy for industrial concentration, is the statistically stronger of the two measures. To the extent that industrial change proceeded consistently over time, the annual trend variable probably also subsumes such effects. Total volume of new issues and real NNP are both statistically insignificant, suggesting that the overall growth of industry is not closely linked to banking concentration.[35]

Growth of Universal Banking

Although expansion was most pronounced among the largest universal banks, regulatory change may have spurred a more general growth in the universal banking industry. Following a similar methodology as the concentration analysis, I also assess overall growth of universal banking as a function of regulatory and economic variables: real NNP, total face value of new domestic shares in Berlin (millions of 1913 marks), average face value of new domestic shares in Berlin (millions of 1913 marks), an annual stock exchange index, subperiod indicator variables (for regulatory events), the turnover tax rate, and a trend variable. Average face value of shares and stock price levels are expected to correlate only weakly with growth, as they pertain disproportionately to the largest banks and their demand for working capital for securities transactions.

Because of the forced smoothing of the estimated private bank assets, this analysis focuses on the joint-stock banks. The inclusion of private banks has little impact on the conclusions of the analysis, however, since estimated private-bank assets increased little throughout the period from 1884 to 1913. The dependent variable is the real value of total joint-stock universal bank assets, but average values of these banks' assets produce nearly the same results. Regressing the log of assets, in real terms, on a constant and time trend yields annual average growth rate estimates of less than 0.5 percent per year for the private banks, compared with a rate of 6.8 percent for the joint-stock universal banks. The growth in joint-stock universal bank assets stemmed both from the setup of new banks and from increases in the size of banks. Average assets per joint-stock universal bank grew at an estimated average of 3.6 percent per annum in this period. Given the historical record describing the absorptions of private bankers by joint-stock banks, it is likely that the number of private banks was declining, at least in the decade

---

[35] See Fohlin (2002b) on the differences between these findings and those in Tilly (1995) and Wetzel (1996). It may prove fruitful in future work to analyze the relationship between direct measures of industrial concentration and concentration in the universal banking industry.

before World War I. Thus, the fact that estimated private-bank assets grew at all in real terms suggests that the remaining private bankers were actually growing as well. Not surprisingly, given the previous discussion, great-bank and provincial-bank assets demonstrate similarly strong trends.[36] This result further demonstrates the extent to which the trend toward concentration (measured with private-bank assets) hinges on the relative lack of growth of private-bank assets.

Based on regulatory events, 1892, 1894, 1896, and 1900 should be the primary inception points for growth spurts in the universal banking sector. As with concentration, however, none of these dates marked the beginnings of growth spurts (see Table 7.6).[37] On the face of it, this statistical fact implies that the legal changes of the late-nineteenth century made no perceptible impression on the growth of the universal banking sector. The stock exchange tax variable (see the last column of Table 7.6), however, tells a more complex story.[38] Universal banking assets increased in line with the turnover tax rate, even though assets were not significantly higher overall in the post-1894 subperiod. Interestingly, however, the significance of the tax variable in the regression hinges on controlling for the real volume of new issues. The volume of new issues grew rapidly over the period but was slightly, though not significantly, dampened by the imposition of stock taxes. Only after controlling for this underlying force for expansion, and its negative relationship to tax rates, does the growth effect of the tax rate increases emerge.

In line with expectations, particularly in light of the immediately preceding discussion, the volume of new issues of domestic shares relates significantly (positively) to joint-stock universal bank assets. This variable produces the strongest effect, both in magnitude and statistical significance, after controlling for the overall trend. The inclusion of the trend variable, of course, ensures that the "new issues" effect is not simply a proxy for a trend variable. The importance of new issues of stocks, along with the

---

[36] When the log of real universal bank assets is regressed solely on a constant and a trend variable, the estimated coefficients are 0.073 for great banks and 0.063 for provincial banks. Part of this difference comes from the apparent movement of two banks from the provincial-bank category to the great-bank category in the source (Deutsche Bundesbank, 1976).

[37] In other words, the subperiod indicator variables yield statistically insignificant coefficients both on their own (indicating a shift in the constant) and when interacted with the trend variable (indicating a change in the slope).

[38] The regressions use the turnover tax, or the tax on transfer of securities (averaging the various rates imposed by the split in 1900). The issue tax rate is calculated as the sum of domestic shares and debt rates. That variable yields insignificant results and is not reported (regression estimates are available from the author).

Table 7.6. *Determinants of Growth in German Universal Banking*

	Total Real Assets of German Universal Banks (1913 marks)							
	Post-1892	Post-1894	Post-1896	Post-1892* yr	Post-1894* yr	Post-1896* yr	Post-1900* yr	
Real NNP	0.001	0.001	0.001	0.001	0.001	0.001	0.001	0.001
	0.07	*0.08*	*0.06*	*0.07*	*0.08*	*0.06*	*0.12*	*0.02*
New domestic shares, Berlin (total face value, millions of 1913 marks)	0.02	0.02	0.02	0.02	0.02	0.02	0.02	0.02
	0.00	*0.00*	*0.00*	*0.00*	*0.00*	*0.00*	*0.00*	*0.00*
Subperiod indicator variable	−0.02	0.02	0.06	0.00	0.00	0.00	0.00	
	0.66	*0.69*	*0.22*	*0.66*	*0.69*	*0.22*	*0.52*	
Turnover tax rate								3.09
								0.05
Year	0.06	0.05	0.05	0.06	0.05	0.05	0.05	0.05
	0.00	*0.00*	*0.00*	*0.00*	*0.00*	*0.00*	*0.00*	*0.00*
Constant	101.52	−99.63	−94.80	−101.54	−99.61	−94.74	−99.09	−82.68
	0.00	*0.00*	*0.00*	*0.00*	*0.00*	*0.00*	*0.00*	*0.00*
Number of observations	29	29	29	29	29	29	29	29
F (Prob > F)	129.95	137.14	175.6	129.9	137.22	176.00	185.41	300.19
	0.00	*0.00*	*0.00*	*0.00*	*0.00*	*0.00*	*0.00*	*0.00*
Adjusted R^2	0.95	0.95	0.96	0.96	0.95	0.96	0.96	0.98
D-W statistic	0.80	0.69	0.83	0.80	0.69	0.83	1.37	1.03
Transformed	*1.92*	*2.00*	*1.96*	*1.92*	*2.00*	*1.96*	*1.98*	*1.99*
Rho	0.68	0.67	0.64	0.68	0.67	0.64	0.62	0.54
	0.00	*0.00*	*0.00*	*0.00*	*0.00*	*0.00*	*0.00*	*0.00*

Notes: Dependent variable is the natural log of real joint-stock universal bank assets. P-values of t-tests (two-sided) are entered in italics below coefficient estimates.

Sources: Total assets calculated from Deutsche Bundesbank (1976) and Goldsmith (1969); NNP from Hoffmann (1965); stock issues from Wetzel (1996); tax rates from Gömmel (1992).

247

impact of the turnover tax, underscores the importance of the securities business to the universal banking sector and, more broadly, to the interdependence between universal banking and securities market institutions. These results also bolster the finding (from Chapter 4) that a large proportion of universal bank profits – in some cases as high as one-third of the total – stemmed from commissions on trading and underwriting of securities in the early-twentieth century.[39] Provincial banks, as a whole, depended less on the securities business, and this fact is borne out in growth regressions that use only provincial-bank assets. If we consider only provincial banks, both the new issues variable and the tax rate lose their magnitude and significance.

General economic prosperity also appears to explain a greater part of the observed trend in universal banking growth than do regulatory events. In contrast to concentration of assets, logged levels of real universal bank assets relate positively to changes in real net national product. So, precisely in line with the findings in Chapter 4, growth in the real economy goes hand in hand with development in the financial sector – or at least in those financial institutions most responsible for financing industry. The results here allow further qualification of the causal importance of financial institutions for real growth. Provincial-bank assets are unrelated to real NNP, so that the link between real and financial variables is weaker than expected. That is, if financial growth were a primary impetus for real development, then surely the provincial universal banking sector, not just the great banks, should contribute significantly.[40]

Universal Banks versus Stock Markets

While it is now clear that German universal banks, and especially the largest such institutions, expanded operations over the period 1884–1913, the question remains whether banks simultaneously usurped business from the exchanges and, if so, whether regulatory change encouraged this displacement. The relevant line of business, of course, is securities trading, since bankers could partially substitute for the exchanges in these transactions. Unlike concentration or size, quantity of business done by the banks is very

---

[39] For a smaller set of banks and years, see also Riesser (1910 [1911]) and Weber (1915).

[40] Besides Chapter 4, refer to Fohlin (1999a), Fohlin (2000a), and the many references cited in those papers. Note that two final variables that related positively to universal banking concentration (average value of new issues and share price levels) provide no explanatory power for growth of the universal banking sector overall and are therefore excluded from the reported regressions. Both of these variables were expected to be weaker correlates, and this expectation is borne out by the results. The other findings are robust to these specification changes.

difficult to measure, particularly for securities trading. It is nearly impossible to quantify trading volumes outside official secondary markets in Germany, and the universal banks themselves did not report the volume of such business. The business turnover of universal banks may serve as a useful, though obviously imperfect, proxy for securities trading within the universal banking system. The variable at least reflects the growing business of the universal banks, a significant portion of which was devoted to brokerage transactions, and may be compared to the volume of turnover on the exchange.[41]

There is little theoretical work on the determinants of trading volume, and at least one prominent theory implies that there should be no trading at all: Prices provide 100 percent of portfolio adjustment.[42] Though the current literature offers no standard, empirically testable, structural model of stock exchange volume, it is possible to investigate the relative strength of identifiable correlates. Annual stock exchange turnover fluctuated dramatically throughout the period, but a significant negative trend in real turnover is still evident over the period. The idea of a trend suggests a gradual process over the twenty-eight years, but that interpretation presents a false perception of events. Much of the negative trend results from the combination of the extreme upswing in 1888–90 and the similarly dramatic drop in 1907–8.

Relative turnover of the banks and markets can be seen as an outgrowth of economic and financial variables (real NNP per capita and an annual stock exchange index), subperiod indicators representing regulatory changes, tax rates, and a trend variable (see Table 7.7). Reflecting the growth patterns of the previous two variables, universal bank turnover did rise relative to market turnover over the course of the late-nineteenth and early-twentieth centuries, and the rate of change averaged a substantial 10 percent per year.[43] While the trend toward greater relative universal bank business over the period is clear, there is also noticeable fluctuation throughout the period. No significant increases emerge for 1892, 1896, or 1900, either in overall levels or break in trend. Yet the post-1894 variable is significant on its own and when interacted with the trend variable – suggesting once again that tax measures were the primary area in which regulatory change made a palpable impact.

---

[41] In addition, using this variable allows comparison with Tilly's (1995) results, since he uses a similar measure.

[42] See Milgrom and Stokey (1982). See also Lo and Wang (1998).

[43] A regression of the logged ratio on a trend variable from 1884 to 1913 produces the estimated annual average rate of increases.

Table 7.7. *Determinants of Universal-Bank Turnover/Berlin Exchange Turnover*

	Universal-Bank Turnover/Berlin Exchange Turnover									
	(post-1892)	(post-1894)	(post-1896)	(post-1900)	(post-1892*yr)	(post-1894*yr)	(post-1896*yr)	(post-1900*yr)	(issue)	(turnover)
Annual stock exchange index	−0.02	−0.02	−0.02	−0.02	−0.02	−0.02	−0.02	−0.02	−0.02	−0.02
	0.06	*0.06*	*0.05*	*0.06*	*0.06*	*0.05*	*0.06*	*0.05*	*0.01*	*0.05*
Real NNP per capita	165.03	119.63	122.98	128.72	164.99	119.61	122.98	128.68	24.19	115.06
	0.20	*0.30*	*0.05*	*0.26*	*0.20*	*0.30*	*0.28*	*0.26*	*0.78*	*0.33*
Year	0.06	0.05	0.05	0.06	0.06	0.05	0.05	0.06	0.15	0.06
	0.03	*0.04*	*0.06*	*0.06*	*0.03*	*0.05*	*0.06*	*0.06*	*0.00*	*0.10*
Constant	−104.31	−99.32	−101.23	−111.86	−104.53	−99.23	−101.18	−111.86	−273.96	−113.78
	0.02	*0.04*	*0.05*	*0.06*	*0.02*	*0.04*	*0.05*	*0.06*	*0.00*	*0.10*
Subperiod indicator	−0.23	0.07	0.02	0.06	−0.00	0.00	0.00	−0.00	0.00	
	0.41	*0.80*	*0.96*	*0.06*	*0.41*	*0.80*	*0.96*	*0.78*		
Turnover/issue tax rate									−0.34	−2.14
									0.00	*0.82*
# obs.	28	28	28	28	28	28	28	28	28	28
F	6.89	5.86	5.98	5.79	6.88	5.86	5.98	5.79	11.31	6.02
(Prob > F)	*(0.001)*	*(0.002)*	*(0.002)*	*(0.002)*	*(0.000)*	*(0.002)*	*(0.002)*	*(0.002)*	*(0.000)*	*(0.002)*
Adjusted R²	0.47	0.42	0.42	0.42	0.47	0.42	0.42	0.42	0.60	0.43
D-W statistic	1.03	1.04	1.04	1.04	1.03	1.04	1.04	1.04	0.84	1.03
Transformed	*1.41*	*1.40*	*1.40*	*1.40*	*1.41*	*1.40*	*1.40*	*1.40*	*1.52*	*1.41*
Rho	0.51	0.55	0.54	0.56	0.51	0.55	0.54	0.56	0.72	0.54
	0.01	*0.00*	*0.00*	*0.00*	*0.01*	*0.00*	*0.00*	*0.00*	*0.00*	*0.00*

Notes: P-values of two-sided t-tests are reported in italics below the coefficient estimates.

Sources: Turnover ratio calculated from Eistert (1970) and Wetzel (1996); stock exchange index from Gielen (1994); NNP from Hoffmann (1965); tax rates from Gömmel (1992).

In the multivariate regressions, however, universal banking business decreased relative to the exchanges as tax rates or percentage changes in those rates increased. Viewed in isolation, relative turnover is clearly positively correlated with both kinds of tax rates, and simple ordinary least-squares (OLS) regression yields very significant positive coefficients of taxes. Yet there is a great deal of autocorrelation in the series, and Durbin-Watson statistics are extremely low. Once trend is accounted for, the additional effect of the taxes (in levels or differences) is negative. The causal link, however, may run in the opposite direction. Cochrane-Orcutt regressions that replace the turnover ratio with the numerator and denominator of that ratio, and control for the same influences controlled for in the ratio regressions, indicate that the tax effect comes from a very significant positive relationship between issue tax rates and stock exchange turnover. One might reasonably speculate from this result that bursts of activity on the stock exchange allowed the implementation of tax increases. But since volume is composed of price and quantity, it is still technically possible that increasing the tax on issuing securities increased the measured volume of trading on exchanges through a price effect.

Despite the significance of the post-1894 indicator, the only discontinuous increases in the ratio appear after 1907, when there were no regulatory measures introduced that could be expected to have produced such an effect. Joint-stock universal bank turnover began 1907 at 84 percent of Berlin stock exchange turnover, but ended the year at over 171 percent of the market's turnover. The ratio then increased over 20 percent in 1908, but returned to its pre-1907 course in 1909. By 1910, universal bank turnover fell back to 80 percent of market turnover, but it began another upswing to 149 percent in 1913. The majority of changes in the turnover ratio stem from large changes in the turnover of the exchange, and 1907 was a particularly troublesome year for the German stock markets (see Figure 7.3). For the most part, universal banking turnover progressed rather steadily after the beginning of the economic expansion starting in 1894.

Not surprisingly, given the presence of stock exchange turnover in the denominator of the turnover ratio, the stock price index offers strong, negative predictive power in the regression analysis. Since market turnover, or volume, is real price times quantity, the real price of securities must be a component of that variable. In the current analysis, however, the correlation between stock exchange turnover and securities prices is weakened, because trading volume is estimated from tax receipts rather than from direct records of trading activity. Indeed, curiously, Berlin market turnover itself is hardly correlated with the stock price index (less than 8 percent for real volume

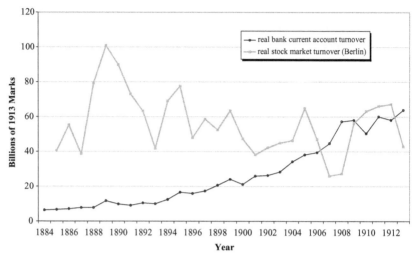

Figure 7.3. Real Turnover of Universal Banks and Stock Markets.
Sources: Eistert (1970) and Wetzel (1996).

and 28 percent for nominal volume). The much tighter correlation comes between universal bank turnover and the stock price index (70 percent). Thus, the turnover ratio is actually positively related to the stock price index in a simple correlation. The exclusion of the stock price index from the regressions has one effect: It renders the post-1894 variable insignificant (both alone and when the trend variable interacts with it).

Real indicators of economic activity, represented here by real NNP per capita, also fail to explain relative bank turnover. Given the lack of theoretical modeling for bank or market turnover, this result is not unexpected. The fact that the regulatory variables provide little statistical power is at least in line with the findings for concentration and universal banking industry development. Thus, if the joint-stock universal banks were gaining business at the expense of the exchanges, it is difficult to tie that development closely to the regulatory changes of the 1890s.

The Impact of Regulation versus General Trends

The findings here suggest that, even though regulatory changes and tax levies on securities business in theory may spur universal banking concentration, growth of the corporate banking sector overall, or displacement of business from markets to banks, the new German laws of the 1890s made little observable impact. Such a finding may result from a number of circumstances. First, the laws may really have had little impact, either because the changes were small or because the provisions were not fully implemented. Second, the laws may have only added to other factors – such as new efforts to capture economies of scale and scope in financial services itself and responses to the growing scale of industrial firms financed by the universal banks – that were already encouraging changes in the industrial organization of universal banking. In other words, the laws may have actually had some discrete impact, but their impact may have been masked by the other changes in the economy of the time. Third, the laws may have had the expected impact, but the effects may have been spread over several years, giving the impression of a general trend.

It is difficult, of course, to differentiate among these three possible interpretations, but international comparison may help. Comparing Germany with countries that did not impose such stock market regulations and did not levy similar taxes at the same time offers insight into general trends in the banking sector over this period. From this perspective, it appears that changes in the German universal banking industry did not hinge on the implementation of the 1896 stock exchange law or even on the levying of taxes throughout the 1884–1913 period. In the case of universal banking concentration, for example, it is commonly argued that several other European countries underwent similar adjustments to their banking industry structure over the same years, despite the wide variation in their regulatory systems.[44]

The English financial system (and that of the U.K. more broadly) makes a particularly useful comparison. It was unconstrained by regulations like the Germans', maintained a very active stock market, and had specialized commercial banks rather than universal banks. By the turn of the twentieth century, the government imposed no significant barriers to deposit banking growth and concentration, having eliminated size restrictions during the liberalization of banking laws in the 1820s. Two points are clear from a comparison of concentration ratios in Chapter 4 (Figure 4.4 and Table 4.3). First, despite the apparent divergence in system design, the British commercial banking industry was just as concentrated as the German universal banking industry between 1884 and 1913. In 1890, estimated five- and ten-firm ratios were very similar in the two countries – 17 and 29 percent in Germany and 21 and 32 percent in the United Kingdom. By 1910, the top five and ten commercial banks held 36 and 56 percent of assets, respectively,

---

[44] See, for example, Freitag and Pohl (1994).

in the U.K. (43 and 65 percent in England and Wales only), but the top five and ten universal banks in Germany held 31 and 44 percent of assets, respectively.[45] Second, in both countries, the greatest surge in banking concentration came during and after World War I – long after Germany's regulatory changes in the late-nineteenth century. By 1920, both countries had five-firm ratios of over 60 percent, and England and Wales were still slightly ahead of Germany (65.5 versus 62 percent). For Germany, this change represents a tripling of the growth rate of concentration (including estimated private-bank assets), from 2.9 to 8.7 percent per year on average, in the 1884–1912 versus 1913–20 periods.

Evidence on the expansion of the two banking systems also suggests that Germany was not propelled toward extreme bank orientation by the 1890s' taxes and regulations. Indeed, observing the total size of the universal and deposit banking sectors relative to the size of the economy (measured as national product), it appears that the German banking industry merely began to catch up with the British over the course of the late-nineteenth and early-twentieth centuries. Even by the start of World War I, the point at which most scholars acknowledge that the German economy had successfully industrialized, the German universal banking sector (including estimated private-bank assets) was still smaller than the U.K. deposit banking sector, relative to national product.[46] The comparison with Britain, as well as the extension of the time series to 1920, suggests that forces other than stock market regulation played the major part in the industrial organization of the German universal banking sector. Thus, even if it is impossible to prove conclusively that regulation had no impact, it is possible to surmise reasonably that universal banking concentration and growth would have progressed rapidly even without the growing regulation of the stock exchanges.[47]

---

[45] The English data are estimated using linear interpolation between the points given in Capie and Rodrik-Bali (1982).

[46] The German ratio is calculated using NNP from Hoffmann (1965), whereas the U.K. figures use the gross national product (GNP). The discrepancy means that, if anything, the German ratio is overestimated compared to the U.K. ratio. See Fohlin (2001a) for further details and comparisons of the German and British banking sectors. Edwards and Ogilvie (1996) also question the exceptionalism of the German universal system, while Baker and Collins (1999) revise the traditional view on English banks.

[47] Clearly, in light of the different regulatory regimes in the two countries, nonregulatory explanations should be explored. In particular, the connection between industrial and banking concentration requires further investigation. In Britain, the existing evidence for a causal link is weak, but for Germany, the proposition has yet to be tested rigorously. On England and Wales (and the U.K. more generally), see Capie and Rodrik-Bali (1982).

Listing Decisions

Stock markets and universal banks developed together in the later stages of industrialization, and the primary link that connected them was the securities of joint-stock corporations. Not all joint-stock firms listed their shares on the exchanges, but even firms without official stock quotes often registered bond issues for public trading. And it was usually the universal banks, or possibly a private bank, that managed the flotation of those shares and bonds and the registration of shares for listing when a firm decided to do so.

Chapter 5 detailed the close ties between stock market listing and bank board representation in seeking explanations for the presence of bank directors in company supervisory boards and the broader networks of interlocking directorates. Having quoted shares was one of the strongest predictors of having a banker on one's board. But that discussion left open the question of causality: The existence of a stock market listing might plausibly be viewed as both a cause and an effect of bank affiliation. Firms wishing to become listed may have gained bank affiliation, or attached firms may have been encouraged to become listed by their bankers. The possibility of endogeneity, therefore, would suggest direct modeling of the decision to list.[48]

Joint-stock firms enjoyed a range of choices regarding stock market quotation, just as they faced manifold stipulations about their company form, financial status, reporting standards, share capital subscription, and responsibilities to shareholders. There is little quantitative assessment of the factors leading to stock market listings, even though the decision to list must be based on not only qualifications, but also an assessment by the firm management that the firm will gain in net from opening up trading to the market. In the context of recent American experience, firms systematically list more often in the exchange where firms in their industry list, and larger, less risky

---

[48] If the right-hand variables in the listing-choice model were the same as those in the attachment-choice model (substituting the attachment variable for the listing variable), the results would be essentially the same as in Chapter 5. That is, simply reversing the positions of the listing and bank-attachment variables would yield little new information. It is theoretically possible to estimate a two-stage model that accounts explicitly for the possible endogeneity of the listing variable. Since the attachment choice variable is multinomial and assumed to have an extreme-value distribution, but the potentially endogenous variable is binomial (assumed to be a latent variable with the normal distribution), the error distributions are incompatible. This complicates the implementation of instrumental variables. Even if an instrumental-variables procedure can be implemented, however, the difficulty of correctly specifying the structural equations often renders two-stage model estimates untrustworthy in practice.

firms tend to list on the New York Stock Exchange.[49] Firms also tend to move to the more established exchange after a period of strong performance.[50]

The German markets of the late-nineteenth and early-twentieth centuries differ, of course, from American institutions in the late-twentieth century. Nonetheless, the same types of incentives existed. One would expect, for example, that firms would have to demonstrate sufficient past success to attract investors on the market. As a result, past returns and dividends should predict stock market listings; dividends possibly carry the greater weight in this context, since at that time they provided the most assured way of gaining from an investment. Firm size (total assets) may also predict listing, since larger firms tend to be more diversified (and thus carry a lower risk) and can also spread the fixed costs of listing over more shares. Firms choosing to list are also more likely to seek outside shareholders and would have relatively dispersed ownership, since firms with large, continuing stakeholders – the Krupps of the world – prefer to maintain insider control.[51] In line with such reasoning, propensity to issue new equity ought to relate positively to stock market listings – especially on the Berlin exchange.

In examining the listing decisions of German firms before World War I, it is useful to consider the differences between the Berlin market and those in the provinces. Many of the provincial markets remained very small during the period and provided little additional exposure to potential investors that the firms would not have accessed through their local bank. Examining the Berlin market on its own, and evaluating the characteristics associated with listing there, reveals several differences between the capital and the provinces. In a simple cross section of firms in the middle of the period (1904), most of the hypothesized factors turn out to be highly indicative of listing (see Table 7.8). Lagged dividends are particularly strong in predicting stock market listings, regardless of location. And overall, listed firms pay over double the dividends paid by unlisted firms (nearly 5.9 percent compared to 2.7 percent). Controlling for the several other characteristics, past accounting performance (ROA) provides no indication of listing in the provinces, and a negative prediction of listing in Berlin.

---

[49] Corwin and Harris (2001).

[50] Cowan, Carter, Dark, and Singh (1992).

[51] When Krupp incorporated (became an AG) in 1903, almost all of the equity remained under the ownership of Bertha Krupp, the daughter of the patriarch. Only enough additional shareholders were added in order to meet the stipulations of incorporation as an AG. According to the father's wishes, the firm was never to be listed on the stock exchange, and ownership was to remain in the family and under close, concentrated control. See the history of Krupp by Gall (2002).

Table 7.8. *Factors Associated with Stock Market Listings*

	Berlin Listed	Listed Provincial Market	Listed Berlin	Listing Decision	Gain Listing
Lagged dividends	0.02	0.14	0.26	0.05	0.04
	0.01	*0.03*	*0.02*	*0.00*	*0.00*
Financial assets	0.02				
	0.15				
Lagged ROA	−0.36	−0.34	−3.77	−0.23	−0.11
	0.01	*0.37*	*0.03*	*0.00*	*0.18*
Total assets	0.01	0.12	0.13	0.01	0.02
(millions)	*0.07*	*0.22*	*0.25*	*0.57*	*0.00*
Share capital	0.26	−0.06	2.66	0.94	0.34
increase	*0.01*	*0.96*	*0.07*	*0.09*	*0.17*
Long-term debt	−0.40	2.98	−3.68	−0.46	0.33
	0.03	*0.07*	*0.09*	*0.66*	*0.55*
Short-term debt	0.04	0.72	1.27	−1.54	−2.03
	0.84	*0.64*	*0.60*	*0.23*	*0.04*
Age	−0.00	0.05	0.01	−0.04	−0.03
	0.31	*0.00*	*0.70*	*0.00*	*0.01*
Trend				−0.09	−0.09
				0.03	*0.00*
Bank attachment:					
Private bank	0.13	0.89	1.71	0.92	0.83
	0.16	*0.15*	*0.06*	*0.01*	*0.00*
Provincial bank	0.14	0.14	1.41	0.51	0.60
	0.09	*0.79*	*0.11*	*0.31*	*0.02*
Great bank	0.12	1.94	2.56	0.31	0.86
	0.38	*0.01*	*0.05*	*0.60*	*0.11*
Combined	0.02	0.75	0.30	−0.46	0.54
	0.92	*0.50*	*0.88*	*0.53*	*0.15*
Machinery,	−0.13	−2.73	−4.11	0.26	
metalworking	*0.10*	*0.21*	*0.06*	*0.74*	
Printing,	−0.12	−3.12	−4.53	−0.40	
woodworking	*0.04*	*0.24*	*0.04*	*0.61*	
Rail transport	−0.11	−2.69	−4.17	−0.81	
	0.12	*0.21*	*0.07*	*0.30*	
Ship transport		−3.42	−49.74	−0.68	
		0.12	*0.00*	*0.39*	
Electrical	−0.12	−49.5	−7.62	2.10	
	0.07	*0.00*	*0.16*	*0.01*	
Gas, petroleum		−3.02	−48.81	0.08	
		0.20	*0.00*	*0.93*	

(continued)

Table 7.8 *(continued)*

	Berlin Listed	Listed		Listing Decision	Gain Listing
		Provincial Market	Berlin		
Water		−48.060	−49.199	−0.70	
		0.00	*0.00*	*0.38*	
Chemicals	−0.15	−3.34	−4.95	0.12	
	0.04	*0.13*	*0.02*	*0.89*	
Stones, cement,	−0.17	−4.33	−6.99	0.17	
earthenware	*0.01*	*0.05*	*0.01*	*0.84*	
Textiles	−0.14	−1.78	−5.18	−0.78	
	0.02	*0.40*	*0.05*	*0.52*	
Food processing,		−3.49	−50.74	−1.01	
milling		*0.10*	*0.00*	*0.30*	
Brewing	−0.21	−2.10	−4.28	−0.24	
	0.03	*0.32*	*0.05*	*0.78*	
Schools, charities	−0.083	−47.72	−3.31	1.04	
	0.49	*0.00*	*0.17*	*0.23*	
Hospitality,		−49.67	−47.71	−0.13	
entertainment		*0.00*	*0.00*	*0.87*	
Constant		−1.22	0.73		−1.57
		0.57	*0.73*		*0.00*
Observations	153	209	209	2809	1727
Model	Probit	Multinomial logit	Multinomial logit	Ordered logit	Panel probit

Note: Robust p-values in italics.
The first three columns use the year 1904 only and are static variables (listed in the specified market or not), while the last two columns use all years. The coefficients in the first column represent the change in the probability of being listed in Berlin (versus not listed in Berlin or not listed at all) for an infinitesimal change (discrete change) in the continuous (dummy) variables. The middle columns give logit (multinomial or ordered) coefficients. The listing decision variable (fourth column) takes the values 1 for gaining a listing (anywhere), 0 for no change, and −1 for de-listing. The "gain listing" variable equals 1 if the firm gains a listing anywhere and is 0 if the firm chooses to remain unlisted. Firms with preexisting listings are excluded. Financial assets and debt are normalized by total assets.

Firm capital structure helps explain much of the variation in stock market listings, especially for the primary stock exchange, Berlin. Propensity to issue new capital predicts Berlin listings but not provincial listings. Notably, the growth rate of share capital as a percentage of existing capital is less important than the mere existence of new issues of shares (a binary choice variable). At the same time, high levels of long-term debt, primarily bonds and mortgages, lower the likelihood of listing in Berlin. These findings underscore the importance of the Berlin market as a center for equity trading.

Size relates positively to listing in both Berlin and elsewhere, but industrial branch accounts for most of the effect. Thus, diversification or stability is important for listing, but it is subsumed partly by the nature of the firms' line of business. Also a sign of stability or diversification, age relates positively to stock market listing, but is particularly strong for the provincial markets. As Chapter 5 noted, firms with provincial listings tend to use bond financing, and they are likely to be older firms in the industries indigenous to the geographical region surrounding the exchange on which they list. These results suggest a complementarity of services or customer bases between the Berlin and provincial exchanges.

Many of the firms in the sample gained listings before the start of the sampling period, but enough firms joined the exchanges during the period to allow some assessment of the factors associated with listing at the time of the decision.[52] Compared to firms that chose to remain unlisted, firms that opted to list at an exchange during the sample period were both large and young; they held much less short-term debt, and they paid out higher dividends in the preceding period – despite having similar accounting profitability. The fact that age relates negatively to the decision to gain listing may seem to contradict the previous finding that older firms are more likely to be listed overall in the sample. The difference, of course, is that the first variable represents a snapshot of all firms at one point in time, while the second provides a dynamic view of the decisions made at several points in time for firms that were not already listed. The negative relationship between age and the choice to gain listing (as opposed to staying unlisted) means that firms tended to list fairly shortly after they were incorporated, if they planned to list at all. In the sample overall, however, it is still the case that listed firms tended to be older than unlisted firms; it's just that the older firms gained listings before the start of the sample period. Unlike the static models, issuing new share capital does not predict the decision to gain listing. The lack of significance could stem only from statistical weakness: the small number of firms making a change in their listing status. But when viewed together with the static models, the result here also suggests that firms list

---

[52] The listing variable includes all exchanges, since the number of cases is too small to permit differentiation.

on an exchange if they are likely to want to issue additional equity at some point, and do not necessarily list at the precise year in which they issue the shares.

While these firms were gaining access to the markets, a number of other firms made the opposite decision and removed their shares from the exchanges. A couple of firms even listed and de-listed repeatedly. Examining the full choice set at once provides a richer understanding of the listing decision along with further support for the idea that stock market listings help differentiate among types of firms. The findings for a multiple-choice decision variable (negative for de-listing, zero for no change, and positive for gaining listing) view listing and de-listing as opposite ends of a continuum, with retention of existing status falling in between the two extremes. Despite the difference in approach, the new models uphold most of the previous results, albeit with some modification. Past dividend payouts continue to provide the strongest indication of listing decisions. Firm size still relates positively and accounting profits still relate negatively to listing decisions, but the statistical power of both are reversed. Firms that issue new equity and hold low proportions of debt are still more likely to be listed, but again, the statistical power is weakened. These results stem partly from the small number of de-listing firms, but they also indicate the possibility that de-listing is less closely associated with these firm characteristics than is listing. Age and trend are still very negatively related to listing. Thus, firms are both less likely to list and also more likely to de-list when they are old. Moreover, the firms in the sample listed sooner rather than later, if they were going to at all, but they were more likely to de-list later in the period. This finding seems almost obvious at first glance, but it is not necessarily so, when we consider that most of the listed firms were already listed at the start of the period.

Taken together, these findings provide strong evidence for the supposition that more dispersed firms, desirous of marketing their securities to a relatively dispersed group of investors, make their way to the stock markets. Investors in these firms clearly demand higher payouts, as demonstrated in the much larger dividends paid. By comparison, the unlisted firms seem to have less pressure to please investors (they pay lower dividends) but apparently perform better in terms of accounting returns on assets. The securities markets are also clearly tied to the universal banks; an increased tendency for firms with bank directors on their boards to be listed evidences this connection. While causal interpretations remain risky, it is safe to correlate involvement with universal banks to entrance into the exchanges. Unlisted firms with bankers on their boards are more likely to become listed than are firms without bankers on board.[53] And at a given point in time, bank-affiliated firms are more likely to be listed than are unaffiliated firms. These connections bolster the previous inference (see Chapter 5) that formal bank relationships result from firm capital structure and listing decisions – particularly, the issuing and listing of equity shares. While bankers sitting on the supervisory board may advise and assist a firm in issuing and listing its shares, the connections among stock market listing, bank positions, and capital structure are complex and multidirectional. These connections, regardless of causality, underscore the importance of the German exchanges in providing a market for corporate securities, particularly for industrial firms at a time of rapid technological progress and economic growth more generally.

Prices and Returns

So far, it appears that stock and bond markets thrived in Germany in the pre–World War I period. Though embattled after crises, and encumbered by regulation, the markets prospered, attracted thousands of companies to list their shares and bonds, and handled a growing turnover of securities. At the same time, little is known about the functional efficiency in the German exchanges before World War I. While some researchers have maintained that the German secondary markets remained largely underdeveloped during even the later stages of industrialization, empirical evidence is insufficient to support this claim.[54] Indeed, the story in this chapter thus far paints a more favorable picture of the German markets, particularly the Berlin exchange in the three decades before World War I. Despite growing regulation and taxation, the market bolstered trading, listed thousands of new shares, and rebounded robustly in the aftermath of local and international crises (for example, 1891, 1900–1, and 1907). Likewise, international comparisons suggest that the Berlin market trailed only London in size and liquidity in 1913.[55]

Yet we still know almost nothing about efficiency and the pricing of risk in the German markets, since past studies have scarcely raised such questions. To the extent that researchers have investigated the functioning of the German stock exchanges, they have focused on risk-return trade-offs and efficient portfolio diversification or they have examined market

---

[53] The variable for combined great- and small-bank attachment is positive but statistically weak.

[54] See, for example, DeLong and Becht (1992), Kennedy (1987), and Michie (1988).

[55] See Fohlin (2000a) and Rajan and Zingales (2003).

volatility.[56] Naturally, because of the German practice of combining securities underwriting and trading with commercial banking services, the idea of bank intervention in markets or bank internalization of markets pervades these studies. Since interrelations between the universal banking system and securities markets have been poorly understood, the idea of bank domination has been allowed to persist. Some have suggested that universal banks were able to convince wary investors of the desirability (stable yields and market values) of the firms that the banks promoted and ensured this outcome by actively managing share prices. Such was the argument of W. Prion (1910, 1929), who claimed at least for the latter part of the period that nearly all securities on the exchanges had a *Schutzpatron* (literally, a patron saint), typically a bank, that consulted daily with the exchange brokers on the determination of the price.[57]

Market Efficiency and the Predictability of Returns

Clearly, large holes remain in our understanding of the German markets. Thus, the goal of this section is to investigate market efficiency and rationality based on modern analytical tools. In theory, expected excess returns ought to relate proportionally to the covariance with the return on the market portfolio.[58] Assuming that the market's expectations are unbiased, this implies that historical average returns in excess of the risk-free rate should be proportional to estimated risk, or "beta" (the covariance with the market portfolio, normalized by the variance of the latter). For most of the twentieth century, however, common stocks listed on the NYSE, AMEX, and NAS-DAQ have failed to follow the model's predictions. Other characteristics, in particular, size (market capitalization) and the ratio of book value of equity over market value provide additional explanatory power, marginalizing the

---

[56] See the series of works by Kennedy (1991), Kennedy and Britton (1985), and Tilly (1986) examining portfolio behavior in Germany. These studies hypothesize that by providing both investment and commercial services, the German universal banking system ameliorated problems of asymmetric information and thereby improved risk management. DeLong and Becht (1992) take a different tack by estimating excess volatility in the Berlin market over the periods 1876–1913 and 1951–90. They find that perfect foresight fundamentals overpredict volatility in the prewar period but underpredict in the more recent period. Wetzel (1996) assesses the impact of the 1896 stock exchange law, comparing volatility ratios for Berlin before and after the ban on futures trading.

[57] See Becht and DeLong (1992). The postwar appearance of excess volatility, in their view, follows from the demise of the banks' role in the exchanges and the concurrent spread of speculators in the securities markets.

[58] Most of this discussion of the cross section of returns comes directly from Bossaerts and Fohlin (2000), an unpublished working paper. Fohlin and Reinhold (2006) provides additional analysis using monthly data.

effect of beta. Average returns relate positively to book-to-market equity (BE/ME) and negatively to size, though the latter effect tends to be comparatively weak and unstable. More recent studies show that size and book-to-market ratios reflect risk, because historical average returns on portfolios formed on the basis of size and book-to-market ratio are well explained by the covariance with the market portfolio, the covariance with a portfolio long in small firms and short in large firms (SMB), and the covariance with a portfolio long in firms with high ratios of book value to market value of equity and short in firms with correspondingly low ratios (HML).[59] Controversy remains, because newer work finds that the book-to-market ratio itself still explains variation in average returns beyond these covariances.[60] That is, the book-to-market ratio explains part of the error left by the three-factor model. Moreover, an additional characteristic, momentum, has explanatory power beyond the three-factor model (Fama and French, 1996).

This section examines the relationship between average excess returns on common stock listed on the Berlin exchange in the period 1881–1913 and the three traditional characteristics (beta, size, and book-to-market ratio). In the process, the analysis assesses the HML covariance (book-to-market factor) and also investigates whether the identified factors proxy for risk and whether any momentum effect remains after taking these effects into account. By investigating the rationality of pricing in German secondary markets, this study goes to the roots of both the universal banking system and the Berlin stock market; demonstrating the viability of markets within a universal banking system.

Stock Returns in the Berlin Market, 1880–1913

The sample used in this analysis includes fifty firms traded on the Berlin stock exchange between 1880 and 1913 (see Table 7.9).[61] The time series

---

[59] Fama and French (1993, 1996). This model has become known as the Fama-French three-factor model. Most authors distinguish between the two approaches as follows: When market beta, size, and book-to-market ratio are to explain the cross section of average returns, the model is the "three-characteristic model." If betas with respect to the market, the SMB, and HML portfolio are to explain average returns, then the model is the "three-factor model." Evidence has emerged that the relationship is far from constant (Davis, Fama, and French, 2000), and, more specifically, that it varies quite substantially across stock markets in the world (Hawawini and Keim, 1995).

[60] Daniel and Titman (1997), but see Davis, Fama, and French (2000) for evidence that this finding is period-specific.

[61] See the data appendix at the end of this chapter. One outlier, with returns of 1,303.33 percent in 1884, was omitted.

Table 7.9. *Size, Book-to-Market Ratio, and Returns: Fifty Long-Lived Firms, 1880–1913*

Year	Market Equity (Millions of Marks)				Book-to-Market Ratio				Dividend-Adjusted Returns (Percent per Annum)			
	Avg	Sd	Min	Max	Avg	Sd	Min	Max	Avg	Sd	Min	Max
1880	4.99	6.39	0.31	28.88	1.55	1.45	0.57	9.30	–	–	–	–
1881	5.64	7.46	0.22	31.78	1.54	2.10	0.53	13.79	16.50	23.95	–32.56	91.50
1882	6.71	8.95	0.13	41.33	1.68	3.75	0.55	25.64	17.86	27.09	–46.21	94.33
1883	7.11	9.00	0.09	40.02	1.77	4.85	0.50	33.33	14.87	20.87	–23.08	66.69
1884	7.80	9.70	0.31	38.97	0.97	0.56	0.42	2.38	14.22	25.34	–41.14	82.80
1885	7.84	9.82	0.33	41.56	1.05	0.64	0.37	3.22	7.49	14.70	–26.13	41.03
1886	8.89	11.73	0.54	53.13	0.92	0.53	0.17	2.78	22.35	35.23	–30.49	154.93
1887	8.67	11.38	0.49	47.67	1.02	0.66	0.27	3.57	4.89	19.75	–47.17	57.13
1888	10.86	12.89	0.69	60.26	0.79	0.53	0.26	3.51	33.07	29.58	–7.38	127.62
1889	14.60	20.21	1.06	107.29	0.68	0.29	0.26	1.51	28.79	49.78	–20.14	296.49
1890	14.51	19.28	0.92	79.00	0.80	0.37	0.27	1.72	–5.50	16.07	–44.47	25.32
1891	12.41	15.66	0.69	65.42	0.97	0.57	0.40	3.70	–3.63	16.05	–52.53	30.58
1892	11.41	13.87	0.51	54.96	0.92	0.45	0.31	2.36	14.43	39.69	–39.43	236.41
1893	12.58	15.93	0.36	63.19	0.93	0.54	0.31	2.99	11.74	13.76	–27.42	40.59
1894	13.48	16.79	0.36	67.71	0.82	0.46	0.26	2.90	19.47	21.80	–36.92	91.50
1895	15.49	19.92	0.94	82.87	0.71	0.37	0.22	2.38	21.75	15.87	–5.31	61.55
1896	17.85	23.48	0.41	93.88	0.66	0.33	0.19	2.17	18.20	14.46	–12.38	52.06
1897	20.92	30.66	0.56	128.69	0.66	0.34	0.21	1.50	16.52	20.51	–36.08	69.39
1898	24.79	39.61	0.45	176.56	0.65	0.33	0.21	1.59	13.80	15.74	–18.51	74.62
1899	28.26	44.13	0.56	210.41	0.63	0.32	0.21	1.79	13.99	18.35	–37.34	77.82

1900	24.37	38.15	0.40	161.13	0.72	0.34	0.20	1.63	0.65	15.30	−32.04	50.15
1901	24.68	38.34	0.52	174.17	0.78	0.38	0.22	1.84	1.21	12.91	−24.99	35.78
1902	26.68	41.19	0.34	184.69	0.73	0.36	0.21	1.79	14.82	14.28	−9.29	60.26
1903	30.88	47.74	0.37	189.62	0.70	0.37	0.17	1.83	18.91	15.54	−10.89	59.38
1904	34.16	54.10	0.57	246.99	0.64	0.36	0.17	1.86	19.42	17.08	−20.33	57.23
1905	36.68	57.41	0.56	241.73	0.60	0.33	0.19	1.61	14.00	12.31	−21.21	45.82
1906	38.44	63.26	0.61	295.18	0.62	0.35	0.18	1.90	10.81	15.67	−42.10	45.39
1907	35.78	57.27	0.42	269.79	0.69	0.38	0.19	2.25	0.15	15.39	−33.02	50.71
1908	36.26	61.16	0.35	301.53	0.73	0.47	0.20	2.70	8.46	18.09	−50.34	45.25
1909	41.47	67.26	0.45	311.17	0.63	0.34	0.18	1.95	20.28	13.51	−19.42	52.62
1910	39.91	68.77	0.41	360.32	0.67	0.33	0.25	1.59	7.02	12.94	−23.11	32.33
1911	45.71	82.30	0.42	472.59	0.67	0.41	0.18	2.19	10.78	17.70	−32.29	76.62
1912	43.55	79.27	0.45	464.03	0.78	0.64	0.20	3.64	0.28	14.75	−44.78	28.59
1913	46.43	92.79	0.30	582.30	0.88	0.96	0.20	6.62	7.37	23.83	−52.81	98.18
All years	22.81	45.30	0.09	582.30	0.86	1.21	0.17	33.33	12.51	22.90	−52.81	296.49

Notes: Market equity is the price of shares times the book value of shares and reserves. B/M ratio is book value of equity divided by market value of equity. Dividend-adjusted return is the percentage increase in share price plus dividend (as a percentage of market value) and omits one observation of 1,303.33 percent in 1884. Marks during this time can be multiplied by three to obtain a rough estimate of 2000 dollar values.

Sources: Bossaerts and Fohlin (2000). Data from Rettig (1978), *Saling's Börsen-Jahrbuch* (1881–1914), and Fohlin (1994).

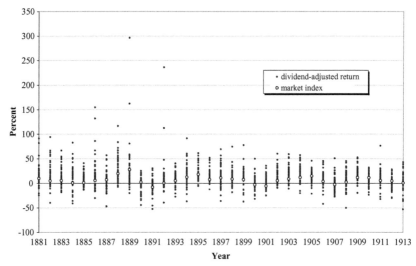

Figure 7.4a. Dividend-Adjusted Returns.

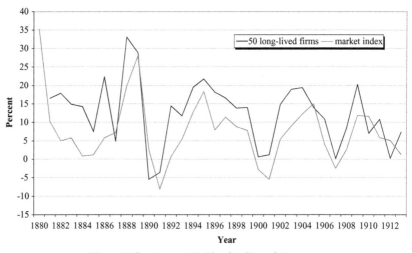

Figure 7.4b. Average Dividend-Adjusted Returns.

of dividend-adjusted returns on the sampled firms and the market index, particularly the spread of the returns on the fifty firms around the return of the market, suggests that the sampled firms typify the market more broadly (see Figure 7.4). There is, however, a survivorship bias in the sample of fifty firms. Figure 7.5 highlights this bias: The average return on the fifty firms is higher than those on the index in earlier years. One could conjecture that

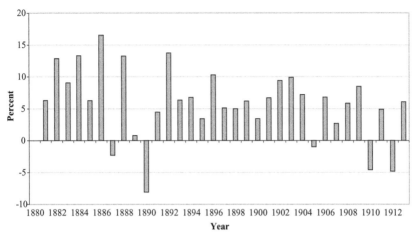

Figure 7.5. Difference in Average Dividend-Adjusted Returns.
Notes: Difference is calculated as the returns for sampled firms minus the market index return.

part of the difference in average returns may have to be attributed to the fact that the average return on the fifty firms is based on equal weighting, while the market index we use is value-weighted. Equal weighting imposes a relatively higher weighting on smaller firms, which in recent U.S. history have outperformed larger firms.

Contrary to conjecture, however, in this sample small firms (quintile 1) in fact earned a lower average return than larger firms (quintile 2): 7.46 percent per annum versus 14.03 percent per annum (see Table 7.10). The results contrast markedly with recent U.S. data. Returns for the small firms in the sample vary more than those for larger firms, and therefore appear riskier, but they generate smaller average returns than their larger counterparts. Moreover, unlike the pattern in recent U.S. data, size does not relate monotonically to risk (beta). The largest firms produce higher betas than the smallest firms, and the middle quintiles generate the lowest betas of all. Still, as in U.S. data, the book-to-market ratio of the smallest firms is substantially higher than that of other firms. The net income (as a percentage of book value of equity) is lower for small firms, indicating that some of them are really firms in distress.[62] Also in line with U.S. experience, there is a slight negative relationship between mean return and beta (the measure of risk).

---

[62] Similar findings appear in recent U.S. data (Fama and French, 1995).

Table 7.10. *Descriptive Statistics by Size and Beta Ranking*

	1 Mean	1 Sd	2 Mean	2 Sd	3 Mean	3 Sd	4 Mean	4 Sd	5 Mean	5 Sd
Panel A: Ranked by Size										
Dividend-adjusted returns	7.46	34.07	14.45	19.43	11.87	14.44	15.14	20.23	14.03	20.01
Dividend-adjusted beta	1.26	1.17	0.60	0.42	0.70	0.41	0.61	0.59	1.46	0.85
Ln(market equity)	14.21	0.63	15.31	0.62	15.82	0.74	16.65	0.75	17.78	1.01
Market equity (millions of marks)	1.77	1.01	5.26	2.93	9.30	5.56	22.30	17.23	81.68	79.84
Ln(book-to-market)	0.19	0.42	−0.33	0.48	−0.53	0.42	−0.63	0.49	−0.58	0.43
Book-to-market	1.33	0.67	0.81	0.47	0.64	0.27	0.60	0.33	0.62	0.31
Net income/book equity	0.05	0.10	0.11	0.08	0.10	0.06	0.12	0.08	0.10	0.05
Dummy variable (NI/BE neg=1)	0.09	0.29	0.01	0.08	0.01	0.09	0.01	0.09	0.01	0.11
NI+/BE	0.06	0.08	0.11	0.08	0.11	0.06	0.12	0.07	0.10	0.05
Average N	290		338		324		332		305	
Panel B: Ranked by Beta										
Dividend-adjusted returns	16.25	24.53	9.38	17.68	14.80	16.83	11.89	20.09	10.75	31.31
Dividend-adjusted beta	0.06	0.19	0.49	0.12	0.82	0.12	1.17	0.14	2.27	0.87
Ln(market equity)	15.83	1.02	15.70	1.45	16.08	1.26	16.29	1.43	15.86	1.75
Market equity (millions of marks)	11.98	12.13	20.84	42.05	20.56	29.44	36.12	72.42	28.58	48.42
Ln(book-to-market)	−0.51	0.57	−0.36	0.41	−0.46	0.56	−0.43	0.50	−0.10	0.54
Book-to-market	0.70	0.42	0.77	0.40	0.75	0.51	0.75	0.54	1.05	0.59
Net income/book equity	0.11	0.08	0.09	0.06	0.11	0.06	0.10	0.07	0.07	0.10
Dummy variable (NI/BE neg=1)	0.02	0.15	0.01	0.11	0.00	0.05	0.03	0.18	0.06	0.23
NI+/BE	0.12	0.08	0.09	0.06	0.11	0.06	0.10	0.06	0.08	0.08
Average N	335		329		335		313		275	

Notes: In panel A, the sample is divided into five groups of ten firms each, ranked in increasing order of size (measured as market value of equity). In panel B, the firms are similarly ranked based on dividend-adjusted beta. One outlier firm is eliminated from the sample (size rank 1 and beta rank 5). B/M ratio is book value of equity divided by market value of equity. Dividend-adjusted return is the percentage increase in share price plus dividend (as percent of market value).

Sources: Bossaerts and Fohlin (2000). Data from Rettig (1978), *Saling's Börsen-Jahrbuch* (1881–1914), and Fohlin (1994).

Table 7.11. *Pair-Wise Correlation Coefficients for Pooled Cross Section/ Time Series*

	Dividend-Adjusted Return	Dividend-Adjusted Beta	Market Value of Equity	Book-to-Market Value of Equity
Dividend-adjusted beta	−0.04			
	0.17			
	1,480			
Market value of equity	0.02	0.17		
	0.54	*0.00*		
	1,480	1,557		
Book-to-market value of equity	−0.33	0.21	−0.25	
	0.00	*0.00*	*0.00*	
	1,480	1,557	1,557	
Net income/book equity	0.46	−0.17	0.05	−0.57
	0.00	*0.00*	*0.04*	*0.00*
	1,479	1,597	1,556	1,556

Notes: Significance levels of correlation coefficients are in italics. The bottom number in each row is the number of observations available for each correlation. One outlier firm is removed. B/M ratio is book value of equity divided by market value of equity. Dividend-adjusted return is the percentage increase in share price plus dividend (as percent of market value).

Sources: Bossaerts and Fohlin (2000). Data from *Saling's Börsen-Jahrbuch* (1881–1914), Rettig (1978), and Fohlin (1994).

A more complete picture of the correlations between the various return and firm characteristics (see Table 7.11) indicates that returns relate somewhat negatively to beta, but from a statistical standpoint, the relationship is insignificant ($p = 0.17$). Size correlates positively with both beta and returns, but only the former achieves statistical significance ($p < 0.01$). More striking is the significant, negative correlation between book-to-market and return: Contrary to recent U.S. data, firms with high levels of book value relative to market value of equity generate lower returns. High book-to-market firms also demonstrate higher risk (beta).

Multicharacteristic Models

Analyzing these correlations within a Fama-Macbeth (1973)–type two-step regression offers a more complex understanding of the relative strength of the statistical relationships (see Table 7.12).[63] Stock returns do relate negatively to risk (beta), as they do in U.S. data, but the statistical significance in

---

[63] Robust-regression and OLS-regression results are displayed, although the differences are minor. See Skoulakis (2005) for a comparison of this method with panel regression methods.

Table 7.12. *Average Coefficient Estimates from Annual Cross-Sectional Regressions*

	Robust	OLS	Robust	Robust	Robust
Beta	−0.90	1.88	1.84	1.42	1.08
	0.27	*0.17*	*0.09*	*0.15*	*0.21*
ln(ME)		−1.96	−1.43	−0.36	−1.24
		0.00	*0.00*	*0.19*	*0.00*
ln(BE/ME)		−18.83	−19.44	−8.50	−19.26
		0.00	*0.00*	*0.00*	*0.00*
E/BE dummy				−7.80	
				0.01	
E(+)/BE				76.36	
				0.00	
Beta (BM beta)					1.50
					0.20

Notes: Coefficients are averages over annual observations. All models include a constant (not reported). P-values of one-sided t-tests are in italics below the coefficient means. Beta is estimated for each firm over the full period. ME is the market value of equity, and BE/ME is the ratio of book-to-market values of equity. E/BE is the ratio of net income to book value of equity. E/BE dummy is 1 when E/BE is negative and 0 otherwise. E(+)/BE is equal to E/BE when that value is positive and is 0 otherwise. "Robust" in the column heading indicates the use of a limited-influence estimator (Huber/bi-weight) in the underlying cross-sectional regressions. The estimator is described in the text.
Sources: Bossaerts and Fohlin (2000). Data from Rettig (1978), *Saling's Börsen-Jahrbuch* (1881–1914), and Fohlin (1994).

this sample is weak. The multivariate approach, including the additional firm-specific variables, is clearly important. When we control for all three characteristics – beta, firm size, and book-to-market ratio – the relationship between stock returns and beta becomes positive. Higher risk firms yield higher returns, but the statistical power is low.

Still, the coefficient of beta in the cross-sectional regression of return on beta, size, and book-to-market is estimated fairly accurately. In principle, it should recover the actual return on the market index, and there is indeed little difference between the estimated coefficients to beta and the annual market return (see Figure 7.6). This small difference might indicate that the volatility of the market index drives the lack of statistical significance of the average coefficient, but we can rule this possibility out: Over the thirty-three-year period, the average return on the market index was 7.6 percent. With a volatility of 8.7 percent per annum, this average return is clearly positive.[64] Hence, the weakness of the relation between return and beta must stem from

---

[64] The mean is statistically significant at the $p < 0.01$ level.

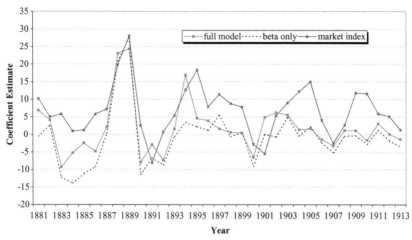

Figure 7.6. Robust Coefficient Estimates of Beta.
Notes: Coefficients of beta are estimated from robust regressions of dividend-adjusted returns on beta, logged market equity, and logged book-to-market ratios.

something other than the volatility in the market index. The capital asset pricing model (CAPM), it seems, performs poorly in this sample, but there is no purely statistical reason for this failure. At the same time, the results for beta do not suggest any systematic alternative to rational pricing. Even if higher risk yields insignificantly higher returns, the converse relationship would fail even more seriously. Low risk clearly does not produce higher stock returns in this market. Thus, arguments about the interventions of banks in price setting cannot be entirely dismissed, but the findings here at least suggest that bank involvement did not turn the normal risk-return trade-off on its head.

Like beta, the size effect commonly found in the U.S. context also appears, but is likewise subject to skepticism: Small firms generate significantly higher returns on average. Further investigation, however, suggests that size may proxy for firm earnings. Firms with negative earnings produce much lower stock returns. More generally, over the positive range of values, earnings as a share of a firm's equity (at book value) predict higher stock returns. These two relationships overshadow the size effect: When they are included in the analysis, size still relates negatively to stock returns, but the impact is much smaller and weaker. We should also view the size effect with caution in this sample, because of the possible survivorship bias.[65] If the size effect

---

[65] See the earlier discussion as well as the complete discussion in Bossaerts and Fohlin (2000).

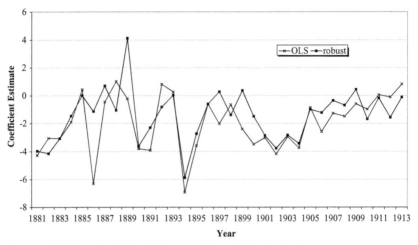

Figure 7.7. Robust Coefficient Estimates of Logged Market Equity.
Notes: Coefficients of logged market equity are estimated from robust regressions of dividend-adjusted returns on beta, logged market equity, and logged book-to-market ratios.

does indeed result from the longevity of the firms, then the magnitude of the effect ought to decline over time, as the firms approach the end of the sampling period. A detailed look at the statistical coefficients bears out this hypothesis (see Figure 7.7).[66] In other words, the size effect apparently picks up the survivorship bias.

The book-to-market value of equity also relates very negatively to stock returns in the Berlin market during this time. Controlling for the other factors, firms with relatively high market value (low BtM) continue to increase their market value at a comparatively rapid pace. Those that have low market value (high BtM) tend to produce smaller percentage returns, thus persisting in low values. The result runs counter to recent U.S. experience, and it does survive further scrutiny. Unlike the size effect, we cannot attribute the book-to-market effect to survivorship bias, because the coefficient's sign runs the opposite of expectations. Moreover, the book-to-market effect follows no perceptible trend over time, and the regression coefficient stays negative in every year of the sample (see Figure 7.8).[67]

[66] The figure plots the evolution of the coefficient in the multivariate regressions of return onto beta, size, and book-to-market.

[67] Coefficients are all negative when the analysis uses robust regression; there is one year with a positive coefficient in a standard OLS analysis. The robust regression is preferred, since it prevents the extreme values from disproportionately influencing the results.

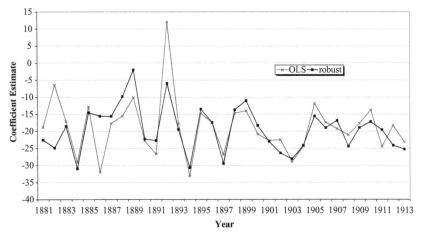

Figure 7.8. Robust Coefficient Estimates of Logged Book-to-Market Ratio.
Notes: This figure presents the estimated coefficients of logged book-to-market ratio from robust regressions of dividend-adjusted returns on beta, logged market equity, and logged book-to-market ratios.

The book-to-market ratio is clearly significant, but it could simply represent an additional proxy for risk. Beta, the covariance of a stock's returns with that of the market portfolio, provides the most widely accepted measure of a stock's risk. But it may capture only part of a stock's risk. One way to evaluate the extent to which book-to-market ratios embody firm-level risk is to create a new beta that estimates covariance of returns relative to the Fama-French HML portfolio.[68] In this sample, HML is an equally weighted portfolio containing relatively more of the top quintile of firms ranked by book-to-market ratio, and fewer of the firms in the bottom quintile. If the book-to-market effect reflects risk, the HML beta should help explain stock returns. As it turns out, however, the inclusion of the new HML beta leaves the book-to-market effect unchanged (see Table 7.12). Moreover, the new beta itself, though positive, is insignificant on average.[69]

Momentum Portfolio Returns

Over the last several years, evidence has been growing that there is a strong momentum effect in U.S. stock returns at least since the late 1920s. That is, a portfolio long in recent winners and short in recent losers generates

---

[68] Bossaerts and Fohlin (2000) cover the methodology fully.
[69] This corroborates recent U.S. history (Daniel and Titman, 1997), but is contrary to earlier U.S. history (Davis, Fama, and French, 2000).

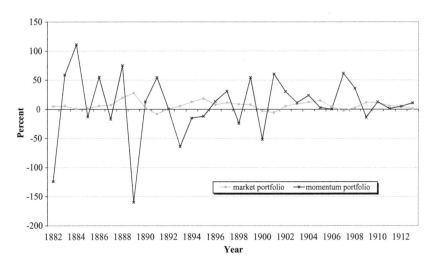

Figure 7.9. Return on Momentum Portfolio.
Notes: This figure presents the dividend-adjusted return on the momentum portfolio
(long in the top 20 percent, short in the bottom 20 percent stocks using regression
residuals) as well as the dividend-adjusted return on the market portfolio.

significant positive returns. This momentum effect is to be expected when-
ever there is any cross-sectional variation in mean returns. Indeed, the spread
(variance) of mean returns in a cross section determines directly the expected
return on a momentum index. The bigger the error of the asset pricing
model, the more the momentum index outperforms the market. The performance of specific momentum portfolios provides a diagnostic test for
an asset pricing model.[70] To determine whether the three-characteristic
model (market beta, size, and book-to-market) captures the cross-sectional
variation in mean returns, I implement the momentum portfolio and test
whether its average return is zero.

The momentum portfolio averages an annual return of 7.3 percent;
yet, with a standard error of 54 percent, the return is hardly significant
($p = 0.23$). The momentum portfolio is decidedly more volatile than the
market overall, but the lack of significance of the average momentum return
cannot be attributed to a few outliers (see Figure 7.9). Positive returns pre-
dominate only in later years (after 1900). This result suggests that the three-
characteristic model captures most of the cross-sectional variation in mean
returns.

[70] Bossaerts and Fohlin (2000) demonstrate this point. That is, payoffs on momentum indices
can be used as the basis of specification tests.

Stock Returns and Bank Involvement

The analysis here permits some preliminary conclusions about the pricing of risk in the Berlin market of the later industrialization period. For a start, size and book-to-market effects offer significant value in predicting returns, while beta performs only weakly. Crucially, however, the book-to-market effect runs the opposite of recent experience in the United States and captures far more than covariance with the portfolio long in high book-to-market firms and short in low book-to-market firms. Moreover, the momentum portfolio yields an insignificant return. In addition, the size effect, since it disappears by the end of the sample period, is attributable to selection bias. While further research is needed to bolster these conclusions and better distinguish between system effects and time-period effects, the analysis here reveals important differences between these historical German markets and more recent U.S. markets.

For the current analysis, differences in pricing and returns provoke questions about the impact of outside influences – such as financial system design or market microstructure. One line of thinking might suggest that the German universal banks, because of their active involvement with firms listed on the stock exchanges, altered pricing to such an extent that they weakened the normal link between beta and stock returns. But to do so, the banks would have had to have consistently influenced prices over many decades and to have done so contrary to firms' fundamentals. Moreover, the many banks, hypothetically representing each of the one thousand or more stocks listed on the exchanges, would have had to act in concert in their lobbying of official brokers. It is more likely that a small number of banks, perhaps the largest Berlin banks, along with a handful of influential private bankers, wielded the greatest power in the marketplace and led to some periodic alteration of prices. In that case, the overall effect on the market would be considerably smaller, though far more plausible. Whether these bank tactics caused the negative relationship between book-to-market values of equity and common stock returns remains an open question – one deserving further investigation.[71]

Price Discovery and the Costs of Trading

One final piece of evidence, effective spreads on share trading, sheds a little more light on the performance of the early stock markets in Germany. The

---

[71] Such research is under way. See, for example, Fohlin and Reinhold (2006).

results bolster the argument that the German financial system supported highly functioning securities markets within its universal banking framework. Moreover, the findings also support the idea of symbiosis – not just coexistence – between the banks and the markets.

Price discovery is a primary function of stock exchanges, and the cost of that service is often represented by the spread on individual securities transactions. That is, the difference between the bid and ask prices (as a percentage of price) gives a measure of trading costs; the higher the spread, the higher the cost. In the absence of quoted spreads – as in the case of Berlin's auction-based market – direct calculations are impossible and require estimation of "effective" spreads.[72] While the results remain provisional, and further research is needed, the early findings suggest that trading costs in the Berlin market ranged around 0.3 percent on average, falling generally in line with the standards of more recent markets.[73]

CONCLUSIONS

This chapter presents an overview of the development of the German securities markets up to 1913 and offers a variety of evidence on its structure, performance, and place within the financial system of the time. The primary point of the story is the impressive development and performance of the German markets, especially the principal stock market in Berlin, despite growing regulation and taxation. The historical record is particularly striking in its revelation of strong markets working in concert with strong, universal banks – a combination that runs counter to the still prevalent notion of a "banks versus markets" dichotomy. The idea of banks and markets as substitutes rests on more recent observation of German and other continental European financial systems. But, as this chapter shows, the schema fits poorly to the German history; and that history, in turn, demonstrates the possibility of a symbiotic relationship between universal banks and active stock markets that could well emerge in financial systems of the future.

---

[72] See Madhavan (2000) for a more technical survey on the empirical estimation of transaction costs.

[73] See Fohlin and Gehrig (forthcoming) on estimating spreads for Berlin. Computation of effective spreads requires long series of high-frequency data. For Berlin at this time, prices were quoted on a daily frequency, six days per week, giving over three hundred data points per firm each year. For a large sample of firms, covering an extended period of interest (at least 1880 to 1910) means gathering hundreds of thousands of observations.

APPENDIX: DATA USED IN THE STUDY OF
THE CROSS SECTION OF RETURNS

This analysis used a sample of fifty firms selected by R. Rettig (1978) and augmented by Fohlin (1994, 1998b). The time period, 1880–1913, is constrained on the early side by the availability of the necessary financial data and on the later end by World War I. The sample is stratified to represent the regional, sectoral, and size variation of Berlin-listed companies and is restricted to firms in continuous existence (and listing) throughout the period. This last criterion imparts an obvious selection bias to the data, discussed in the text.

The analysis requires several types of data: share prices, dividends, book capitalization, total assets, reserves, and other financial information. Annual share prices, along with the remainder of the necessary data (capitalization, total assets, reserves, annual dividend, and other financial data) come from the annual reports of the companies, reported in *Saling's Börsen-Jahrbuch*, Part II. The former covers all firms listed on the Berlin exchange (beginning in 1876).

The German stock markets and reporting agencies during this period reported share prices as the ratio of the market value to the par value of the share, multiplied by 100 (known as the *Kurs*). Dividend-adjusted return is the annual percentage change in Kurs plus annual dividends (as a percentage of market value). Dividend-adjusted beta is the coefficient estimate from a regression of dividend-adjusted returns on the dividend-adjusted market return (taken from Gielen, 1994). For the current sample, the book value of total equity (the sum of par value of total share capital and reserves) is reported in aggregate, so the total number and par value of shares are not available separately. Thus, market value of equity is calculated as the product of the Kurs and the book value of equity. This method obviously overestimates the market value of all firms. The book-to-market ratio is calculated as 100/Kurs. Financial performance is the ratio of net income to book equity (NI/BE), and a dummy variable is defined as 1 when the NI/BE ratio is negative and 0 otherwise. NI+/BE is equal to NI/BE when positive and 0 otherwise.

8

Upheaval and Recovery

This book has related a story that is by and large one of great prosperity and fortune. In 1913, Germany stood at the vanguard of science, technology, and industry. The country had progressed from an economically and politically "backward" patchwork of states to become one of the world's great powers. In the spring of 1914, it would have been hard to imagine that Germany was about to endure more than three decades of upheaval, crisis, tyranny, and war. And it is doubtful that anyone could have predicted the profound and lasting changes that would take place in the structure of Germany's economy and financial system.

THE FIRST WORLD WAR AND THE EARLY WEIMAR REPUBLIC

The Economic, Political, and Legal Environment

When war broke out in August 1914, German politicians figured on a short engagement and planned accordingly. As it turned out, they had miscalculated, and the unexpectedly high war demands strained the German productive capacity. The difficulties stemmed largely from domestic supply shortages, compounded by the British blockade starting in November 1914. Export volume declined by half in the first two years of the war and by 1918 fell to 15 percent of the 1913 level.[1] Private consumption and investments fell, and many imports were blocked by embargo. While a trickle of imports

---

[1] Maddison (1982), p. 250, table F4. The export volume index took the following values: 1913 = 100; 1914 = 80; 1915 = 50; 1916 = 20; 1917 = 20; 1918 = 15. For income and expenditure of the Reich, see Feldman (1993), p. 40, table 2; industrial production, p. 78, table 5.

continued, Germany fell into near autarky. At the same time, as farmers were conscripted, agricultural production contracted, essential supplies ran short, and food prices increased.[2]

As war requirements escalated, the German government began to increase its involvement in industry and more generally tightened its control over the economy. The Hindenburg program of August 1916 formalized state and even military power in the German economy, and the creation of the *Reichswirtschaftsamt* in July 1917 further increased the government's direction of economic matters.[3] To increase armament production, the government instituted conscription of all male workers between the ages seventeen and sixty for work in crucial industries.[4] The *Zwangswirtschaft* had begun.[5] The chemicals, heavy industry, and engineering industries expanded as they turned to war-related production.

The war costs mounted quickly and brought severe problems of war finance as well as a decline in production. Within one year, GDP fell to 85 percent of its 1913 level, and the slide continued unabated through the war years. By 1919, GDP had dropped to 72.3 percent of the 1913 level.[6] Industrial production declined even further over the same period, to 42 percent of the 1913 output.[7] War costs amounted to about 150 billion reichsmarks, nearly 40 billion dollars in real terms, the vast majority of which was financed by internal debt.[8] The remaining funds came from taxes and monetary expansion – printing money. The circulation of Reichsbank notes increased from 2.9 billion marks at the start of the war to 18.6 billion marks at the

---

[2] See Hardach (1987). Grain production, for example, fell by at least half by 1917.

[3] See Feldman (1993), pp. 72, 88, and Hau (1988), p. 91. Even prior to the war, Germany was already moderately centralized, but the war marked a new era of concentration of government at the national level. This ministry of economic affairs (renamed *Reichswirstchafstminitserium* or RWM in 1919) took over economic duties of the Reich office of the interior.

[4] Hardach (1987), p. 13.

[5] See Braun (1990), p. 26.

[6] Maddison (1982), p. 174, table A7. The GDP index takes the following values: 1913 = 100; 1914 = 85.2; 1915 = 80.9; 1916 = 81.7; 1917 = 81.8; 1918 = 82.0; 1919 = 72.3.

[7] Hardach (1987).

[8] In 1919, there were approximately 32.85 marks to the U.S. dollar, so the cost in 1919 dollars was 4.6 billion, or about 38.6 billion 2004 U.S. dollars. (See www.eh.net for currency and deflator calculation tools.) Hardach (1987), p. 10, gives the debt percentage at 70 percent. Braun (1990) has a slightly different analysis and argues that the war expenditure "was almost completely financed by loans" (p. 31). The debt constituted primarily war bonds and treasury bills bought by the public a result of the law of August 4, 1914, requiring the Reichsbank to provide short-term credits to the Reich.

war's end.[9] While seignorage provided a convenient source of war finance, it proved difficult to slow the presses once started. The quintupling of the money supply during the war created inflationary pressures that would eventually spell disaster. Throughout the war, the mark stayed at 50 percent of its 1914 value.[10]

The costs of the war and reconstruction exceeded all expectations, and it proved catastrophic for the German economy. The country lost 10 percent of its population and 13.5 percent of its prewar territory. Moreover, Germany lost regions that were particularly rich in agricultural and industrial resources (the colonies, Upper Silesia, Alsace-Lorraine, and the Saar district above all): 15 percent of the arable land, 75 percent of iron ore deposits, 44 percent of pig iron production capacity, and 38 percent of steel production capacity. Agricultural production fell to about 55 to 60 percent of the 1913 level. Simultaneously, 10 million returning soldiers flooded the labor market.[11]

The greatest financial consequence of the war was the 132 billion gold marks of reparations imposed by the Allies in April 1921. This burden, added to the costs of prosecuting the war itself, led the German government to issue enormous amounts of debt that held little hope of repayment. In the short term, as the German government continued along the previous path of inflationary monetary policy, industrial production grew and the world recession of 1920–1 largely passed without notice. The labor force reached full employment, and workers received substantial wage increases in the first postwar years.[12]

Substantial amounts of foreign, especially American, short-term investment capital flowed into Germany in 1921 and the first part of 1922.[13] But Germany's financial position was insufficient to keep up: Little gold and foreign exchange reserves remained, foreign securities were confiscated and transferred to the reparation creditors (according to the Treaty of Versailles), and domestic investment declined – partly in reaction to the reparation demands. The reparations produced a massive external deficit,

---

[9] Born (1983), p. 26, based on Statistisches Reichsamt (1925). After one month the circulation hit 4.24 billion. One year into the war, in August 1915, the circulation was 8 billion marks; two years after that, in September 1917, it passed 10 billion marks.

[10] Born (1983), p. 28. The U.S. dollar cost 4.3 marks on July 1, 1914, but on November 9, 1918, the U.S. dollar was quoted at 7.43 marks.

[11] See Braun (1990), p. 34.

[12] See Hau (1988), p. 115 on the creation of the *Arbeitsgemeinschaft* in November 1918, in which unions and the employers agreed to settle labor conflicts.

[13] Braun (1990), pp. 37–8, citing Holtfrerich (1988). Also, see Huck (1993), p. 123.

and the struggling German economy could not support repayment without even more debt and further inflation. Inflation increased the risk of foreign exchange trading, and such dealing came under increasing regulation.[14] The transfer, however, would have required an increase in exports to earn the amounts needed for the reparations.[15] But the tense international situation and the mistrust in the German government prevented healthy development of foreign trade. State expenditures were rising, and taxation could not stop inflation.[16] As early as the summer of 1921, it became clear that the currency could not be stabilized without external debt (foreign bonds) and without a reparations moratorium. The resulting loss of confidence and devaluation lit the fire of hyperinflation that wreaked havoc in 1922 and 1923.[17]

The situation escalated during the occupation of the Ruhr. In January 1923, Allied troops marched into the Ruhr in order to force Germany to pay its reparations. The state lost further tax income (a coal tax and export duties) and tried to support the "passive resistance" in which it had encouraged the population to participate. The currency declined, and a "Ruhr tax," based on a stable dollar-denominated bond, failed.[18] The creation of additional currency seemed the only way to save the government, but it could not save the mark.[19] Such a drastic inflationary policy had only a limited period of success before the natural repercussions began. On November 9, 1923, the mark had fallen to one-trillionth of its prewar value.[20]

---

[14] Henning (1992), p. 228. Forward exchange contracts were permitted for the Reichsbank starting on December 16, 1919, because the reparations had to be dealt with to make export possible.

[15] Braun (1990), p. 35, citing Hardach (1987) that the cash payments of reparation sums accelerated the inflation. In April 1921, the Allied Reparation Commission fixed the reparation obligation at 132 billion gold marks, which amounted to 33 billion U.S. dollars. Braun (1990), pp. 34–5.

[16] See Huck (1993), p. 110, for figures.

[17] Others point out additional, interrelated factors, such as more general tendencies to oversupply money, dating back even to World War I; external deficits, reparations being the most important; and substantial wage increases in 1918–19. See Hardach (1987), p. 23: "...though weakness and indecision on the part of the German government were partly responsible for the complete collapse of the currency..., the reparation burden was primarily responsible for the catastrophic hyperinflation of 1923." Braun (1990), pp. 39–40, is more cautious.

[18] Haller (1976), p. 148.

[19] Ibid.

[20] See Balderston (2002), pp. 34–60, summing up the main theories on the hyperinflation. See Feldman (1993) for an exhaustive discussion and Sargent (1982) on the economics of ending the hyperinflation.

The hyperinflation irreparably damaged public confidence in the mark, and no government promises of fiscal and monetary restraint could stem the tide. On September 25, 1923, the Ebert government stopped the Ruhrkampf (the military engagement specifically in the Ruhr region, involving the occupation by Allied troops) and shortly thereafter began serious stabilization measures – introducing new intermediate currencies (the roggenmark and then rentenmark), giving the Reichsbank its legal independence from the central government in early August 1924, and ultimately creating the gold-backed reichsmark at the end of August 1924.[21] These critical currency reforms coupled with the more reasonable reparations schedule under the Dawes Plan finally stalled the hyperinflation. As the government focused its energies on reconstruction, the German economy quickly recovered from the crisis of the hyperinflation period.

Industrial production increased steadily between 1924 and 1929; averaging 7.9 percent growth per year, in spite of an interruption in 1926. Germany became the second largest industrial nation, producing about 12 percent of world industrial output, or about 26 percent of the U.S. level.[22] Rates of growth trailed those of other similarly developed countries (the United States, France, Italy, and the U.K.), but a period of relative stability and seeming prosperity was under way.[23]

At the same time, the concentration and cartelization of industry took on new vigor. The major chemical firms combined into the IG Farbenindustrie in 1925, for example, while the steel industry formed the Vereinigte Stahlwerke trust in 1926. Individual firms, such as Siemens and AEG in the electrical industry, built up enormous concerns, and about 2,500 cartels came into existence.[24] These changes in industry structure represented, in part, a rationalization process necessitated by mechanical and technological change – especially in mining and in the iron and steel industry. In most branches, rationalization created new unemployment. It may have also led to suboptimal distribution of investment, with overcapacity in branches

---

[21] Born (1983), pp. 45–6. In November, 1 billion marks equaled 1 gold mark. Braun (1990), p. 36. See also Born (1983), p. 69. In addition to the banking law (independence for the Reichsbank), reforms included a law of private-bank notes, a law on coins (Münzgesetz), and a law eliminating circulation of rentenmark notes (*Rentenbankscheine*).

[22] Hardach (1987), p. 39.

[23] Braun (1990), pp. 46–52.

[24] See Feldman (1993), p. 810. The legislature did attempt to bolster competition, for example, with its Decree Concerning Abuses of Economic Power of November 1923, but the efforts remained weak. See also Feldenkirchen (1992) and Wunderlich (1938).

such as the heavy industries and textiles.[25] Massive state intervention began anew in an effort to resolve many of these labor problems, but these efforts deepened the government deficits and sowed new seeds of instability.

Throughout the period, political stabilization proved difficult to achieve. The war defeat, along with the abdication of the kaiser, left Germany in political, economic, and social chaos and created a power vacuum that was filled in 1919 by the newly formed Weimar Republic. Momentous and well conceived as this first effort at democracy was, the surrounding turmoil – economic dislocation, political in-fighting, attempted coups – weighed heavily on the nascent republic and ultimately doomed it to failure.[26] The Weimar Republic was, by its own definition, a social welfare state, striving for the creation of public employment, development of social housing, public education, and social security benefits. As with the economy, relative stability came only during the middle years of the republic, from late 1923 until late 1929.

Developments in Banking and Finance

The Banking Industry

World War I disrupted the banking business as it had interrupted many other facets of the economy. The banks weathered the significant withdrawals in the first couple of weeks of the engagement, but the situation normalized quickly and a run never materialized.[27] As the war progressed, however, certain services came to a near-halt: international and real estate businesses, foreign exchange dealings (banned until 1916 and seriously restricted thereafter), and new issues of securities.[28] As it did in the industrial sectors, concentration accelerated rapidly among the universal banks during and after the war. The mergers that had provoked so much hand-wringing over excessive concentration in the prewar era paled in comparison to what followed. The largest universal banks, the great banks, swallowed up hundreds of smaller commercial and private banks and, with the 1922 acquisition of

---

[25] Braun (1990), p. 52: "In Germany, rationalization contributed to a sectoral maldistribution of investment with overcapacity in branches such as the heavy industries and textiles." He relies here on James (1986), p. 149.

[26] See Feldman's (1993) authoritative work on the war and early Weimar (1914–24), revolving mainly around the theme of the inflation.

[27] Born (1983), p. 24.

[28] Ibid., p. 31, based on data from Deutsche Bundesbank (1976), pp. 56–9. While the joint-stock banks (with a balance of more than 1 million marks) had 459 million marks in syndicate securities (*Konsortialbeteiligungen*) in 1914, they had only 370 million marks in 1916 and 331 million marks in 1918.

the Nationalbank für Deutschland by the Bank für Handel und Industrie (Darmstädter Bank), took the first steps toward combining among themselves. The byproduct of this process, of course, was the increasingly national reach of the largest banks' networks of branch offices, which together had grown from the low one hundreds at the start of the war to the thousands by the mid-1920s.[29]

The war and hyperinflation proved difficult for the universal banking sector. The great banks certainly gained ground over the provincial and private banks, but their financial position in absolute terms deteriorated significantly with the onset of World War I and the inflation. When the banks reopened their accounts under the new currency (the *Goldmarkeröffnungsbilanz*) on January 1, 1924, they showed only one-fifth the level of assets of December 31, 1913.[30] In the end of 1924, they owned just one-fifth of their equity capital of 1913; by 1929, they had reached only 56 percent. Their ratio of equity capital to external funds stood around 1:3 in 1913; in 1929 it was 1:13 and heavily based on short-term foreign loans.[31] Provincial banks suffered heavier losses in equity capital than the great banks, and over the same period, they lost more than two-thirds of their prewar equity capital. Since they had merely half of the amount of foreign investment (of 1913) in their deposits, however, their ratio of equity capital to external funds, at 1:6, remained much more favorable than that of the great banks. Of the external funds, as much as 24 percent was long-term investments in 1930.[32] Decreasing capitalization ratios hastened the universal banks' move toward discount credits that they could rediscount with the Reichsbank.[33]

Despite the increasing concentration among universal banks, costs remained a major problem for them, through slower growth of transaction volume and reduced profit margins. The problem grew over the following

---

[29] Pohl (1982), pp. 67–8. For a contemporary appraisal of the concentration and decentralization processes, see Fendler (1926). See also Zorn (1976). While 50 new provincial banks had appeared during the inflation, a third of them disappeared, and by the end of 1929, only 211 provincial banks were left. The great banks also targeted the smaller private banks in their concentration movement. The number of private bankers declined markedly after the start of the war, and 180 private banks became branches of the joint-stock banks between 1913 and 1925.

[30] Ibid., p. 865. See also Whale (1930).

[31] Born (1983), p. 76.

[32] Figures come from Untersuchung des Bankwesens (1933). Born (1983), p. 78, notes that this fact goes quite a ways in explaining the safety of the provincial banks, compared to the great banks, during the ensuing crisis.

[33] For more details, see Lüke (1958), p. 209. Quoted in Pohl (1982), p. 86.

years, despite an increase in business activity.[34] While costs took up 30 percent of total profits in 1913, they had risen to 85 percent in 1924.[35] Cost problems continued, as did the pressure for further consolidation in the banking industry. Oscar Schlitter, director of the Deutsche Bank, based his argument for mergers on this cost question (*Kostenfrage*) and on the concentration process in industry. In his view, the banks were to create a "bank-bloc," the power of which would govern the German market.[36]

The war and its aftermath brought changes in the services provided by the banks as well. The joint-stock banks, particularly the great banks, dealt comparatively little in war bonds, though their holdings of short-term loans of the Reich and Länder increased considerably over the second half of the war.[37] Industry also moved more into long-term foreign bonds for its funding, thus avoiding business with the banks.[38] The war and the inflation had caused serious damage to the financial markets, and the securities business of the universal banks had lost its grounding and integrity through the war and the inflation. So, while many new stock corporations were founded, and existing stock corporations increased their capital, industry had become less dependent on the universal banks as intermediaries of its securities. The receding issuing business became apparent in the banks' balance sheets: Consortium securities holdings of the great banks doubled between 1918 and 1921, but total bank assets quintupled over the same period.[39] In 1913, the great banks had held stocks and bonds with a value of 812 million marks, 373 of which were Konsortialbeteiligungen. After the currency reform, only RM 141 million were left. Up to 1929, securities holdings grew to merely RM 379 million – less than half of the holdings of 1913. As the universal banks decreased these lines of business, however, they also began to move into insurance services.[40]

The structural changes in the universal banking sector prompted a corresponding counter move by the savings banks.[41] These politically

---

[34] Idem (1986), pp. 86, 88–9.
[35] See idem (1982), p. 87, for more on this.
[36] Born (1983), p. 81, quotes Pohl (1980), p. 38, quoting Schlitter.
[37] Born (1983).
[38] Ibid., pp. 84–5, has numbers for this funding.
[39] Ibid., p. 51.
[40] Ibid., pp. 31–2, gives numbers for takeovers and capital expansion of the three great banks during the war.
[41] Pohl (1982), pp. 72–4. Johann Christian Eberle, whose idea it was to protect the smaller companies through local credits from the strong concentration in the industry, also thought it would be possible to avoid a capital concentration in Berlin through setting up central giro institutions. (Pohl refers to Hoffmann [1966].) See Feldman (1991) on competition within the banking sector – private versus savings banks.

promoted institutions were created to serve the credit demands of small and medium-sized companies that had insufficient access to financial services via the commercial/universal banks.[42] Due to their primary role in issuing and holding the massive amounts of war bonds that financed the war – more than 8 billion marks worth by the end of 1918 – the savings banks gained vital experience in securities issue that they had previously largely avoided or ignored.[43] During the inflation, the savings banks continued their path toward universal banking, partly because of their need for the liquidity of short-term business in order to adapt to the unstable value of the currency.[44] The loss of the war bond business necessitated a transition to other lines of business, and the government granted the savings banks more freedom, permitting, for example, the storing and administration of securities starting in 1920 and securities transactions on commission starting in 1925.[45] As the savings banks and credit cooperatives encroached more and more into universal banking territory, the latter finally responded by introducing savings accounts.[46]

Banks and Corporate Governance

World War I and its aftermath fundamentally altered the structure of shareholding within German corporations. The late-nineteenth century trend toward shareholder democracy came to an end, the separation of ownership and control grew, and the role of banks in corporate governance underwent marked change. After the war, members of the management and supervisory board often held a large amount of managers' shares in order to tie them to the fate of the company. To secure management control over the company, firms often distributed preferred stocks, extending more than one vote per share on these stakeholders.[47] Some companies also issued shares to workers, but imposed specific conditions and constraints on them. For example, in 1919, the Rheinische Möbelstoff-Weberei offered its workers 280 new shares but attached the condition that the bank that issued them exercise the voting

---

[42] Born (1983), p. 52.

[43] The savings banks held 5.7 billion marks worth of war bonds among their deposits at this time. See Pohl (1982), p. 71.

[44] Born (1983), pp. 51–2. For numbers on the sorts of banks that existed in 1925, see pp. 72–3.

[45] See Pohl (1986), p. 73.

[46] Ibid. refers to Walb (1933).

[47] See Passow (1922), p. 260 ff, for examples, including the AG Ferd. Rueckforth Nachfolger in Stettin, where the managing and the supervisory board members held preferred stocks, and members of the supervisory board were required to hold at least twenty of the preferred stocks (which carried multiple voting rights).

rights for these shares.[48] Not altogether representative of general patterns, but certainly interesting, the giant but closely held Krupp AG decided in 1921 to issue new shares especially designed for workers.[49] These shares were not given directly to workers, but rather distributed in the workers' name to the "Krupp'sche Treuhand," which represented the workers' shares at the general meetings. In other words, the Treuhand exercised the voting rights according to the outcome of the members' meetings. More generally, unions often bought shares in order to represent their members at the general meetings.

With the enormous upswing in corporations at the end of the war and during the inflation, banks boosted their proxy holdings as well as their presence in the supervisory boards of these firms. The impact was particularly noticeable for the largest banks, as they had taken over many of the smaller banks and along the way gathered further board positions. Thus, by 1927, representatives of the large banks held 2,514 seats in nonfinancial firms' supervisory boards, out of which 1,785 (70 percent) were in industry and infrastructure.[50] In 1912, by contrast, Deutsche Bank held 159 seats, Disconto-Gesellschaft 143, Berliner Handelsgesellschaft 123, and Dresdner Bank 120.[51] Marked as these increases were, the corporate governance system would undergo even more change as Germany fell into economic depression and war.

Financial Markets

By the spring of 1914, the markets were beginning to show signs of nervousness, and price fluctuations increased. The unease intensified with the assassination in Sarajevo on June 28; tensions mounted, leading up to the outbreak of the war a month later. Insurance stocks declined markedly early on, as did bond prices.[52] Stocks suffering the greatest declines stopped trading first, and futures trading stopped at the Berlin stock exchange on August 25. Five days later, all official quotation halted when the bourses were closed and written quotations were prohibited.[53]

---

[48] Ibid.

[49] The maximum amount for one worker was five hundred shares (ibid., p. 261).

[50] See Hagemann (1931), p. 74, as quoted in Brendel (2001), p. 86.

[51] Hagemann (1931), p. 81.

[52] Henning (1992) provides the most thorough survey of this period in the German securities markets. He notes (p. 218), on August 20, one of the major German banks advised its privileged customers to sell their stocks. See also Helten (1928), used in Henning (1992).

[53] Kronenberger (1920), cited in Henning (1992), p. 218.

Stocks continued to trade over the counter, both through the banks and in the stock exchange buildings themselves. Off-board trading flourished once it became clear that the war would last longer than a few months. The government tolerated this unofficial trading, with the idea that it would allow customers to exchange their corporate stocks for war bonds and to transfer foreign securities into the banking system, thereby strengthening German foreign currency holdings.[54] At the same time, however, off-board trading weakened the transparency and security of the trading process and led to increased speculation – particularly in industrial shares of companies producing war goods.[55] As bankers took over the price-setting functions from official brokers, the banks seemingly gained increasing power in the markets.[56] Official price quotations resumed in November 1917 and returned the brokers to their position as the market's chief price setters.[57] The situation began to normalize further after January 1, 1918, when markets reopened under the prewar regulations. Forward exchange contracts were permitted for the Reichsbank in December 1919, in order to deal with reparations payments and to facilitate exports.[58]

During the war, prices had doubled and many stocks had lost substantial real value. This tendency continued for several years following the war, though most commodity-based stocks retained their value.[59] Demand for stocks, and the level of speculation, increased, partly because of the ready availability of financial resources. By December 1918, investors had grown optimistic about a transition out of the war economy, and prices rose. A bull market gathered steam in August 1921, when the managing committees of the stock exchanges reduced trading to three days.[60] The growing trade

---

[54] Ibid., p. 219.
[55] Ibid., p. 223. Henning also notes that as prices rose for war-related stocks, they became strong competitors for war bonds.
[56] Ibid.
[57] Banks could only trade fixed-interest–bearing securities, since the Department of Commerce realized that the banks had become competitors among each other instead of working as commissioners. Fendler (1926), p. 16, argues that the Reich government grew concerned that the increase in unofficial stock trading – first by private bankers, then also by the large universal banks – amounted to speculation that tied up financial resources needed in production of war-related goods. Moreover, unofficial stock trading was arguably part of the reason for the lack of reliability of the treasury securities (*unverzinslichen Schatzanweisungen*) from the fifth war bond on, and subsequently as part of the reason for inflation and thus for concentration of capital (from 1917 on).
[58] Henning (1992), p. 228.
[59] Ibid., pp. 226–7.
[60] Kronenberger (1920), p. 9, cited in Henning (1992), p. 227.

volume and the dangers that came with speculation and inflation led to organizational and legal changes for the stock markets in both 1920 and 1921. The new regulations, reflecting a policy of favoring large enterprises, placed a minimum par value on shares and reduced banks' stock exchange turnover tax rate by half. The growing volume of trading also required institutional changes, such as the creation of security deposit associations (*Kassenvereine*) in 1923.[61]

As inflation raged out of control in mid-1923, foreign exchange trading was prohibited altogether, unofficial trading was stopped, and standard quotations were fixed by the Reichsbank in Berlin. The currency reforms of October 1923 (rentenmark) and August 1924 (reichsmark), along with the Dawes Plan, finally allowed the return to normal stock market transactions and the abatement of speculation. In the spring of 1925, futures trading in securities was permitted again (with limitations), in an effort to remove it from the purview of the banks. A listing board was set up, in order to assist joint-stock companies in the transition to the new currency.[62] With the improving economy, stock prices increased about 60 percent between 1924 and 1927.[63]

After the stabilization, Germany was especially attractive to foreigners' investment, because interest rates were high.[64] But the credit market's dependence on foreign investment represented a serious danger, since a short-term withdrawal of the external funds would spell disaster.[65] That scenario came to pass in May 1927, when the Reichsbank president Hjalmar Schacht warned about the run-up in the market during a speech at the Reichstag.[66] Foreign capital responded by evacuating the market, and foreign exchange holdings dropped by half. On May 13, the stock market fell precipitously.[67] It was just the first step toward the string of disasters that would follow.

---

[61] Other changes included, for example, the admission of women to the stock exchanges. Because of rising trade volume, the boards of directors were enlarged. (The members of the boards were elected; at this point, the stock exchanges were self-governing bodies under the supervision of the Ministries of Commerce of the Länder.) Also, the number of entrants rose. At the Berlin stock exchange, for example, the number of visitors doubled between 1914 and 1924.

[62] Ibid., pp. 242–3.

[63] Ibid., p. 249, based on Deutsche Bundesbank figures.

[64] Born (1983), p. 71, gives figures.

[65] Ibid., p. 72.

[66] Henning (1992), p. 246, based on *Berliner Börsenzeitung*.

[67] See Prion (1929), p. 81. Henning (1992), p. 248, has some figures on this for the years 1925–9.

DEPRESSION AND WAR

The Economic, Political, and Legal Environment

The relative calm of the mid-1920s was tenuous at best and could not withstand the subsequent economic and political shocks. Real gross national output declined more than 25 percent over the worst years of the depression, from 1928 to 1932.[68] Unemployment doubled from 1.5 million in 1929 to 3 million in 1930 and doubled again to 6 million in 1932. Output returned to predepression levels around 1937, and unemployment dropped back to 1.8 million by 1935.[69] While some debate continues over the causes of the depression, it probably resulted from a confluence of several domestic and international problems: the drop in investment, particular inventory investment, high real wages accompanied by declining factor productivity, as well as "sunspot" phenomena – that is, psychological or nonfundamental factors.[70]

The political unrest arguably worsened the situation, particularly when the Reichstag elections of September 1930 brought yet more Nazis and Communists into the government and prompted a massive recall of short-term funds by foreign creditors.[71] A run on the German banks followed and in turn triggered numerous banking failures or near failures and the stepping up of German government intervention in the system.[72] The massive reparations payments continued to strain Germany's economy and financial system, and deflation was seen as the best way to regain economic activity.[73] At the same time, the general credit squeeze in Germany increased the deflationary tendencies.[74] The mounting crisis demonstrated Germany's inability to cope with reparations demands, and finally prompted their termination in the Treaty of Lausanne of July 9, 1932.[75] In an attempt to pull the economy

---

[68] Fisher and Hornstein (2001), p. 1, and Weder (2006), p. 1.

[69] See Balderston (2002), p. 79, and James (1986), p. 371. Also see Temin (1990), contrasting the U.S. and German patterns of unemployment.

[70] See Fisher and Hornstein (2001) on real wages and productivity, Temin (1971) on investment, and Weder (2005) on "sunspot" phenomena.

[71] Hardach (1987), p. 41.

[72] The next section, on developments in banking and finance specifically, takes up this issue in a bit more depth.

[73] Braun (1990).

[74] Hardach (1987). See Feldman (1991) on overcapacity in production, that is, reinflation. On international factors in the crisis, see the works of Eichengreen (1992) and Kindleberger (1986).

[75] Born (1983), p. 139.

out of depression, Heinrich Brüning and the two subsequent administrations (Franz von Papen and Kurt von Schleicher) undertook massive job creation programs financed by exchange bills – an instrument of government finance that would reappear with some alteration under the Nazi regime.[76]

Capitalizing on the popular fear of the rising Communist Party, and with the support of well-known industrial leaders (Gustav Krupp, Fritz Thyssen, Albert Voegler, and others), President Paul von Hindenburg appointed Adolph Hitler Chancellor in January 1933. By then, the National Socialist German Workers' Party (NSDAP) held fewer Reichstag seats than it had earned in its largest vote thus far – slightly more than 37 percent – in the elections of July 1932.

Despite their lack of coherent economic doctrine or theory (Hitler himself was proud of declaring, "the basic feature of our economic theory is that we have no theory at all"), the National Socialists pursued a range of economic policies, the underlying goal of which was to grow out of recession.[77] Their ideology prescribed, first and foremost, the withdrawal from the world market and economic self-sufficiency. The Nazi thinking involved the extension of German "living space" (*Lebensraum*): expanding the country in order to feed the German people.[78] With that goal in mind, the regime imposed centralized control of the economy and eliminated state input into financial decision making. Likewise, the Nazi government promoted agricultural autarky, and agricultural production increased substantially over the mid- to late-1930s. This growth, in turn, increased self-sufficiency in Germany.[79] In 1936, the National Socialist Four Year Plan established agricultural reforms and instituted new measures to extend the raw material base. Yet Germany remained dependent on imports for much of its raw materials – two-thirds of iron ore and oil requirements, for example, with only about half of the latter coming from European sources.[80]

A second main tenet of Nazi policy was the rearmament of its military – a policy goal that naturally also spilled over into the economic sphere. Several industrial branches – primarily chemical engineering, iron and steel,

---

[76] Von Papen ruled from June 1932 to December 1932; Von Schleicher governed from December 1932 to January 1933.

[77] Quoted by Braun (1990), p. 78. Original citation in Zilbert (1981).

[78] The expression "living space" comes from the Nazi economic program of 1920. See Braun (1990), p. 79.

[79] Ibid., p. 99.

[80] Hardach (1987), p. 77.

and machinery – benefited considerably from the buildup effort. And in 1936, as a result of the heavy emphasis on rebuilding, military spending exceeded 10 percent of GNP for the first time. The military buildup was in turn financed by the Mefo-Wechsel from 1934 to 1936.[81] Beyond its obvious political motivations, therefore, the rearmament spending, and the corresponding government debt, played a significant part in Germany's economic recovery.

Raising employment – particularly that of blue-collar workers – represented another important component of the Nazi economic policy. Piggybacking on the work creation programs of von Papen and von Schleicher, the Nazi administration set up new programs focused on construction and motor transport – including not only the motor vehicle industry, but also the entire surrounding infrastructure.[82] While unemployment had dropped by about one-third by the end of 1933, 4 million people remained unemployed. It took another three years for Germany to reach just short of full employment. As the economic recovery progressed, industrial production rose and by 1938 was 22 percent higher than the level a decade earlier. The industries targeted by the work projects – construction and transport – played a major role in generating the growth necessary for the economic recovery. Still, while employment increased over the mid-1930s, and the economy did recover, considerable doubt remains about the effectiveness of the Nazi plans themselves in creating the employment recovery.[83]

Despite the military buildup over the mid-1930s, as well as the focus on self-sufficiency in raw materials production, the German economy was inadequately prepared for war. It could supply its own food and raw materials only for a short engagement. The war dramatically increased demand for certain goods and required shifts in production along with considerable

---

[81] Mefo was an acronym for Metallurgische Forschungs-GmbH, which Braun (1990), p. 91, describes as: "a straw firm" with Deutsche Werke, Krupp, Rheinmetall, and Siemens as stockholders. Mefo bills carried a three-month maturity that could be extended to six months. The bills were issued by firms with limited capital that were supplying material to the armed forces, and they were accepted by the Mefo and then discounted at the Reichsbank or sold in the open market. Hardach (1987), p. 63, estimates that the Mefo bills accounted for approximately one-fifth of all military expenditures from 1933 until the outbreak of the war.

[82] The programs were largely the work of Fritz Reinhardt, the state secretary in the Ministry of Finance. Ibid., p. 57, refers to Reinhardt as "the party's leading theorist on economic stimulation." See also Temin (1990) on the use of military and investment spending (over consumption) in rapidly reducing unemployment.

[83] See Ritschl (2002) and Weder (2005).

reallocation of labor inputs. Between 1938 and 1944, the building industry dropped from 25 to 5 percent of production; consumer-goods industries declined from 30 to 25 percent; and capital-goods industry fell from 19 to 10 percent. The armaments industry absorbed all of the difference, rising from 7 to 40 percent of production in the same years. This restructuring toward and expansion of the armaments industry required significant increases in labor productivity along with active government centralization of control.[84] More broadly, however, while industrial production increased somewhat over the war years, the increases were small compared to the requisite war production.

The massive redirection of resources required an infusion of funds, and the Nazi regime was compelled to raise taxes of various types – nearly half (48 percent) of the state expenditure came from these sorts of "regular income." And, to be sure, the Reich exploited occupied countries in its war effort. The regime also borrowed from the public, sometimes indirectly, through a variety of government-backed or -controlled securities.[85] The Reichsbank, which was subordinated to the Führer from 1937 onward, accepted part of the short-term bonds itself. [86] But the Reich also financed the war, as the World War I government had done before it, with the expansion of the money supply. Effective rationing of foodstuffs and consumer goods and controls on prices and wages sufficed to stabilize the reichsmark's purchasing power for quite a while, in spite of the enormous increase in the volume of currency.

The war mobilization also required enormous labor inputs, and it needed to make up for the loss of workers entering into military service – nearly 6 million men just in the two years between May 1939 and May 1941. The civilian labor force decreased only 10 percent, as millions of foreigners and prisoners of war filled much of the gap.[87] Women also replaced some of the missing labor force, and industrialists happily employed them for below-market (male) wages and without the benefits that the government

---

[84] Hardach (1987), p. 81.

[85] Wandel (1993), pp. 284–5, provides figures: RM 117 billion of medium and long-term credits, and RM 225.5 billion of short-term credits.

[86] In 1944 the Reichsbank held RM 64 billion in treasury bills (*Wechseln* and *Schatzwechseln*). For more on the development of the Reichsbank from 1918 onward, see Holtfrerich and Iwami (1999). Zorn (1976), p. 190, indicates that the total debt amounted to RM 390 billion (including Mefo-bills) at the war's end, RM 290 billion of which were deposited in German banks, of which 250 billion RM was short-term.

[87] Hardach (1987), p. 80. These segments of the workforce increased from 3 million to over 7 million by 1944.

mandated for men.[88] But women's labor participation stayed within a fairly narrow range, between 14.1 and 14.8 million, during the war.[89]

Developments in Banking and Finance

The Banking Industry

Financial fragility went hand in hand with the economic problems. Debates over the precise causes of the German financial crisis continue still, with some arguing that the problem was one of currency, not bank instability.[90] External factors – the war reparations, the high interest rates in Germany, and excessive short-term borrowing from abroad that was invested long term – played some role. Domestic influences – a shortage in domestic capital for long-term investment, the government's poor tax policy, capital flight, and forced rationalization and cost reduction in industry (*Zwangsbewirtschaftung*) – contributed as well.[91] The American contraction has often been targeted as a cause, but its role is disputed as well. While perhaps not a direct causal factor, it probably did worsen the German situation.[92] And the interwar version of the gold standard, also insufficient as root cause, did constrain its adherents and prevent domestic policies that would promote economic recovery.[93]

The first year of the depression was relatively harmless for the banks. Compared to industry, which earned less than one-third of its total 1929 profit in 1930, the banks made a total profit of 69 percent of the previous year.[94] But the crisis forced reduction of credit to industry.[95] In 1929, it became apparent that many industrial companies held too much productive capacity and could not pay their debts. The inability to pay revealed the faults in the screening and monitoring policies of the universal banks;

---

[88] See Braun (1990).

[89] Hardach (1987), p. 81, explains the phenomenon based on "Nazi conception of women's role in society, but also due to the financial support extended to servicemen's wives and their reluctance to leave their homes."

[90] See Ferguson and Temin (2003), who also argue that the German crisis was largely one of domestic political unsoundness. For further details and debates over the 1931 crisis (or crises), see Adalet (2005), Ferguson and Temin (2004), Petri (1998), and Schnabel (2004a, b).

[91] Pohl (1982), pp. 91–2.

[92] Temin (1971), p. 248, concludes that "the fall in American capital exports in 1929 could not have initiated the German depression." See also Balderston (1994) and James (1986).

[93] Eichengreen (1992).

[94] Born (1983), p. 105, reports numbers for stocks of banks.

[95] Ibid., p. 137, gives numbers for this as well.

they had granted loans without sufficient credit checks. As a result, many bank credits were converted into equity stakes (*Kapitalbeteiligungen*), and these growing stocks of untradable equities further reduced the banks' liquidity. Strong competition among the banks continued to hold down profit margins.[96] After the war and the inflation, the equity capital of the banks proved insufficient for their volume of business.[97]

The growing power of the National Socialists – with their seats in the Reichstag increasing by more than 150 percent in the elections of September 1930 – prompted further retraction of foreign credit. In the first few weeks after the election, foreigners withdrew RM 700 million of deposits and loans; the Reichsbank lost more than RM 1 billion of gold reserves and foreign currency holdings.[98] And from January 1931 on, the banks had to worry about the prices of their own stocks. The Berliner Handelsgesellschaft was able to support its share price by dealing with foreign countries, but other great banks resorted to buying their own stock in order to stabilize their prices.[99]

Preceding the German banking crisis – if not the actual trigger for it – was the collapse of the largest Austrian commercial bank, the Oesterreichische Creditanstalt, on May 11, 1931. As it collapsed, it withdrew RM 288 million of short-term loans from German banks.[100] This may have affected the German banks, because of their relative illiquidity, particularly considering their high foreign debt; 40 percent of it being American. In the second half of May, RM 288 million short-term loans were withdrawn.[101] On July 13, the Danat Bank stopped payments (*Zahlungseinstellung*), and bank holidays on the following two days did not ease the situation. Among other things, the Danat Bank (along with Dresdner) had been involved in the textile group Nordwolle's undertakings, and the latter lost RM 200 million on speculative dealings. Danat had actually lost more on the Nordwolle disaster than it held in available equity capital.[102] Further credit withdrawals followed

---

[96] Schneider (1984), p. 87.

[97] Pohl (1982), p. 92.

[98] Braun (1990), p. 65, citing Blaich (1985).

[99] Such price support was in accordance with the shareholder law (*Aktienrecht*) of the time, in which AGs and KGs were allowed to buy their own stocks "outside of regular business transactions." This law was changed with the Aktienrechtsnovelle of September 19, 1931. See Born (1983), p. 107.

[100] See Braun (1990), p. 68, who refers to Henning (1973). On international factors in the crisis, see the works of Eichengreen (1992) and Kindleberger (1986).

[101] Braun, p. 68, citing Henning (1973). Also see Born (1983), pp. 108–9.

[102] Around RM 50 million, or RM 18 million more than the bank's available net worth, according to ibid., p. 111.

and endangered the Reichsbank's position as lender of last resort.[103] The massive credit drain had become a political issue, particularly in light of Reichskanzler Brüning's apparent unwillingness to cover the reparations payments.[104]

After the Hoover Moratorium (July 1, 1931, to June 30, 1932) and the three bank holidays, it became clear that the banking sector needed urgent change. The government took control of the situation, creating the Akzeptanz- und Garantiebank AG on July 20, 1931, to support banks in trouble. The Reich's stake in the great banks amounted to RM 839 million in 1931 (at that stage, the Reich owned 91 percent of the share capital of Dresdner Bank and 70 percent of Commerzbank).[105] The majority of the credit sector was not only under government control, but after an emergency decree of September 1931, it came under direct supervision as well. From December 1931 onward, the Reichskommissar began to set interest rates in order to curb destructive competition among the banks and effectively create a forced cartel among them.[106] In the wake of the crisis, the central credit committee (*Zentraler Kreditausschuss*) also ensured that banks adhered to rate arrangements. Starting in 1931, the government began to impose stringent regulation of foreign exchange dealing. The national money and capital markets were isolated once again, and the foreign exchange and securities business, which had been important for the great banks, lost much of its volume.

The depression and banking crisis set off a new process of reduction and selection within the banking industry.[107] In 1929, Deutsche Bank and Discontgesellschaft merged into Dedi-Bank, later renamed Deutsche Bank. In the 1931–2 crisis, Dresdner Bank and Danat Bank combined, while Commerz- und Privatbank merged with the Bremer Bankverein.[108] After the dust settled, three great banks emerged, along with an unprecedented amount of government involvement in regulation, supervision, and even ownership. The takeover of the Nazi regime further increased the level of government involvement in the financial sector, based largely on a series of "emergency" acts. Soon after their assumption of power, the market came under additional regulation and restriction of traditional business. On September 4, 1934, the government prohibited the founding of new

---

[103] Ibid.
[104] Braun (1990), p. 68, citing Henning (1973).
[105] Zorn (1976), pp. 187–8.
[106] Pohl (1982), p. 94, quotes Bähre (1982) and Schneider (1984), p. 89.
[107] Born (1983), p. 137, provides some figures.
[108] Zorn (1976), p. 850.

banks and branches.[109] And on December 15, 1934, it passed a law on the credit business (*Kreditwesengesetz*). Designed by the banking inquiry commission, the act granted public control of credit institutions and legally instituted the supervisory board for the banking industry.

As the crisis faded, however, the bank inquiry commission concluded that the German banking industry was soundly organized, and the government ultimately abandoned its nationalization plans for the banks. By 1937, the great banks, the equity capital of which had mostly fallen into the hands of the Reich (via the stated-owned Golddiskontbank), once again returned to private ownership.[110] In the same year, a collective agreement (*Mantelvertrag*) was established among all credit institutions that remained essentially valid until 1967.[111]

The chief aim of the Nazi government regarding the credit sector was to find a means for financing a war, and the government gradually forced the banks to provide credit to the state and to offer services in furtherance of state policy.[112] To avoid the unpopular war loans that the Reich had issued in World War I, the new Reich employed a regime of "silent finance" (*geräuschlose Finanzierung*).[113] The state encouraged, if not forced, citizens to deposit their money into savings accounts, the balances of which were lent to the Reich government as bonds. These proceeds then went to pay for the workers in the war industry.[114] Much of the financing through Mefo-Wechsel happened via the public banking sector – the savings banks (*Sparkassen*) – that the Nazi government had subsumed under its administrative umbrella after 1933.[115] In effect, savers provided credit to the Reich without being fully aware of it.[116]

The savings banks (*Sparkassen*), the credit banks, and the cooperatives held just over half of the Reich's debts at the end of the war; the Reichsbank (21 percent), and insurance companies (6.4 percent) also provided significant sums.[117] The remaining share (17 percent) came from other lenders, mainly in the occupied territories.[118] The role of the universal banks,

---

[109] Pohl (1982), p. 94.

[110] Ibid., p. 95, quotes Peckolt (1937), p. 37, and Stucken (1933), p. 7.

[111] Zorn (1976), p. 865.

[112] Ibid., p. 186. For statistics (to be read carefully) on the years 1930 to 1937, see Peckolt (1937).

[113] Braun (1990), p. 114. The term translates literally as "noiseless," but indicates a means of financing without making the public aware of the huge financial costs of the war.

[114] Frank (1993), p. 193.

[115] Pohl (1982), p. 98, quotes Ashauer (1983).

[116] Wandel (1993), p. 282.

[117] Ibid.

[118] Ibid.

particularly the great banks, in the war finance effort remains open to debate. Some argue that they took part only hesitantly in financing armament production.[119] But the fact of the banks' financing is clear. The universal banks not only accepted and redistributed bonds, but they also participated in the prewar finance (*Vorfinanzierung*). Since only half of the RM 12 billion in Mefo-bills ended up at the Reichsbank, the other RM 6 billion worth were either kept by the suppliers or by the banks as investments with interest. Here the Berlin great banks surely became involved, because they dealt far more with the armament industry than did the savings banks or other segments of the banking industry.[120] Through the silent war finance, the banking industry evolved toward *Hofbankwesen*.[121]

The banking industry structure continued its transformation during the Nazi years, but the overriding influence became the policy of aryanization, or the elimination of Jewish ownership.[122] Because of the traditional predominance of Jews in the banking professions, the aryanization program dramatically reduced the number of private banks. Many of the Jewish bank houses turned to the great banks to help meet the new regulations. In one example, the Deutsche Bank took over the private banker Mendelssohn & Co.[123] After a particularly harsh round of aryanization in 1938, the number of private bankers stood at only 565. Ultimately, of the 1,406 private banks in 1925, only 491 remained in 1942.[124]

Corporate Governance

The Great Depression of the 1930s hit German corporations hard and sent large numbers of them into insolvency. It also threw the banks more and

[119] Pohl (1982), p. 98, quotes Ashauer (1983). See also Wandel (1993), p. 282. Wandel's analysis of the role of banks in financing the armament of World War II aims at refuting the opinion that the great banks played a major part in financing armament production and the war. See also Wandel (1983).

[120] Wandel (1993), p. 281. On the role of the Deutsche Bank specifically, see the chapters (the one by Harold James in particular) on the interwar and war years in Gall et al. (1996). The universal banks' management was apparently not selected based on party identity; however, the Sparkassen managers were.

[121] Zorn (1976), quoting Terhalle (1952). The term *Hofbankwesen* refers to the idea of a house banking arrangement (*Hausbankwesen*), but invokes the idea of a feudal court with the bank as a subservient subject.

[122] For the achievements of individual Jewish bankers (Max Warburg, Oscar Wassermann, Jakob Goldschmidt, and Georg Solmssen), see Feldman (1995).

[123] Pohl (1982), p. 99. For more details, particularly of Deutsche Bank's involvement with the Nazi economy, see James (2001) and OMGUS (1987).

[124] Brendel (2001). See also Zorn (1976), p. 851. Statistics mostly come from Deutsche Bundesbank (1976), p. 118.

more into the position of holding equity positions in nonfinancial firms, largely as a result of nonperforming loans that had been made on little tangible collateral. The crisis revealed a number of problems with the existing system of corporate governance. For example, it had been possible for corporate managers to hide the true status of their companies from shareholders, supervisory boards, and creditors. The Nordwolle case was only one of the more extreme examples of a larger problem. Many corporations, including joint-stock banks, bought their own stocks and thus reduced their liable equity capital.

The wave of corporate failures prompted new calls for reform to the corporation laws (*Handelsgesetzbuch*, or HGB) as well as the desire to create a code (*Aktiengesetz*) specifically addressing shareholding and attendant rights and restrictions.[125] Ultimately, the debates led to an emergency order (*Notverordnung*, or NotVO) on stock companies. The act, set into force outside of the parliamentary process, included a tax credit, stronger regulation of banks, and stronger disclosure rules. Legitimized by an overriding principle of acting for the good of the whole (known as the *Führerprinzip*), the new law weakened the position of the shareholders – in particular, the general assembly – in favor of the management board (*Vorstand*). The management was no longer responsible specifically for the shareholders' interests but for all groups having a stake – figuratively – in the company, including the Reich (§70 I AktG 37).[126] The new laws eased the process of transforming stock corporations into partnerships (*Umwandlungsgesetz*), while a higher minimum share capital of RM 500,000 impeded the founding of new stock corporations. While the law undermined the use of the *Aktiengesellschaft* form, it simultaneously required greater public disclosure of corporate information.[127]

Although both the HGB and the AktG considered registered shares (*Namensaktien*) as the norm, in practice the market was dominated by bearer shares, because they allowed shareholders to remain anonymous.[128]

---

[125] See Fohlin (2005), from which this section borrows, for an extended survey of these issues.

[126] It is easy to assume that the law represented standard Nazi thinking, given the date of its promulgation. Yet the president of the commission for preparing the new *Aktiengesetz* in 1965, Wilhelmini (1965), p. 153, argued that the 1937 law was not a piece of Nazi work. It seems that the main components of the law were actually articulated under the previous administration, the Weimar Republic. For more on corporate governance, see Fohlin (2005).

[127] See Kübler (1994), p. 12.

[128] See von Falkenhausen (1967), p. 69.

Under the shareholder law of 1937, votes could not be cast by mail. This law made it even more likely that shareholders, especially small stakeholders, would be unable or unwilling to exercise their ownership rights directly. As accommodation, the law provided two ways for shareholders to cast their votes by proxy. First, shareholders could give their bank a *Stimmrechtsvollmacht*, allowing the bank to cast the votes in the shareholders' name but also forcing shareholders to reveal their identity. Second, and more important in practice, the *Stimmrechtsermächtigung* ceded shareholders' voting rights to the bank.[129] A *Stimmrechtsermächtigung* had to be given in written form and, while valid for up to fifteen months, it could be revoked anytime. This form of proxy voting was later called *Bankenstimmrecht* or *Depotstimmrecht*, due to the heavy use of banks as the proxy holder.[130] It is worth noting that the new regulation actually weakened the banks' position, since some banks had previously required customers to turn over *Stimmrechtsermächtigungen* automatically upon opening securities accounts. Even with the new law, banks could still do more or less whatever they wished with the voting rights that continued to be ceded to them.[131] Thus, the pre–World War I phenomenon of bank proxy voting remained strong and may have increased somewhat among large, publicly listed companies. But the tendency away from the public corporation diminished the population of public companies in the course of the Nazi years.

Financial Markets

Stock prices had begun to drop in 1927 and continued their decline through the fall of 1929. Despite the poor performance, companies interpreted the weak market as a normal market cycle and kept their dividend payouts optimistically high.[132] The seriousness of the German crisis became clear with collapse of the Allgemeine Versicherungs AG in Frankfurt in August, and after the heavy withdrawals of foreign capital from the German market starting in September.[133] The Reichsbank had no effective response, and by the time the realization of the problem came, investors had lost enormous

---

[129] See Hüffer (2002), p. 694. Though similar to *Stimmrechtsvollmacht*, the *Stimmrechtsermächtigung* gave banks much more power. See also von Falkenhausen (1966), p. 69.

[130] Hopt (1996) calls the *Depotstimmrecht* a misnomer for that reason. The correct word is *Vollmachtsstimmrecht*, but at the moment these words are used synonymously.

[131] See von Falkenhausen (1966), p. 71.

[132] See Blaich (1985), p. 76.

[133] The German banks could not cope with the withdrawals of American deposits (Braun [1990], p. 78, citing Blaich [1985]). Temin argues that the problem was not so much the withdrawal, but rather "a fall of inventory investment in Germany in 1929." (See Braun [1990], p. 64).

sums.[134] The crash of the New York Stock Exchange on October 25, 1929, really only emphasized the severe flaws in the German market.

As difficult as the situation was in 1929, the real blow to the stock exchanges came in 1931 with the banking crisis.[135] As the banks fell into crisis, the stock exchanges ceased trading on July 11, 1931. Exchange controls were introduced the same month, in reaction to the alarming lack of gold and foreign currency reserves. The markets resumed operations in the beginning of September but stopped again a few weeks later and remained closed until the following April. Meanwhile, futures trading was prohibited (until 1933), though spot transactions (*Kassageschäft*) remained possible for a while. The government began enforcing more stringent controls on new issues, and even stocks that had already been admitted to trading were withdrawn.

The Nazi regime brought with it an anticapitalist mindset that dictated "the abolition of income not earned by work and toil," and distinguished between "rapacious" and "productive" capital. The latter constituted capital invested in projects with socially beneficial ends. The Nazis considered financial capital unproductive, particularly that used in international finance and securities market transactions, and often termed it "Jewish capital."[136] The speculative character of stock trading fed the negative propaganda. As with other areas of public policy, the regime worked to adjust the stock exchanges to their own concept of the "new order," rather than to reform existing institutions based on competent, expert analysis.[137] First and foremost, this approach meant the appointment of new people, whose main qualification was adherence to the National Socialist ideology. Thus, the stock exchanges were reorganized according to the tenets of the *Führerprinzip*. The managing committees were now appointed, rather than elected. And a new law on price

---

[134] Henning (1992), p. 260 ff.

[135] "The ensuing collapse of the German capital market in the summer of 1931 turned a 'normal' temporary crisis into a crisis of the whole economic and political system" (Braun [1990], p. 68).

[136] Ibid., p. 79, citing Hardach (1980), p. 54.

[137] In his "Abhandlung über die Börse" of 1937, Peter Graf Czernin expressed the resentment toward the big banks and finance capitalism that were prevalent in those years. See Henning (1992), p. 271. There were also voices critical of the government policy in terms of finances. Willi Prion, an economist, wrote eight "dialogues" about the financial system in which he let, for example, *Reichswirtschaftsminister* und *Reichsbankpräsident* Walter Funk and Hermann Göring (*Beauftragter für den Vierjahresplan*) set out their positions, and in which he laid out his own skeptical stance toward the government financing and also spoke out for private financing. Also there was a chapter on "Effekten aus jüdischem Besitz." But Henning (1992), p. 271, concludes, not surprisingly, that the Nazis did not listen to critical and competent voices.

setting moved the power to the official brokers (*Makler*) and away from the managing committees. Brokers came under tighter controls, and Jewish brokers were banned.

Many legal provisions enacted during the Great Depression could be used with little alteration to achieve the Nazi regime's political ends. Additional laws in September of 1934 transferred many functions of individual states (*Länder*) to the Reich, and generally attempted to structure the financial system to channel resources into the rearmament effort. The new laws turned over stock exchange supervision to the *Reichswirtschaftsminister* (who was *Reichsbankpräsident* Schacht).[138] With inflation fears lurking, Schacht introduced plans to limit trading in foreign currency, but he was unable to prevent the outflow: Foreign currency holdings dropped from RM 2.7 billion to RM 396 million between 1933 and 1935.[139] The new law on securities trading (*Gesetz über den Wertpapierhandel*) of December 1934 imposed minimum paid-in capital for new issues, a policy that favored large companies. Also in December 1934, the *Anleihestockgesetz* limited the distribution of dividends to 6 percent, so that profits would be reinvested into companies.[140] In general, Schacht's policies favored big corporations and the transformation of smaller corporations (*juristische Personengesellschaften or Körperschaften*) to private firms (*Personalgesellschaften*) through tax incentives.

Once the Olympic games ended in 1936, the Nazi regime could operate out of the international spotlight, and they began to push their policies more forcefully. They did so in a variety of ways. They prohibited the quotations of foreign stocks on German stock exchanges, and all owners of foreign stocks had to register such ownership with the Reichsbank.[141] While the Nazis relaxed the ban on dividends in 1937, thus permitting distributions after four years, they simultaneously required that payments be reinvested in tax certificates, which were traded at the stock exchange. In December 1938, they blocked foreign exchange dealings at the stock exchanges

---

[138] Henning (1992), p. 275, explains that it was part of the general strategy to bring the economy, particularly heavy industry needed in war preparation, under state control. Starting in 1934, new regulations came into force; for example, women were excluded again. The number of stock exchanges was reduced from twenty-one to nine by January 1935, and stocks were to be traded only at the local or regional stock exchanges (*Wirtschaftsbezirke*). Also the number of persons with access to the stock exchanges was reduced – from 3,000 in 1933 to 1,350 in 1938 at the Berlin stock exchange, for example.

[139] See Irmler (1976) on the *Devisenzwangswirtschaft*.

[140] Braun (1990, p. 89) indicates that the government decreed the capital stock law in December 1934 specifically to reserve a large share of the capital market for public bonds.

[141] Irmler (1976), p. 326.

completely.[142] In addition, the government raised corporate taxes and forced Jewish shareholders to sell their stakes. Meanwhile, new issues came under even tighter restrictions.

The Nazi policies obviously hampered the functioning of the markets and produced a restructuring of corporate capital. Between 1933 and 1939, the capital of the joint-stock companies remained nearly constant, and stock exchange turnover stagnated, despite the fact that the economy overall expanded by about 50 percent.[143] Securities issues rose minimally: from RM 31.3 billion in 1931 to RM 32.6 billion in 1936.[144] The new laws prompted a drastic thinning among the ranks of joint-stock companies, from ten thousand in 1933 to five thousand in 1939.[145] By the late 1930s, the stock exchanges had largely become an instrument of capital mobilization by the state.[146]

The trend only intensified during the war. As the war started, stock prices began to climb, reaching 1927 levels by 1941.[147] All sectors profited from the demand for war goods.[148] To keep prices in check and for fear of a flight into resource-based assets, the state implemented many new regulations. On October 15, 1941, the Reich government created a stock exchange monopoly that would prevent stock trading outside of the exchanges – especially by the banks – in order to gain centralized control over the market. Only official brokers were allowed to trade according to official quotations. In December of that year, the stock exchange law was revised to give preference to loans of the Reich, and a decree on the ownership of stocks, the *Verordnung über Aktienbesitz*, attempted to reduce the public demand for stocks.

The strategy of indirect war finance intensified in 1943, and the government set out new provisions to facilitate its access to capital markets. Price controls (caps) appeared in January 1943, and two months later price setting became the responsibility of the *Reichswirtschaftsminister*. The government reduced trading to three days per week, though by some accounts

---

[142] Ibid., pp. 280, 301.

[143] See Henning (1992), p. 213, for a graph of the stock exchange turnover tax 1910–44.

[144] Irmler (1976), p. 321.

[145] See Fohlin (2005) for the number of corporations throughout the twentieth century. According to Frank (1993), p. 152, around twenty thousand joint-stock corporations (*Aktiengesellschaften*) and limited liability corporations (*Gesellschaften mit beschränkter Haftung*) were converted to *offene Handelsgesellschaften* or other *Personengesellschaften* by 1940.

[146] According to Henning (1992), government debt for armament took on increasing importance at the exchanges.

[147] Deutsche Bundesbank (1976), p. 295.

[148] Henning (1992), p. 281.

one day would have sufficed to complete all the transactions that took place. The new regulations curtailed the admission of new issues but provided exceptions for all loans taken by the Reich. The next year (September 14, 1944), turnover taxes were eliminated, which encouraged more trading in the government-issued and -backed securities that were left.[149]

By the end of the war, the Nazi regime had turned the stock market into one more tool for dealing with its extraordinary government expenditure. The government encouraged, if not forced, the public to deposit their money into bank accounts, and the banks would then transfer the funds in the form of bonds to the Reich.[150] The market was essentially reserved for trading the debts of the Reich.[151] It was part and parcel of the "silent finance" plan to fund the war effort. This fundamental alteration probably helps explain why the markets were kept open through most of the war: Trade did not stop when the rooms of the Frankfurt stock exchange were destroyed but only shortly before the American troops arrived.[152] Trade continued in Berlin until April 18, 1945.[153]

THE POST–WORLD WAR II ERA

The Economic, Political, and Legal Environment

The Nazi regime and World War II devastated Germany, killing 8 million of its inhabitants and injuring another 4 million. By dividing Germany into four zones ruled separately by the United States, France, Great Britain, and the Soviet Union, the victorious powers divided the capital, Berlin, and fragmented the whole country as well. Moreover, Germany lost important territory, amounting to one-quarter of the former Third Reich area. Meanwhile, the loss of housing was catastrophic, and the lack of energy sources reached crisis proportions.

Despite the general level of disaster, industry emerged relatively unscathed. Indeed, fixed industrial assets at the end of the war probably exceeded those existing in 1939.[154] The problem of food shortages notwithstanding, the influx of refugees created an inexpensive labor force. The allies, however, imposed the policies of "De" and "Dis" – demilitarization, denazification, administrative decentralization, economic deconcentration, and

---

[149] Ibid., p. 282.
[150] Frank (1993), p. 193.
[151] Braun (1990), p. 114.
[152] See Baehring (1985) and Gielen (1994), p. 45.
[153] Rudolph (1992), p. 294.
[154] Braun (1990), p. 149.

industrial disarmament – with the goal of restructuring German industry in such a way as to prevent Germany from waging war in the future.[155] The allies endeavored to abolish excessive concentration in the economy, targeting primarily the chemical industry (IG Farben), iron and steel (Montan), and banking. While the allies succeeded to some extent in the first two areas, they failed to break up the banking industry permanently.[156]

The lessons of World War I and its consequences propelled the allies to a more reasonable course of action in the wake of the Second World War. To stabilize the shaky economic and political situation in Western Europe and particularly in West Germany, the U.S. Secretary of State George Marshall announced the European Recovery Program (ERP), or Marshall Plan, on June 5, 1947.[157] While the Marshall Plan provided aid to several countries besides Germany (indeed, Germany's share of aid was smaller than that of Britain or France), the ERP smoothed the way for the West German economy to be reintegrated into the international economy. The next spring, on April 16, 1948, the Organization for European Economic Cooperation (OEEC) was also founded, with the goal of ensuring that American aid would have the desired economic and political effects.[158]

Concomitant with redevelopment came a focus on preventing another monetary disaster. On top of the inflationary war spending, high demand and a paucity of goods heightened inflationary tendencies in the early postwar years. Thus, once again, the German currency required reform. Immediately following the war, state central banks (*Landeszentralbanken*) in the three Western occupational zones were organized for each state, but the British insisted on one coordinating bank. With that goal, the Bank deustcher Länder was created on March 1, 1948. Given the past experiences of inflation, particularly the political interests that had infiltrated and influenced the Reichsbank, legal autonomy and independence from the federal government

---

[155] Hardach (1987), pp. 90–1.
[156] The next section takes up the evolution of the banking industry and of corporate governance and finance.
[157] See Ritschl (2004) for a brief survey of the Marshall Plan as well as useful references, including DeLong and Eichengreen (1993).
[158] The original eighteen OEEC participants were the following: Austria, Belgium, Denmark, France, Greece, Iceland, Ireland, Italy, Luxembourg, the Netherlands, Norway, Portugal, Sweden, Switzerland, Turkey, United Kingdom, and Western Germany (represented by both the combined American and British occupation zones [the Bizone] and the French occupation zone). The Anglo-American zone of the Free Territory of Trieste was also a participant in the OEEC until it returned to Italian sovereignty. See the OECD website (www.oecd.org) for additional details, including an annotated bibliography, *The European Reconstruction 1948–1961: A Bibliography on the Marshall Plan and the Organisation for European Economic Co-operation and Development*.

lay at the core of the new central bank. On June 20 and 21 of that year, the deutsche mark replaced the reichsmark as the national monetary unit.[159] The exchange rate of old to new currency varied according to the nature of the claim: Wages, salaries, and rents exchanged at a 1:1 ratio; mortgages and other private debts at the rate of 1:10. Having reined in inflation, the German government abolished price controls in July 1948. Certain difficulties remained – moderate inflation and insufficient production, for example – but the Marshall Plan and currency reform together created a solid foundation for growth.

The *Wirtschaftswunder* was on its way in Germany, with a new "mixed economy" that emphasized, on the one hand, the restoration of market institutions, and yet maintained, on the other hand, a control on certain sectors. The Allied law of 1947 prohibiting cartels remained in force until 1957, when the German version, the "law against restraint of competition" (*Gesetz gegen Wettbewerbsbeschränkungen*), appeared. The new law prohibited cartel agreements in principle, but it also granted many exceptions. Likewise, the law created a federal cartel office (*Bundeskartellamt*) to watch for abuses of monopolistic power, but the impact was apparently minimal.[160] Thus, government attempts at lessening industry concentration succeeded only to a limited extent, and even with the drive toward renewed market forces and competition, industry again became progressively more concentrated.

Of the 100,000 or so enterprises in Germany throughout the 1950s and 1960s, about 60,000 were small units with fewer than 20 employees; 35,000 were medium-sized with 20 to 199 employees; and only roughly 7,000 were large enterprises with 200 or more employees. But by the late 1960s, the share of these three categories in total industrial employment and sales was about 5 percent, 25 percent, and 70 percent, respectively. It was precisely the very large companies that, to an increasing extent, represented the most important factor in German industry. By the mid-1950s, concentration was already high in many industries, judging by the market shares (based on sales) of the sectors' top ten firms: 70 percent in shipbuilding, oil, and tobacco processing; about 60 percent in the automobile industry and in rubber and asbestos processing; close to 50 percent in the pig iron–producing and

---

[159] See Buchheim (1993). James (1999) provides further discussion of the development of the new central bank in the early postwar era. See also Pohl (1983), p. 224 ff, on the reorganization of central banking after the war.

[160] Hardach (1987), p. 149. Braun (1990), p. 180, likewise says that the law permitted so many exceptions that "it proved unable to stop the continuing trend towards increasing oligopolistic and quasi-monopolistic structures."

glass industries; and slightly under 40 percent in chemicals and electrical equipment.[161] In almost all branches, however, concentration ratios rose further, with as few as four firms earning half of the sales income in shipbuilding, electrical, chemical, rubber, and asbestos and as much as 80 percent of sales in the automobile industry and oil processing.[162]

The idea of government coordination of the economy appeared in the context of monetary authority as well. On July 26, 1957, the Bundesbank became the Federal Republic's central bank and lender of last resort, replacing the Bank deutscher Länder and ushering in an era of great monetary stability.[163] Though the German federal government intended for the Bundesbank to be more dependent on the government than its predecessor had been, it never became a tool of government policy, and government officials had no official say (that is, no votes) in central bank decisions and policies.[164] The Bundesbank remained one of the most independent central banks in the world, and the deutsche mark remained one of the most stable currencies in the postwar period right up to the introduction of the euro. Instead, the government used state-owned financial institutions, such as the Kreditanstalt für Wiederaufbau (the fourth largest German credit institution in the late 1960s), to further its political-economic agenda.[165]

The government also returned to its prior roles in industry. Certain sectors of the German economy – agriculture, housing, and transport – remained regulated. And public ownership and control by the government in certain areas where such activity had been traditional (transportation, communications, and utilities) persisted in the postwar era. While these sectors, along with banking and insurance, fell outside the purview of the cartel law, the state organized its own "cartel-like arrangements."[166] Indeed, in the 1950s, state-operated plants produced 60 percent of the electricity and over 90 percent of gas and electricity distribution, and produced about half of all automobiles, iron ore, lead, and zinc. The state owned firms both directly (for example, Lufthansa airlines and Volkswagen works) and indirectly through holding companies (for example, Vereinigte Elektrizitäts- und Bergwerks AG, or VEBA, and Vereinigte Industrie-Unternehmungen AG, or VIAG). By the late 1960s, the government held an interest in some three thousand enterprises despite some previous privatizations. Even more

---

[161] Hardach (1987), p. 147.
[162] Ibid.
[163] See Holtfrerich (1988), pp. 139–41.
[164] See Dickhaus (1996).
[165] Hardach (1987) provides additional information.
[166] Ibid., p. 150.

than its ownership role, the government – federal, state, and local – played a major part as administrator.[167]

Whether or not attributable to the institutional arrangements in place, or simply the inevitable return to its prior standing, Germany experienced remarkable economic growth between 1949 and 1985. The most impressive growth came in the 1950s, during which time real output grew by more than 8 percent per annum on average and fell below 6 percent only once.[168] By 1960, unemployment hovered around 1 percent, inflation was low, and the balance of payments current account had shown a decade of continuous surplus.[169] Exceeding the performance of its European counterparts, Germany returned to primacy in industrial production within the same timeframe. The leading growth industries of the 1950s and the 1960s – plastics, synthetic fibers, automobiles, and electrical engineering – based their expansion on innovation in process and products.

Industrial structure changed somewhat after World War II, but the evolution was relatively gradual. Postwar German industry supported firms of all sizes, depending on the sector. In some areas, large-scale, capital-intensive, heavy industry dominated, but in many others, small, highly skilled, craft-oriented firms prevailed – just as had been the case in the prewar era. Still the number of small firms did fall almost by half, from 886,500 in 1950 to 492,200 in 1982; but the number of people employed in these firms actually increased (from 3.3 million to almost 4 million, in the same period). Moreover, sales volume of these firms grew rapidly over the period.[170]

But the economic miracle could not last forever. Growth rates declined continuously from the 1950s onward, and by the 1970s growth and conditions for growth deteriorated. Between 1961 and 1996, West Germany lost its edge over many of its European neighbors, averaging real growth rates of 2.8 percent, compared to the European Union average of 3.1 percent.[171] Inflation and unemployment increased, and income grew at a diminishing rate.[172] In the early 1970s, a shortage of labor – especially skilled labor – created a serious obstacle to growth; a situation that was

---

[167] Ibid., p. 150.

[168] Braun (1990), p. 168, and sources cited there.

[169] See Lindlar and Holtfrerich (1996), who argue that Germany's postwar prosperity stemmed primarily from its great success in export markets.

[170] Braun (1990), p. 230, and sources cited there. On postwar industrial structure, see Herrigel (1996).

[171] Funk (2000), p. 21.

[172] Braun (1990), p. 169.

partly remedied by the substitution of capital for labor. Circumstances changed with the first oil price shock of October 1973 and the beginning of the recession of 1974–5; unemployment rose as vacancies fell, and in the early 1980s, real GNP growth slowed considerably. Unemployment plagued Germany, with 1 million out of work in 1975, and 2.3 million unemployed in 1985. By early 1983, however, the West German economy had begun a recovery, and unemployment decreased in the late 1980s, falling to 1.7 million in 1991. But recession returned in the 1990s, following reunification with the East. In the 1990s, manufacturing industry declined consistently as a share of GDP, and the restructuring dislocated workers further. Unemployment reached 3 million by 1993 and 4 million by 1997. As manufacturing declined, the former West Germany evolved into a service economy.[173]

While the former West German areas suffered in the aftermath of reunification, the eastern *Länder* faced even worse economic stagnation and unemployment. From 1991 to 1997, the former East German economy grew at a rate of about 8 to 9 percent. Yet the dramatic productivity boost over the period most likely stemmed from the 80 percent decline in employment.[174] Moreover, since 1997, growth rates fell to 1 to 2 percent – even below those in the West German areas.[175]

Developments in Banking and Finance

The Banking Industry

The banking industry continued its structural change after the war. At the war's end, the Allies closed all banks, and in the end of 1945, J. M. Dodge demanded that the German banking sector be decentralized and that the big banks be destroyed. The American military government broke the Deutsche Bank, Dresdner Bank, and Commerzbank into thirty separate institutions on May 6, 1947.[176] The Allies could not sustain the dissolution of these "big three" banking groups; the status quo quickly returned.[177] With the Gesetz über den Niederlassungsbereich von Kreditinstituten passed on March 29, 1952, the previously separated institutions that had been created out of the

---

[173] Lindlar and Holtfrerich (1996), p. 30.
[174] Real labor productivity in East Germany increased by nearly 80 percent, according to Sinn (2002), p. 115.
[175] Ibid., p. 118.
[176] See Braun (1990) and Owen-Smith (1994).
[177] Braun (1990), p. 151, and Owen-Smith (1994), p. 16. See also Pohl (1983), p. 231 ff, on a wide variety of banking institutions after 1945.

great banks were recombined into just three institutions for each of the great banks.[178]

While the German banking sector moved toward horizontal concentration until the reconstruction of the great banks in 1957, vertical concentration began to take hold thereafter.[179] The three great banks held shares in the private mortgage banks, and large banking and insurance companies became more and more entangled with one another. And from 1960 onward, bank groups (*Konsortialbanken*) formed with the prospect of founding a European Economic Union. The regional and other credit banks held fairly steady but expanded their network of branches, growing from 96 institutions with 1,020 branches in 1957 to 103 institutions with 2,501 branches by the end of 1984.[180] Private banking, by contrast, met a different fate. Even with some recovery in the early 1950s, the sector continued to decline, particularly after the mid-1950s. Between 1954 and 1974, the number of private banks dropped from 252 to 138, and by 1984 there were only 73. Even by the late 1960s, only a handful of private banks could be considered large institutions, and they were almost all already part of or affiliated with a larger financial conglomerate.[181]

Even more than structural change in various sectors of the banking industry, the important developments in the financial system involved diversification of bank services and the gradual disappearance of differentiation among bank types. While the credit banks expanded their business into savings and to small private customers, particularly after 1959, the more remarkable changes came in the savings bank segment.[182] The savings banks and credit cooperatives intruded more and more into the classical business of the universal or credit banks. New laws to spur savings (the *Sparprämiengesetz* of 1959 and the second *Vermögensbildungsgesetz* of 1965) helped the savings banks grow by ensuring a steady flow of long-term savings. The savings banks also began to issue long-term depository notes (the *Sparkassenbriefe* in 1976 and the *Sparkassenobligationen* in 1970) after similar products (*Volksbanksparbrief* and *Sparbrief der Bank für Gemeinwirtschaft*) met with success in the mid-1960s. Even securities trading took hold with the savings banks after the introduction of *Volksaktien*: Preussag issued *Volksaktien* in

---

[178] See Pohl (1982), pp. 104–5, for specifics.

[179] Ibid., p. 105 ff, finds it significant that at about the same time that the three great banks were set up again, the convertibility of the mark was secured and that on August 1, 1957, the Bank deutscher Länder was changed to Deutsche Bundesbank.

[180] Ibid., p. 111; numbers from *Monatsberichte der deutsche Bundesbank*, July 1985, p. 45.

[181] Zorn (1976), p. 851. Data come from Deutsche Bundesbank (1976).

[182] See Pohl (1982), p. 118, on the changing business of the joint-stock credit banks.

1959, Volkswagen in 1961, and VEBA in 1965. The securities deposit business was also strengthened through the increasing importance of investment saving.[183]

Other related institutions also transformed into quasi-universal banks. Mergers of central giro institutions in North Rhineland and Westphalia in 1969 led to the creation of Westdeutsche Landesbank, a development that turned what was previously a sort of savings bank into a universal bank and a direct competitor of the three great banks. In 1969, the Westdeutsche Landesbank (WestLB) became Germany's largest credit institution, and the next year, the Norddeutsche Landesbank reached a similar status. Among the 150 largest AGs in the Federal Republic (in terms of capital stock), there were nine banks in 1974, two insurance companies, six trading firms, and seven transportation companies.[184]

Although the liquidity of the banks declined after the war and sank even further in the 1970s, monetary and financial stability generally reigned. The Allied Banking Board and the Land Central Bank Commission were set up for coordinating the Landeszentralbanken, stabilizing the German currency, and supervising the banking system. On March 1, 1948, the Allies formed the Bank Deutscher Länder, establishing a minimum reserve ratio for the banking system.[185] With the currency reform (the Colm-Dodge-Goldsmith Plan) of 1948, and the creation of the deutsche mark, bank deposits and cash exchanged at a ratio of DM 6.5 to RM 100. Some 93.5 percent of the former stock of reichsmarks was withdrawn from circulation.[186] The reform, along with the London debt agreement (*Schuldenabkommen*), stabilized the currency and the reconstruction of foreign lines of credit.[187] The situation of the banks had remained unclear until this point. They had not collapsed, despite their heavy losses on loans to the Reich; they were expanding and increasing their employees; and they were covering their costs. In the very early postwar years, the banks focused heavily on reorganizing business, cleaning up the mess of the war, and reconstructing business documents. As a result, the true status of the banks after the war still remains difficult to determine, particularly given the apparent political influences that may have intruded on their accounting following the currency reform.[188]

---

[183] Ibid., p. 130.
[184] Zorn (1976), p. 850.
[185] Pohl (1982), pp. 101–2.
[186] Braun (1990), p. 155.
[187] Pohl (1983).
[188] Zorn (1976) p. 871.

Currency policy represents one of the key factors in the development of the great banks in West Germany after the war.[189] In the 1950s, investment accelerated and deposits poured into the banks. The capital market, however, remained subject to many conditions and restrictions until 1955.[190] After the deutsche mark had reached convertibility in 1957–8, the international business, which had been nonexistent since 1931, started to develop anew: The first German foreign bonds were issued in 1959, and Germany soon began to participate in the Euro-dollar market. Only after the exchange rate of the deutsche mark was liberalized in 1973 did the banks experience major losses on foreign currency trading. But even the best-known example, the collapse of the private bank J. D. Herstatt, failed to prompt a run on the banks – thanks in part to the security systems (*Einlagegarantiesysteme*) that the government had established in the aftermath of the banking crisis and to the assistance of other banks through additional guarantees.[191]

In the 1960s, incomes rose and the changing distribution of wealth led to the increasing flow of money and capital from private households through the banks.[192] But as the economic "miracle" waned, globalization and technological advances presented new challenges for the German banks. Concentration and consolidation continued among smaller institutions, but the market position of the largest banks changed little over the period.[193] The great banks in particular fought a certain stagnation over the last two or three decades of the twentieth century and into the twenty-first.[194] Bank customers began to demand more in-depth advice, pressuring banks to increase their services. Growing competition both domestically and internationally hit all segments of the banking industry, not just the larger, universal banks. Electronic banking in particular has raised the costs of retail banking, for example, and has dissolved much of the small banks' advantage in personalized customer service and information about customers and their needs. Accelerating competition has pushed the small banks into cooperative arrangements.[195]

Banks and Corporate Governance

After the war, American occupation forces in particular saw the need to restructure Germany's corporate governance system, partly as a way to

---

[189] Tilly (1993), p. 315.
[190] Zorn (1976), p. 871.
[191] Ibid., p. 872.
[192] Pohl (1982), p. 119.
[193] Moser (1999), pp. 3–4.
[194] Ibid.
[195] Ibid., pp. 5, 39.

prevent the country from reconstituting the type of military-industrial complex that had fueled the war. The plan involved the introduction of shareholder democracy with the intent of limiting excessive concentration of power.[196] The reforms, directed largely at the mining industry, included registration of shares, restriction of proxy voting by banks to its weaker form (*Stimmrechtsvollmachten*), and the abolishment of anonymous voting. The law enacted specifically for the privatization of Volkswagen in 1960 (*Gesetz zur Privatisierung des Volkswagenwerkes vom* 22.7.1960) contained similar provisions, and the Schuman plan likewise imposed restrictions on proxy voting by banks involved with mining firms.[197] Along the way, smaller reforms, called *kleine Aktienrechtsreform* tightened accounting standards and rules for accumulating reserves.

The more general atmosphere of reform that emerged during the reconstruction period favored a number of alterations to the status quo.[198] Significantly, the 1965 reform bill abolished the *Führerprinzip* and, while retaining important powers for the management board, imposed a norm of majority rule for that body. The new law included provisions aimed at eliminating the practice of "silent reserves" that allowed corporations to hide their true returns, strengthening the general assembly of shareholders vis-à-vis the management board – especially its director – and increasing oversight and control of management by the supervisory board. It also targeted greater dispersion of share ownership, improved access to company information for small shareholders, and tightened regulations on industrial groups (*Konzern*).[199]

One of the major changes of the 1965 law (AktG 65) concerned the process of proxy voting via banks. Under the new law, banks were allowed to cast votes as a proxy only when they received a written authorization (*schriftliche Vollmacht*) (§135 I AktG 65). Valid for up to fifteen months, the authorization could be given for individual posts in an account or for all shares in it, and could be revoked at any time (§135 II AktG 65). The new law allowed shareholders to remain anonymous and required banks to ask customers for specific voting instructions (§128 II AktG) and to inform their

---

[196] See von Falkenhausen (1967), p. 70.

[197] The Schuman plan, named after the French foreign minister, Robert Schuman, created a coal and steel union between France and Germany and then included other European nations (Italy, Belgium, Netherlands, and Luxembourg being the first to join).

[198] Many German politicians did not view the 1937 shareholder law (*Aktiengesetz*) as seriously flawed, and even modern scholars note that arguments for reform stemmed from a desire to improve the lot of small shareholders and to promote a society based on democracy and capitalism, rather than somehow to right a wrong that was imposed under the Nazi regime. See Gessler (1965), p. 344, and Kübler (1994), p. 13.

[199] See Hopt (1996), p. 210.

customers on how the bank intended to vote. In the absence of customer instructions, the bank could vote according to its own plan (§135 V AktG, §128 II AktG).

As important as the 1965 reform was, it left the banks with widespread, easy access to corporate control rights. Pressure for reform began to build anew as Germany's postwar economic miracle faded. As Germany slid into recession in the 1990s, political debates focused once again on the power of the banks in Germany's corporations, and the government enacted a string of three new laws to modify the existing shareholder law (AktG).[200] The new laws stipulated important alterations of corporate ownership and control rights and responsibilities, especially the use of registered shares and the exercising of proxy voting rights. Current law requires banks to inform shareholders yearly of their option to revoke their proxy authorization and of their opportunities for alternative representation. Notably, to prevent banks from refusing instructed votes in favor of unrestricted voting rights, any institution that offers to cast proxy votes must offer the services to all of its customers (*Kontrahierungszwang*). In an effort to avoid conflicts of interests, banks must create organizational units exclusively for managers who prepare voting plans, separate from other divisions of the bank (in particular lending divisions). Banks must also inform their customers about relationships, such as bank employees in the supervisory boards or major equity holdings in target companies. Moreover, banks must also inform shareholders if the bank is a member of a consortium that prepared an IPO or any issue of shares for the company. The most recent law (TransPubG 02) aims at increasing the transparency of corporate governance, particularly by raising the information requirements imposed on companies and their managers, thereby bringing the system into line with international standards and increasing the attractiveness of German firms in world markets.[201]

Political and public debates continue over further legislative changes in these areas, and further recommendations of the commission on corporate

---

[200] The three laws were the 1998 law on control and transparency in corporations (KonTraG 98), the 2001 law on registered shares and the facilitation of exercising voting rights (NaStraG 01), and the 2002 law on transparency and publicity (TransPubG 02).

[201] For example, the law requires corporations to declare whether they comply with the so-called Corporate Governance Codex; strengthens the supervisory board by increasing the information provision to that body; strengthens the general assembly of shareholders by, among other things, granting greater control over the distribution of profits; and specifically identifies new ways for companies to communicate with shareholders and the market – for example, by broadcasting major meetings on television or via the Internet.

governance remain under discussion.[202] Whether Germany will retain a relationship-oriented system of corporate ownership and governance remains to be seen. Whether such a system is desirable, or has in fact been widespread in Germany, is another question. Data on share ownership in the direct aftermath of World War II are scarce for (West) Germany. Still, the published figures go back to 1960 (from the Deutsches Aktieninstitut) and therefore allow some broad patterns to emerge.

Nonfinancial firms as a group are the most important shareholders in Germany, owning a substantial plurality of shares during the past several decades, despite some decline over the 1990s. Since the 1960s, private households and the state have decreased equity participation, while foreigners and financial firms, including the newer investment funds, took up the slack.[203] While financial services firms increased equity holdings over the 1990s, they have not typically taken the form of majority stakes, especially for larger corporations. Equity ownership in the one hundred largest corporations in Germany was remarkably stable, and highly concentrated, in the 1990s. Out of the one hundred companies with the highest value added, slightly more than half were owned by one large shareholder, and another 16 to 21 percent of the sample had moderately concentrated ownership (that is, they had no majority owner, but less than half of shares were dispersed). Fewer than one-third of the firms had widely dispersed ownership.[204] In all but four of the fifty-four firms with concentrated ownership, the majority stakeholders were foreign investors, public entities, or a private individual, family, or endowment. This picture does depend to some extent on the population of firms being examined, but the high concentration of ownership extends to companies across a broad range of sizes. Between 1993 and 1997, the largest share block for large manufacturing firms averaged 81 percent; even in the case of the listed AGs, the biggest shareholder held a 53 percent stake on average.[205] In stark contrast to the largest one hundred firms, over 60 percent of manufacturing firms had another nonfinancial enterprise as their largest shareholder.[206] However, some argue that cross-ownership

---

[202] Proposals have included measures to increase supervisory and management board liability and more generally to strengthen disclosure rules and informational rights of shareholders. Other possible adjustments include restricting supervisory board members to a maximum of five supervisory board positions and establishing a central database of information on all corporations (see Bundesregierung, 2001).

[203] For detailed data, see Fohlin (2005) and sources cited there.

[204] See Brickwell (2001), p. 52, table 3.8.

[205] Köke (2001), p. 285.

[206] Ibid.

among nonfinancial firms is not widespread in the German manufacturing sector and seems to be of minor relevance in Germany overall.[207]

Given the often heated discussion about banks' power and influence in Germany, the available evidence on banks' stakes is surprising: Along with the state, financial enterprises hold the fewest large share blocks in manufacturing firms.[208] Neither banks nor insurance companies held a stake of 50 percent or more in any of the listed companies studied as of 1990.[209] Moreover, banks and insurance companies rarely held stakes greater than 25 percent that were also the largest stake in the respective companies.[210] In the 1980s and 1990s, banks and insurance companies only owned stakes larger than 5 percent in those companies from the top one hundred that did not have a majority stakeholder.[211] The vast majority of these equity stakes constituted long-term investments, with one-third being older than twenty years, and ranged between 5 and 25 percent. Holdings larger than 25 percent have been scaled back since the mid-1980s, so that by 1990 the thirty principal banking institutions averaged fewer than sixteen stakes (in fourteen firms) per bank.[212] These firms represent a tiny proportion of the 2,682 AGs and 433,731 limited liability companies (*Gesellschaft mit beschränkter Haftung*) in Germany at the time.[213] Moreover, the handful of these banks' stakes that constituted majority positions involved smaller companies.[214]

The current level of bank shareholdings in nonfinancial firms remains comparatively low. In 2002, the German government abolished capital gains

---

[207] Ibid.

[208] Data from ibid. See Adams (1994, 1999), Baums and Fraune (1995), and Wenger and Kaserer (1998) on the power of banks.

[209] Franks and Mayer (2001) report similar results for a sample of 171 large industrial quoted companies in 1990.

[210] Yet, Santucci (2002), p. 513, asserts: "In sum, due to their unique position as equity holders, banks and financial institutions are in a position to substantially control German companies."

[211] According to Brickwell (2001). Forty-three companies fell into this category in 1998, and banks and insurance companies held stakes in twenty-eight of those (65 percent). In 1980, banks and insurance companies held stakes in twenty-three of the one hundred major companies. This figure rose to thirty-five in 1996 before falling back to twenty-five in 2000.

[212] Haas (1994), pp. 32–3, covers the ten largest private banks, public banks, and credit cooperatives. These held a total of 202 direct stakes (172 firms) and 276 indirect stakes (236 firms) among all capital companies (AG and GmbH form).

[213] Ibid., p. 38. The affected firms represent 3.62 percent of all AGs and *Kommanditgesellschaften auf Aktien* (KGaAs) and 0.06 percent of all GmbHs. Since there are other banks not considered in the sample, the total proportion of companies with bank-held stakes is likely somewhat higher.

[214] Ibid., pp. 32–3.

taxes in a widely publicized effort to encourage banks to divest themselves of equity stakes. But given the lack of major holdings, the banks have not sold enormous amounts of shares. Moreover, the trend toward disentangling the dense business networks in Germany began before the tax changes took effect, with ownership concentration and cross-holdings falling significantly between 1997 and 2001, and with financial sector institutions diminishing their position as blockholders at the same time.[215] Recent annual reports of the top four banks confirm that even though all banks have myriad holdings in other, often unrelated companies, the stakes are rarely significant, and overall the participations make up much less than 5 percent of the respective banks' assets.[216] Taken together, the empirical evidence seriously undermines the claim that over the past decade big finance has been running Germany's economy via its equity stakes.

Because of their proxy shareholding, however, the banks' effective voting power far exceeded their direct equity stakeholding, all the more so as small shareholders participated in annual meetings at declining rates, particularly at the largest German firms, from the mid-1970s to the early 1990s.[217] As a result, the proxy stakes of the banks carry the greatest weight in these cases. In 1961, for example, on the basis of proxy rights (*Depotstimmrecht*), banks held approximately 70 percent of the votes (*Aktienstimmen*) of the general assemblies of almost four hundred nonfinancial firms (AGs). Of these, the three great banks alone held 70 percent, and thus they could place votes for about one-half of the total share capital (*Aktienkapital*).[218] And the banks' proxy voting remained strong for much of the period to follow. In 1986, in the thirty-two largest corporate firms with dispersed ownership, on average, 64.5 percent of shares received representation at the annual general meeting of shareholders.[219] Taken together, the big three banks often held a majority of votes cast (45 percent share on average), and even held substantial pluralities at their own general meetings. Moreover, with the notable exception of Volkswagen, banks as a group always held

---

[215] Wójcik (2001), p. 15. He finds that when compared to individuals and families and non-financial corporations, the holdings of the financial sector were significantly lower and declining sharply over the period from December 31, 1997, to May 2, 2001. See also Beyer (2002), who finds similar patterns in the prevalence of interlocking directorates.

[216] Brickwell (2001), p. 53, table 3.9.

[217] Adams (1994), p. 156, reports data for five of the largest German companies for 1975 and 1992, while Brickwell (2001), p. 62, provides an overview of turnout at the general meeting of shareholders of four financial services companies in 1998 and 1999.

[218] Tilly (1993) quotes from Deutscher Bundestag (1964). See also Cable (1985) on bank involvement through proxy voting in the 1970s.

[219] See Gottschalk (1988) for details and methods.

a majority of represented votes (83 percent share on average).[220] Notably, however, individual banks rarely dominated general annual meetings on their own.

Interestingly, when banks owned their own stakes in the firms, they did also hold proxy votes, but they averaged lower total vote percentages (for the big three alone, 25 percent of the total or 33 percent of votes present at the meeting) compared to widely held firms.[221] Not surprisingly, the banks held the fewest proxy votes in firms with dominating blockholders: The big three held only 6 percent of votes (7 percent present at the annual meeting), and all banks together held 13 percent (15 percent of those cast at the meeting). For smaller firms, those with more concentrated share ownership, or unlisted companies, banks exercised significantly less control.[222] As of the early 1990s, proxy votes accounted for a greater share (8.5 percent) of banks' total votes than did actual equity ownership (6.7 percent).[223] Banks rarely held any proxy votes in unlisted firms, but held at least some in the majority of the listed firms. The big three banks continued to play the dominant role in proxy voting.

The banks held many votes, and they certainly exercised them. While the causal link is not definitive and the midcentury evidence is spotty, the presence of the great banks was clearly evident in the supervisory boards of nonfinancial firms. One study in the 1950s showed that certain representatives from Deutsche Bank, Dresdner Bank, and Commerzbank each held more than twenty positions in various boards of directors. These numbers were remarkably high considering that regulations limited to eighteen

---

[220] Ibid. The big three banks are Deutsche, Dresdner, and Commerzbank. Gottschalk also included the Bayrische Vereinsbank, Bayrische Hypo, the state banks (*Landesbanken*) and savings banks (*Sparkassen*), the credit cooperatives (*Genossenschaftsbanken*), and other financial institutions. Though it is unwise to infer any kind of trend, the data for 1990 show a slight reduction (to 72 percent) in the average share of votes held by the banks in dispersed top one hundred firms, and the big three banks continued to hold substantial voting percentages at their own meetings (Baums and Fraune, 1995). Their sample contains only twenty-four companies, so it's possible that fewer firms had dispersed ownership, though data availability could also explain part of the difference in sample sizes.

[221] Böhm (1992) and Perlitz and Seger (1994). The latter find total proxy voting by banks of less than 10 percent in over one-third of their firms; but also found 30 percent of firms (seventeen of fifty-seven) had at least a majority of represented votes held in proxy by banks. Also, 83 percent of the 110 firms had at least one banker on its supervisory board.

[222] The influence is constrained further when instructed proxy votes are excluded, though only about 2 to 3 percent of bank customers take advantage of the opportunity, according to Baums (1996).

[223] Edwards and Nibler (2000) used a sample based on 156 of the 200 largest nonfinancial firms as measured by 1992 sales volume, and the figures are far lower than for the more restricted samples used in other studies.

the number of seats (mandates) that one individual could hold.[224] Shortly thereafter, in 1961, the three great banks held just over half (297 of 573) of bank-seated supervisory board positions in 318 nonfinancial firms, amounting to about one-sixth of the firms' supervisory board seats as a whole.[225] Throughout the 1960s and 1970s, banks held seats in all branches of industry but gradually shifted focus to mandates in larger corporations by 1978.[226]

Over the past two to three decades, the banks shifted their strategy from quantity toward quality – gaining power in the most important firms rather than via a large number of mandates in smaller companies.[227] Even among the largest one hundred firms, the proportion of mandates held by bankers has fallen gradually since the late 1970s – from 8.6 percent in 1978 to 6.4 percent in 1996.[228] Still, even among these large companies, the banks held relatively few board seats – never more than 15 percent of any board.[229] And the majority of banks engage infrequently in these relationships: Half of the bank-held positions traced back to just two banks – Deutsche and Dresdner – with Deutsche holding twice as many mandates as Dresdner. Banks have also decreased the number of firms on whose supervisory boards they sit. In 1986, over two-thirds of the top one hundred firms, and forty-three of the top fifty, had bankers on their boards. The Deutsche Bank alone sent representatives to forty of the top one hundred in 1980 but only seventeen in 1998. Deutsche Bank and Allianz, two of the primary participants in board representation, have enacted clear plans to dissolve their formerly strong and thick ties with German companies – Deutsche, in particular, announcing in March 2001 that members of the bank would no longer take up supervisory board chairs (*Aufsichtsratsvorsitze*).[230]

Financial Markets

Though the German stock exchanges remained open for much of the war, they had not functioned freely for many years and perhaps decades

---

[224] See Linsel (1956), p. 225.

[225] Tilly (1993), p. 336, provides other related figures.

[226] Albach and Kless (1982), p. 977. Samples in these studies are often small and heavily biased in one direction or another (such as using only large firms or only listed firms – tending to overstate the presence of bankers in supervisory boards).

[227] Ibid.

[228] Bokelmann (2000).

[229] Böhm (1992), pp. 194–5. Size is measured by revenue as of 1986. Half of the mandates are elected by labor, which automatically halves the number of seats available to bankers. At the same time, this power-sharing arrangement may lessen the banks' influence via the supervisory board seats.

[230] Beyer (2002).

by that point. Thus, while attempts at reconstruction began shortly after the war, the process was long and difficult and – one could argue – still incomplete.[231] Eight exchanges reopened after the war: Hamburg, Bremen, Hanover, Düsseldorf, Munich, Stuttgart, Berlin, and Frankfurt. Those in the eastern zone of the former Reich remained closed. Despite their official opening in the months following the war, the process of relisting securities and operating normal trade took several more years.

Proper functioning of the exchanges hinged on the establishment of ownership rights for securities being traded. This process was greatly complicated by the widespread loss, theft, and destruction of security certificates that had very often taken the form of bearer – and therefore anonymous and unregistered – shares. The dispossession and murder of so many securities holders during the war obviously compounded the difficulty of establishing ownership rights. Having taken such a large volume of these securities on deposit before the war, the banks were now put in the position of validating ownership, and securities could therefore enter trade only after a bank had issued an official affadavit, or certificate of deliverability (*Lieferbarkeitsbescheinigung*), attesting to the owernship rights of the bearer. Starting in October 1947, these validated securities could be traded, and the process was then formalized in the *Wertpapierbereinigungsgesetz* of 1949.[232]

The abandonment of the prewar currency created its own difficulties in setting the value of securities for trade on the exchanges. The currency reform and conversion (*Währungsumstellungsgesetz*) in 1948 effectively invalidated all reichsmark-denominated equities that were issued before 1945 and that lacked certification (*Lieferbarkeitsbescheinigung*).[233] The transition to the new currency, lasting until 1953 or even 1955 in some cases, depended on a number of different organizations with varying functions and origins. The *Arbeitsgemeinschaft der Deutschen Wertpapierbörsen* (founded November 28, 1952) coordinated trading in securities and represented the stock exchanges on a federal and later on an international level. The *Notgemeinschaften der Wertpapierbesitzer*, literally an emergency collective of equity owners, worked with considerable influence to speed the validation process and see that it acted in their interests.[234] The *Arbeitsgemeinschaft Deutscher*

---

[231] See Rudolph (1992) for a thorough survey of markets in Germany from the end of World War II to that point.

[232] The English translation sounds awkward but would be "securities settlement law" or "securities validation law." The law was not valid for the zone that became the German Democratic Republic (GDR) and the issue was only addressed at reunification (in the *Einigungsvertragsgesetz* of 1990). See Gielen (1994) and Rudolph (1992).

[233] Gielen (1994).

[234] Rudolph (1992), p. 295.

Kassenvereine, which organized the giro transfers of equities, assisted in the validation process, and also helped return the exchanges back to structured trading.[235]

A number of other factors hampered the revival of active securities markets after the war and simultaneously strengthened the position of the banks.[236] The popular emphasis on low-risk saving and aversion to high levels of personal debt compounded the general preference for personal savings over conspicuous consumption.[237] In the late 1940s, it proved difficult to convince the public to invest via the securities market, so the first issues – offered in the fall of 1948 – comprised fixed-interest–bearing securities and industrial bonds. Registered bonds with variable rates appeared from 1949 onward, but the first public bond, a DM 500 million bond by the Deutsche Bahn in June 1949, met with some hesitation: The banks could only sell DM 400 million. The so-called Baby-Bonds, premium/lottery treasury bonds with a value of DM 10 each, failed as well.

The government's policies at times also appeared contradictory: The Law on Capital Transactions (*Kapitalverkehrsgesetz*) continued the course of strong regulations into the 1950s. Renewed several times, the law stipulated that all securities issues must be registered with the government and could only be traded if approved by the Committee for Capital Transactions (*Kapitalverkehrsausschuss*). Despite its intent, the law led to considerable growth of the "gray" and "black" markets, and the government eventually abolished it in December 1953.[238] The German financial market also lacked a central supervisory agency, an issue that arose mainly in the (loose) handling of insider trading. Though calls for something resembling the United States' Securities Exchange Commission (SEC) began early on, no such commission appeared for several decades.[239]

At the same time, the government hoped to revitalize the capital market by increasing public interest and trust in the market and by loosening regulations on market operations. In December 1951, legislators promulgated a new law on the admission of securities that had been transferred to the new currency (*Gesetz über Börsenzulassung umgestellter Wertpapiere*). The law

---

[235] Ibid., p. 297. The securities deposit associations were united in 1989 when they were integrated in the Frankfurter Kassenverein AG, which in turn was turned into the Deutsche Kassenverein AG.

[236] Häuser (1997), p. 120. Häuser is also quoted in Rudolph (1992), p. 299: "The securities market has become a bank market."

[237] Wadhwa (1996), p. 77. She notes that these patterns are changing, but only slowly, and that German savings ratios remain high.

[238] Baehring (1985), p. 205, and Rudolph (1992), p. 298.

[239] See Wadhwa (1996), p. 82.

simplified access to the stock exchanges by permitting share companies – in circumvention of the stock exchange law – to maintain official notation of their stocks even in the absence of a new prospectus.[240] Additionally, the Capital Market Promotion Act (*Kapitalmarktförderungsgesetz*) provided tax relief for certain bonds that were used to pay for construction of cheap housing.[241] And the central capital market committee (*Zentraler Kapital-marktausschuss*), combining representatives from the Ministry of Economic Affairs with others from the banking sector, essentially took up a position to mediate between the markets and the public sector.[242] The committee negotiated and organized demands on the market with the goal of stabilization and expansion.[243]

By the early 1950s, loosening strictures on the market took effect, and demand for capital began to grow; by the middle of the decade, the market for securities began to boom. In 1956 there were 2,515 share companies (AGs) in Germany, 686 of which were listed on the exchange. Also in the mid-1950s, the German market began to integrate more noticeably into the international market, particularly in 1956, when the acquisition of and off-floor trading in foreign stocks (at first, six U.S. industrial securities) resumed. The first issue of a foreign currency bond since 1930 made its debut on September 10, 1957, while the first DM-denominated foreign bond (*DM-Auslandsanleihe*) appeared in October 1958.[244]

As measured by the volume of net issues, the German market became one of the largest worldwide and eventually took second place only to the U.S. market. Total net volume (turnover) of securities in 1965 reached DM 17.8 billion, or 4.4 percent of the net national product (NNP).[245] As interest rates and capital demand rose, companies found alternative ways to attract financing, such as securities carrying the so-called *Degussa-Klausel*, named

---

[240] Gericke (1992), p. 135, and Rudolph (1992), p. 297.

[241] See the discussion of Baehring's (1985, p. 205) arguments in Rudolph (1992, p. 298), suggesting that the law facilitated the reintroduction of flexible interest rates, but discriminated against stocks. The Capital Market Promotion Act was active only between 1952 and 1954, but when the Tax Reform Act (*Steueränderungsgesetz*) abolished the tax exemption in 1991, more than DM 4 billion tax-exempted bonds were still in circulation. The result was a plunge in prices for public bonds and even a temporary halt of notation.

[242] Rudolph (1992), p. 303.

[243] The negotiated demands resulted in the February 1968 Gentlemen's Agreement, which lasted until 1985, whereby the banks agreed to act in cooperation with the Bundesbank. See Franke (1999).

[244] Rudolph (1992), p. 302.

[245] See Häuser (1997), p. 119, who gives additional figures.

after a bond issued by the chemical giant Degussa that offered creditors the right to exit the contract (*Gläubigerkündigungsrecht*).[246] Another major step came in the early 1960s in the form of several so-called *Volksaktien* issues, used to sell off parts of public entities and simultaneously place equities in the hands of the public. The first of these, Preussag and VW, met with substantial success, though the third issue, by VEBA, encountered some difficulty in placement.[247]

Legal reforms of the exchanges finally appeared only in 1959 and 1965, in the form of the so-called Small and Large Stock Corporation Law Reforms (*Kleine und Große Aktienrechtsreform*).[248] The new laws mainly aimed at improving the position of stakeholders, and critics frequently cited their lack of progress toward unifying the various laws impinging on the capital market; corporate governance law, shareholder rights, and stock exchange regulation remained largely disconnected.[249] The new laws also could not counteract the growing weakness in the market for stocks and bonds starting in the mid-1960s, and as the market declined, efforts at reform continued. In July 1966, the Ministry of Economic Affairs published a plan to improve the operation of the stock exchanges (*Plan zur Verbesserung des Börsenwesens*), in an effort to increase the equity base of German companies and to attract new investors in the market. Among other things, the plan called for a stock exchange monopoly (*Börsenzwang*), semi-annual reports by joint-stock companies, publication of the trading volume data of the official brokers, and a general rule to quote prices in DM per share.[250] It also recommended a harmonization of admissions rules with constitutional law, the reintroduction of forward trading, and a serious attempt to address insider trading. The government never produced the recommended reforms, as discussions dragged out for years and the elections in 1972 finally pushed the issue off the agenda.[251] Only in 1975 did the government finally enact the

---

[246] Rudolph (1992), p. 300.

[247] Ibid., p. 305.

[248] See the discussion in the previous section on corporate governance as well as Fohlin (2005).

[249] Rudolph (1992), p. 307.

[250] Ibid., p. 310. Wadhwa (1996), p. 79, notes that the larger exchanges, most notably Frankfurt, joined with the leading German banks in favoring a single centralized exchange, arguing that the fragmentation of the German market put them at a competitive disadvantage compared to London, Paris, or Milan. The smaller exchanges argued that regional exchanges would play a crucial role in channeling locally based finance to the hundreds of thousand of small and medium-sized companies that made up the bulk of German output.

[251] Rudolph (1992), p. 311. Some of the interest groups involved, however, did voluntarily make many of the suggested changes. For example, the suspicious price movements of 1970, which some saw as evidence of insider trading, prompted voluntary self-regulation

Stock Exchange Amendment (*Börsennovelle*), and even then, the law brought few changes that had not previously appeared under self-regulation.[252]

In the 1970s, observers began commenting on the widening equity gap (*Eigenkapitallücke*) – an unwillingness of companies to invest and a simultaneous drought of investment supply, especially in the high-technology sector. Once again, the government stepped in, this time abolishing the double taxation of stocks with the Corporate Tax Reform Act (*Körperschaftssteuerreformgesetz*) on August 31, 1976. The number of companies listed at the stock market continued to decline. In 1979, only eight new joint-stock companies gained admission to trading, while another ten companies de-listed.

Numerous new laws also appeared in the mid- to late-1980s. The Stock Exchange Law Amendment of 1986 attempted to provide easier access to stock exchanges for small companies by setting up the regulated market (*Geregelter Markt*), to fill the gap between the officially listed companies and the over-the-counter market. In addition, the Stock Exchange Admission Act (*Börsenzulassungsgesetz*) of 1988 eliminated the banks' monopoly over admission to the regulated market and also prohibited double listing in order to ensure a single price for any given stock.[253] In April 1987, a new regulation on Stock Exchange Admission (*Börsenzulassungsverordnung*) finally replaced the ones that had remained in place since 1910 (*Zulassungsbekanntmachung*). Mainly designed to protect investors, the Act set a minimum of DM 2.5 million for share capital and required companies to exist for three years before admission to the exchange.[254] In the summer of 1986, the eight exchanges united in an effort to strengthen their capacity and create *Finanzplatz Deutschland*. By some accounts, this step signaled the start of serious attempts at stock exchange reform.[255]

Common stock issues experienced a slight revival after 1983, at which point only 442 companies remained listed. That same year, 11 new AGs went public and another 21 joined the exchange in 1984. As in the 1950s, stocks financed one-fourth of all long-term investment in the producing sector.[256] Yet the IPO market still lagged that of the United States by

by the exchange. See also Wadhwa (1996) on the long delays and the stimulus of the 1986 reorganization of the London Stock Exchange (in the "Big Bang") and the establishment of the London International Financial Futures and Options Exchange (LIFFE).

[252] Rudolph (1992), pp. 316–17.
[253] Neubauer (2002), p. 8.
[254] See Rudolph (1992), p 331, for additional details.
[255] Ibid., p. 327.
[256] Ibid., p. 323.

a huge margin.[257] And to the extent that equity investments increased, the issuers remained mainly large companies – typically, well-established firms in mature industries – not small firms with high growth potential.[258] The markets generally expanded during the 1980s, despite the temporary crashes in 1987 and 1989, enough so that the Bundesbank deemed it the "Decade of the Stock" (*Jahrzehnt der Aktie*).[259] Private investment continued to decline, and by 1990 individuals and families owned only 17 percent of stocks.[260] The German system of public old-age pensions may explain part of the low rates of equity holding, since it lessened the need for personal retirement savings. Substantial fees charged by the banks may have also pushed small investors into investment funds instead of direct stockholding.[261]

Still, even among investment funds, equity funds seemed to lose acceptance among the public by the late 1980s.[262] While the equity funds clearly dominated the investment sector from the 1950s to the late 1960s in terms of sales volume and fund assets, they stagnated in the 1980s.[263] At the end of 1989, equity funds made up less than 40 percent of all funds open to the general public (96 out of 258), and over the previous decade, their assets grew at 70 percent of the rate achieved by other fund types. In many cases, equity funds did not even match the performance of the equity price indexes in Germany at that time.[264] Observers of investment fund performance predicted that the opening of the European investment market (March 1, 1990) would improve the situation, and some expected a substantial increase in the demand for investments as savings rates remained high and major blocks of assets were expected to come onto the market.[265] In addition, some hoped that the end of the Stock Exchange Turnover Tax would not be offset by

---

[257] Franzke et al. (2002), p. 11, mark the year 1983 as a turning point for IPOs, and point to a positive investment climate and euphoric reports from the United States to explain the shift.

[258] Ibid., p. 5, provides details.

[259] Rudolph (1992), pp. 322–4, provides figures on numbers of new issues for the period between 1980 and 1991.

[260] Mathes (1992), p. 30, indicates that as of 1989, only 7 percent of citizens over fourteen years old owned stocks, and little more than 5 percent of private assets were invested in equities or equity funds.

[261] Rudolph (1990), p. 337.

[262] Mathes (1992), p. 28.

[263] Ibid., p. 30, presents a table of the development of funds open to the general public between 1979 and 1989.

[264] Ibid.

[265] Ibid., pp. 29, 40.

increases in banking fees and would therefore stimulate some interest in equity investing.[266]

The fall of the Berlin Wall in 1989 changed almost all facets of the German economy, including the securities markets, even if the impact became fully apparent only over time. After reunification the number of newly established businesses increased as the government offered special funds to encourage start-ups and promote investment in the new states.[267] Once again, government policy targeted small and private investors, this time with the official introduction of *Kleine AG* (small-share companies) as well as decreases in the minimum share price from DM 50 to DM 5 in 1994 and then to € 1 during the transition to the euro.[268] With the security of the general investing public increasingly a stated government priority, the Second Financial Market Promotion Act (*Finanzmarktförderungsgesetz*) passed on August 1, 1994. Eventually, it officially outlawed insider trading and introduced the concept of ad hoc publicity.[269] On January 1, 1995, the federal government finally established a commission to deal with issues related to insider trading in the form of the Federal Securities Supervisory Office (*Bundesaufsichtsamt für Wertpapierhandel*); the *Deutsche Gesellschaft für Ad-hoc-Publizität* (DGAP) came into being in 1996. Furthermore, a new law on securities trading (*Gesetz über den Wertpapierhandel* [WpHG]) strengthened information and publication requirements regarding share ownership in other companies.[270]

The introduction of the Neuer Markt (NM) in Frankfurt in March 1997 constituted the most significant change in the shape of German financial markets. Organizationally a segment of the broader market, the Neuer Markt specifically targeted young innovative high-tech (growth) firms. The new segment imposed more stringent listing, reporting, and disclosure requirements, in order to ensure parity with international standards.[271] With the first IPO issued – that of Mobilcom AG – the Neuer Markt appeared positioned to compete with NASDAQ and EASDAQ.[272] The German IPO market at last showed signs of life, with a major expansion appearing immediately

---

[266] Carl and Förster (1990), p. 42.

[267] Franzke et al. (2002), p. 4.

[268] Schander and Lucas (1998). As of January 1, 1999, all quotations appeared in euros.

[269] *Ad-hoc-Publizität* involves publication of a new fact that may, due to its effects on the asset or financial situation or on the path of business itself, have an influence on the price at the exchanges.

[270] Schander and Lucas (1998), p. 78, and Wadhwa (1996), p. 82.

[271] Franzke et al. (2002), p. 4.

[272] Neubauer (2002), p. 1.

in 1997 and with more IPOs hitting the market in 1999 than in the ten years prior to 1997.[273] As promising as the NM looked by the end of the 1990s, however, prospects looked poor as the twentieth century began. The crisis of 2000–1 led to drastic price declines and, despite parallel phenomena world-wide, prompted regulatory change at the Neuer Markt. The legal structuring of the markets hindered reorganization, as the Deutsche Börse AG – owner of the Neuer Markt – could not unilaterally change its legal framework.[274] Unable to find compromise among the various interested and cognizant parties, the Neuer Markt closed only six years after its initiation, on March 24, 2003. The companies that had been listed moved over to two new segments of the main exchange: Prime Standard and General Standard. The former carried higher transparency standards for companies seeking international placement.[275]

CONCLUSIONS

This chapter places the analysis of the preceding seven chapters into a long-run perspective. By continuing the story into the post-industrialization period, we can appreciate even more fully the great industrial, financial, and political development that Germany achieved between the mid-nineteenth century and 1913. It also becomes clear how dramatically the subsequent forty years altered the structure and performance of the German economy – particularly its corporate finance and governance system.

As much as the financial system has changed, the banks' involvement in corporate governance at the start of the twenty-first century – at least on the surface – looks much like it did a hundred years ago. In particular, recent patterns of bank involvement in corporate ownership and control are remarkably similar to those of the late industrialization period. The figures on banks' equity shareholding for the last few decades mirror those of the largest banks a century ago. Banks do not – and never did – control most of the corporate economy. Broadly speaking, the idea of the banks' domination of corporate ownership or control is just as much a myth for present-day Germany as it is for the industrialization period.[276] Still, the

---

[273] Franzke et al. (2002), p. 3.
[274] See Neubauer (2002), p. 164, on the peculiarities of the law that prevented its integration either into the regulated market or into the official market.
[275] http://deutsche-boerse.com/dbag.
[276] There is some evidence, however, that banks largely control themselves through cross-shareholdings, and have thus effectively managed to shield themselves from outside influences. Given the less useful securities markets as a means of restructuring control,

banks do participate actively – as they always have – in the ownership and control of a notable minority of corporations. Bank involvement continues to relate significantly to dispersion of corporate ownership, firm size, securities issue, and stock market listing – all pointing at proxy voting for customers depositing shares with the bank. It is safe to say that proxy voting by banks, especially by the largest banks, has been a key feature of the connection of banks to corporate ownership in Germany since the industrialization period. The recent movement away from bank representation on boards, when placed in this much longer perspective, appears as a historical low point. The war period, roughly 1915–45, represents an aberration from long-run patterns of corporate governance, with obvious connections to economic dislocation and political upheaval – particularly the latter.

Three decades of political and economic turbulence has left lasting marks on the German economy and financial system. While the country quickly reconstructed its infrastructure following World War II, the financial system has never fully returned to its pre–World War I mix of strong banks and vibrant markets. While some of the developments, especially the growing vertical and horizontal integration in commercial-investment banking, mirror economic rationalization patterns found in other highly developed economies after 1913, the subjugation of markets and mass expropriation of ownership rights stain the German record to an unusual extreme. More recently, the adjustment to reunification, along with the structural realignment of the productive capacity of the German economy, has proven arduous. From the standpoint of the early-twenty-first century, the rejuvenation of Germany's securities markets to their pre–World War I standing appears unlikely in the near future. Still, by many metrics, and despite the periods of havoc and upheaval, the German economy has shown remarkable resilience and success over the past ninety-two years since the start of World War I.

the system differs significantly from the pre–World War I period. See Adams (1994), p. 151, and Brickwell (2001), pp. 60–5. See also Boehmer (2000), p. 117, for a critical view on the role of banks in corporate takeovers; Jenkinson and Ljungqvist (2001), pp. 430–1, for a more favorable view of banks aiding nonfinancial firms in equity stake building; and Köke (2004) for related arguments and a more extensive discussion of block trading in Germany.

9

Conclusion

German industrialization has always attracted the attention of scholars and policy makers – even as it was under way – because it seemingly progressed through the development process with great speed and success. In striking an appealing balance of public and private control, the German system created what appears to have been particularly effective and efficient political, economic, legal, and financial institutions. This sense of beneficial institutional and systemic design continues to influence modern thinking about the best ways to promote economic advancement and prosperity, particularly in light of the late-twentieth-century political and economic transitions from communism to capitalism, as well as the broader post–World War II goals of achieving industrial development in the many economically disadvantaged regions of the world. Even on the theoretical front, the German case has inspired numerous ideas about modeling the role of financial institutions, corporate governance relationships, and their impact on firms, industries, and the economy as a whole.

With this substantial foundation of past literature and thinking in mind, the first chapter of this book laid out three primary motivations for undertaking an in-depth, historical study of the German corporate finance and governance system: first, gaining a clearer understanding of Germany's rise to financial and economic power; second, using the empirical evidence of the German case as a means of informing and refining general theories of financial intermediation and economic growth; and third, using that historical knowledge and experience to draw out lessons for financial policy today. The wide-ranging historical analysis of this book has provided many contributions on all of these fronts.

HISTORICAL FINDINGS

On the first count, the book offers new insights into the development of the German financial system – its structure, performance, and influence on firms and the economy. To set the stage, Chapter 2 provided a critical review of much of the past work on German financial history since the mid-nineteenth century. Of primary importance, the chapter chronicles the evolution of the German financial system through its phases of development, tracking shifts in institutional forms and acknowledging their wide variety. As dominant a position as the joint-stock universal banks would take in Germany's twentieth-century corporate financial system, the longer-run view reveals a relatively late take-off in this sector and the importance of other financial institutions in the early stages of industrialization. The rapid expansion of the corporate form in the early 1870s, and of markets to trade corporate securities, opened up far greater possibilities for universal banking growth than had ever existed. Thus, the political and technological advances of the mid- to late-nineteenth century clearly played an enormous role in shaping the German financial system of the time.

Alexander Gerschenkron's work looms large in this literature; one could hardly write a book about German financial history without addressing his contributions. Gerschenkron's many suppositions about financial and industrial development continue to influence modern thinking on the subject, and his conception of the issues often still frames the debates over the role of the universal banks in the industrialization of Europe's "moderately backward" economies of the nineteenth century. Ultimately, however, I concluded that while the Gerschenkron-inspired paradigm and debates over its validity should certainly play some role in formulating the historical investigation, numerous problems weaken the standard approach to German financial history – most notably the lack of testable hypotheses about the role of specific financial institutions and the common emphasis on a limited range of often nonrepresentative historical cases. That chapter argued for a more theoretically informed structuring of the historical investigation that would thereby allow for rigorous empirical testing of well-specified propositions. This sort of approach could not only create a more accurate picture of the historical experience but could also provide evidence on general propositions about corporate finance and governance relationships.

With this view in mind, Chapter 3 surveyed the most relevant theoretical literature, ranging from the motivation for the existence of banks to the incentives that corporations face in choosing financing. The chapter lays out some of the hypothetical benefits of combining banking services within universal banks and also raises some potential costs that may arise. Because of the long-standing emphasis on the role of German bankers in the ownership and control of their client firms, the theoretical discussion focuses heavily on the potential impact of these relationships on firms. While the focus remains primarily on the level of firms and industries, the chapter also offers a cursory examination of the theoretical links between financial system design and overall economic growth. This survey highlights the shortage of growth theories that differentiate among various forms of institutions and markets.

Having built this historical and theoretical foundation, the subsequent four chapters undertook a methodical study of German corporate finance and governance over the late-nineteenth and early-twentieth centuries, ranging in scope from the individual loan to the volume of securities issues to the rate of economic growth. The investigation began with a reexamination of the size and shape of the financial system, with particular attention to the universal banks and their development of characteristic practices, especially the formalization of banking relationships. The analysis moved on to a more detailed investigation of the reasons for the creation of bank–firm relationships, uncovering both differences and similarities among firms, depending on their engagement in such relationships. Taking the analysis one step further, the chapters looked for the hypothesized impact of banks on firm financing, investment, growth, and performance. Throughout, the chapters uncovered many new patterns, phenomena, and relationships of historical importance and modern relevance. The most critical among these can be summed up as follows.

Structure and Development of the Universal Banking Sector

The German joint-stock banks began to appear in the mid-nineteenth century, but they accounted for a small proportion of the financial system for several decades. This fact should come as no surprise, if we consider the main clientele of a universal bank: corporate firms. During this period – the 1850s and 1860s – the banks themselves, along with railroads and mining companies, comprised the primary customers for large-scale underwriting services. Cumbersome concession processes kept most firms small and family-controlled, so that there was little demand for securities issues. The joint-stock universal banking sector took off most rapidly during the latest stages of industrialization, not as a precursor to it. The combined effects of new technologies (electricity and its many applications, for example) and loosening regulation on incorporation provided the necessary impetus.

While some of the universal banking sector's growth came from the creation of new institutions, most of it arose from the expansion of existing ones. Particularly around the turn of the twentieth century, the largest universal banks began to build up national networks of branches and subsidiaries, very often doing so by absorbing smaller banks. As a result, the largest banks grew even faster than the banking industry as a whole, and concentration increased over time. Like many other facets of German financial history, however, the phenomenon has been somewhat exaggerated. Concentration increased at a moderate pace in this period and did so in step with similar developments in the British commercial (deposit) banking sector. Moreover, these prewar developments would pale in comparison with those that followed over subsequent decades.

Even more crucial to understanding institutional structure, this book shows that the German joint-stock banks did not as a general rule do all the things that traditional accounts – or subsequent retellings – indicate they did.[1] The characteristics and functions that they developed did not appear to the extent, as soon as, or in the manner in which the standard view holds. And the financial structure of the joint-stock banks differs somewhat from the traditional view and also changed markedly over the period of heavy industrialization between the 1850s and World War I. The banks did combine commercial and investment banking services, so it is certainly true that they became universal banks. But the corporate banks of the 1850s looked very different from those active in the years leading up to the war, even when they were nominally the very same bank.

At their inception, the joint-stock banks generally operated almost entirely on the basis of equity capital, though they did accept some current account deposits held for short terms. As the country unified and industrialized, the universal banks evolved from primarily investment to majority commercial banks, building up national branch networks and expanding their deposit base starting at the turn of the twentieth century. The increasing use of deposits shifted the banks' business from underwriting to commercial lending, in order to preserve strong reserve ratios. All forms of securities underwriting still remained within the purview of the universal banks and even grew over the pre–World War I period, but the commercial business simply grew more rapidly, absorbing an increasing share of banking assets. The investigation into individual banks' financial structure demonstrates as well a wide variation in the scope of services provided. Many of the

---

[1] See Chapter 4.

joint-stock banks played little role in underwriting, and they very likely had little business in brokerage either.

Overall, and increasingly over time, the universal banks structured their assets and liabilities conservatively. At least by the early 1880s, they held few industrial stocks in their portfolios, and they covered short-term liabilities (deposits) with substantial reserves of short-term assets. Their ratios look surprisingly conservative, given the central bank's reputation as a strong lender of last resort, which should have mitigated the universal banks' risk of insolvency. Indeed, the joint-stock banking sector remained highly stable throughout the late-nineteenth and early-twentieth centuries. It is likely, as well, that the banks adjusted their investment banking practices in response to their increasing deposit base, so that they moved more and more invest- ment banking activities off of their balance sheets. The banks' rates of return reflect their moderate levels of risk taking and increasing competition, to the extent that their returns roughly matched those of the comparable com- mercial banks in the United States and the United Kingdom and declined considerably after the early 1890s.

At the broadest level, I have provided new insights into the question of universal banking's impact on the economy, showing that no discernable sta- tistical connection emerges between the expansion of the universal banking sector and the growth of the German economy overall. In other words, the universal banks did not cause the macroeconomic growth of the industrial- ization period. Thus, the common perception that German industrialization depended on the institutional innovation of joint-stock universal banking or on the overall growth of that sector of the financial system clearly exag- gerates the universal banks' role. They were more a product than a primary cause of rapid economic growth, and coevolution of industry and finance is probably the best characterization of what happened prior to World War I.

Corporate Governance Relationships

Corporate governance relationships stand out as one of the most heavily emphasized attributes of the German universal banking system. Yet this study finds that the German universal banks played a significant but not overwhelming role in the ownership and control of corporate firms. The common idea that the universal banks behaved like modern, American- style venture capitalists – taking large, long-term stakes in high-risk, start-up firms – is quite far from reality. On the contrary, the banks owned few such stakes in nonfinancial firms, particularly after the major industrialization push of the 1870s. By the 1880s, equity stakes comprised a small part of most banks' portfolios and constituted a minor portion of total corporate capital at the time.

When large, prolonged equity stakes arose, they did so largely because a bank had decided to underwrite a new issue of shares – using the common method of buying the entire amount of the issue with the intent of a subsequent resale – and then encountering poor reception in the market. This phenomenon appeared most notably in the early years, when the corporate underwriting business and the banks engaged in it were new. The experience of one well-known bank that took on a couple of enormous, unplanned stakes in mining companies just prior to the bearish market of the early 1850s at least temporarily steered that bank and others toward more conservative decisions and may have spurred the use of underwriting consortia to spread risk. Certainly, the boom and bust cycle of the early 1870s – and to a lesser extent later in the period – left banks holding stakes they did not want. Contemporary commentators noted, moreover, that banks' investors looked disapprovingly on large stakeholding, seeing it as a sign of poor underwriting, as I believe it for the most part was.

Thus, the banks did not normally use equity holdings to tie themselves to or to hold sway over their client firms; rather, they held on to securities in the hope of improving their returns on the securities they underwrote, and they often held such securities in smaller amounts simply as an investment in their own portfolios. Large equity stakes, particularly as a share of the banks' assets, became less common as industrialization progressed and markets expanded and improved. The fact that the banks typically held shares either as an investment for their own portfolio or as a result of an unsuccessful underwriting attempt undermines the venture capital interpretation of their activities. That conclusion is strengthened by the fact that during this period, companies tended to undergo securities issues only after they were established, not usually in their start-up phases, as is the typical practice among modern venture capital organizations.

The banks' underwriting and stakeholding practices relate closely to the broader issues of corporate governance. German corporate governance institutions, executive and supervisory boards, grew up along with the phenomenon of incorporation itself and with the markets that arose to deal in the resulting securities. Corporate governance institutions remained quite underdeveloped in Germany until the last quarter of the nineteenth century. Many early corporations had no supervisory board at all, and the rights of shareholders as well as the responsibilities of managers and large stakeholders were poorly defined. Regulation on corporate governance remained lax even after the move toward free incorporation around 1870, but legislators began to take action as the population of outsider shareholders grew and demanded clearer and stronger rights of representation and protection. The idea of shareholder democracy largely held sway by the 1880s, with widespread use of common stock carrying one vote per share. Yet boards were generally small and grew little over the decades before World War I.

Largely due to this pattern of institutional evolution, the placement of bank directors in the supervisory boards of nonfinancial firms – one of the features most clearly identified with the German universal banks – emerged late in the industrialization period and well into the development of the universal banking sector itself. Thus, the emphasis on formal relationships between banks and firms during the early phases of industrialization turns out to be something of an anachronism. Eventually, many firms did have bank representatives on their boards, but the expansion of this practice came toward the end of the nineteenth century. In addition, interlocking directorates between banks and firms very often involved non-bankers who simultaneously held seats on both a bank's and a firm's (or multiple firms') supervisory board. To be sure, some bankers collected board positions in an enormous number of companies, but these individuals represent the extreme rather than the norm. Nevertheless, they are usually singled out as examples of bank power and influence even though they do not at all describe a common practice for the banking community overall. Indeed, there is no one truly typical pattern of bank representation on corporate boards: Some companies placed multiple representatives from different banks on their boards, while others maintained more exclusive arrangements with particular banks. At the same time, however, many bankers never sat on any industrial firms' boards at all, and many companies never placed a banker on their boards.

The historical literature highlights the active governance and oversight roles of the great banks – the elite handful of the largest and ultimately Berlin-centered universal banks of the late-nineteenth and early-twentieth centuries. This book shows that, in certain branches of industry, particularly the electricity sector, the largest banks were present in the boards of the largest firms, comprising a substantial majority of equity capital. From this standpoint, the emphasis on the great banks seems warranted. But this book also demonstrates that the positions of the great banks in industrial boards, while certainly more prevalent and extensive than those of most of their smaller, provincial counterparts, never did grow to imagined proportions among the corporate population at large. Perhaps even more importantly, the book undermines the strict notion of house banking between banks and firms. Especially where the largest firms and largest banks were concerned, multiple-bank representation and indirect links were more common than single-bank, direct representation. In fact, exclusive relationships appeared rarely. When they did, they more typically formed between a smaller firm and a provincial or private bank.

Of key importance for understanding this subject is the general evidence I have found to help explain why the universal banks held these positions on company boards – or more precisely, why they ended up with these board seats. Traditional explanations of German bank–firm relationships focus on banks' intervention in investment decisions and direct monitoring of debt contracts, but this book finds spotty support for these kinds of explanations. Instead, my analysis demonstrates that formal bank relationships were linked closely to company equity structure.[2] Factors associated with ownership dispersion or the marketing of company securities to the public – especially equity securities – count among the most consistent and robust predictors of bank board memberships. Large companies with stock market listings were much more likely to have bankers sitting on their boards; the tendency toward such relationships increased for firms undertaking new equity offerings. This new evidence fits well with the older accounts of widespread use of proxy voting and the virtually automatic access banks had to the voting rights of the many bearer shares they held on deposit. Piecing together the various bits of indirect evidence, along with the logic that small shareholders in widely held firms are the most likely source of proxy voting rights, leads to the conclusion that banks gained access to boards via a confluence of their underwriting and brokerage activities, the legal phenomena of bearer shares and deposited voting rights, and the flourishing securities markets of the turn of the twentieth century. Put in modern terms, the evidence suggests that banks substituted for "rationally apathetic" small shareholders. Whether they successfully advocated for the interests of those shareholders or simply took advantage of their privileged access to voting rights is yet another question, and one that is partially addressed in the next section.

Firm Financing and Performance

Financial system development is important for its own sake, that is, for its impact on the circulation of money and financial assets and the financial wealth it can create. But financial institutions are also crucial to the mobilization of capital that provides nonfinancial firms access to outside funds

---

[2] See Chapter 5.

that can help them expand their production of goods and nonfinancial services. Financing choices may influence firm performance, and in the extreme, may dictate whether or not a firm survives. Financial intermediaries, to the extent that they participate as well in firm governance, may also alter firm performance through decisions on company strategy, structure, and management. Thus, to paint the complete picture of German corporate financial development, it is necessary as well to study the clients of financial institutions and markets.

The German universal banks' reputation for active involvement in relationships with their clients has led to the idea that the banks promoted these firms' interests, resolved liquidity problems, and provided strategic advice, and in various other ways has led to superior outcomes for firms, industries, and the German economy as a whole. Given the results on corporate governance relationships, it should come as little surprise that this book finds considerable exaggeration in the standard view of corporate financing and performance. That traditional perspective is essentially static. It misses the evolution of the nature and roles of the banks and their links to business. It gives too little attention, as well, to the shifting nature and complexities of the firm and of industries.

German corporations of the late-nineteenth and early-twentieth centuries certainly performed well, but perhaps not as remarkably in terms of investment and growth rates or profitability as one might imagine given the growth of the overall economy at the time.[3] Growth rates differed markedly among firms and sectors, with small, young firms outpacing their larger and older counterparts. As we should expect, firms at the vanguard of the industrial revolution tended to expand far more than those in the "old economy" sectors, though the variability of growth rates was also greater. Failure rates fluctuated with the business cycle, but overall rates remained relatively low throughout the period. Small, old firms, in old-technology sectors failed most, particularly those with significant debt burdens and poor profitability. Corporate profit rates ranged widely as well, but the general tendency was solid, if not spectacular. Similar patterns emerge for returns on assets (ROA) and stock returns; a significant proportion of firms performed poorly, but the strength of the rest yielded handsome rewards overall. Average dividends far exceeded modern rates, and many more firms paid out dividends than typically seen in recent years. A substantial proportion of firms paid no dividends at all, but they tended to be smaller firms without

---

[3] See Chapter 6.

stock market listings – more likely closely held firms with less pressure for distributions.

Studying the financing patterns of these firms gives the strong sense that the German financial system functioned well at this time, directing resources to a diverse range of fruitful undertakings. Financial decision making operated very much as we would expect a modern system to operate. Firms structured their liabilities according to their relative costs and benefits and within the constraints of availability of collateral and insiders' desire to maintain control over firm strategy and management. Over the period, debt cost more in Germany relative to the United Kingdom but was comparable in price to that offered in the United States, which was undergoing a similar stage of development in the pre–World War I era. Debt may have been somewhat expensive, but joint-stock firms decreased their equity capitalization over the period, gradually using more debt financing on average. At the same time, firms also relied considerably upon internal funds to finance new investment in fixed capital, and they also paid down debt with newly generated funds – a sign that liquidity constraints did not bind and credit rationing presented few problems to firms.

Of particular note, the study reveals that the German system, despite its apparently strong insider-relationship orientation, did experience frequent management changes when performance was weak. In that sense, the system included a successful corporate control mechanism. Shareholders (or their representatives) ousted management teams when their firms performed poorly, particularly when accounting profits appeared subpar. On this year-by-year basis, shareholders reacted less severely to low dividends or stock returns, perhaps signaling a longer-term perspective on equity stakeholding. Interestingly, managerial turnover also responded less to poor firm returns when the broader environment was bearish, so that shareholders tended not to change management teams when the corporate population overall performed poorly. This may have been a function of a distinctive German management or business culture, one pervaded by a sense of national rivalry (with England), but my data do not reveal anything about that dimension of the corporate setting.

These findings focus our attention on the issue of bankers' influence on firm decision making. We could expect that the presence of bankers in the supervisory board might weaken the connection between firm performance and managerial turnover, because a banker could perhaps distinguish better between managerial performance and performance that was outside of even a good manager's control. And yet there is no such impact of bank board membership. Instead, there is a very significant difference between firms with stock market listings and those without. More broadly, formalized banking relationships had an uneven impact on the firms involved in them. The apparent influence also depended on the type of bank sitting on the board – or at least on unobservable characteristics that such differences signal. Few, if any, downsides of bank relationships appear on the firm or economy level. At the same time, however, hardly any noticeable benefits appear either. In many cases, relationships are decidedly neutral: The search for a tangible or observable impact turns up nothing of significance. In essentially all areas of corporate financing studied, stock market listings made much more difference in firm behavior and performance than the presence of bankers in company boards. Stock market listings are key, particularly those in the national market in Berlin, because they very likely indicate a greater dispersion of ownership and more engagement with outside shareholders.

These results in no way suggest that the banks played an inconsequential role in firm finance or the redistribution of the economy's resources. The findings also do not exclude the possibility that the banks had very significant impact on some individual firms and sectors. It would be difficult to imagine that none of the firms that received financing or underwriting services from the universal banks depended heavily on that funding or on the board input from bankers. But this study focuses more intently on issues of institutional design, asking whether particular features of the universal banks – most importantly their formalized relationships with firms – promoted superior performance for those firms that were involved. Even on this point, the findings cannot refute a possible influence for individual firms or entrepreneurs. But the critical point to bear in mind is the overall patterns and general phenomena – and in that respect, the consistency of the results speaks very clearly. It also points us once again to the importance of securities markets as they operated within the context of the universal-relationship banking system.

Securities Markets

The universal banks far overshadow the securities markets in traditional accounts of Germany's industrialization experience, particularly – but certainly not exclusively – in the English-language literature. One possible explanation for this phenomenon is simply historical accident – that the great banks attracted so much popular and scholarly attention early on that subsequent researchers continued on these already-laid research paths. Such persistence is not an uncommon historiographical paradigm. Once a style of analysis becomes firmly planted in the literature, it is likely to have a half life of several generations of scholars. The lack of vibrant markets in Germany during the last several decades of the twentieth century also compounds the problem, in that modern researchers have been lured into the sense that universal banking somehow substituted for securities markets. Based on my findings, however, it is clear that Germany's pre–World War I history tells quite another story.

Financial markets developed sooner, faster, and better than the traditional view of Germany's industrialization suggests or than modern conceptions of "civil-law" tradition would imply.[4] Late-twentieth-century thinking set up a stark dichotomy between bank-based and market-based financial systems, and in doing so assumed that markets could not flourish in systems where large-scale, universal-relationship banking prevailed. This study shows that, far from being a natural impediment to markets, the universal banks depended on the vitality of markets to produce a significant share of their profits. In the German system of the pre–World War I era, banks and markets operated not only in tandem but also in symbiosis with one another.

The first German exchanges appeared in the mid-sixteenth century, just as they did in a handful of other countries in northwestern Europe. As elsewhere, the stock exchanges increased in importance as the availability of tradable securities expanded in the mid- to late-nineteenth century. With the liberalization of incorporation around 1870, and the burgeoning corporate population that resulted, stock markets boomed. The foundation-era bubble soon burst, and demands for regulation gained momentum. New laws tightened listing requirements and trading practices, and the markets became safer places to transact business. Contrary to some accounts, the advent of securities and corporate governance regulation did not stand in the way of market expansion and performance. Growing taxation likely impinged somewhat on market dealings, and certain loopholes in the tax code did temporarily permit the largest banks to profit on internal trading among their customers and affiliates. But there was clearly a functional dual system of banks and markets circulating capital through the rapidly growing economy.

None of these regulatory changes signaled the end of markets and the takeover of universal banks. Indeed, stock market listings grew rapidly over the period – and into the postwar years – and firms opted to list their shares

---

[4] See Chapter 7.

if they were involved in or planning securities issues, typically managed by the universal banks. Once again, the study reveals close ties between securities markets usage and universal banking relationships, given the notably elevated likelihood of listing for firms with bank directors on their boards. The new laws actually attempted to reduce the role of banks in the trading process. Whether or not they were successful is difficult to say, but it is clear that the market's price discovery mechanism was at least as efficient in terms of transactions costs as modern securities markets in highly developed economies. Moreover, fewer anomalies – size, value, or momentum effects, for example – appeared in the cross section of stock returns in the Berlin market than have been identified in more recent markets.

REFINING THEORIES OF FINANCIAL INTERMEDIATION

From the perspective of corporate finance and banking theory, this study underscores the fundamental difficulty of developing unambiguous empirical tests of theoretical models hinging on asymmetric information and the abuse of that situation by the better-informed side. In most cases, the best we can do is to seek testable implications of the theories and then determine whether or not the data reject those hypotheses. This problem, of course, applies as much in the analysis of current practice as it does in studying the historical experience. With this caveat in mind, the theoretical foundation laid out at the start of the book yielded numerous empirical predictions – some well established in the literature, others new to this study – concerning the financing of corporations, the monitoring functions of financial intermediaries, the impact of relationship banking, and the overall effect of financial system architecture on aggregate-level industrial development, productivity, and economic growth.

Based on these hypotheses, the analysis has provided support for existing theory on some fronts, yet has raised concerns on others. For example, firms generally structured their funding in line with a pecking-order theory, altering that structure according to changes they faced over time. Moreover, firms with greater access to or input from outside shareholders paid greater attention to performance, management, and the connection between them. At the same time, however, firms did not always behave badly, even when they had no formal oversight from bankers, undermining the hypothesized debt-monitoring role of formal banking relationships. This point also raises a curious feature of the mixed system that conflicts with the standard paradigm of delegated monitoring: Banks simultaneously held debt, controlled equity via proxy votes, but did not often own the cash-flow rights to the shares. What forces bound the banks to behave in the interest of equity owners while defending their position as debt holders, and how the banks' actions depended on the balance between their debt holdings and equity control rights is an area in need of further research. All of these findings suggest the importance of developing theories that incorporate societal norms, trust, informal relationships, and other behaviorally oriented approaches to economic relationships.

At a broader level, the German experience also demonstrates that banks and markets are not substitutes and should not be modeled as such. There is no true dichotomy between banks and markets, so there is no solid premise for modeling a binary choice between two financial system types. While the goal of theoretical modeling is naturally to strip down economic relationships to the essential ingredients, discarding this level of complexity renders models uninformative. Instead, it is important to find ways to model the synergies between banks and markets, explain the functional areas in which these different institutions overlap, and clarify the means by which external forces – such as economic, political, and legal systems – shape them. These new approaches, with their implicit added complexity, should in turn cause some adjustment to theories linking financial development and economic growth. Because banks and securities markets differ in form and function, and because they seem to evolve in symbiotic fashion – at least the evidence on the one major case studied here suggests they can – their relative levels of advancement may influence how industry and the economy develop. Moreover, growth theory has little to say about the impact of banking scope or about the impact of formalized relationship banking practices, despite the emphasis placed on these features by the corporate finance literature. It seems likely, in light of this study, that the empirical impact is either small or it is difficult to capture. Theoretical modeling may help in distinguishing between these two conclusions and may offer guidance in refining further empirical studies.

LESSONS FOR TODAY

Beyond their historical and theoretical interest, the results in this book cover a wide range of issues that still confront all countries, whether economically advanced, transitioning, or still working toward financial and industrial development. As such, the findings offer insights for modern problems of financial development and regulation, most of which harken back to the two key questions raised in the introductory chapter: First, does expansion of the financial system encourage economic growth? Second, does the structure of banking and financial systems matter for economic development? The findings in this book offer at least partial answers to these questions and provide the basis for cross-country comparisons that may shed even more light on these issues.

On a purely statistical level, it seems clear that broadly measured financial asset growth relates to expansion in the real sector over most periods and countries that have been examined. In some cases, it also appears that financial development leads real growth – a relationship that some interpret as causal. The results in this book provide more insight into these statistical relationships. The fact that expansion of the German universal banking sector does not significantly predict future growth of the German economy suggests that the finance-growth link is more complicated than a simple statistical model allows. Universal banking growth is correlated to output growth, but there are almost certainly feedback mechanisms that get in the way of clearly causal statistical relationships.

Because of the complexity of the finance-growth relationship, the microeconomic study of firm financing is all the more important. This book's investigation into banking relationships, credit provision, and firm performance indicates clearly that German financial institutions played an active role in the financing of industry. Banks may have provided crucial working capital or business connections at key points in time for certain firms. In isolated cases, banks and bankers may have even dictated the activities or strategies of individual firms. In general, however, financial institutions did not cause firms to innovate, grow, and prosper. Bankers did not create the new products or processes that made the economy grow; entrepreneurs did. Thus, the finer-grained portrait of corporate financing demonstrates the manner in which the financial system helps promote growth by facilitating the flow of financial capital in the economy, directing it to its most productive uses. And this understanding clarifies the oft-observed macro-level connection between finance and growth.

This book's analysis is even more informative on the question of financial system design – why systems develop different organizational forms and whether certain types of financial systems are more effective and efficient than others. Perhaps most importantly, the study demonstrates that a universal banking system does not necessarily take one, static shape, and it does not necessarily differ dramatically from a system comprised of specialized financial institutions. Universal banking systems do not exclude the possibility of specialized commercial banking institutions, nor do they necessarily create unusually high levels of financial institution assets or banking industry concentration. They do not necessarily hinge on a system of equity stakeholding or other formalized relationships, but when such relationship practices do emerge, they may or may not have a pronounced effect. Relationship banking systems may not provide marked improvements in firm performance, but they are also not necessarily rife with inefficiencies stemming from lack of transparency, expropriation of shareholders, or other abuses by insiders.

German corporate finance institutions changed substantially, along with the customers they served, over the nineteenth and twentieth centuries. As they continued to evolve in the late-twentieth century, the universal banks have moved toward functional disintegration, providing different services within distinct parts of the organization. At the same time, securities markets have struggled and have failed to keep pace with those in rival economies. This book does not solve this conundrum, but it does serve as a reminder that the system can be changed and that powerful banks and vibrant markets can coexist comfortably and efficiently in one system.

These ideas of systemic complexity and diversity – in particular, the finding that securities markets may play a vital role within a universal-relationship banking system – lead directly to the issues of legal and political environments and their influence on financial system design. First, it is worth reemphasizing the importance of these results to the "law and finance" literature, given the still prevalent notion that common law tradition provides a superior environment for the growth of financial markets. At the same time, it is true that governments, or the politicians who comprise them, often feel tempted to intervene in the design and operation of financial systems, particularly in times of crisis or situations of economic underdevelopment. Interventions appear in almost all countries at one time or another, but this book cannot address the broader question of how government involvement differs depending on legal or political systems.[5] Nonetheless, the German experience studied in this book warns against attempts to dictate financial structure from above – for example, to quash market activity under the assumption that the government can organize optimal financial institutions. Germany's industrialization highlights how complexity in the system governing the flow of capital to industry can favor rapid expansion. That is, allowing financial systems to evolve a diverse array of institutional forms may create the most nurturing environment for industrial development.

---

[5] Fohlin (forthcoming) addresses the questions of political and legal factors in financial system design and economic growth.

FINAL THOUGHTS

In writing this book, I have kept three types of readers in mind: specialist scholars of German history or of finance and business history; economists interested in a long-term analysis of German corporate finance and governance; and also general readers with a more casual interest in some or all of these areas of study. The book, I hope, offers much food for thought to all of these readers and produces results of broad interest and impact. Taken together, the analysis should convince readers of three overarching principles:

- *The weight of history.* The structure of modern financial institutions in industrialized economies is rooted in the past and normally changes only slowly over time.[6] The presence of this phenomenon means that understanding recent developments in the financial systems of long-since-developed economies requires a long-term perspective. For example, this study demonstrates the importance of the last 150 years of history in dictating the current issues faced by the German financial system and its economy as a whole. Thus, analyses that consider only the recent past miss much evolution that helped determine the system's current shape.
- *The importance of context.* Society, culture, politics, legal tradition, and economics all combine to mold institutions, through both implicit norms and explicit regulation. Because of variation in the underlying context, different types of financial systems emerge to solve similar problems in different countries. Political machinations, and other exogenous events, may distort institutions and prevent their adaptation to changing economic needs. These complexities undermine attempts to define an optimal financial system to fit all, or even most, situations. This book highlights the need – for both economists and historians – to consider and appreciate the complete range of these factors in the analysis of long-run financial system development.
- *The limits of institutional design.* The structure of the financial system, particularly the choice between universal and specialized banking, may have little impact on real economic growth at a first-order approximation. In the German case, the development of the financial system differs markedly from the stylized view of history. This book raised a number of ways in which the universal banks in particular did not perform the functions

---

[6] Some might refer to this phenomenon as path dependency or hysteresis, though these terms carry certain technical connotations that may not apply.

normally assumed. But an equally important point to remember is that it did not really matter: Some features likely promoted growth, while others possibly hindered it; but in net, the system worked well as it was structured.

Despite the periodic ups and downs, overall the economy and the financial sector generally succeeded and grew during the industrialization period. The financial system changed rapidly between 1870 and 1913, yet it continued to provide industry with the capital it needed to become one of the most advanced and efficient economies in the world. By any measure, Germany reached the pinnacle of industrialization at the start of the twentieth century. The three keys to this prewar system were balance – between regulation and liberalization, between banking scope and market independence, and between bank relationships and bank domination; complexity – with securities markets and universal banks sharing the key corporate financing functions; and evolution – a situation in which neither the banks nor the markets were locked in.

This beneficial equilibrium in the prewar German financial system turned out to be temporary.[7] Like many systems of the time, it could not withstand the forces that buffeted it starting with the First World War. In the face of such political and economic upheaval, the balance of the prewar era crumbled. The Weimar Republic could not prevail over economic and political volatility. Worse yet, the relative political and economic stability of the Nazi regime brought unthinkable human atrocities. The political reconstruction of the early post–World War II era struck a new balance and targeted different objectives from those of earlier periods, sharing much greater power with the working classes and providing far-reaching social programs for the least fortunate in the population. Political forces and societal interests once again dominated in decisions surrounding the German reunification, and the west took on enormous new economic burdens as a result.

Germany has paid dearly for its political choices over the past century, but we cannot say what would have happened to the German financial system after 1913 if there had be no wars, no hyperinflation, and no totalitarian regime – or if Germany had instituted a completely free market system following World War II. We cannot prove which if any of these factors resulted in the system taking its current shape. It is clear, however, that

---

[7] See the extended discussion in Chapter 8.

the highly successful system that arose before 1913 was fundamentally and apparently irrevocably altered thereafter. The concentration, opaqueness, and insider orientation that became the identifying features of the German financial system for much of the past half-century prevented the return to the pre–World War I equilibrium path.

At the same time, German firms have continued to grow and prosper, and – outside of the obvious periods of extreme crisis – the German economy has performed on par with the wealthiest nations of the world. Even as it emerged from a brutal and destructive political regime and war in 1945, the country's productive capacity had increased. And even under the control of foreign occupation and its strict limitations on industry, the German economy rebounded. Despite the severe pressure of reunification, Germany has managed to keep up with most and even surpass many other European economies.

We cannot know for sure whether the German economy could have expanded faster, if the pre–World War I financial system had been fully restored after World War II. Perhaps it could have, but its somewhat lower recent growth path must also stem largely from the system's postwar political trade-offs – its preference for more equal distribution over greatest possible total wealth. As political priorities have shifted, partly in reaction to the economic consequences of earlier choices, the financial and corporate governance systems have continued to evolve. The largest banks' recent unwinding of corporate stakeholding, efforts to return to greater openness and transparency in corporate governance, and the attempts to build new issues markets seem promising signs for future financial system development. Even if these changes come slowly, the long-run perspective on the German system suggests that it would be unwise to underestimate the resilience of the German economy and its ability to adapt to and thrive under varying institutional arrangements for corporate finance and governance.

Ultimately, this book leads to the very strong conclusion that, for overall industrial development, the existence of some effective mechanism to mobilize capital and solve information problems is more important than the precise form that those institutions take.[8] Financial systems that appear

---

[8] I made this same point in Fohlin (2000a), which examines the economic growth rates of most countries that industrialized before World War I, and finds that long-run performance bears no relationship to financial system structure or legal tradition. Short-run growth rates do vary, but differences are mostly explained by wars and stage of economic development

endogenously will naturally take varying forms depending on national contexts and will evolve over time in response to changing environments. Transplanting certain institutional arrangements may prove useless and even undesirable. This conclusion may dash the hope for regulatory optimization from above, but it should also assuage many fears about the same.

(for example, universal banking countries, such as Germany and Italy, grew faster right after World War II because they required major reconstruction). This working paper is now part of a UFJ monograph, Fohlin (forthcoming). Levine (2002) comes to a remarkably similar conclusion based on very recent data.

References

Adalet, Muge (2005). "Fundamentals, Capital Flows and Capital Flight: The German Banking Crisis of 1931." Working Paper, Victoria University of Wellington, New Zealand. Available at http://www.ata.boun.edu.tr/ehes/Istanbul%20Conference%20Papers-%20May%202005/adalet.pdf.

Adams, Michael (1994). "Die Usurpation von Aktionärsbefugnissen mittels Ringverflechtung in der 'Deutschland AG.'" *Die Aktiengesellschaft* 39: 148–58.

——— (1999). "Cross Holdings in Germany." *Journal of Institutional and Theoretical Economics* 155: 80–109.

Albach, Horst and Heinz-Peter Kless (1982). "Personelle Verflechtungen bei deutschen Industrieaktiengesellschaften." *Zeitschrift für Betriebswirtschaft* 52 (10): 959–77.

Allen, Franklin (1992). *Stock Markets and Resource Allocation in Capital Markets and Financial Intermediation.* New York: Cambridge University Press.

Allen, Franklin and Douglas Gale (1999). *Comparing Financial Systems.* Cambridge, MA: MIT Press.

Allen, Franklin and Anthony M. Santomero (1998). "The Theory of Financial Intermediation." *Journal of Banking and Finance* 21: 1461–85.

Altman, Edward I. (1991). "Techniques for Predicting Bankruptcy and Their Use in a Financial Turnaround." S. N. Levine (ed.). *Investing in Bankruptcies and Turnarounds: Spotting Investment Values in Distressed Businesses.* New York: Harper-Collins.

Aoki, Masahiko (1988). *Information, Incentives, and Bargaining in the Japanese Economy.* New York: Cambridge University Press.

Arestis, Philip, Panicos O. Demetriades, and Kul B. Luintel (2001). "Financial Development and Economic Growth: The Role of Stock Markets." *Journal of Money, Credit and Banking* 33 (1): 16–41.

Arnold, Anton (1903). *Die Bilanzen der großen deutschen Kreditbanken und der deutschen Notenbanken seit 1894 in tabellarischen Übersichten.* Leipzig: Duncker und Humblot.

Ashauer, Günter (1983). "Entwicklung der Sparkassenorganisation ab 1924." Manfred Pohl (ed.). *Deutsche Bankengeschichte.* Frankfurt am Main: Fritz Knapp Verlag.

Astebro, Thomas B. and Joachim K. Winter (2001). "More Than a Dummy: The Probability of Failure, Survival and Acquisition of Firms in Financial Distress." Paper presented at the EFA Annual Meeting, London.

Augustine, Dolores L. (1992). "The Banker in German Society, 1890–1930." Youssef Cassis (ed.). *Finance and Financiers in European History, 1880–1960.* New York: Cambridge University Press, Editions de la Maison des Sciences de l'Homme, pp. 161–85.

Baehring, Bernd (1985). *Börsen-Zeiten. Frankfurt in vier Jahrhunderten zwischen Antwerpen, Wien, New York und Berlin.* Frankfurt: Frankfurter Wertpapierbörse.

Bähre, Inge Lore (1982). *Der Zusammenhang zwischen wirtschaftlicher Entwicklung und Bankenaufsicht von 1934 bis zur Gegenwart.* Frankfurt: Fritz Knapp Verlag.

Baker, Mae and Michael Collins (1999). "English Industrial Distress before 1914 and the Response of the Banks." *European Review of Economic History* 3/1: 1–24.

Balderston, Theo (1994). "The Banks and the Gold Standard in the German Financial Crisis of 1931." *Financial History Review* 1: 43–68.

——— (2002). *Economics and Politics in the Weimar Republic.* Cambridge, MA: Cambridge University Press.

Barro, Robert J. (1991). "Economic Growth in a Cross Section of Countries." *Quarterly Journal of Economics* 106: 407–43.

Baskin, Jonathan and Paul J. Miranti, Jr. (1997). *A History of Corporate Finance.* New York: Cambridge University Press.

Baums, Theodor (1996). "Vollmachtstimmrecht der Banken Ja oder Nein?" *Die Aktiengesellschaft* 41: 11–26.

Baums, Theodor and Christian Fraune (1995). "Institutionelle Anleger und Publikumsgesellschaft: eine empirische Untersuchung." *Die Aktiengesellschaft* 40: 97–112.

Benston, George J. (1994). "Universal Banking." *Journal of Economic Perspectives* 8: 121–43.

Berglöf, Erik (1997). "Reforming Corporate Governance: Redirecting the European Agenda." *Economic Policy* 12: 91–123.

Berk, Jonathan B. (2000). "Sorting Out Sorts." *Journal of Finance* 55: 407–27.

Beyer, Burkhard and Lothar Gall (2002). *Krupp im 20. Jahrhundert: Die Geschichte des Unternehmens vom Ersten Weltkrieg bis zur Gründung der Stiftung.* Berlin: Siedler.

Beyer, Jürgen (2002). "Deutschland AG a.D.: Deutsche Bank, Allianz und das Verflechtungszentrum Großer Deutscher Unternehmen." MPIfG Working Paper.

Bhattacharya, Sudipto and Anjan Thakor (1993). "Contemporary Banking Theory." *Journal of Financial Intermediation* 3: 2–50.

Blaich, Fritz (1978). *Grenzlandpolitik im Westen 1926–1936: die "Westhilfe" zwischen Reichspolitik und Länderinteressen.* Stuttgart: Deutsche Verlags-Anstalt.

——— (1985). *Der Schwarze Freitag: Inflation und Wirtschaftskrise.* Munich: DTV.

Board of Governors of the Federal Reserve System (1959). *All Bank Statistics: United States, 1896–1955.* Washington, DC: Library of Congress.

Boehmer, Ekkehart (2000). "Business Groups, Bank Control, and Large Shareholders: An Analysis of German Takeovers." *Journal of Financial Intermediation* 9: 117–48.

Böhm, Jürgen (1992). *Der Einfluß der Banken auf Großunternehmen.* Hamburg: Steuern- und Wirtschaftsverlag.

Bokelmann, Bettina (2000). *Personelle Verflechtungen über Aufsichtsräte: Aufsichtsratsmitglieder mit hauptberuflicher Vorstandsfunktion.* Frankfurt: Lang.

Boot, Arnoud W. A. (2000). "Relationship Banking: What Do We Know?" *Journal of Financial Intermediation* 9: 7–25.

Boot, Arnoud W. A., Todd T. Milbourn, and Silva Dezelan (2001). "Regulation and the Evolution of the Financial Services Industry." Anthony Santomero, S. Viotti, and A. Vredin (eds.). *Challenges for Central Banking.* Massachusetts: Kluwer, pp. 39–58.

Boot, Arnoud W. A. and Anjolein Schmeits (2002). "Incentives and Market Discipline." A. Meyendorff and A. V. Thakor (eds.). *Designing Financial Systems in Transition Economies.* Cambridge, MA: MIT Press, pp. 261–81.

Boot, Arnoud W. A. and Anjan V. Thakor (1997a). "Banking Scope, Financial Innovation." *Review of Financial Studies* 10: 1099–1131.

——— (1997b). "Financial System Architecture." *Review of Financial Studies* 10: 693–733.

——— (2002). " Banking Scope and Financial Innovation." B. Biais and M. Pagano (eds.). *New Research in Corporate Finance and Banking.* Oxford, UK: Oxford University Press, pp. 181–210.

Borchardt, Knut (1963). "Zur Frage des Kapitalmangels in der ersten Hälfte des 19. Jahrhunderts in Deutschland." *Jahrbuch für Nationalökonomie und Statistik* 173: 401–21.

——— (1968). "Staatsverbrauch und öffentliche Investitionen in Deutschland, 1780–1850." Unpublished Ph.D. thesis, University of Göttingen.

Borchardt, Knut, with Cornelia Meyer-Stroll (1999, 2000). *Max Weber Börsenwesen: Schriften und Reden, 1893–1898.* Tübingen: J. C .B. Mohr (Paul Siebeck).

Born, Karl Erich (1967). *Die deutsche Bankenkrise 1931. Finanzen und Politik.* Munich: R. Piper.

——— (1983). "Vom Beginn des Ersten Weltkrieges bis zum Ende der Weimarer Republik (1914–1933)." Manfred Pohl (ed.). *Deutsche Bankengeschichte.* Frankfurt: Fritz Knapp Verlag.

Bosenick, Alfred (1912). *Neudeutsche gemischte Bankwirtschaft.* Berlin: J. Schweitzer Verlag.

Bossaerts, Peter and Caroline Fohlin (2000). "Has the Cross-Section of Average Returns Always Been the Same? Evidence from Germany, 1881–1913." Social Science Working Paper No. 1084, California Institute of Technology.

Bösselmann, Kurt (1939). *Die Entwicklung des deutschen Aktienwesens im 19. Jahrhundert.* Berlin: W. de Gruyter.

Boyd, John H. and Edward C. Prescott (1986). "Financial Intermediary-Coalitions." *Journal of Economic Theory* 38: 211–32.

Boyd, John H. and Bruce D. Smith (1994). "Capital Market Imperfections, International Credit Markets, and Nonconvergence." *Journal of Economic Theory* 73: 335–64.

——— (1995). "The Evolution of Debt and Equity Markets in Economic Development." Working Paper No. 542, Federal Reserve Bank of Minneapolis.

—— (1996). "The Coevolution of the Real and Financial Sectors in the Growth Process." *World Bank Economic Review* 10: 371–96.

Braun, Hans-Joachim (1990). *The German Economy in the Twentieth Century.* London and New York: Routledge.

Brendel, Gregor (2001). *Zur Macht der Banken in Deutschland.* Münster: Lit.

Brickwell, Daniel M. (2001). *"Zu den Einflusspotenzialen der Großbanken,"* Ph.D. thesis, Freie Universität.

Broadberry, Stephen (1997). "Anglo-German Productivity Differences, 1870–1990: A Sectoral Analysis." *European Review of Economic History* 1: 247–67.

—— (2003). "Human Capital and Productivity Performance: Britain, the United States and Germany, 1870–1990." P. A. David and M. Thomas (eds.). *The Economic Future in Historical Perspective.* London: Oxford University Press (for the British Academy).

Broder, Albert (1991). "Banking and the Electrotechnical Industry in Western Europe." V. I. Bovykin and R. Cameron (eds.). *International Banking, 1870–1914.* New York: Oxford University Press.

Brown, Stephen, J., William N. Goetzmann, and Stephen A. Ross (1995). "Survival." *Journal of Finance* 50: 853–74.

Buchheim, Christoph (1993). "The Currency Reform in West Germany in 1948." *German Yearbook on Business History 1989–92.* Munich: K.G. Saur, pp. 85–120.

Buchwald, Bruno (1909). *Die Technik des Bankbetriebs,* fifth edition. Berlin: Springer Verlag.

Bund der Landwirte (1908). *Das neue Börsengesetz.* Berlin.

Bundesregierung (2001). "Kurzfassung des Berichts der Regierungskommission 'Corporate Governance.'" Available at www.bundesregierung.de.

Buss, Georg (1913). *Die berliner Börse von 1685–1913.* Berlin: Gedenktage der ersten Versammlung im Neuen Hause.

Cable, John (1985). "Capital Market Information and Industrial Performance: The Role of West German Banks." *Economic Journal* 95: 118–32.

Calomiris, Charles W. (1993). "Financial Factors in the Great Depression." *Journal of Economic Perspectives* 7: 61–85.

—— (1995). "The Costs of Rejecting Universal Banking: American Finance in the German Mirror, 1870–1914." Naomi Lamoreaux and Daniel Raff (eds.). *Coordination and Information: Historical Perspectives on the Organization of Enterprise.* Chicago: University of Chicago Press, pp. 257–315.

—— (2000). *U.S. Bank Deregulation in Historical Perspective.* New York: Cambridge University Press.

Calomiris, Charles and Charles Himmelberg (1993). "Directed Credit Programs for Agriculture and Industry: Arguments from Theory and Fact." *Proceedings of the World Bank Annual Conference on Development Economics.* Washington, DC: World Bank.

Cameron, Rondo E. (1961). *France and the Economic Development of Europe.* Princeton, NJ: Princeton University Press.

—— (1967) "England, 1750–1844." Cameron et al. (eds.). *Banking in the Early Stages of Industrialization. A Study of Comparative Economic History.* New York: Oxford University Press, pp. 15–59.

———— (1972). "Introduction." Cameron (ed.). *Banking and Economic Development.* New York: Oxford University Press.

Capie, Forrest (1988). "The Mechanism of the Supply of Money in the United Kingdom, 1873–1913." P. L. Cottrell and Donald E. Moggridge (eds.). *Money and Power: Essays in Honour of L. S. Pressnell.* Hampshire, UK: Macmillan.

Capie, Forrest and Michael Collins. (1992). *Have the Banks Failed British Industry? A Broad Historical Survey, 1870–1990.* London: Institute of Economic Affairs.

Capie, Forrest and Ghila Rodrik-Bali (1982). "Concentration in British Banking, 1870–1920." *Business History* 24: 280–92.

Capie, Forrest and Alan Webber (1985). *A Monetary History of the United Kingdom, 1870–1982.* London: Allen and Unwin.

Carl, Dieter and Wolfgang Förster (1990). *Das neue Recht der Investmentfonds. europarechtlicher Rahmen und nationale Gesetzgebung: die Bedeutung für den europäischen Finanzraum und den Finanzplatz Deutschland.* Göttingen: WiRe Verlagsgesellschaft.

Carlson, John B. (2001). "Why Is the Dividend Yield So Low?" *Economic Commentary* (Federal Reserve Bank of Cleveland), April 1.

Champ, Bruce and Scott Freeman (1994). *Modeling Monetary Economies.* New York: John Wiley.

Chandler, Alfred D. (1990). *Scale and Scope: The Dynamics of Industrial Capitalism.* Cambridge, MA: Belknap Press of Harvard University Press.

Chemmanur, Thomas J. and Paolo Fulghieri (1994). "Reputation, Renegotiation, and the Choice between Bank Loans and Publicly Traded Debt." *Review of Financial Studies* 7: 475–506.

Chordia, Tarun and Lakshmanan Shivakumar (2002). "Momentum, Business Cycle and Time-Varying Expected Returns." *Journal of Finance* 57: 985–1019.

Collins, Michael (1991). *Banks and Industrial Finance in Britain: 1800–1939.* Hampshire, UK: Macmillan.

———— (1998). "English Bank Development." *Economic History Review* 51: 1–24.

Confalonieri, Antonio (1975). *Banca E Industria in Italia Dalla Crisi Del 1907 All'agosto 1914,* Vol. 1. Milan: Banca Commerciale Italiana.

———— (1979). *Banca E Industria in Italia 1894–1906,* Vol. 2. Milan: Banca Commerciale Italiana.

Cottrell, Peter (1980). *Industrial Finance, 1830–1914.* New York: Methuen.

Corwin, Shane A. and Jeffrey H. Harris (2001). "The Initial Listing Decisions of Firms That Go Public." *Financial Management* 30: 35–56.

Cowan, Arnold R., Richard B. Carter, Frederick H. Dark, and Ajai K. Singh (1992). "Explaining the NYSE Listing Choices of NASDAQ Firms." *Financial Management* 21, Winter: 73–86.

Craine, Roger B. (1995). "Fairly Priced Deposit Insurance and Bank Charter Policy." *Journal of Finance* 50: 1735–46

Däbritz, Walther (1931). *Gründung und Anfänge der Disconto-Gesellschaft Berlin.* Leipzig: Verlag Von Duncker und Humblot.

Daniel, K. and Sheridan Titman (1997). "Evidence on the Characteristics of Cross Sectional Variation in Stock Returns." *Journal of Finance* 52: 1–33.

Da Rin, Marco and Thomas Hellmann (2002). "Banks as Catalyst for Industrialization." *Journal of Financial Intermediation* 11: 366–97.

Davis, James L., Eugene F. Fama, and Kenneth R. French (2000). "Characteristics, Covariances, and Average Returns: 1929 to 1997." *Journal of Finance* 55: 389–406.

Davis, Lance (1965). "The Investment Market, 1870–1914: The Evolution of a National Market." *Journal of Economic History* 25: 355–99.

————— (1966). "The Capital Markets and Industrial Concentration: The U.S. and U.K.: A Comparative Study." *Economic History Review*, second series 58: 255–72.

DeLong, J. Bradford and Marco Becht (1992). "Excess Volatility and the German Stock Market, 1876–1990." Harvard University mimeo, Cambridge, MA.

DeLong, J. Bradford, and Barry Eichengreen (1993). "The Marshall Plan: History's Most Successful Structural Adjustment Program." Rudiger Dornbusch et al. (eds.). *Postwar Economic Reconstruction and Lessons for the East Today.* Cambridge, MA: MIT Press, pp. 189–230.

Demirgüç-Kunt, Asli and Ross Levine (eds.) (2004). *Financial Structure and Economic Growth: A Cross-Country Comparison of Banks, Markets, and Development.* Cambridge, MA: MIT Press.

Demirguc-Kunt, Asli and Vojislav Maksimovic (1998). "Law, Finance, and Firm Growth." *Journal of Finance* 53: 2107–37.

Deutsche Bundesbank (1976). *Deutsches Geld- und Bankwesen in Zahlen 1876–1975.* Frankfurt: Fritz Knapp Verlag.

Deutscher Bundestag (1964). Bericht über das Ergebnis einer Untersuchung der Konzentration in der Wirtschaft vom 29. February 1964, Drucksache IV/2320, Bonn.

Devereux, Michael B. and Gregor Smith (2004). "Transfer Problem Dynamics: Macroeconomics of the Franco-Prussian War Indemnity." Working Paper. Available at http://ssrn.com/abstract=575681.

Dewatripont, Mathias and Eric Maskin (1990). "Contract Renegotiation in Models of Asymmetric Information." *European Economic Review* 34: 311–21.

————— (1995). "Credit and Efficiency in Centralized and Decentralized Economies." *Review of Economic Studies* 62: 542–55.

Diamond, Douglas (1984). "Financial Intermediation and Delegated Monitoring." *Review of Economic Studies* 51: 393–414.

————— (1991). "Monitoring and Reputation: The Choice between Bank Loans and Directly Placed Debt." *Journal of Political Economy* 99: 689–721.

Dickhaus, Monika (1996). *Die Bundesbank im westeuropaeische Wiederaufbau.* Munich: Oldenbourg.

Dietrich, J. Richard and Robert S. Kaplan (1982). "Empirical Analysis of the Commercial Loan Classificiation Decision." *Accounting Review* 57: 18–38.

Donaubauer, Klaus A. (1988). *Privatbankiers und Bankenkonzentration in Deutschland von der Mitte des 19. Jahrhunderts bis 1932.* Frankfurt: Fritz Knapp Verlag.

Dumke, Rolf H. (1976). "The Political Economy of German Economic Unification: Tariffs, Trade and Politics of the Zollverein Era." Ph.D. dissertation, University of Wisconsin, Madison.

————— (1981). "Die Wirtschaftlichen Folgen des Zollvereins." W. Abelshauer and D. Petzina (eds.). *Deutsche Wirtschaftsgeschichte im Industriezeitalter.* Königstein/Ts.: Athenäum, pp. 341–73.

—— (1991). "Tariffs and Market Structure: The German Zollverein as a Model for Economic Integration." W. R. Lee (ed.). *German Industry and German Industrialisation. Essays in German Economic and Business History in the Nineteenth and Twentieh Centuries.* London and New York: Routledge, pp. 77–115.

Dunlavy, Colleen (1998). "Corporate Governance in Late 19th-Century Europe and the U.S.: The Case of Shareholder Voting Rights." Klaus J. Hopt, Hideki Kanda, Mark J. Roe, Eddy Wymeersch, and Stefan Prigge (eds.). *Comparative Corporate Governance: The State of the Art and Emerging Research.* Oxford, UK: Clarendon Press, 1998.

Dunne, Timothy, Mark J. Roberts, and Larry Samuelson (1989). "The Growth and Failure of U.S. Manufacturing Plants." *Quarterly Journal of Economics* 104: 671–98.

Edwards, George T. (1987). *The Role of Banks in Economic Development.* London: Macmillan.

Edwards, Jeremy and Marcus Nibler (2000). "Corporate Governance in Germany: The Role of Banks and Ownership Concentration." *Economic Policy* 31: 239–67.

Edwards, Jeremy, and Sheilagh Ogilvie (1996). "Universal Banks and German Industrialization: A Reappraisal." *Economic History Review* 49: 427–46.

Eichengreen, Barry (1992). *Golden Fetters: The Gold Standard and the Great Depression, 1919–1939.* New York: Oxford University Press.

Eistert, Ekkehard (1970). *Die Beeinflussung des Wirtschaftswachstums in Deutschland von 1883–1913 durch das Banksystem.* Berlin: Duncker und Humblot.

Enquete Ausschuß (1933). *Untersuchung des Bankwesens.* Berlin: Carl Heymanns Verlag.

Ericson, Richard and Ariel Pakes (1995). "Markov-Perfect Industry Dynamics: A Framework for Empirical Work." *Review of Economic Studies* 62: 53–82.

Fama, Eugene. F. and James D. MacBeth (1973). "Risk, Return and Equilibrium: Empirical Tests." *Journal of Political Economy* 81: 607–36.

Fama, Eugene F. and Kenneth R. French (1993). "Common Risk Factors in the Returns on Stocks and Bonds." *Journal of Financial Economics* 33: 3–56.

—— (1995). "Size and Book-to-Market Factors in Earnings and Returns." *Journal of Finance* 50: 131–55.

—— (1996). "Multifactor Explanations of Asset Pricing Anomalies." *Journal of Finance* 51: 55–84.

Fear, Jeffrey (2005). *Organizing Control: From August Thyssen to Heinrich Dinkelbach.* Cambridge, MA: Harvard University Press.

Feldenkirchen, Wilfred (1979a). "Banken und Stahlindusrie im Ruhrgebiet. Zur Entwicklung ihrer Beziehungen 1873–1914." *Bankhistoriches Archiv* 2: 27–52.

—— (1979b). "Kapitalbeschaffung in der Eisen- und Stahlindustrie des Ruhrgebiets." *Zeitschrift für Unternehmensgeschichte* 24: 39–81.

—— (1991). "Banking and Economic Growth: Banks and Industry in Germany in the Nineteenth Century and Their Changing Relationship during Industrialisation." W. R. Lee (ed.). *German Industry and German Industrialisation: Essays in German Economic and Business History in the Nineteenth and Twentieth Centuries.* London and New York: Routledge, pp. 116–47.

—— (1992). "Competition Policy in Germany." *Business and Economic History*, second series 21: 257–69.

Feldman, Gerald (1991). "Banks and the Problem of Capital Shortage in Germany, 1918–1923." Harold James (ed.). *The Role of Banks in the Interwar Economy.* New York: Cambridge University Press, pp. 49–79.

——— (1993). *The Great Disorder.* New York: Oxford University Press.

——— (1995). *Jewish Bankers and the Crisis of the Weimar Republic.* New York: Leo Baeck Institute.

——— (1997). "Responses to Banking Concentration in Germany, 1900–1933." Mimeo, University of California, Berkeley.

——— (1998). *Hugo Stinnes: Biographie eines Industriellen, 1870–1924.* Munich: Beck.

Fendler, Arnold (1926). *Zur Kapitalkonzentration der berliner Großbanken, 1914–1923.* Berlin: W. Christians.

Ferguson, Thomas and Peter Temin (2003). "Made in Germany: The German Currency Crisis of July 1931." *Research in Economic History* 21: 1–53.

——— (2004). "Comment on the German Twin Crisis of 1931." *Journal of Economic History* 64 (3): 872–6.

Fischer, Wolfram (ed.) (1968). *Wirtschafts- und sozialgeschichtliche Probleme der frühen Industrialisierung.* Berlin: Colloquium-Verlag.

Fisher, Jonas D. M. and Andreas Hornstein (2001). "The Role of Real Wages, Productivity, and Fiscal Policy in Germany's Great Depression, 1928–37." Working Paper 01-7, Federal Reserve Bank of Richmond.

Fohlin, Caroline (1994). "Financial Intermediation, Investment, and Industrial Development: Universal Banking in Germany and Italy from Unification to World War I." Dissertation, University of California, Berkeley.

——— (1997a). "The Universal Banks and the Mobilization of Capital in Imperial Germany." Forthcoming in P. Cottrell, G. Feldman, and J. Reis (eds.). *Finance and the Making of Modern Capitalism.* Aldershot, UK: Scolar Press.

——— (1997b). "Universal Banking Networks in Pre-War Germany: New Evidence from Company Financial Data." *Research in Economics* 51: 201–25.

——— (1997c). "The Rise of Interlocking Directorates in Imperial Germany." *Economic History Review* 52: 307–33.

——— (1997d). "Bank Securities Holdings and Industrial Finance before World War I: Britain and Germany Compared." *Business and Economic History* 26: 463–75.

——— (1998a). "Fiduciari and Firm Liquidity Constraints: The Italian Experience with German-Style Universal Banking." *Explorations in Economic History* 35: 83–107.

——— (1998b). "Relationship Banking, Liquidity, and Investment in the German Industrialization." *Journal of Finance* 53: 1737–58.

——— (1999a). "Capital Mobilization and Utilisation in Latecomer Economies: Germany and Italy Compared." *European Review of Economic History* 2: 139–74.

——— (1999b). "The Rise of Interlocking Directorates in Imperial Germany." *Economic History Review* 52 (2): 307–33.

——— (1999c). "Universal Banking in Pre-World War I Germany: Model or Myth?" *Explorations in Economic History* 36: 305–43.

———— (2000a). "Economic, Political, and Legal Factors in Financial System Development: International Patterns in Historical Perspective." Social Science Working Paper No. 1089, California Institute of Technology.

———— (2000b). "IPO Underpricing in Two Universes: Berlin, 1882–1892, and New York, 1998–2000." Social Science Working Paper No. 1088, California Institute of Technology.

———— (2000c). "Banking Industry Structure, Competition, and Performance: Does Universality Matter?" Social Science Working Paper No. 1078, California Institute of Technology.

———— (2001a). "The Balancing Act of German Universal Banks and English Deposit Banks, 1880–1913." *Business History* 43: 1–24.

———— (2001b). "A Comprehensive Panel Database for 400 German Stock Companies, 1895–1913." Mimeo, California Institute of Technology.

———— (2002a). "Corporate Capital Structure and the Influence of Universal Banks in Pre-World War I Germany." *Jahrbuch für Wirtschaftsgeschichte* 2: 113–34.

———— (2002b) "Regulation, Taxation, and the Development of the German Universal Banking System," *European Review of Economic History* 6: 221–54.

———— (2005). "The History of Corporate Ownership and Control in Germany." R. Morck (ed.). *The History of Corporate Governance around the World: Family Business Groups to Professional Managers.* Chicago: University of Chicago Press, pp. 223–77.

Fohlin, Caroline and T. Gehrig (forthcoming). "Price Discovery in an Early Emerging Market: the Case of the Berlin Stock Exchange, 1880–1910," *Review of Finance.*

Fohlin, Caroline and Steffen Reinhold (2006). "The Cross-Section of Common Stock Returns in a Relationship Banking System: Evidence from Pre-World War I Germany." Working Paper, Johns Hopkins University.

Frank, Harald (1993). "Wirtschaftspolitik in der NS-Zeit." Richard H. Tilly (ed.). *Geschichte der Wirtschaftspolitik: vom Merkantilismus zur sozialen Marktwirtschaft.* Munich and Vienna: R. Oldenburg Verlag, pp. 148–98.

Franke, Günter (1999). "The Bundesbank and the Financial Markets." Deutsche Bundesbank (ed.). *Fifty Years of the Deutsche Mark: Central Bank and the Currency in Germany since 1948.* Oxford, UK: Oxford University Press, pp. 219–66.

Franks, Julian and Colin Mayer (2001). "Ownership and Control of German Corporations." *Review of Financial Studies* 14 (4): 943–77.

Franzke, Stefanie, Stefanie Grohs, and Christian Laux (2004). "Initial Public Offerings and Venture Capital in Germany." Jan Pieter Krahnen and Reinhard H. Schmidt (eds.). *The German Financial System.* Oxford, UK: Oxford University Press, pp. 233–61.

Freitag, Sabine and Manfred Pohl (eds.) (1994). *Handbook on the History of European Banks.* Aldershot, UK: Edward Elgar.

Freixas, Xavier and Jean-Charles Rochet (1997). *Microeconomics of Banking.* Cambridge, MA: MIT Press.

Fremdling, Rainer (1975). *Eisenbahnen und deutsches Wirtschaftswachstum, 1840–1879.* Dortmund: Gesellschaft für westfälische Wirtschaftgeschichte.

——— (1977). "Railroads and German Economic Growth: A Leading Sector Analysis with a Comparison to the United States and Great Britain." *Journal of Economic History* 37 (3): 583–604.

——— (1983). "Germany." P. O'Brien (ed.). *Railways and the Economic Development of Western Europe*. New York: St. Martin's Press, pp. 121–47.

Fremdling, Rainer and Richard H. Tilly (1976). "German Banks, German Growth and Econometric History." *Journal of Economic History*, 36: 416–24.

——— (1979). *Industrialisierung und Raum: Studien zure regionalen Differenzierung im Deutschland des 19. Jahrhunderts*. Stuttgart: Klett Cotta.

Funk, Lothar (2000). "Economic Reform of *Modell Deutschland*." Rebecca Harding and William E. Paterson (eds.). *The Future of the German Economy: An End to the Miracle?* Manchester, UK, and New York: Manchester University Press, pp. 16–35.

Gale, Douglas and Martin Hellwig (1985). "Incentive-Compatible Debt Contracts: The One-Period Problem." *Review of Economic Studies* 52: 647–63.

Galetovic, Alexander (1996). "Finance and Growth: A Synthesis and Interpretation of the Evidence." *BNL Quarterly Review* 196: 59–82.

Gall, Lothar (ed.) (2002). *Krupp im 20. Jahrhundert: die Geschichte des Unternehmens vom ersten Weltkrieg bis zur Gründung der Stiftung*. Berlin: Siedler.

Gall, Lothar, Gerald D. Feldman, Harold James, Carl-Ludwig Holtfrerich, and Hans E. Büschgen (1995). *Die Deutsche Bank, 1870–1995*. Munich: C. H. Beck.

George, Thomas J., Gautam Kaul, and Mahendrarajah Nimalendran (1991). "Estimation of the Bid-Ask Spread and Its Components: A New Approach." *Review of Financial Studies* 4: 623–56.

Gerschenkron, Alexander (1962). *Economic Backwardness in Historical Perspective*. Cambridge, MA: Harvard University Press.

——— (1970). *Europe in the Russian Mirror*. New York: Cambridge University Press.

——— (1977). *An Economic Spurt That Failed*. Princeton, NJ: Princeton University Press.

Gericke, Horst (1992). *Handbuch für die Börsenzulassung von Wertpapieren*. Frankfurt: Verlag Börsen-Zeitung.

Gessler, Ernst (1965). *Aktiengesetz: Kommentar*. Munich: F. Vahlen.

Gibrat, Robert (1931). *Les Inégalités Économiques*. Paris: Sirey.

Gielen, Gregor (1994). *Können Aktienkurse noch Steigen? langfristige Trendanalyse des deutschen Aktienmarktes*. Wiesbaden: Gabler.

Glagau, Otto (1876). *Der Börsen- und Gründungs-Schwindel in Berlin*. Leipzig: Verlag von Paul Frohberg.

Goldsmith, Raymond W. (1969). *Financial Structure and Development*. New Haven, CT: Yale University Press.

——— (1985). *Comparative National Balance Sheets: A Study of Twenty Countries, 1688–1978*. Chicago: University of Chicago Press.

Gömmel, Rainer (1992). "Entstehung und Entwicklung der Effektenbörse im 19. Jahrhundert bis 1914." H. Pohl (ed.). *Deutsche Börsengeschichte*. Frankfurt: Fritz Knapp Verlag.

Goodhart, Charles A. E. (1972). *The Business of Banking, 1891–1914*. London: Weidenfeld and Nicolson.

Gottschalk, Arno (1988). "Der Stimmrechtseinfluß der Banken in den Aktion-ärsversammlungen von Großunternehmen." *WSI-Mitteilungen* 41 (4): 294–304.

Greenbaum, Stuart I., George Kanatas, and Itzhak Venezia (1989). "Equilibrium Loan Pricing under the Bank–Client Relationship." *Journal of Banking and Finance* 13: 221–35.

Greenwood, Jeremy and Bruce D. Smith (1997). "Financial Markets in Development, and the Development of Financial Markets." *Journal of Economic Dynamics and Control* 21: 145–81.

Guinnane, Timothy (2001). "Cooperatives as Information Machines: German Rural Credit Cooperatives, 1883–1914." *Journal of Economic History* 61 (2): 366–89.

Haas, Wolfgang (1994). *Die Auswirkungen des Betriebsübergangs insbesondere bei der Fusion von Kapitalgesellschaften auf Betriebsvereinbarungen*. Mainz: Dissertations Druck.

Hadi, Ali S. (1992). "Identifying Multiple Outliers in Multivariate Data." *Journal of the Royal Statistical Society*, series B, 54: 761–71.

——— (1994). "A Modification of a Method for the Detection of Outliers in Multivariate Samples." *Journal of the Royal Statistical Society*, series B, 56: 393–6.

Hagemann, Wilhelm (1931). *Das Verhältnis der deutschen Großbanken zur Industrie*. Berlin: Christians.

Haller, Heinz (1976). "Die Rolle der Staatsfinanzen für den Inflationsprozess." Deutsche Bundesbank (ed.). *Währung und Wirtschaft in Deutschland, 1876–1975*, second edition. Frankfurt: Fritz Knapp Verlag, pp. 115–55.

Handbuch der deutschen Aktiengesellschaften (various years). Berlin: Verlag für Börsen- und Finanzliteratur.

Hardach, Gerd (1987). "The Marshall Plan in Germany, 1948–1952." *Journal of European Economic History* 16 (3): 433–85.

Hardach, Karl (1980). *The Political Economy of Germany in the Twentieth Century*. Berkeley, CA: University of California Press.

Harris, Milton and Artur Raviv (1991). "The Theory of Capital Structure." *Journal of Finance* 46: 297–355.

Hau, Harald (1998). "Competitive Entry and Endogenous Risk in the Foreign Exchange Market." *Review of Financial Studies* 11: 757–87.

Häuser, Karl (1997). *Börse und Kapitalmarkt*. Frankfurt: Fritz Knapp Verlag.

Hauswald, Robert (1995). "On the Origins of Universal Banking: An Analysis of the German Banking Sector 1848 to 1910." Working Paper, Stanford University.

Hawawini, Gabriel and Donald Keim (1995). "On the Predictability of Common Stock Returns: World-Wide Evidence." R. Jarrow, V. Maksimovic, and W. Ziemba (eds.). *Handbooks in Operations Research and Management Science – Finance*, Vol. 9. Amsterdam: Elsevier, pp. 497–544.

Hayashi, Fumio (1982). "Tobin's Marginal Q and Average Q: A Neoclassical Inter-pretation." *Econometrica* 50: 213–24.

Hellman, Thomas and Joseph Stiglitz (2000). "Credit and Equity Rationing in Mar-kets with Adverse Selection." *European Economic Review* 44: 281–304.

Hellwig, Martin (1991). "Banking, Financial Intermediation and Corporate Fin-ance." A. Giovannini and C. Mayer (eds.). *European Financial Integration*. New York: Cambridge University Press, pp. 35–63.

——— (1998). "Banks, Markets, and the Allocation of Risks." *Journal of Institutional and Theoretical Economics* 154: 328–51.

——— (2000). "Financial Intermediation with Risk Aversion." *Review of Economic Studies* 67: 719–42.

Helten, J. (1928). *Die Kölner Börse 1553–1927.* Köln: Kölner Verl.-Anst. u. Druckerei A.G.

Henderson, William O. (1975). *The Rise of German Industrial Power, 1834–1914.* London: Temple Smith.

——— (1984). *The Zollverein,* third edition. London: Frank Cass.

Henning, Friedrich-Wilhelm (1973). "Die Liquidität der Banken in der Weimarer Republik." Harald Winkel (ed.). *Währungs- und Finanzpolitik der Zwischenkriegszeit.* Berlin: Duncker und Humblot.

——— (1990). "Die Unternehmensfinanzierung in der Bundesrepublik Deutschland von 1952 bis 1965, unter Besonderer Berücksichtigung der Industrie-Aktiengesellschaften." Dietmar Petzina (ed.). *Zur Geschichte der Unternehmensfinanzierung.* Berlin: Duncker und Humblot, pp. 99–117.

——— (1992). "Börsenkrisen und Börsengesetzgebung von 1914 bis 1945 in Deutschland." Hans Pohl (ed.). *Deutsche Börsengeschichte.* Frankfurt: Fritz Knapp Verlag, pp. 211–90.

Herrigel, Gary (1996). *Industrial Constructions: The Sources of German Industrial Power.* London: Cambridge University Press.

Heyn, Udo (1981 [1969]). *Private Banking and Industrialization: The Case of Frankfurt am Main, 1825–75.* New York: Arno.

Hilferding, Rudolf (1910). *Das Finanzkapital.* Vienna: Wiener Volksbuchhandlung (English translation: *Finance Capital.* Tom Bottomore (ed.). Boston: Routledge and Kegan Paul, 1981).

Hoffmann, Walther G. (1965). *Das Wachstum der deutschen Wirtschaft seit der Mitte des 19. Jahrhunderts.* New York: Springer-Verlag.

Hoffmann, Joseph (1966). "Sparkassen und Konzentration." J. Hoffmann (ed.). *Der Weg der Sparkassenpolitik.* Stuttgart: Deutscher Sparkassenverlag.

Holtfrerich, Carl-Ludwig (1988). "Relations between Monetary Authorities and Governmental Institutions: The Case of Germany from the 19th Century to the Present." Gianni Toniolo (ed.). *Central Banks' Independence in Historical Perspective.* Berlin and New York: de Gruyter, pp. 105–59.

Holtfrerich, Carl-Ludwig and Toru Iwami (1999). "Post-War Central Banking Reform: A German-Japanese Comparison." Carl-Ludwig Holtfrerich, Jaime Reis, and Gianni Toniolo (eds.). *The Emergence of Modern Central Banking from 1918 to the Present.* Aldershot, UK: Ashgate, pp. 69–109.

Hopenhayn, Hugo A. (1992). "Entry, Exit, and Firm Dynamics in Long Run Equilibrium." *Econometrica* 60: 1127–50.

Hopt, Klaus J. (1996). "Corporate Governance und deutsche Universalbanken." Feddersen Dieter (ed.). *Corporate Governance: Optimierung der Unternehmensführung und der Unternehmenskontrolle im deutschen und amerikanischen Aktienrecht.* Cologne: Otto Schmidt, pp. 243–63.

——— (1998). "The German Two-Tier Board: Experience, Theories, Reforms." Klaus J. Hopt et al. (eds.). *Comparative Corporate Governance: The State of the Art and Emerging Research.* Oxford, UK: Clarendon Press, pp. 227–58.

Horn, Norbert (1979). "Aktienrechtliche Unternehmensorganisation in der Hochindustrialisierung (1860–1920): Deutschland, England, Frankreich und die USA im Vergleich." N. Horn and J. Kocka (eds.). *Recht und Entwicklung der Großunternehmen im 19. und frühen 20. Jahrhundert.* Göttingen: Vandenhoeck and Ruprecht.

Horn, Norbert and Jürgen Kocka (eds.) (1979). *Recht und Entwicklung der Großunternehmen im 19. und frühen 20. Jahrhundert.* Göttingen: Vandenhoeck and Ruprecht.

Houston, Joel and Christopher James (2001). "Do Relationships Have Limits?" *Journal of Business* 74: 347–74.

Hübner, Otto (1968 [1853]). *Die Banken,* Band 2. Frankfurt: Sauer und Auvermann Verlag.

Huck, Norbert (1993). "Wirtschaftspolitik zwischen Weltkrieg und Weltwirtschaftskrise." Richard H. Tilly (ed.). *Geschichte der Wirtschaftspolitik: Vom Merkantilismus zur sozialen Marktwirtschaft.* Munich and Vienna: R. Oldenburg Verlag, pp. 104–47.

Hüffer, Uwe (2002). *Aktiengesetz.* Munich: Beck.

Irmler, Heinrich (1976). "Bankenkrise und Vollbeschäftigungspolitik (1931–1936)." Deutsche Bundesbank (ed.). *Währung und Wirtschaft in Deutschland, 1876–1975.* Frankfurt: Fritz Knapp Verlag, pp. 280–329.

James, Christopher and Peggy Wier (1990). "Borrowing Relationships, Intermediation and the Cost of Issuing Public Securities." *Journal of Financial Economics* 28: 149–71.

James, Harold (1986). *The German Slump: Politics and Economics, 1924–1936.* Oxford, UK: Oxford University Press.

——— (1992). "Banks and Economic Development: Comments." Youssef Cassis (ed.). *Finance and Financiers in European History, 1880–1960.* Cambridge, UK: Cambridge University Press, pp. 113–18.

——— (1999). "The International Monetary Fund and Central Banking." Carl-Ludwig Holtfrerich, Jaime Reis, and Gianni Toniolo (eds.). *The Emergence of Modern Central Banking from 1918 to the Present..* Aldershot, UK: Ashgate.

——— (2001). *Die Deutsche Bank and the Nazi Economic War against the Jews. The Expropriation of Jewish-Owned Property.* Cambridge, UK: Cambridge University Press.

Jappelli, Tullio and Marco Pagano (1994). "Saving, Growth, and Liquidity Constraints." *Quarterly Journal of Economics* 109: 83–109.

——— (2000). "Information Sharing in Credit Markets: A Survey." Centre for Studies in Economics and Finance (CSEF) Working Paper No. 36.

Jayaratne, Jith and Philip E. Strahan (1996). "The Finance-Growth Nexus: Evidence from Bank Branch Deregulation." *Quarterly Journal of Economics* 111: 639–70.

Jeidels, Otto (1905). *Das Verhältnis der deutschen Großbanken zur Industrie.* Leipzig: Duncker und Humblot.

Jenkinson, Tim and Alexander Ljungqvist (2001). "The Role of Hostile Stakes in German Corporate Governance." *Journal of Corporate Finance* 7: 397–446.

Jensen, Michael and W. Meckling (1976). "The Theory of the Firm: Managerial Behavior, Agency Costs, and Ownership Structure." *Journal of Financial Economics* 3: 305–60.

Jovanovic, Boyan (1982). "Selection and the Evolution of Industry." *Econometrica* 50 (3): 649–70.

Kanatas, George and Jianping Qi (2003). "Integration of Lending and Underwriting: Implications of Scope Economies." *Journal of Finance* 58: 1167–91.

Kaplan, Steven N. and Luigi Zingales (1997). "Do Investment-Cash Flow Sensitivities Provide Useful Measures of Financing Constraints." *Quarterly Journal of Economics* 112: 169–215.

Kaserer, Christoph and Ekkehard Wenger (1997). *The German System of Corporate Governance: A Model Which Should Not Be Imitated*. Washington, DC: American Institute for Contemporary German Studies.

Kennedy, William P. (1987). *Industry Structure, Capital Markets, and the Origin of British Economic Decline*. Cambridge, UK: Cambridge University Press.

——— (1991). "Portfolio Behavior and Economic Development in Late Nineteenth-Century Great Britain and Germany: Hypotheses and Conjectures." *Research in Economic History* 6: 93–130.

——— (1992). "Historical Patterns of Finance in Great Britain: A Long-Run View." V. Zamagni (ed.). *Finance and the Enterprise*. London: Academic Press.

Kennedy, William P. and Rachel Britton (1985). "Portfolioverhalten und Wirtschaftliche Entwicklung im späten 19. Jahrhundert. Ein Vergleich zwischen Großbritannien und Deutschland. Hypothesen und Spekulationen." Richard Tilly (ed.). *Beiträge zur Quantitativen Vergleichenden Unternehmensgeschichte*. Stuttgart: Klett-Cotta, pp. 45–93.

Kindleberger, Charles P. (1984a). *A Financial History of Western Europe*. London: George Allen and Unwin.

——— (1984b). "Financial Institutions and Economic Development: A Comparison of Great Britain and France in the Eighteenth and Nineteenth Centuries." *Explorations in Economic History* 21: 103–24.

——— (1986). *The World in Depression, 1929–1939*. Berkeley, CA: University of California Press.

King, Robert G. and Ross Levine (1993). "Finance and Growth: Schumpeter Might Be Right." *Quarterly Journal of Economics* 108: 717–37.

Klarmann, Norbert, Ernst Klein, and Manfred Pohl (1980). *Deutsche Bankengeschichte*. Frankfurt: Fritz Knapp Verlag.

Kocka, Jürgen. (1978). "Entrepreneurs and Managers in German Industrialization." Peter Mathias and M. M. Postan (eds.). *The Cambridge Economic History of Europe*, Vol. 7: *The Industrial Economies: Capital, Labor, and Enterprise*. Cambridge, UK, and New York: Cambridge University Press, pp. 492–589.

——— (1999). "Big Business and the Rise of Managerial Capitalism: Germany in International Comparison." Idem (ed.). *Industrial Culture and Bourgeois Society: Business, Labor, and Bureaucracy in Modern Germany*. New York and Oxford, UK: Berghahn, pp. 156–73.

Köke, Jens (2001). "New Evidence on Ownership Structures in Germany." *Kredit und Kapital*, 34: 257–92.

——— (2004). "The Market for Corporate Control in Bank-Based Economy: A Governance Device." *Journal of Corporate Finance* 10 (1): 53–80.

Komlos, John (1978). "The Kreditbanken and German Growth: A Postscript." *Journal of Economic History* 38: 476–9.

Krengel, Jochen (1980). "Zur Berechnung von Wachstumswirkungen konjunkturell bedingter Nachfrageschwankungen nachgelageter Industrien auf die Produktionsentwicklung der deutschen Roheisenindustrie während der Jahre, 1871–1882." W. Schröder and R. Spree (eds.). *Historische Konjunkturforschung.* Stuttgart: Klett-Cotta.

Kronenberger, Fritz (1920). "Die Preisbewegung der Effekten in Deutschland während des Krieges." *Betriebs- und Finanzwirtschaftliche Forschungen,* Vol. 2. Berlin: Verlag von Emil Ebering.

Kroszner, R. and R. Rajan (1994). "Is the Glass Steagall Act Justified? A Study of the US Experience with Universal Banking before 1933." *American Economic Review* 84: 810–32.

Krupke, Franz (various years). *Krupkes Konversations-Lexikon der Börse und des Handels und praktischer Führer für Kapitalisten.* Berlin: Franz Krupke.

Kübler, Friedrich (1994). *Gesellschaftsrecht,* fourth edition. Heidelberg: C. F. Müller Juristischer Verlag.

Kuh, Edwin (1963). *Capital Stock Growth: A Microeconometric Approach.* Amsterdam: North-Holland.

Kuh, Edwin and John R. Meyer (1957). "How Extraneous Are Extraneous Estimates." *Review of Economics and Statistics* 39: 380–93.

Kunze, Walther (1926). *Der Aufbau des Phoenix-Konzerns.* Dissertation, University of Frankfurt am Main.

Lansburgh, Alfred (1909). *Das deutsche Bankwesen.* Berlin-Charlottenburg: Bank Verlag.

Laux, Frank (1998). *Die Lehre vom Unternehmen an Sich: Walther Rathenau und die aktienrechtliche Diskussion in der Weimarer Republik.* Berlin: Duncker und Humblot.

Lavington, Frederick E. (1921). *The English Capital Market.* London: Methuen.

Lesmond, David A., Joseph P. Ogden, and Charles A. Trzcinka (1999). "A New Estimate of Transaction Costs." *Review of Financial Studies* 12: 1113–41.

Levine, Ross (1997). "Financial Development and Economic Growth: Views and Agenda." *Journal of Economic Literature* 35: 688–726.

——— (1998). "The Legal Environment, Banks, and Long-Run Economic Growth." *Journal of Money, Credit and Banking,* second series 30: 596–613.

——— (2002). "Bank-Based or Market-Based Financial Systems: Which Is Better?" *Journal of Financial Intermediation* 11: 398–428.

——— (2003). "More on Finance and Growth: More Finance, More Growth?" *Federal Reserve Bank of St. Louis Review* July/August: 31–46.

Levine, Ross and Sara Zervos (1998). "Stock Markets, Banks, and Economic Growth." *American Economic Review* 88: 537–58.

Lëvy Leboyer, Maurice (1964). *Les Banques Europeennes et l'Industrialisation Internationale dans la Premiere Moitie du XIX Siecle.* Paris: Presses Universitaires de France.

Liefmann, Robert (1921). *Beteiligungs- und Finanzierungsgesellschaften: eine Studie über den modernen Effekten-Kapitalismus in Deutschland, den Vereinigten Staaten, der Schweiz, England, Frankreich und Belgien.* Jena: G. Fischer.

Lindlar, Ludger and Carl-Ludwig Holtfrerich (1996). "Four Decades of German Export Expansion." German Institute for Economic Research Discussion Paper 130, pp. 1–34.

Linsel, Hermann (1956). *Die Aufrechterhaltung und Entwicklung des Bankmonopols in Westdeutschland.* Berlin: Verlag Die Wirtschaft.

Lo, Andrew W. (1995). "Implementing Option Pricing Models When Asset Returns Are Predictable." *Journal of Finance* 50: 87–129.

Lo, Andrew W. and Jiang Wang. (1998). "Trading Volume: Definitions, Data Analysis, and Implications of Portfolio Theory." Working Paper No. LFE-1028-97, Massachusetts Institute of Technology, Laboratory for Financial Engineering.

Loewenstein, Arthur (1912). *Geschichte des württembergischen Kreditbankwesens und seiner Beziehungen zu Handel und Industrie.* Tübingen: Verlag von J. C. B. Mohr.

Lucas, Robert E., Jr. (1988). "On the Mechanics of Economic Development." *Journal of Monetary Economics* 22: 3–42.

Lüke, Rolf E. (1958). *Von der Stabilisierung zur Krise.* Zürich: Polygraphischer.

Maddison, Angus (1982). *Phases of Capitalist Development.* New York: Oxford University Press.

——— (1995). *Monitoring the World Economy 1820–1992.* Paris: OECD.

Madhavan, Ananth (2000). "Market Microstructure: A Survey." Social Science Research Network (SSRN) Working Paper Series, ITG Inc.

März, Eduard (1968). *Österreichische Industrie- und Bankpolitik in der Zeit Franz Josephs I.* Frankfurt: Europa-Verlag.

Marx, Erich (1913). *Die Entwicklung der deutschen Provinzbörsen.* Berlin: Verlag für Fachliteratur.

Mathes, Manfred (1992). "Investmentsparen in Deutschland: eine Idee setzt sich Durch." Georg Bruns and Karl Häuser (eds.). *Deutschland als Finanzplatz: Analysen und Perspektiven.* Frankfurt: Fritz Knapp Verlag, pp. 7–44.

Mathias, Peter (1973). "Capital, Credit, and Enterprise in the Industrial Revolution." *Journal of European Economic History* 2: 121–43.

——— (1989). "Financing the Industrial Revolution." P. Mathias and J. A. Davis (eds.). *The First Industrial Revolutions.* Oxford, UK: Basil Blackwell, pp. 69–85.

Mayer, Colin (1988). "New Issues in Corporate Finance." *European Economic Review* 32: 1167–88.

McKinnon, Ronald (1973). *Money and Capital in Economic Development.* Baltimore, MD: Brookings Institution.

Meier, Johann Christian (1993). "Die Entstehung des Börsengesetzes vom 22. Juni 1896," *Studien zur Wirtschafts- und Sozialgeschichte,* Vol. 9. Munich: St. Katharinen.

Meyer, John R. and Edwin Kuh (1957). *The Investment Decision.* Cambridge, MA: Harvard University Press.

Michie, Ranald (1988). "Different in Name Only? The London Stock Exchange and Foreign Bourses, c. 1850–1914." *Business History* 30: 46–68.

Milgrom, Paul and Nancy Stokey (1982). "Information, Trade, and Common Knowledge." *Journal of Economic Theory* 26: 17–27.

Mitchell, Brian R. (1992). *International Historical Statistics: Europe, 1750–1988,* third edition. New York: Stockton Press.

Modigliani, Franco and M. H. Miller (1958). "The Cost of Capital, Corporation Finance, and the Theory of Investment." *American Economic Review* 48: 261–97.

Moser, Fritz (1999). *Die Bedeutung der Wettbewerbsveränderungen im Finanzdienst-leistungssektor für die Entwicklungsperspektiven internationaler Fenanzzentren und die Zukunft der deutschen Großbanken.* Regensburg: Transfer Verlag.

Motschmann, Gustav (1915). *Das Depositengeschäft der berliner Grossbanken.* Munich: Duncker und Humblot.

Myers, Stewart J. (1977). "Interactions of Corporate Financing and Investment Decisions: Implications for Capital Budgeting." *Journal of Finance* 32: 218–20.

Myers, Stewart and Nicholas S. Majluf (1984). "Corporate Financing and Investment Decisions When Firms Have Information That Investors Do Not Have." *Journal of Financial Economics* 13: 187–221.

Narayanan, M. P. (1985). "Managerial Incentives for Short-Term Results." *Journal of Finance* 40 (5): 1469–84.

Neubauer, Sven (2002). "Zulässigkeit und Grenzen der einseitigen Änderung des Regelwerks Neuer Markt durch die Deutsche Börse AG." Dissertation, University of Kiel.

Neuberger, Hugh (1977 [1974]). *German Banks and German Economic Growth from Unification to World War I.* New York: Arno Press.

Neuberger, Hugh and Houston Stokes (1974). "German Banks and German Growth 1883–1913: An Empirical View." *Journal of Economic History* 34: 710–31.

O'Brien, Patrick K. (1986). "Do We Have a Typology for the Study of European Industrialization in the XIXth Century?" *Journal of European Economic History* 15: 316–19.

Office of Military Government–United States (OMGUS) (1987). Gesamtregister: Ermittlungen gegen die Deutsche Bank, Ermittlungen gegen die Dresdner Bank. Nördlingen: F. Greno.

Overy, Richard J. (1989). "Hitler's War and the German Economy: A Reinterpretation." Clive Emsley, Arthur Marwick, and Wendy Simpson (eds.). *War, Peace and Social Change in Twentieth-Century Europe.* Philadelphia, PA: Open University Press, pp. 208–32.

——— (1994). *War and Economy in the Third Reich.* Oxford, UK: Clarendon Press.

Owen-Smith, Eric (1983). *The West German Economy.* New York: St. Martin's Press.

——— (1994). *The German Economy.* London: Routledge.

Pagano, Marco (1993). "Financial Markets and Growth: An Overview." *European Economic Review* 37: 613–22.

Passow, Richard (1922). *Die Aktiengesellschaft. Eine wirtschaftswissenschaftliche Studie.* Jena: G. Fischer.

Peckolt, Horst (1937). *Strukturverschiebungen im deutschen Bankwesen.* Stuttgart: C. E. Poeschel.

Perlitz, Manfred and Seger, Frank (1994). "The Role of Universal Banks in German Corporate Governance." *Business and the Contemporary World* 6 (4): 49–67.

Peters, Stephen R. and Anjan V. Thakor (1995). "A Rationale for the Functional Separation of Qualitative Asset Transformation Services in Banking." Working Paper, Indiana University.

Petersen, Mitchell (1999). "Banks and the Role of Lending Relationships: Evidence from the US Experience." Working Paper, Northwestern University, Kellogg Graduate School of Management.

Petersen, Mitchell and Raghuram Rajan (1994). "The Benefits of Lending Relationships: Evidence from Small Business Data." *Journal of Finance* 49: 3–37.

Petri, Martin H. (1998). "The Causes of the German Banking Crisis of July 1931 Viewed from Bank Balance Sheets and the Contemporary Financial Press." Ph.D. dissertation, University of California, Berkeley.

Pfannschmidt, Arno (1995). "Mehrfachmandate in deutschen Unternehmen." *Zeitschrift für Betriebswirtschaft.* 65 (2): 177–203.

Pohl, Hans (ed.) (1986). *Gewerbe- und Industrielandschaften vom Spätmittelalter bis ins 20. Jahrhundert.* Stuttgart: Franz Steiner Verlag.

——— (ed.) (1992). *Deutsche Börsengeschichte.* Frankfurt: Fritz Knapp Verlag.

Pohl, Manfred (1980). "Der Zusammenschluß der Deutschen Bank und der Disconto-Gesellschaft im Oktober 1929." *Beiträge zu Wirtschafts- und Währungsfragen und zur Bankgeschichte* 18: 31 ff.

——— (1982). *Konzentration im deutschen Bankwesen, 1848–1980.* Frankfurt: Fritz Knapp Verlag.

——— (1983). "Die Entwicklung des privaten Bankwesens nach 1945: Die Kreditgenossenschaften nach 1945." Manfred Pohl (ed.). *Deutsche Bankengeschichte.* Frankfurt: Fritz Knapp Verlag, pp. 207–76.

——— (1986). *Entstehung und Entwicklung des Universalbankensystems. Konzentration und Krise als Wichtige Faktoren.* Frankfurt: Fritz Knapp Verlag.

Pollard, Sidney (1979). *Regionen und Industrialisierung.* Göttingen: Vandenhoeck and Ruprecht.

Pollard, Sidney and Dieter Ziegler (1992). "Banking and Industrialization: Rondo Cameron Twenty Years On." Youssef Cassis (ed.). *Finance and Financiers in European History, 1880–1960.* New York: Cambridge University Press, pp. 17–38.

Preussische Statistik (1865). Berlin.

Prion, Willi (1910). *Die Preisbildung an der Wertpapierbörse.* Liepzig: Verlag von Duncker und Humblot.

——— (1929). *Die Preisbildung an der Wertpapierbörse.* Munich: Verlag von Duncker und Humblot.

Rajan, Raghuram (1992). "Insiders and Outsiders: The Choice between Informed and Arm's Length Debt." *Journal of Finance* 47: 1367–1400.

——— (1995). "The Entry of Commercial Banks in the Securities Business: A Selective Survey of Theory and Evidence." Paper presented at the conference on Universal Banking held at the Solomon Center at New York University.

Rajan, Raghuram and Luigi Zingales (1995). "What Do We Know about Capital Structure? Some Evidence from International Data." *Journal of Finance* 50: 1421–60.

——— (1998). "Financial Dependence and Growth." *American Economic Review* 88: 559–86.

——— (1999). *The Politics of Financial Development.* Working Paper, University of Chicago.

——— (2003). "The Great Reversals: The Politics of Financial Development in the Twentieth Century." *Journal of Financial Economics* 69: 5–50.

Reich, Norbert (1979). "Auswirkungen der deutschen Aktienrechtsreform von 1884 auf die Konzentration der deutschen Wirtschaft." Norbert Horn and Jürgen

Kocka (eds.). *Recht und Entwicklung der Großunternehmen im 19. und Frühen 20. Jahrhundert.* Gottingen: Vandenhoeck and Ruprecht, pp. 255–73.

Rettig, Rudi (1978). "Das Investitions- und Finanzierungsverhalten Deutscher Größunternehmen, 1880–1911." Dissertation, University of Münster.

Riesser, Jakob (1910). *Die deutschen Großbanken und ihre Konzentration.* Jena: Verlag von Gustav Fischer. (English translation: *The German Great Banks and Their Concentration.* Published by the National Monetary Commission. Washington, DC: Government Printing Office, 1911.)

Ritschl, Albrecht (2002). "Deficit Spending in the Nazi Recovery, 1933–1938: A Critical Reassessment." *Journal of the Japanese and International Economies* 16 (4): 559–82.

——— (2004). "The Marshall Plan, 1948–1951." Robert Whaples (ed.). *EH.Net Encyclopedia.* http://eh.net/encyclopedia/?article=Ritschl.Marshall.Plan.

Rousseau, Peter (2002). "Historical Perspectives on Financial Development and Economic Growth." National Bureau of Economic Research (NBER) Working Paper No. W9333, Vanderbilt University.

Rousseau, Peter and Richard Sylla (2001). "Financial Systems, Economic Growth, and Globalization." NBER Working Paper No. W8323, New York University.

Rousseau, Peter L. and Paul Wachtel.(1998). "Financial Intermediation and Economic Performance: Historical Evidence from Five Industrialized Countries." *Journal of Money, Credit and Banking,* second series 30: 657–78.

Rudolph, Bernd (1992). "Effekten- und Wertpapierbörsen, Finanztermin- und Devisenbörsen seit 1945." Hans Pohl (ed.). *Deutsche Börsengeschichte.* Frankfurt: Fritz Knapp Verlag, pp. 291–375.

Saling's Börsen-Jahrbuch (various years).

Santucci, Tanja (2002). "Extending Fair Disclosure to Foreign Issuers: Corporate Governance and Finance Implications for German Companies." *Columbia Business Law Review* 2: 499–539.

Sargent, Thomas J. (1982). "The Ends of Four Big Inflations." Robert E. Hall (ed.). *Inflation: Causes and Effects.* Chicago: University of Chicago Press, pp. 41–97.

Sattler, Heinrich (1977 [1890]). *Die Effektenbanken.* Vaduz, Liechtenstein: Topos Verlag.

Schönitz, Hans (1912). *Der kleingewerbliche Kredit in Deutschland.* Karlsruhe: G. Braunsche Hofbuchdruckerei and Verlag.

Schander, Albert A. and Johannes H. Lucas (1998). "Veränderungen an den Börsen: der zunehmende Stellenwert der Information." Michael Müller and F.-J. Leven (eds.). *Shareholder Value Reporting: veränderte Anforderungen an die Berichterstattung börsennotierter Unternehmen.* Vienna: Ueberreuter, pp. 75–102.

Schnabel, Isabel (2004a). "The German Twin Crisis of 1931." *Journal of Economic History* 64 (3): 822–71.

——— (2004b). "Reply to Thomas Ferguson and Peter Temin's Comment on 'The German Twin Crisis of 1931.'" *Journal of Economic History* 64 (3): 877–8.

——— (2005). "The Role of Liquidity and Implicit Guarantees in the German Twin Crisis of 1931" (formerly entitled "The Great Banks' Depression: Deposit Withdrawals in the German Crisis of 1931"). Max Planck Institute (MPI) Preprint #2005/5. Available at http://www.mpp.rdg.mpg.de/schnabel/greatbanks.pdf.

Schneider, Uwe H. (1984). *Die Entwicklung des Bankenaufsichtsrechts, in: Standortbestimmung, Entwicklungslinien der deutschen Kreditwirtschaft.* Stuttgart: Deutschen Sparkassen- and Giroverband, p. 83.

Schreyögg, Georg and Hieke Papenheim-Tockhorn (1995). "Dient der Aufsichtsrat dem Aufbau zwischenbetrieblicher Kooperationsbeziehungen?" *Zeitschrift für Betriebswirtschaft* 65 (2): 205–30.

Schulz, Wolfgang (1994). *Das deutsche Börsengesetz. Die Entstehungsgeschichte und wirtschaftlichen Auswirkungen des Börsengesetzes von 1896.* Frankfurt: Peter Lang.

Schumacher, Hermann (1911). *Weltwirtschaftliche Studien: Vorträge und Aufsätze.* Leipzig: Veit.

Schumpeter, Joseph (1912). *Theorie der Wirtschaftlichen Entwicklung.* Leipzig: Duncker und Humblot.

———— (1930). *Theory of Economic Development.* Cambridge, UK: Harvard University Press.

Sharpe, Steve A. (1990). "Asymmetric Information, Bank Lending, and Implicit Contracts: A Stylized Model of Customer Relationships." *Journal of Finance* 45: 1069–87.

Shaw, Edward S. (1973). *Financial Deepening in Economic Development.* Oxford, UK: Oxford University Press.

Sheppard, David K. (1971). *The Growth and Role of UK Financial Institutions, 1880–1962.* London: Methuen.

Shumway, Tyler (2001). "Forecasting Bankruptcy More Accurately: A Simple Hazard Model." *Journal of Business* 74 (1): 101–24.

Sinn, Hans-Werner (2002). "Germany's Economic Unification: An Assessment after Ten Years." *Review of International Economics* 10 (1): 113–28.

Skoulakis, Georgios (2005). "Panel Data Inference in Finance: Least-Squares vs. Fama-MacBeth." Working Paper, Northwestern University, Kellogg School of Management.

Sombart, Werner (1903). *Die Deutsche Volkswirtschaft im neunzehnten Jahrhundert.* Berlin: Georg Bondi.

———— (1909 and 1913). *Die Deutsche Volkswirtschaft im neunzehnten Jahrhundert*, second and third editions. Berlin: Georg Bondi.

Spence, Michael A. (1974). "Job Market Signaling." *Quarterly Journal of Economics* 87: 355–74.

Statistisches Bundesamt Wiesbaden (1972). *Bevölkerung und Wirtschaft 1872–1972.* Stuttgart: W. Kohlhammer.

Statistisches Reichsamt (various years). *Statistik des deutschen Reichs.* Berlin.

———— (various years). *Statistisches Jahrbuch für das deutsche Reich.* Berlin.

———— (1925). "Zahlen zur Geldentwertung in Deutschland 1914 bis 1923." *Wirtschaft und Statistik* [Sonderheft I], Berlin. p. 5.

Stein, Jeremy C. (1989). "Efficient Capital Markets, Inefficient Firms: A Model of Myopic Corporate Behavior." *Quarterly Journal of Economics* 104: 655–69.

Stiglitz, Joseph E. (1985). "Credit Markets and the Control of Capital." *Journal of Money, Credit and Banking* 17: 133–52.

Stiglitz, Joseph E. and A. Weiss (1981). "Credit Rationing in Markets with Imperfect Information." *American Economic Review* 71: 393–410.

Stucken, Rudolph (1933). "Die Konzentrationsbewegung im deutschen Bankgewerbe und deren Gegenkräfte und die Tendenzen zur Dekonzentration und Spezializierung." *Untersuchung des Bankwesens.* Berlin: Heymann, pp. 7–40.

Stulz, Rene (1990). "Managerial Discretion and Optimal Financing Policies." *Journal of Financial Economics* 26 (1): 3–28.

Sylla, Richard (1969). "Federal Policy, Banking Market Structure, and Capital Mobilization in the United States, 1863–1913." *Journal of Economic History* 39 (4): 657–86.

——— (1991). "The Role of Banks." Richard Sylla and Gianni Toniolo (eds.). *Patterns of European Industrialization: The Nineteenth Century.* London and New York: Routledge, pp. 45–63.

Taeuber, Rudolf (1911). *Die Börsen der Welt.* Berlin: Verlag für Börsen- und Finanzliteratur A.-G.

Temin, Peter (1971). "The Beginning of the Depression in Germany." *Economic History Review* 24: 240–8.

——— (1990). "Socialism and Wages in the Recovery from the Great Depression in the United States and Germany." *Journal of Economic History* 50 (2): 297–307.

Terhalle, Fritz (1948). *Die Finanzwirtschaft des Staates und der Gemeinden: eine Einführung in die Staatsfinanzwirtschaft.* Berlin: Duncker und Humblot.

——— (1952). "Geschichte der deutschen öffentlichen Finanzwirtschaft vom Beginn des 19. Jahrhunderts bis zum Schlusse des Zweiten Weltkrieges." Erwin von Beckerath et al. (eds.). *Handbuch der Finanzwissenschaft,* Vol. 1. Tübingen: J. C. B. Mohr, pp. 274–327.

Thakor, Anjan V. (1996a). "Capital Requirements, Monetary Policy, and Aggregate Bank Lending: Theory and Empirical Evidence." *Journal of Finance* 51: 279–324.

——— (1996b). "The Design of Financial Systems: An Overview." *Journal of Banking and Finance* 20: 917–48.

Thieme, Horst (1960). "Statistische Materialien zur Konzessionierung von Aktiengesellschaften in Preussen bis 1867." *Jahrbuch für Wirtschaftsgeschichte* 2: 285–300.

Tilly, Richard H. (1966). *Financial Institutions and Industrialization in the Rhineland, 1815–1870.* Madison, WI: University of Wisconsin Press.

——— (1967). "Germany, 1815–1870." Rondo Cameron (ed.). *Banking in the Early Stages of Industrialization: A Study in Comparative Economic History.* New York: Oxford University Press, pp. 151–82.

——— (1986). "German Banking, 1850–1914: Development Assistance for the Strong." *Journal of European Economic History* 15: 113–51.

——— (1992). "An Overview of the Role of the Large German Banks up to 1914." Youssef Cassis (ed.). *Finance and Financiers in European History, 1880–1960.* London: Cambridge University Press, pp. 93–112.

——— (1993). "Geschäftsbanken und Wirtschaft in Westdeutschland seit dem Zweiten Weltkrieg." Eckart Schremmer (ed.). *Geld und Währung in der Neuzeit vom 16. Jahrhundert bis zur Gegenwart.* Stuttgart: F. Steiner, pp. 315–43.

——— (1994a). "German Banks and Foreign Investment in Central and Eastern Europe before 1939." D. Good (ed.). *Economic Transformations in East and Central Europe.* London and New York: Routledge, pp. 201–30.

———— (1994b). "Banks and Industry: Lessons from History." Paper presented at the conference European Economic Integration as a Challenge to Industry and Government. Münster, Germany.

———— (1995). "The Berlin Securities Exchange in National Context: Actors, Rules and Reforms to 1914." Working Paper, University of Münster.

———— (1999). "Policy, Capital Markets and Supply of Industrial Finance in Germany in Nineteenth-Century Germany." R. Sylla, R. Tilly, and G. Tortella (eds.). *The State, the Financial System and Economic Modernization.* New York: Cambridge University Press, pp. 134–57.

Townsend, Robert (1979). "Optimal Contracts and Competitive Markets with Costly State Verification." *Journal of Economic Theory* 21: 265–93.

Trebilcock, Clive (1981). *The Industrialization of the Continental Powers, 1780–1914.* New York: Longman.

U.S. Bureau of the Census (1960). *Historical Statistics of the United States, Colonial Times to 1957.* Washington, DC: U.S. Government Printing Office.

Utrero González, Natalia (2002). "Legal Environment, Capital Structure and Firm Growth: International Evidence from Industry Data." Working Paper, Universidad Carlos III de Madrid, Department of Business Administration.

Vagts, Detlev F. (1979). "Railroads, Private Enterprise and Public Policy: Germany and the United States, 1970–1920." N. Horn and Jürgen Kocka (eds.). *Recht und Entwicklung der Großunternehmen im 19. und frühen 20. Jahrhundert.* Gottingen: Vandenhoeck and Ruprecht, pp. 604–18.

Verdier, Daniel. (1997). "The Political Origins of Banking Structures." *Policy History Newsletter* 2: 1–6.

———— (2002). "Explaining Cross-National Variations in Universal Banking in 19th-Century Europe, North America and Australasia." Douglas Forsyth and Daniel Verdier (eds.). *The Origins of National Financial Systems.* London: Routledge, pp. 23–42.

von Falkenhausen, Bernhard Freiherr (1966). "Das Bankenstimmrecht im neuen Aktienrecht." *Die Aktiengesellschaft* 11 (3): 69–79.

———— (1967). *Verfassungsrechtliche Grenzen der Mehrheitsherrschaft nach dem Recht der Kapitalgesellschaften (AG und GmbH).* Karlsruhe: C. F. Müller.

von Poschinger, Heinrich (1971 [1879]). *Bankwesen und Bankpolitik in Preussen.* Glashütten im Taunus: Verlag Detlev Auvermann.

von Reden, Friedrich Wilhelm Otto (ed.) (1848). *Zeitschrift des Vereins für deutsche Statistik,* Vol. 2. Berlin: F. Schneider.

von Thadden, Ernst-Ludwig (1995). "Long-Term Contracts, Short-Term Investment and Monitoring." *Review of Economic Studies* 62: 557–75.

———— (2004). "Asymmetric Information, Bank Lending and Implicit Contracts: The Winner's Curse." *Finance Research Letters* 1: 11–22.

von Thadden, Rudolf (1990). *Deutschland von Aussen Gesehen.* Esslingen: Neckar.

Wadhwa, Sylvia (1996). *Finanzplatz Deutschland.* London: Euromoney Publications PLC.

Wagenblass, Horst (1973). *Der Eisenbahnbau und das Wachstum der Deutschen Eisen- und Maschinenbauindustrie, 1835 bis 1860.* Stuttgart: Gustav Fischer.

Walb, E. (1933). "Übersetzung und Konkurrenz im deutschen Kreditapparat." *Untersuchungen für das Bankwesen.* Berlin.

Wallich, Paul (1905). *Die Konzentration im deutschen Bankwesen.* Stuttgart: Union Deutsche Verlagsgesellschaft.

Wandel, Eckhard (1983). "Das deutsche Bankwesen im Dritten Reich 1933–1945." Manfred Pohl (ed.). *Deutsche Bankengeschichte.* Frankfurt: Fritz Knapp Verlag.

———— (1993). "Die Rolle der Banken bei der Finanzierung der Aufrüstung und des Krieges 1933 bis 1945." Eckart Schremmer (ed.). *Geld und Währung in der Neuzeit vom 16. Jahrhundert bis zur Gegenwart.* Stuttgart: F. Steiner.

Warburg, Paul M. (1910). *The Discount System in Europe, 61st Congress, 2nd Session Senate Document 402.* National Monetary Commission. Washington, DC: U.S. Government Printing Office.

Warschauer, Otto (1905). "Die Deutsche Börsensteuer und die Versuche ihrer Umgestaltung." *Jahrbücher für Nationalökonomie und Statistik* 30: 57–66.

Watson, Katherine (1995). "The New Issue Market as a Source of Finance for the U.K. Brewing and Iron and Steel Industries, 1870–1913." Youssef Cassis, Gerald D. Feldman, and Ulf Olsson (eds.). *The Evolution of Financial Institutions and Markets in Twentieth-Century Europe.* London: Scolar Press, pp. 209–48.

Weber, Adolf (1915). *Depositenbanken und Spekulationsbanken,* second edition. Leipzig: Duncker und Humblot.

Webster's Dictionary (1913). Springfield: Merriam-Webster.

Weder, Mark (2005). "A Heliocentric Journey into Germany's Great Depression." Working Paper 2005–13, University of Adelaide, School of Economics.

———— (2006). "Some Observations on the Great Depression in Germany." *German Economic Review* 7: 113–33.

Wehler, Hans Ulrich (1987). *Deutsche Gesellschaftsgeschichte.* Munich: C. H. Beck.

Wellhöner, Volker (1989). *Großbanken und Großindustrie im Kaiserreich.* Göttingen: Vandenhoek and Ruprecht.

Wengenroth, Ulrich (1986). *Unternehmensstrategien und technischer Fortschritt: die deutsche und britische Stahlindustrie, 1865–1895.* Göttingen: Vandenhoeck and Ruprecht.

———— (1991). "Iron and Steel." V. I. Bovykin and R. Cameron (eds.). *International Banking, 1870–1914.* New York: Oxford University Press.

Wenger, Ekkehard and Christoph Kaserer (1998). "German Banks and Corporate Governance: A Critical View." K. J. Hopt, H. Kanda, M. J. Roe, E. Wymeersch, and S. Prigge (eds.). *Comparative Corporate Governance. The State of the Art and Emerging Research.* Oxford, UK: Clarendon Press, pp. 499–536.

Wessel, Horst A. (1990). "Finanzierungsprobleme in der Gründungs- und Ausbauphase der Deutsch-Österreichischen Mannesmannröhrenwerke A.G., 1890–1907." D. Petzina (ed.). *Zur Geschichte der Unternehmensfinanzierung,* Vol. 196. Berlin: Schriften des Vereins für Sozialpolitik, pp. 119–71.

Wetzel, Christoph (1996). *Die Auswirkungen des Reichsbörsengesetzes von 1896 auf die Effektenbörsen im deutschen Reich, Insbesondere auf die Berliner Fondsbörse.* Münster: Lit Verlag.

Whale, P. Barrett (1930). *Joint-Stock Banking in Germany.* London: Macmillan.

White, Eugene N. (1986). "Before the Glass-Steagall Act: An Analysis of the Investment Banking Activities of National Banks." *Explorations in Economic History* 23: 33–55.

Wiener, Fritz A. (1905). *Die Börse*. Berlin: Puttkammer and Mühlbrecht.

Wiethölter, Rudolf (1961). *Interessen und Organisation der Aktiengesellschaft im deutschen und amerikanischen Recht*. Karlsruhe: C. F. Müller.

Wilhelmini, Hans (1965). "Das neue Aktiengesetz." *Die Aktiengesellschaft* 10 (6): 153–5.

Wilson, P. (1994). "Public Ownership, Delegated Project Selection and Corporate Financial Policy." Working Paper, Indiana University.

Wójcik, Dariusz (2001). "Change in the German Model of Corporate Governance: Evidence from Blockholdings, 1997–2001." Working Paper, University of Oxford, School of Geography and the Environment.

Wormser, Otto (1919). *Die Frankfurter Börse*. Tübingen: J. C. B. Mohr.

Wunderlich, Frieda (1938). "Germany's Defense Economy and the Decay of Capitalism." *Quarterly Journal of Economics* 52: 401–30.

Ziegler, Dieter (1993). "Zentralbankpolitische Steinzeit? Preußische Bank und Bank of England im Vergleich." *Geschichte und Gesellschaft* 19: 475–505.

——— (1997). "Die 'Industrielle Revolution' in den Staaten des Deutschen Zollvereins." *Beiträge zur Historischen Sozialkunde: Zeitschrift für Lehrerfortbildung* 3.

——— (2000a). "Das Zeitalter der Industrialisierung, 1815–1914." M. North (ed.). *Deutsche Wirtschaftsgeschichte: ein Jahrtausend im Überblick*. Munich: C. H. Beck, pp. 192–281.

——— (2000b). "Die Wirtschaftsbürgerliche Elite im 20. Jahrhundert: eine Bilanz." D. Ziegler (ed.). *Großbürger und Unternehmer: Die Deutsche Wirtschaftselite im 20. Jahrhundert*. Göttingen: Vandenhoeck and Ruprecht, pp. 7–29.

——— (2000c). "Kontinuität und Diskontinuität der deutschen Wirtschaftselite 1900 bis 1938." D. Ziegler (ed.). *Großbürger und Unternehmer: die deutsche Wirtschaftselite im 20. Jahrhundert*. Göttingen: Vandenhoeck and Ruprecht, pp. 31–53.

Zilbert, Edward R. (1981). *Albert Speer and the Nazi Ministry of Arms. Economic Institutions and Industrial Production in the German War Economy*. London: Fairleigh Dickinson University Press.

Zorn, Wolfgang (1976). "Staatliche Wirtschafts- und Sozialpolitik und öffentliche Finanzen 1800–1970." Hermann Aubin and Wolfgang Zorn (eds.). *Handbuch der deutschen Wirtschafts- und Sozialgeschichte*, Vol. 2: *Das 19. und 20. Jahrhundert*. Stuttgart: Klett-Cotta, pp. 148–97.

Index

For EU product safety concerns, contact us at Calle de José Abascal, 56–1°,
28003 Madrid, Spain or eugpsr@cambridge.org.

www.ingramcontent.com/pod-product-compliance
Ingram Content Group UK Ltd.
Pitfield, Milton Keynes, MK11 3LW, UK
UKHW042211180425
457623UK00011B/148